# *THRU*

# *MY*

# *EYES*

*MALINDA GUERRERO CASTORENO*

Thru My Eyes

All rights reserved ©2013 by Malinda's Publishing
And the Author, Malinda Guerrero Castoreno

No part of this book may be reproduced or transmitted in any form or by any means whether it be mechanical, electronic, including photo copying, recording or by any information and storage retrieval system without the written consent of the author or the publishing company.

This book is fiction, based on events that are true. This book is a vision of the author. Names have been changed for obvious reasons. Some purely coincidental events are just that, purely coincidental. No two people see things the same way, hence the title.

Cover created by: Sarina Castoreno

For information:
Malindaspublishing@live.com
Or
Malinda's Publishing
2012 Market Ave. Fort Worth, Tx. 76164
817-655-3038

Printed in the United States of America

## DEDICATION

*To My Family: For encouraging me to use my imagination.*

*To you, the reader: For being a part of this spectacular journey.*

*" Much Luv" to you all!*

## *ACKNOWLEDGEMENTS*

To my husband Louis Castoreno for tirelessly reading every single page and not once having a negative comment, and telling me. "I'm on to something."

To my ten kids, Louis Jr., Paul, Monica, Eric, Tony, Stanley, Vanessa, Stefany, Sabrina, Sarina, thank you for the tears and the laughter when I sent you page after page for your opinions sand comments.
And, thank you to your spouses.

To my sister Sheril Tidwell, for your countless hours of input and jokes in creating this story.

To my brother Johnny (Gilbert to me), thank you for the use of your name. Thanks also for the daily laughter every time we talk.

To LLCOOLJ, for your very first word when you read Chapter 1. "Powerful." That single word from you lit the fire that started this journey.

To the ones that have cheered me on, and believed I could do this. "Rah, rah, rah!"

To the readers, thank you for taking the time out of your busy lives to read a story I wrote from my heart.

I wrote this story with love; I hope you each accept it with love.

I love you all,<br>
Malinda

## INTRODUCTION:

A picture tells a thousand words. What one person sees, another sees differently. The love, the hate, the fears, the acceptance, it was quite a life for such a young girl. The absolute fear of a gangster father, the undeniable love of the most beautiful woman in the world, her mother. Her mom could have been anything; A celebrity, a movie star, a model... anything but his wife.

## SPECIAL DEDICATION

*TO MY MOM:*

*IF IT WEREN'T FOR YOU,*

*THERE WOULD BE NO ME.*

## "Thru My Eyes"

# 1

It was an old house. The type of house, at first glance, you would think to yourself, trash must live there. Rats ran as freely as the family cat, at times not knowing which was the cat, and which was the rat.

Such a shabby disgusting frame of a house, with missing shingles and rotted wood from the front porch steps all the way to the wood siding.

The house was white…possibly, with so much of the seventy-year-old paint peeling off, it was impossible to tell what color the house actually was. There was missing siding on various spots of the outside walls, looking as if someone had punched holes here and there with their fists, and never bothered to fix the damage.

The window trim and doorframes were painted a dark shade of blue, in an attempt to match them with the blue roof shingles.

Yes, it's fair to say it should have been condemned twenty years earlier. Seems all the houses on our block appeared unlivable. But for some reason, ours like the others, still stood. It was a disgusting excuse for a home, if you can even call it a home.

Fourteen years we had been living in that old house; mom, dad, and six kids. Not even the homeless would have considered this a spot to lay their heads at the end of the night, yet it is where I was attempting to sleep, except for the unruly ways of my older sister Sher.

"Malina, Malina." Sher never said my name correctly. It was pronounced Ma-lee-nah, but Sher, though quite beautiful, deliberately said it with a voice that produced the image of the "Dueling Banjo" dudes from the movie "Deliverance."

"Malina, Malina." She repeated my name, then sort of yodeled, to wake me up.

"Get up "Changa." Mom wants you to get up." Sher growled.

Now she was being a smart ass, no need to call me "monkey" this damn early in the morning.

I half opened one eye to see her coming towards me with a glass full of water, and yes she was gonna throw it all over me.

"I'm awake. Don't you dare." I mumbled …But what the hell was I gonna do about it if she did throw it in my face? She was bigger than me, tougher than me, and could take on all five of us kids with one hand tied behind her back, blindfolded.

"Thought so!" She smirked as she took the glass of water back to the kitchen.

I drug myself out of the bed, the one I was forced to sleep on with my three sisters, Sher being one of them.

Unfortunately, we slept four to a bed, on an old four-post bed, with an old mattress that must have been handed down generation after generation. It was made of deteriorated cotton and rusty old springs.

Once in the restroom I examined my back to see if I had been the unfortunate one to wake with a gouge, or scratches, or scrapes on my back thanks to the protruding wires.

Nope, not this time! I smiled knowing I escaped the awful pain of alcohol being poured on my back had there been any marks from that horrific mattress.

If one or more of us wasn't scraped overnight, then one or more of us was kicked in the face from one or the other sister turning over in their sleep. It was always something; we never had the pleasure of an undisturbed nights sleep. I often compared sleeping on that bed as sleeping on a bed of nails.

I saw "Willie Wonka" once, studying so carefully the scene with Charlie's four grandparents were ill in bed. Thinking to myself, damn I know that sardine like felling.

How fortunate my two younger brothers were that they slept on some type of military cot. It didn't have rusty old wires, but what it did have was a squeaky frame. Any time either of them moved even a centimeter during the night that damn old bed would let out a deafening squeak that sounded more like a loud scream of a little child that may have just seen the "Boogie Man." That squeak took many years to adjust to, but we did.

I changed my clothes and washed my face. Something I had to do quickly, because if I let the sink water run too long, it would flood the restroom floor. Not only was the sink fucked up in that dump we called home, everything else was.

I went to the kitchen, another pathetic room in our house, and there stood my mom, with the biggest beautiful smile on her face.

"Morning Malina." Mom said my name correctly, wondered why Sher couldn't?

I walked over and hugged her, and said. "Good morning mommy."

The other kids had already eaten breakfast and were outside by this time. Sher was in the kitchen, not looking directly at me but whispering smart-ass comments mom couldn't hear, but I could.

"Pet!" Sher whispered as she put the breakfast dishes in the sink for someone to wash, other than herself.

Mom placed a bowl of oatmeal and toast in front of me. I looked at the oatmeal, which I knew would taste good. But I also knew my belly craved, eggs, bacon, and possibly orange juice, not fricken powdered milk. I knew I had to eat it whether I wanted to or not. It was all we had; besides, I did not wish to offend my mom. It wasn't her fault we couldn't eat gourmet breakfasts every morning.

Mom began the cleanup of the horrid kitchen, humming as she did. Always in a good mood, always happy and so full of life. Without a doubt, my mom was the most beautiful woman in the world.

Sher looked at me. "Your turn to do the dishes, Changa." She barked.

I remained silent.

"Right mom?' Sher insisted.

"Yes Malina, it's your turn, and Sher, we can do without the name calling. Ok?" Mom said. Her voice almost a calm whisper.

Sher stuck her tongue at me as she stomped out of the kitchen, her ponytail bouncing as she exited the room.

I watched her disappear into the living room; she was tall, long legged, with eyes almost as beautiful as moms.

Sher was dad's favorite, him hers. I could have cared less.

I always felt had Sher been a boy dad would have insisted mom never have another child, I wouldn't be here anyway.

However, he didn't get that first-born son until his fifth child, so, too damn bad…dad.

Though my tummy was longing for an entirely different breakfast, I ate my oatmeal slowly, listening to mom hum one of her favorite songs. She began peeling potatoes, already preparing for lunch, though breakfast had just ended. Mom was always on the go, never taking a second to slow down.

I had to close my eyes for a second while eating my oatmeal, so I wouldn't get sick, because eating the oatmeal and looking at the shabby walls and shabby cabinets completely disgusted me.

Opening my eyes, looking at the beat up old kitchen I remembered so many times I wished the house would burn down, just burn to the ground so we would be forced to move. But where? Where would we go? Another rat infested house?

I got up to put my dish in the bubbly water in the sink; mom walked over to me, touched my forehead, and asked.

"Are you ok?"

"Yes ma'am." I answered and began washing the dishes.

Mom continued peeling potatoes, while I was finishing the breakfast dishes.

Then I heard it! That undeniable sound of my dad entering the house. It just as well could have been an F5 tornado exploding through our front door; it had the same everlasting effect on me.

I literally had to squeeze my legs together to keep from pissing on myself; the sound of his voice always threw me into a frenzy.

Mom glanced over at me, and winked, already suspecting what she knew was more a possibility than not.

I mean seriously! She had been putting up with mine and dads shit for so long she already knew what might happen.

Not three steps past the doorway, he was already bitching about anything and everything. Having my hands in a sink full of water only added to my urge to piss on myself.

I didn't need soapy dish water to further my urge to piss, all I needed was to hear his monstrous voice, and I could piss instantly.

Bladder problems? Hell no! My problem was fear. Pure, "Shakin In Your Boots" type of fear.

Mom put the potato peeler down, which I anticipated picking back up and stabbing him if he came anywhere near me, but rejected that idea because I already knew one look at him might just have me stabbing myself, not vice versa.

Who the hell was I kidding? I was a fucking wimp.

Mom wiped her hands on her old apron and went in the direction of dad's voice. He was already half yelling about where was?... I couldn't even understand what he was bitching about.

"Where are they Shirley?" He was demanding of her.

"I thought you took them with you Johnny." She said in her sweet kind voice. Always the calm quiet wife.

"No, I put that shit right here." He yelled.

Even from the kitchen, I could clearly hear his finger harshly pounding on his dresser, at the exact spot he left whatever the hell he was looking for.

There was no need for me to go near his room to see what I could already hear; him throwing things out of his dresser drawer, like a rushed cat burglar, rummaging through the drawers looking for the "Loot."

I felt sick.

I wondered did he just get home or had he been home, left and came back.

Hell no, it was too early; he must have just got home.

How the hell can such an absolutely handsome man be such a terror of a human being?

So many times I would glance, and I mean glance, not stare, not look, but glance at him and realize just how handsome he was. Then he would speak, reminding me never judge a book by its cover.

Dad had dark black hair, dark piercing eyes, dimples, and a smile that could not be found on any other person on the planet. He was a strong man, not like a body builder, but strong with the physique of a star athlete.

Anyone could understand why mom fell in love with him.

No one could understand why she stayed with him.

I stayed put, knowing he would not come into the kitchen unless he was actually hungry, then I'd be shit out of luck, because once dad starts in on one thing, he takes aim at everyone, one by one, just for kicks.

He rambled on and on for a few minutes, then whatever it was he was looking for, was found, possibly by mom, possibly he himself found it. Nonetheless, the tornado departed leaving a path of destruction from his dresser to the front door.

What was he looking for? I did not care to ask.

I could hear him start that old heap of a car and speed off.

Relief went through my body. I uncrossed my legs.

So, you may wonder, why all the dramatics? Why all the cussing and bitching, and over what?

That wasn't dramatics, that's just the way it was. Any time day or night, that is exactly how my dad behaved.

And then you may wonder why was I, a kid, not quite a teen, so quick to run my mouth about my own flesh and blood.

First off, I never ran my mouth publicly; are you kidding? I was no dumb ass; these were all mere thoughts in my mind, things I was allowed to think to myself and only to myself.

Unless daddy dearest was a mind reader, and many times I believe he just may be. But, until he smacked me for anything I thought, I still stood by my right to express my thoughts to myself and only myself. The day he smacks me, and rightfully so because I cussed more in my mind than any drunken sailor in a bar, then I'm done.

I could hear mom in their room picking up the things dad had thrown about, placing every thing back in its proper place.

She returned to the kitchen to continue peeling the potatoes.

Again, she asked. "You ok?"

Again, I answered. "Yes ma'am."

"Would you please go check on the boys for me?" Mom asked, knowing I would never refuse anything she ever asked of me.

I walked out onto the front porch; saw my two little brothers playing in the dirt with their raggedy old cars. Not dirt like a sand box, but dirt as in, there wasn't any grass in our front yard only dirt and rocks, yet neither seemed to mind.

Hey, they were little boys; they didn't mind playing in dirt, getting all dirty and shit. Besides, there had never been grass in that yard anyway, so they had no idea what they were missing.

My two little brothers, not a single care in the world between them. The most they had to worry about was to get the hell out of the way if our maniac father came back and smashed right into them as they played innocently on the ground.

Four-year-old Danny and Six-year-old J.J.

Yes, we called him J.J. for short; he was after all, Johnny Junior. I couldn't fathom saying Johnny over and over throughout the day, so he was given the nick name J.J. the year we realized just what a fuckin jerk our dad was.

It was obvious J.J. wanted to be like his dad, act like him, go everywhere with him. His face would completely lite-up when mom would dress him just like dad and he'd get to sit right up in the front seat with him, as dad would say. "Come on Junior, let's go paint the town."

Why, I often wondered? Other than dad's handsome looks, why would anyone in the world care to look like him or be like him?

I watched my brothers playing a few minutes longer, noticing just how cute they both were.

Danny four years old, sounded more like a fourteen-year-old teen going through puberty when he talked, than a four-year-old child. His voice so deep, often we mistook his voice for dads. Danny had beautiful brown eyes, and hair that was the identical color of his eyes. He was a spoiled brat, because everyone catered to his every need.

When they played any game or sport together J.J. could never win because if he did, Danny would cry confirming what we all knew, Danny was a big crybaby. It seemed the proper nickname "Baby," and so he was called.

Good ol' big brother J.J. always let Danny have his way and stand defeated, knowing damn good and well he was the victorious one in most of their games.

Rumor has it mom had to ride the bus home after giving birth to Danny, because our "dad" was no where to be found.

J.J. six years old but was very tall making one believe he was closer to ten years old, than six because of his height.

He was blessed with a smile identical to dads, dimples and all, which had us girls pinching and kissing his cheeks several times throughout the day.

J.J. loved attention, same as his dad, and he got it, same as his dad. J.J. also loved baseball more than anything. From the time he could walk and received his first baseball and glove he spent countless hours playing catch, usually with one of us girls. If we were busy or just didn't want to play, it really didn't matter, J.J. would just throw the ball up in the air and play catch all by himself.

My brothers were adorable precious kids, too bad they would have to grow up.

I stood on the porch and looked down at the beat up old steps, which were, for lack of a better word, they were hazardous. Some of the boards were rotted, some were cracked, and some were... just not there anymore. I shook my head in disgust, remembering that we all had to literally walk zigzag up or down these stairs to keep from falling through.

I felt a bit of a breeze, hot breeze, but none the less a breeze that was caused by the two enormous oak trees that had been strategically placed on opposite ends of the front yard.

Those monstrous trees provided plenty of shade on those hot scorching summer days, enough to make me wonder just how hot our old house would be if it weren't for the shade those trees provided.

It is impossible to tell because even with the damn trees, it was hot as the Sahara Desert inside our house every moment through out the day.

As I turned to go back inside, I looked at our disgusting old house, and shook my head.

# 2

I believe when it was first built, our house was quite possibly an eye pleaser, a house anyone would have proudly called home. However, today it was nothing more than an eye sore. Conditions not suitable for the rats our family cat Suzie devoured daily.

Built with a wrap around porch that gave the appearance of a much grander home than it actually was. Somewhere along the line someone, definitely not a carpenter, but someone, took the left side of the porch and made it into a terribly constructed room. The person that built it either had no concept of electricity at all, or just didn't know how to install electrical outlets, so they chose to put nothing, no kind of power what so ever.

"The little room" we called it because it was so damn small, enough room only for a tiny twin sized bed and an even tinier dresser.

Even while standing on the front porch I could hear the old metal oscillating fan trying it's best to cool that old room, which was impossible to do. First off, the extension cord we used to plug from the "Big Room" to the "Little Room," was an electrician's nightmare. With so much electrical tape wrapped around it, it would only be a matter of time before that piece of shit cord would probably catch fire... Besides, I never understood why we ran that old fan anyway. All it did was circulate the heat, and make so much noise from the metal blades rubbing the sides of the cover you couldn't hear yourself talk if you were in the same room with it.

I again, shook my head in disgust, turned to walk back in the house. When I opened the screen door, I was hit in the face with a wave of heat.

An old water cooler in mom's room blew heat throughout the house. Even the timed, every thirty minute, water down of that water cooler could not help cool us down. One of us kids had to literally go outside every thirty minutes and water down that old cooler, and if for some reason we were stupid enough to touch that cooler while holding the water hose, you guessed it, shock the shit right out of us. Water coolers tend to put out funky sticky air rather than nice comfortable, fresh cold air.

The weather conditions in that house could only be described as "Hot as Sahara Desert in the summer time, cold as Siberia in the wintertime." Not comfortable at all.

I headed toward the kitchen, where I could hear my mom still humming.

"Why did you move it?" Carrie was screaming at Becky as I walked past them. Both girls sitting crossed legged on the living room floor playing jacks, the hobby they played religiously twenty-two hours a day.

"Mom, Becky is cheating." Carrie sounded like she wanted to cry.

I'm not sure, but I believe I heard Becky mumble the word "bitch" at Carrie.

"Girls play nice." Mom said from the kitchen.

I half expected Carrie to throw the jacks all over the floor just to piss Becky off.

Carrie was like that, she was a cute little chubby kid, with her hair always in pigtails, hence the nick name "piggy." She loved to draw pictures and she loved to color. Anytime she felt like sketching a portrait of one of us she would insist we stand still, if we refused, she would throw a little temper tantrum.

I often wondered if she were named after the movie "Carrie?"

"Come on "Carrie." Becky insisted. Let's start over, or I'm not playing anymore."

Becky the standout kid, was always jumping around, and dancing around, a little bit of a show off, an attention seeker. She sucked on her thumb as a child and as the myth goes, it caused her to have bucked teeth. So, instead of being called Becky she was tortured with the nickname "Bucky."

Her biggest flaw was her nonstop conversations that continued day and night, literally never shutting the hell up.

She drove us all crazy because most of her conversations were to herself. She budded in on everyone else's conversation, insisting she get the last word in, even if the conversation had nothing to do with her.

When we would go to bed at night she would be carrying on a conversation, with whom, we were not sure, but nonetheless a conversation would be in full force.

And when one of us would ask. "Who are you talking to?"

She would stare up at the ceiling, and say. "I'm talking to the angels."

"What angels?" Being curious kids, we would ask and even look up at the ceiling to see if we could actually see the angels ourselves.

"Right there." She would insist and actually point as if there really were angels on our ceiling.

One of my old aunts said Becky must have been blessed by God to be able to see and talk to angels. I never believed that statement at all. Seemed to me there were no angels looking over anyone in that old house.

The argument would go back and forth and just as I suspected, Carrie started with the name-calling.

So, here goes Carrie yelling. "Bucky, Bucky, Bucky," and even sticking her teeth out to imitate Becky's buckteeth. Then Becky stands up, kicks the jacks, sending the jacks all over the place, yelling "Pig, Pig, Pig" short for Piggy, and even does a squeal sound of a pig.

Just in time, mom walks in the room and says. "Pick up the jacks girls, and go outside for awhile." Becky in tears, Carrie crying, both of them pissed off at the another.

Mom with her soft-spoken voice. That was not punishment I thought to myself. If you really want to punish them? Try sending them to their room and let them sweat it out.

Both girls did as they were told, cleaned up their mess and by the time they finished finding the last jack they were already laughing at one another.

I went to the kitchen to see what I could do for mom. She was making fish sticks and French fries. Oven on and a frying pan full of grease, my poor mom suffering in that old stinky kitchen, which seemed to not bother her at all. I could barely breathe.

It was a Saturday afternoon, clean up day for me and Sher. We always helped mom, and though we put countless hours sweeping, moping and dusting, the house always looked dirty, because it was just so old and wore out. With all that dirt in the front yard, it was impossible to get rid of the dust, but we tried, nonetheless.

Sher always took control of cleaning day, mostly because she was so damn bossy. Sher was fourteen literally going on twenty. She had beautiful green eyes, light skin, and long light brown hair.

Sher and I, were both busy doing our designated chores. I did mine the same every Saturday; Sher on the other hand did hers almost as if she were angry. When sweeping, she would make great big sweeping motions, almost sending the broom flying across the room. When wiping off the table, she would take the cloth and scrub, I mean scrub, as if she was trying to erase permanent marker off the table. She seemed so pissed off to have to do the same chores we did fifty-two weeks out of the year. I smiled to myself, because I knew just what she wanted. She wanted to hurry the process so she could stick her nose in a book. She loved to read and all these chores were interfering with her book reading. How silly she looked to me.

Sher appeared to be flawless, except that she was one bossy ass teenager. She loved the control of bossing the rest of us around, telling each of us what to do and when to do it. Things like, "sit down, shut up, better mind me or I'll beat the crap out of you!" She would actually pretend she was hitting us, though pretending, she managed to get a slight jab in here and there.

More times than not she did make one of us cry.

"I'm just pretending to hit them mom." She would lie as she would actually be hurting one of us. Her nickname was "Murderer" which dad thought was hilarious, Sher did not. It would piss her off even more, and she would simply "pretend" to beat us up again.

Most teen girls go through that awkward, tomboyish stage, not Sher. She was beautiful, flawless and I adored her. That and the fact that I was scared to death of the bitch.

I helped Sher change the sheets on the big bed as mom set up the washing machine for us to do laundry. No, we were not fortunate enough to have a nice convenient washing machine and dryer. Are you kidding? That old house could have only a few electrical items running at a time. Anytime we attempted to plug in more than one thing here and one thing there, the fuses blew, and we would have to mess with the breaker boxes, located on the outside of our house, another pain in the ass.

This washer was an old wringer type machine that was operated manually. It took hours and hours to do all of our laundry, exhausting us by the end of the day.

I'm sure mom would have loved to have some kind of modern convenience in that rat hole of a house.

The kids were in the house now, washing up for lunch.

Would dad be home or wouldn't he? Odds were, not.

We all sat at the table laughing and eating our perfectly crisp fish and fries. Of course, mom set aside a plate for the king, no not "Elvis," rather "dad." Mom always ate with us insisting kids should eat with their parents. I think she meant singular, parent, because if we had been forced to wait on dad, each one of us would have starved to death.

After lunch, the kids went back outside to play, Sher and I continuing our chores.

I was dusting the items in mom's room. Don't get the idea we had gold statues and shit, I mean dusting the half ass furniture and the odds and end collectables mom usually found along side the curb as she walked to the nearby store.

Oh yes, there was a certificate hanging on mom's wall, a certificate that was given dad when he was honorably discharged from the Air force.

"We must keep that nice and clean." Mom would insist.

Therefore, I always gave it my famous "spit shine." Nice and pretty for my dad.

My dad, John Vincent Guetarro… Where do I begin?

Actually, he was always called Johnny. Johnny G. to most.

A name quite becoming such a man. He was the type of man you hated to love, or loved to hate. I was on the receiving end of both.

He was a handsome man, with the most beautiful smile, second only to his dimples. Every strand of his perfectly combed blue-black hair matched his dark piercing eyes. One would have to look away if he were staring at you for fear of being hypnotized by his haunting stare. He had a strong jaw line and cheekbones, a face that could have easily landed him on the cover of any magazine.

He never shied away from showing off the muscles that won him numerous awards and legendary status throughout his military career.

Dad would shadow box while we kids would watch in awe, knowing if someone stood in his path, they would be knocked completely out. Sometimes while showing off his shadow boxing techniques, he would actually get a little to close to the mirror. I often wondered what he would do if he actually knocked the shit out of the mirror. "Ouch."

His nose was surprisingly perfect, never broken in a boxing match because he was so fast and powerful; no one could get close enough to him to hit him.

Someone took notice of his quickness and strength while in the Air Force and introduced him to the boxing team. His career in the Air Force was a firefighter, but his love was being on the boxing team. He did not need the boxing team, they needed him. Actually, dad "WAS" the boxing team.

When dad did something, he loved, he did it good, and he did it correctly.

People say dad was mean as a child, never obeying anyone. It was told, though his step dad loved him, he periodically beat him with battery cables in an attempt to discipline him. All that did was make dad meaner and stronger.

He was the only son to my grandma who had my dad and four daughters. Dad was the protector of his sisters and mom, never allowing anyone to do or say anything to harm them.

Dad was one of those people, you fuck with his family, he fucks with you. Regardless, he always won!

Dad was born while grandma was visiting relatives in Mexico. Being that grandma was a U.S. citizen, dad was automatically given a U.S. citizenship as well.

Family gossip said my grandma was a beautiful young woman who dated a man of power. On her third date with that man he allegedly raped her, hence the conception of my dad. Because of this man's political status and to protect him from prosecution, grandma was sent to the U.S.

It was told by relatives that my dads' dad was a wealthy, prosperous government official, whom grandma had no contact with since this alleged occurrence.

Dad traveled to Guadalajara once in an attempt to find his dad. Turns out the name listed as his father on his birth certificate wasn't even the name of the man grandma knew to be dads' real dad.

Perhaps to save my dad, perhaps to save the man that was my dads' real father, whatever her reason, it was apparent grandma, and even my dads' aunts could have given dad the answers he would spend a lifetime searching for. Whatever the reasons, no one would ever give dad what he really wanted.

The name! The name of his real father.

With a promising career in the military, it was obvious dad had quite a future ahead of him. He had served his four years in the Air Force and was about to reenlist, but as fate and stupidity would have it, he got involved with the wrong people.

Shady ass characters, perhaps, that enticed dad with money and power. With no regards for his military career or his family, dad took a guy for "A Ride" shot him and left him for dead. The man did not die but was paralyzed from the neck down.

Possibly, it was an initiation into organized crime, a way for dad to "Prove Himself." However, it has always been unclear why, but dad did not spend one day in jail for that crime. It's a fact our lives would have changed if he had.

Fate would take many twists and turns throughout dad's life, sometimes on his side, sometimes not.

It was hard to believe he could have done something positive with his life. I guess the illusion of gangster life was positive to him.

Sher was finishing her chores, I watched her knowing she was about to start bitching about something, but what? She was so much like dad, she would bitch about any and everything just like dad, only difference, she would laugh about it afterwards.

Because Sher and I were so close in age, I suppose it was the nature of the beast to pick on me as much as she could. I was a moving target, and there was nothing I could do about it.

Twelve-year-old Malina, pronounced Ma-lee-nah. Quite an exotic name for a skinny, hairy little girl huh?

Yes hairy! My arms were so hairy that my brothers and sisters called me "Monkey." As an added bonus, I was called "Changa." Same difference.

Even on those horrible hot summer days, I would still wear a sweater to conceal my hairy arms. Talk about being self conscience. Thinking to myself, if these kids can not actually see my hairy arms they will not make fun of me.

Did not work! All that theory did was damn near make me pass out from heat exhaustion. Eventually all the hair did fall of, but the nickname to this day remains.

All that hair on my arms, I was also blessed with long hair that went all the way to my waist, actually all four of us girls had very long hair, but mine was the longest and the thickest.. It was a pain in the ass for mom to keep, but dad insisted she never cut it. However, being that I had the hairy arms to match, the second the "Adams Family" came on TV, my fricken brothers and sisters looked directly at me, laughing, pointing, and saying, "There's Malina, Cousin It." Over and over they would tease me, again me the wimpy kid would cry.

I was often teased I was adopted because I looked nothing like my brothers and sisters. Most of them inherited the light skin, light eyes of my mom, me the darker skin tone, dark eyes of my dad.

Sher is the one that teased me the most, with comments like. "Malina you sure weren't born round here."

Insinuating what? I was born on another planet? Which always made me think perhaps I really wasn't one of the "Pack?" Thus enticing all the kids to laugh at me, furthermore, causing me to cry.

I was the shy quiet reserved one and I was always afraid. Afraid of what you may ask? Well, from the time I could walk, the second I heard my dad's voice, I would piss on myself. I was completely terrified of him.

I felt as if I had a miserably unhappy childhood, except when I was with my mom. I absolutely loved her. I always wanted to be with her, be beside her at all times.

When I was in school, I would fake being sick just so I could stay home with her. My dad would see right though my fakeness and hit me and force me to go to school, but I hated it and would always cry in class hoping to be sent home so I could be with my mom. You might think I would have been used to the fact that I had to be in school. Not me! I cried every single day in the first grade.

The principal, Mr. Mann would come to my class and ask.
"Why are you crying?"
"Cause I want my momma." I would cry even more just saying her name.
"But you can't be with your mama; you have to be here in school." He would say in his hateful stern voice, thus making me cry even more. I honestly believe he wanted to knock the shit out of me for wasting his time on such nonsense. Who would blame him if he did? I disrupted the class every day for an entire school year. But I didn't care. I loved my mommy and I wanted to be with her. I hated school and I hated everyone that forced me to go.

Sometimes mom would get upset when she saw me crying, maybe she wanted me to stay home also, but there was no way she would go against my dad. But sometimes I got my way, and I would miss school to be home with my mom.

Shirley, my mom, the most beautiful woman alive. She had a calm mesmerizing beauty about her. The very first thing you would notice about her was her gorgeous emerald green eyes. It was often said she spoke with her eyes; you simply could not help but stare. Mom never wore makeup; she didn't need to, only a touch of mascara if she were to go somewhere.

She had beautiful naturally red lips that gave the impression she had on lipstick, which she did not. When mom spoke, she spoke with class and grace, never yelling or cussing. If she had to discipline any of us, she would simply say. "Go to your room sweetie, until I tell you to come out." Sounding more like a request rather than a demand. Lesser kids might have laughed in her face, not us, we loved and obeyed her.

After having six kids who would have thought she could keep such a beautiful hourglass figure. She had flawless light skin and the softest feminine hands, like those of a model. She had long silky dark hair, which she usually wore back in a ponytail. At times, she would wear it long and flowing. When she accompanied our dad outside our house, she wore it in a French Twist, which made her movie star like.

    This type of rare beauty one does not see every day. Mom should have been a movie star, a celebrity, a model…anything but his wife.

# 3

On the rare occasion dad was going to take mom out, he would tell her what clothes to wear, what shoes to wear, how to fix her hair how much make-up to put on. She never argued, just did as she was told.

I was surprised when I saw her getting dressed one particular night. Already so beautiful, I was in awe as I watched her preparing herself for the night out with dad.

While she was dressing dad came in the room and took something out of his dresser drawer, handed them to mom and said. "Put them in."

Apparently, he didn't realize I saw what he was doing.

Put them in what? I wondered.

She tried to cover them up but I saw them anyway. She looked at me and did a motion with her lips like. "Shhh." I remained quiet, not saying a word. He left the room and she continued getting ready, then she put the things he handed her into her bra. Instantly her boobs became bigger.

Yes, she had given birth to six kids and still maintained a beautiful body. Shapely legs, flat tummy, not one stretch mark at all, and she even had a nice butt. One thing she did not possess were big boobs.

Why the hell would he want her to have big boobs? Was he ashamed of her? Did he want her to look like someone she was not? I did not understand this at all.

She looked somewhat teary eyed and scared. I smiled at her and said. "You look beautiful mom."

She smiled, hugged me, and said. "I love you Malina."

It was about 9:30 when mom and dad left that night. Having such a strict father, we all knew his rules. Never act up, especially if we were in public, as it might embarrass him.

"Always present yourselves as perfect little ladies and gentlemen, even while at home." He would say in his demanding military voice.

We would never dream of misbehaving. Therefore, anytime it was babysitting night, my little brothers and sisters knew they could get away with anything with me and Sher, knowing they could behave as kids, not mini military personnel.

So with our parents gone for the night, in our eyes it was "Party Time." Time for us to be kids, time to simply have fun.

They ran around laughing and screaming, and even dared to say a few cuss words here and there. Sadly, it seemed funny, almost like caged animals being set free.

Since we were poor and didn't live in a beautiful home, we would play a game we created called "Rich House." The concept of the game was to take any half-decent thing we could find in our house and fix up one room to give the illusion of a rich home.

We would get some of my moms' full skirts, spread them on the floor, and pretend they were mink rugs. Then we would use our creative minds and get anything we could find that looked half-nice and fix the one room up and make it look beautiful, then pretend we were rich kids that lived in the most beautiful home in town, without a worry in the world.

Two years earlier when J.J. was four, me and Sher were babysitting; being bored, wanting to do something different, we decided to dress him up as a ballerina.

Why dress J.J. as a girl? Who knows? We were just playing around. Curiosity got the best of us wondering what he might look like had he actually been born a girl.

Sher had been in a school play a few years earlier and still had the ballerina outfit she wore in the play. We put the little pink ballerina outfit on him, rouge on his cheeks, polished his toenails pink, and even put pink lipstick on him.

He was laughing and dancing around like a little ballerina just as Sher had instructed him. It was absolutely hilarious to watch him pretend to imitate Sher. He was so fricken adorable, Sher and I could not resist kissing his cheeks. We were all laughing so loud we didn't hear our parents come into the house.

Just as dad walked into the room he saw his little namesake jumping around like a ballerina, saw his polished toenails, and rouged cheeks. Furious, dad barged into the room and slapped J.J. to the floor.

Instantly Sher and I started crying. "No daddy, don't. We were only playing."

He yelled back. "He's a fucking boy, not a fucking sissy."

Dad was furious with us, furious with J.J.

Needless to say, he whooped J.J., he whooped us all actually, for dressing J.J. like a girl.

Mom begged dad to stop, but he was already beyond furious and never could she cross the devil. We could never just be kids and be happy. Though it was incredibly funny to see my four year old little brother pretend to be a tiny little ballerina, it was not worth the ass whooping we all got that night. As you can imagine, we never did any thing like that again.

We were just kids, simply trying to have fun.

After we played rich house that night, and ate all our snacks, Sher and I put the little kids to bed. We cleaned up our imaginary rich house, putting all the worn out things back in their proper places. Sher and I watched TV. for a while then went to bed. We didn't have a house phone for our parents to call and check on us, they just had to trust that we were ok.

It wasn't often Sher and I had to baby-sit because it was not everyday that dad took mom out with him. Dad did his street running bullshit on a daily basis, but the things he did, he would not allow mom to be a part of.

I really do believe mom loved staying home with her kids, we were her life, and she was ours. Possibly dad took her out, I assume mostly to show off what he had. No wife compared to her, none even came close. Though it was obvious I was not there to see for myself, but I often wondered just how did dad treat mom in public?

I wondered did he open the car door for her, did he stand when she left the room to powder her nose? Did he hold her high on a pedestal where she belonged, or did he do the macho crap, and disrespect her as she were his property rather than his wife? I'm sure many a man would love to have mom as their wife. It was obvious many admired her, but knew she was a lady, a real lady. Dad knew what he had; he also knew no one was stupid enough to cross the line.

Sometimes when mom and dad went out, they would come home laughing and having a good time. I supposed dad encouraged mom to have a drink or two and enjoyed her high with her. Perhaps at times, she drank nothing at all, because after all, as drunk as he got she knew she would have to drive home. I often felt if she had a choice to be home with her kids, or go out on the town with dad, I assumed she would rather be home with us. As much control as dad had, I sometimes got the impression she didn't enjoy all that nightlife. I know when they would come in at night, she would come to our room and make sure we were ok, almost a sigh of relief on her face, that she had made it home safe, and found that we were safe.

I lay awake for the longest time staring at the ceiling, wishing mom and dad were already home.

# 4

I must have fallen asleep for a bit, not quite sure of the time but I was awakened by a noise. I listened for a moment, not really sure what the noise was, scared it might be a prowler in the house.

After a few minutes I realized what I heard was not a prowler at all, but rather it was my mom crying, a soft cry not a hysterical one. I looked toward her room to see her shadow pacing back and forth. It appeared she was alone, because I didn't see or hear my dad.

I thought about getting out of bed to see if she were ok, then suddenly I heard it. From my overcrowded bed, what sounded like dad slamming the brakes of his car to avoid smashing into our house? It was obvious he got out of his car because he slammed the car door so hard it sounded as if someone had slammed into the rear of his car. I could hear him stomping up the five steps, sounding more like an army of men marching up those stairs, not just dad. He pushed the front door open with such force it broke out several of the square glass panels and shattered them to the floor.

Again, I could see moms shadow, now just standing there, paralyzed and unable to move.

A deafening sound was coming from dad, a sound that produced the image of a raging bull in my mind. An endless stream of mumbled cuss words which were impossible to understand.

He rushed into the room, and with no warning whatsoever, he body slammed mom to the floor. The entire house shook with the intensity of an exploding bomb.

From where I was laying I could see into their room, horrified, I closed my eyes hoping it would all go away and not be there when I reopened them.

Then I heard mom crying again and attempting to yell out.

"No Johnny, Please." She begged.

"I'm sorry, please don't. Please." She cried out.

As she was crying and pleading, I could hear a loud pounding, thudding sound. I was horrified, trembling, and so terribly afraid to open my eyes.

Mom was crying and begging over and over. "Please Johnny, no, please don't.

I heard what sounded like mom struggling to get away from him.

"You mother fucking bitch!" My dad was screaming as loud as he possibly could.

I was shaking so badly, completely terrified at what I was hearing.

"Who the fuck do you think you are?" He screamed even louder, if that were at all possible.

"Please don't Johnny, I'm sorry." She pleaded, as her voice seemed to fade.

"You fucking bitch." His voice enraged.

I opened my eyes and looked toward their room. From the foot board posts of my bed, as if looking through a window, with the posts of my bed on either side, I saw the most terrifying thing I had ever seen.

"Please stop Johnny. I'm sorry, I'm sorry." She was begging him to stop.

With my eyes wide open, I saw him on top of her. He had her pinned to the floor with his body straddling her. She was struggling and squirming, trying to get free from his grasp, which was completely impossible for her to do. His fingers wrapped around her throat, at the same time smashing the butt of a pistol into her face, all while choking her.

"You fucking bitch, why did you embarrass me? Don't you ever embarrass me like that again?" He screamed with so much anger.

"Stop Johnny, please stop." The only words she could cry.

"I should kill you Mother Fucker." His words were so clear to me.

"Who the fuck do you think you are?" He screamed and beat her as he would if he were beating someone he had been hired to kill. The actions of a complete mad man, he just kept hitting her, and hitting her, and hitting her.

I was paralyzed, unable to scream, move, or make a sound. I felt as if I were choking to death myself, choking on fear. I was literally petrified and didn't dare attempt to get out of the bed to try and help her. Mom just kept crying and begging him to stop.

He continued yelling. "Don't you ever do that fucking shit to me again."

She was trying desperately to get away from him, though she wasn't actually fighting back, nor attempting to hit him. She was just squirming, trying desperately to get out of the hold he had on her. He had her by her hair shaking and banging her head into the floor.

Mom pleaded over and over. "Please stop Johnny, please, I'm sorry."

Such a horrid cry for her life.

It seemed to go on forever, the cries, the hitting, the begging, the cussing, and the beating.

How could such a frail woman take so many blows and not die from them?

Obviously, she was no match for his brutal strength.

Then there was silence, neither of them moved, no more cussing or hitting. I couldn't even hear her muffled cries anymore. I thought they were both dead.

I guess he wore himself out from the physical motion of beating the hell out of her, because he literally passed out.

Silence! There was complete silence. I believed he had killed her. I stared toward their room...I saw nothing, I heard nothing, then I saw her attempt to get up off the floor. It seemed she lost her balance as she tried to stand up, holding on first to the dresser in front of her, then to the wall as she collected her balance.

For a second I thought she was going to fall back to the floor.

As she turned my way, I saw her face, bleeding with a cut on her forehead, blood dripping down her face. Her lip was swollen and her nose bleeding.

He had pulled out so much of her hair; it was literally falling to the floor. There was blood and hair everywhere. I could see him lying on the floor, just laying there completely passed out. His arms spread out as if he had been nailed to a cross.

Why didn't she pick up that gun and blow his fucking head off... Why?

Mom didn't see me but she heard me crying. She looked in my direction and put her finger to her lips as to tell me to be quiet. I covered my head with the covers then put my pillow over my face to muffle my own cries.

He remained on the floor, passed out as if he had been beat to death.

"Drunken bastard, I hate you, I hate you." I cried to myself, from under my pillow.

Mom somehow managed to drag herself to the restroom to clean her self off. It was obvious she could barely move. I was surprised she was able to get up at all, considering the amount of blows to the head she took.

Finally, she came out of the restroom. Quietly she tiptoed past him. I don't know why she didn't pick up that gun and kill him. Just blow his fucking head off for what he had just done to her. It would have been justified. One look at her face anyone could tell she had just been beat by a fucking mad man.

Instead, she climbed in the bed next to me. Mom grabbed me and hugged me; I buried my face in her chest. As I did I let out a scream.

"Shhhh." She whispered. "Please don't wake him Malina."

She was shaking, I was shaking even more. I hated him; I hated him more than I thought it was possible to hate anyone.

The light was on in the restroom, producing just enough light that I could see the bruises under her eyes, the cuts, the blood.

She literally looked like a monster.

She continued crying; now a very painful cry, then she began to throw up. I suppose he was just so damn drunk he didn't hear her.

She got up, grabbed a towel and the mop to clean the mess. I looked over the edge of the bed to see what she was cleaning up. I cried even more when I saw she had been throwing up blood.

I believe as a child it was just too much for me.

Sick, scared, horrified for our lives, for moms' life. I literally passed out from pure fear.

# 5

Was it possible for him to remain on that floor and die? I had no idea what happened overnight. I wondered, did he stay on the floor all night long? Did he die on the floor? Did he wake up and slither like a fucking snake and sleep on his bed?

I woke the next morning, my father approaching my mom who was still lying next to me.
"If anyone finds out about this, you and these kids are dead." She didn't move.
"Do you hear me?" He snapped. She could only shake her head yes. I smelt liquor still on his breath from the night before, he completely disgusted me. I was so sad for mom, so sad for us all. I simply didn't understand why she didn't get up and run out of that house for help. But run where? We lived across from a cemetery; the nearest house was at least half a block away. She sure wasn't gonna leave her kids with him. She was trapped, and he knew it.

It was just turning light outside, usually the time he would be coming in, not getting up. I could hear him in his room slamming things around; cussing to himself making sure we could hear every word he said. As if he were saying to himself, "All y'all mutha fuckas wake up." I do believe this was a mental form of torture.
Please dear God, I begged to myself. Please make him leave, just get up and leave this house. Within minutes my prayer was answered, he left.
Mom was awake but couldn't move.
"Can I help you mama?" I asked her, wanting so bad to do anything I could to help her.
"No baby." She said and just cried and cried. This was no life for my mother; this was no life for her kids either. This

was a complete horror story, one that seemed impossible to wake from.

He was gone, but for how long, no one knew.

I assumed he stayed gone all day because of his shame, if he even had any. Shame not only for beating his wife but the fact that he used a pistol to do it. My biggest fear was that this bastard was going to come back drunk, start all his shit with mom again, but this time kill us all as he had threatened earlier.

Though he had left, it seemed his evil presence still lingered like smoke from a burned-out building.

No one made a sound at first, though we were all awake we weren't sure what to do. Gradually, one by one, we all got out of bed and got dressed, beginning with Sher.

Eventually mom was able to get herself out of bed also. She moaned with pain, walking so slowly toward the restroom. Me and Sher made cereal for the kids and kept them in the living room so they didn't bother mom or see the masterpiece dad did on her face.

When she was able, she came out of the restroom, stood in the doorway, not knowing whether to come out of the restroom, go back in and throw up, or just hide so we didn't have to see her beaten face and body.

To be perfectly honest I did not recognize my beautiful mom. I screamed the second I saw her, she grabbed me.

"I'm sorry, I'm so sorry you saw all this." She hugged me tightly, trying her best to comfort me. Apologizing to me for what dad had done and knowing that I had seen the absolute worst thing a child could witness. As I screamed, the other kids came running to see just what caused me to scream, but stopped the second they saw moms' face.

They all began screaming and crying. Six different piercing tones of crying, almost like a pack of howling wolves. Mom did everything in her power to comfort all of us, but how could she? How does any woman explain how or why this happened, and that she could have been beat to death, oh and by the way kids, don't hate your dad for doing this because, after all, he is still your father.

Six panicked, screaming crying kids. Almost to much for anyone to console.

It took awhile but she did manage to calm all of us down.

It would be a task to calm one child from being terrified, but to try and calm six kids, it was almost impossible.

The comforting, soothing words that came out of mom's mouth just did not match her monster like face. It was so confusing. The pain her body must have felt. Unimaginable.

The uncontrollable sound of six crying kids. What thoughts must have gone through her mind and the fears for her children if her husband were to come back and carry out his threats? How in the world did she not go insane? No other woman in the world could have calmed six terrorized kids, only our mom.

Once she some-what calmed us down, she went in to take a bath and get out of her bloody clothes. I stood by the restroom door the entire time, my ear pressed against the door listening for signs she may try to cut her wrist, drown her self, or whatever she could in an attempt to get away from him.

Several times I heard her cry out in pain; several times I tapped on the door and asked. "Are you ok mom?"

Each time she would barely speak, "Yes." But I knew better. I suspected she was just trying to make it easier for us. I don't recall exactly how long she stayed in the restroom, an hour it seemed, nonetheless, I stood there the entire time, hoping and praying she would not do anything to harm herself. When she finally did come out, I followed her. Wherever she went, I was right behind her.

She lay down several times throughout the day, never really sleeping, just laying down to rest her weary body. She didn't eat anything, she would insist she was not hungry, I'm sure she really wasn't. How could she be hungry with all the blood she had been throwing up? I believe I was in shock, but remained right by her side. In all honesty, what does a twelve year old know about taking care of a beat and battered woman.

The day seemed an eternity. Every time we heard a car outside, we would cringe, for fear he was back. Could it be possible he left us for good, just walked away before he was put away?

Oh, if only that were true.

I looked at my badly beaten mom and asked over and over to myself, why would she not leave him? With everything I had seen I was aware she did not actually allow him to beat her, but, in a twisted way, perhaps she felt responsible for her own misfortune. What causes a man to beat a woman so severely? What man in his right mind could beat a woman, not slap, but beat and think it to be acceptable. Did mom blame herself for this ass whoopin she had taken?

Does my dad hate her that much? Is that why he did this? There is no way this is love. You don't beat someone so damn severely and call it love. If that were so, then I never wanted to be in love or be loved by anyone. This was worse than a nightmare. I just wished some how some way he would never come back, ever.

No such luck! As much as I never wanted to see him again, as much as I wanted him in jail or better yet, dead. I was horrified when I realized he was back.

At first he did not come inside, rather just sat in his car. He sat there waiting, like a lion waiting to pounce on his prey.

God, what was I gonna do if he tried to beat her again? She was frail and badly beaten. There was no way she could survive another round of his torture. What the hell were we to do? If I screamed for help no one would hear us, and surely, our failed attempts to get help would further enrage him.

The little kids came running to mom when they heard him drive up, fear in all their eyes. I'm very grateful none of the kids woke when he was beating her: I seriously doubt he would have stopped, it probably would have only pissed him off even more, besides what I witnessed was too much for me to handle, let alone a younger kid.

Not knowing what else to do, mom had the kids get ready for bed. She stayed in our room, just sitting on the edge of the bed, waiting. Waiting for the inevitable.

To this day, I believe mom must have had a knife somewhere on her person, just in case that monster decided to beat her again.

Premeditated on her part? Possibly! But why just sit there knowing his capabilities? It is so hard to believe she sat there a sitting duck, waiting for round two.

God or the devil himself must have reached in his car, opened his car door, led him to the front door, opened the door for him, took off his shirt, and made him collapse on his bed.

Oh! Could he have possibly overdosed on some kind of drug, because he wasn't drunk? Was he drowning in self-pity? Feeling sorry that he turned into an uncontrollable monster that escaped having his sorry ass hauled off to jail, and at some point would have to face his wife and kids knowing that he was anything but the image of a perfect man?

Who knows? Who cares? He was asleep, that's all mom cared about, hell that's all I cared about. What ever caused him to just pass out and not say one word to any of us was in fact in our favor?

For the night, as long as he slept and didn't attack we were safe, and we knew at one point we would have to deal with him again.

# 6

The word "bitch" kept ringing in my ears. He was actually calling my mom a bitch. She was a saint in my eyes. She was not like other women, she wasn't vain. She wasn't a show off, she wasn't a demanding wife, and she sure as hell wasn't anything like dad. So why was he calling her such names? Not once did it ever cross my mind that my mother was actually a bitch.

So many fights they had over the years, usually him slapping her or pulling her hair, anything he could do to belittle of humiliate her. Unacceptable acts by society's rules, things we always thought to be normal, like the changing of the weather from spring to summer. It was inevitable.

However, this time it was different. It was more physical, horribly verbal, and almost deadly. As a child, I did not think of her as weak. She was what held us all together, but dear Lord why would she let this good for nothing-bastard damn near kill her and not even attempt to leave him.

I suppose instinct kept all the kids quiet that night.

The next morning we were supposed to go to school, but I knew we weren't going anywhere.

Mom stayed with us in our room, avoiding dad at all costs. She looked even worse now, her face giving the appearance of one mangled in a car wreck.

Her beautiful green eyes were blood shot, red, with purple bruises under each eye, and damn near closed shut. I noticed she intentionally avoided the mirror each time she passed it, yet I could see bald spots in her hair from where dad had pulled so much out... How could she be so strong, yet so weak?

We woke but knew not to make any noise as to wake him, even Danny managed to keep his deep voice to a whisper.

Sher fixed cereal for all of us and even brought it to our room, knowing if we all went to the kitchen to eat, it would surely wake him. It may have been impossible for other kids to remain quiet so that a monster of a man could sleep, not us. Being quiet was the easy part; dealing with his wrath was the worst.

Then, as we all knew it would happen, we heard him wake. I began to shake. I knew if I pissed on myself and he found out, he would, without a doubt go on a rampage. I held it in.

While sitting beside me on the bed, mom took my hand in hers to comfort me. As he walked into our room I swear I thought the bastard was gonna just kill us all.

I didn't look at him as he entered the room, I couldn't, I was just too afraid. I'm not quite sure how much of mom's face he could actually see, though he was a mere two feet in front of her. She squeezed my hand as he approached, an attempt I'm sure on her part to comfort me.

"No one leaves this house till that shit clears up." He demanded.

Stupid me, I thought he meant the mess the kids had made with their cereal bowls and their raggedy toys. I looked up and he was pointing at her face. She did not say a word; she was motionless.

I looked down at her hand, which was holding mine; a tear fell from her cheek right into our hands. I believe God covered my mouth to prevent me from screaming. Dad turned, and walked out of the house.

I cried so much after that, describing my pain only as a bomb exploding in my brain. Mom tried desperately to comfort me, knowing I was the only child of six that had witnessed the brutal attack. Now she stayed by my side, attempting to comfort me the entire day.

It was impossible for mom to cook a meal; we didn't expect it of her. She opened a can of soup and heated it for us, and was able to keep a bit of it in without getting sick herself. We spent the entire day in our room, Danny and J.J. playing with their cars and trucks. Becky and Carrie, playing round after round of jacks. Sher and I did whatever chores we could, knowing damn well there was no way mom could do any of them.

Sher really hadn't said too much during this entire ordeal, which was so unlike her because she was the virtual life of the party. She pretty much kept to herself, yet the smaller kids, though frightened by mom's face, pretty much continued to be kids.

Mom asked Sher if she was ok.

"Yes." She said in what sounded like an angry tone. She was dad's favorite, and for a second I got the horrible feeling she was angry with mom. Sher saw in that animal father of ours what none of us was able to see. Maybe she just felt sorry for him.

"I have to go to school tomorrow, I have tests." Sher announced. Mom tried to explain that none of us would be going anywhere. Really, there was no explanation for any of this.

How could she tell us whether we liked it or not, we were pretty much prisoners until her bruises faded? How the heck was my mom gonna avoid her own mother, which did her weekly visits on Wednesdays? Surely eventually, someone would come calling.

Mom went to the restroom at least ten times before dad returned home. I heard him shut the front door, and fumble around with his personal items on his dresser. Perhaps he changed clothes, perhaps he just made his grand appearance just to make sure mom hadn't packed us all up and left his sorry ass. After ten or fifteen minutes, he left again.

One would have thought this so called "man" would have begged for forgiveness, plead with her, kiss her ass, something remorseful. Instead, he was acting as if he were the victim! Whatever self pity trip he was putting himself through, at least for the moment, he wasn't terrorizing us…...

We had been confined to one bedroom for two days before someone knocked at the front door. Mom knew better than to open it. We knew for a fact that it wasn't our animal father because he had a key.

"Hello." A male voice said.

Mom stood at the front door but didn't open it.

"Yes." She said

"Mrs. Guetarro? I'm from Denver Elementary School. I'm here to find out why the kids aren't in school."

No matter which of us wanted to go to school, and which of us didn't, it pretty much was a given we weren't gonna get out of our house for possibly another week or so...

I wanted to scream Help, help us! But fear kept me quiet.

Mom peeked through the curtain. Sure enough, it was the truancy officer from school Mr. Johnson. He was a short bald man with a big fat nose. His nickname was Mr. Magoo, because he was the spitting image of the cartoon character Mr. Magoo.

I could see the shadow of his nose through the curtain. I almost laughed.

"The kids are all sick, and won't return this week." She lied without opening the door.

"What's the problem?" He asked. (Once before I had missed two days of school, and he came to find out why. He took one look at the chicken pox all over me, turned, and walked away) I couldn't imagine what mom was going to say.

"We all have a stomach virus." She lied again.

"You sure?" He asked. A tone in his voice insinuating he did not believe her.

"Would you like to come in and see?" Seems she was being sarcastic.

Now it goes without saying, and it doesn't take a really smart person to compute: "If you know someone with a stomach virus, stand clear, they are highly contagious."

"No thank you, Mrs. Guetarro. I'll take your word for it. So just send a note when they return to school." He said as he walked off the front porch.

Desperate times, desperate measures. She had made up a good lie. It was senseless to wonder why she didn't scream for help, open the door and scare the shit out of old Magoo, with her smashed up face? Simply put, she knew better.

Dad stayed away for two days, I'm sure a relief for mom, and definitely a relief for me. We had no idea where he was or what he was doing, but one thing was certain, we were grateful he was gone.

# 7

The lifestyle dad had grown accustomed to; if he didn't come home at night, it was usually one of two things. Another woman or dead.

Dad didn't have a job per say, he was a hustler. Every day he went to the neighborhood bar, did his hustling thing; gambling, rolling dice, anything he could do for a quick buck.

Seems no one ever understood why dad gave up his military career to become a gangster. No one had the guts to ask. In fact, I seriously doubt he would have given anyone an honest answer anyway.

Before dad's military and gangster days, dad did what ever he could to make a living. I vaguely remember him working at a warehouse, and driving a snow cone truck. I even remembered him throwing newspapers. Apparently, this was not enough to support his growing family, so he enlisted in the Air Force. But as we all know he took that destructive turn in his life and became the notorious "Johnny G."

Now, I'm not saying he was big time mafia, Chicago, New Jersey style, or wherever it is big time mafia folks migrate from. But nonetheless, he was a gangster. He was not a thug, he was not a punk, and he sure was not a wanna be.

Dad was one hundred percent gangster.

He found a way to be a respected and loved gangster, and he loved the power of it all. He answered to no one, he owed nothing to anyone.

Fort Worth Texas had its share of gangsters and shady characters. It is where dad had lived all his life, where the Air Force base was that dad had been stationed. It is the city he loved.

He lived in the north side of town his entire life. It was his area; it's where he went to Elementary, Junior High, and High School in North Side, where never a prouder North Sider lived.

I'm aware every city has their share of bad asses; our part of town was no exception.

I'm not stupid, though a young child I knew such words as Syndicate, Gangster, Mafia, Hired Killers, Boss, Soldier, though generally these are not words you hear at the dinner table, none the less they were words we grew up with.

Dad loved what he did, he had no shame. I didn't realize in the beginning why, but knew for a fact there was something very special about my dad.

Maybe that's why the gangster life just seemed more appealing to dad than any thing honorable. Dad did what he did, and as far as he was concerned, he owed an explanation to no one. Not his wife, his mother, or his kids.

He made his quick cash, with the help of the crew he formed from old acquaintances, hired hands, and people that had proven them selves by whatever means he asked of them.

Then there were the really bad things he would do for money. Things we kids weren't told about, but we were able to pick up on during those whispering conversations we would over hear him bragging about to his other gangster friends when they would periodically visit our house.

Dad, in a twisted way reminded me of Sonny from "A Bronx Tale," Not classy like Sonny, but the same gangster concept. Only difference, Sonny was not a wife beater.

Dad had his crew following him around, doing as he said. Committing crimes for him, committing crimes right along side him.

Not all things dad and his crew did were bad. I overheard him talking about the people he would help and the things he would do for the neighborhood. Dad liked helping the older women the most; I suppose they reminded him of his own mom, whom he saw only when she would pass through town.

Someone said dad and his men caught two teens taggin a building once, I think it must have been Sal-E bar they were taggin, because dad was furious. So rather than beat the shit out of the two punks, dad took their paint cans away from them, which was silver paint and painted the punks hair, their clothes, and their shoes. The two teens were horrified.

Then dad wrote our address on a piece of paper, and said to the teens. "Go home, give your dad this paper with my address, if he doesn't like what I just did to you punks, tell him to come see me."

They escaped without an ass whooping or being killed. No parent ever showed up to confront dad.

Any time dad or his men would ride through the streets of north side, which it seemed they patrolled the streets more than the cops did. If there were trash on the street in front of a house, dad would send one of his men to knock on the door and tell the resident to clean the mess. The disgusting way we lived who the hell could've ever guessed dad cared about appearances. I must admit, though we had no grass in our front yard, our yard was spotlessly clean. Always.

Dad absolutely loved North Side. If a new family moved into the neighborhood dad personally met them. Mostly to see what kind of people they were, I suppose also to let the new residents know who was boss. Dad and his "Welcoming Committee."

Then there were the haters and I suppose if anyone ever wanted to assassinate him, all they had to do was walk up to the neighborhood bar and blow his fucking head off, but no one dared. He was feared, he was respected, he was loved, and he loved every damn second of it.

Once he took me and Sher with him to the neighborhood bar. Sal-E-'s Bar, dad's second home, actually, it was more of a first home to him, he spent more time there than he ever did at our home, it goes without saying. However, why would he take his daughters to such a place? I suppose he was doing something illegal and needed an alibi. What better alibi then his own two daughters, right?

Whatever his reason, whatever possessed him to take two innocent young girls to a disgusting bar with even more disgusting patrons, is something we will never know. Even as we walked in the bar, instinct told me we had no business being there.

The first thing I noticed was all the smoke. Everyone was smoking a cigarette. I literally couldn't breathe. It was a small place, enough for twenty or thirty people, but this particular night over sixty people were crammed into that small confined space.

Dad always wore a suit and tie, giving the impression he were on a special business trip. As I looked around, surprisingly all the other men had on suits and ties as well. There is just something classy about a man all dressed up, whether he's a banker or a killer.

The very second we entered the bar, dad was greeted, first by the owner of the bar, then like robots each of the other thirty or so men shook his hand then kissed him on the cheek. I suppose it was a gangster ritual, something these men did out of respect for the great and powerful Johnny G.

Dad, smiling with approval as he went from handshake to handshake.

I slowly looked around the room at all the people and noticed all the women's faces were plastered with makeup and most of the women were smoking, which made them look and smell cheap. Several women hugged me and Sher, like you would if you were hugging a long lost relatives. To me these women stunk, they were loud, dirty, and trashy. Not ladies by any means. These were the proverbial "broads" dad often talked about.

Dad "showed us off" to everyone, one by one, saying these are my two oldest daughters.

Several men handed us dollar bills. A bribe? Maybe an attempt to pay us for being somewhere we had no business being. Perhaps it was their clumsy attempt to impress dad.

An old jukebox in the corner, with the volume turned up way too high. There were two couples on the dance floor, but not following the beat too closely. One woman, obviously drunk and showing off appeared to be doing a cheap imitation of a stripper rather than dancing. Embarrassed for her, I looked away.

The bartender handed me and Sher a glass of soda. We were seated at a table while dad took care of business in the back room, where, I now believe the drugs were being dealt, prostitution was being conducted, gambling, and the roughing up of the unsavory characters who may have owed dad money.

He left us alone for all of ten minutes.

I finished my soda and before I swallowed the last sip, the bartender refilled my glass.

I looked around at all the men, and the trashy women with their tight fitting dresses and their clown makeup and thought,

My dad stays away from his family for this shit?
He's mean to his beautiful wife so he can be in this dump with these skanks? This is the place my dad loves to be rather than at home with his family?

I didn't get it, but everyone in that place absolutely loved him. Throughout the bar, you could hear, "Hey Johnny my man."

Someone else would say, "Come here "Compadre" let me buy you a beer."

Throughout the bar dad's name echoed, Johnny this and Johnny that.

I knew for a fact that day dad never spent any money what so ever to buy his own beer. These idiots couldn't stop buying them for him. The beer bottles were lined up on the bar waiting for him to pick one and down it.

Everyone hung on to every word he said, and laughed at his stupid jokes. I knew his jokes weren't funny, hell even he knew his jokes weren't funny, yet they all laughed. They all smiled at him as if he was a king or a prince. Only thing missing was for the women to curtsy, or the men to trip and fall all over their own feet just to offer him their seat.

A disgusting show of loyalty and respect, more like kissing a mother fucker's ass to me. Hell, not even I would kiss his ass, and I was the daughter that feared him the most.

There was a smile on dad's face, ear-to-ear, non-stop from the time we walked in the bar until we left. He was a different person here; actually, he seemed happy, comfortable.

As handsome as I knew he was, he looked even more handsome here, around all these people. Dad stood out compared to all these other men, though they dressed like dad, tried to act like dad, none could ever be dad.

He couldn't stop smiling, the more he smiled, the more his dimples stood out, those pearly whites, a dead give away as to his love for this place and all these people.

At home he was always bitching and in a hurry to leave, to be somewhere else. Apparently, he was always in a hurry to leave his family to be here amongst the fake people that loved him. Maybe they weren't fake people; maybe they really did love and respect him. Because the Johnny G. they knew, was not the Johnny G. I knew.

It was rare to see my dad smile, unless, at the time I had no idea what the smell was. But I knew if I smelled it and looked at him, his eyes would be glassy, his breath would stink, and he would be smiling and happy about nothing.

This was exactly how he smelt and looked as he came out from the back room of the bar. This is how he looked and smelled and acted many times at home. I just didn't know at the time, but my monster father was high on marijuana.

So the day he was throwing shit around in his room, bitching at mom "Where are they, I left them right here." He was bitching and acting like a crazy man over his mother fucking rolling papers." UNBELIEVABLE!

# 8

No show for dad no surprise to us, but just as she always had, and as timely as clockwork, Grandma showed up.

Since we were deprived of a phone, mom was unable to call Grandma and inform her we were all sick with stomach viruses, so just as she had done all my life, she showed up on Wednesday at 9 am.

Now, whether dad was home or not, somewhere with a mistress, away doing his illegal bull shit, or in jail, the same rules always applied. Do not open the door.

We all heard grandma as she drove up, with her loud raggedy car; we even smelled the fumes from her exhaust before she even parked the car.

She was a chubby woman, with grey curly hair and beautiful white false teeth, which she would pop those suckas in and out of her mouth to scare us and or make us laugh. She rather waddled when she walked, like a penguin. Maybe she walked like that because as a nurse, she was always on her feet, and after pulling double shift after double shift, it just hurt for her to walk.

Seldom did I see her with regular clothes and shoes on because ninety percent of the time she was dressed in her nurses' uniform because she was either going to or coming from the nursing home she supervised.

She was a happy woman and wore very sweet perfume, which at times could be nauseating. She always gave big long hugs and kisses every time we saw her, sometime not wanting to let us go, hugging us and telling us just how much she loved us. Once I literally got dizzy because she hugged me so long, her perfume damn near suffocated me.

She was aware there were problems with my father; of course, she did not know the severity of those problems. She warned dad once, "If you ever hurt my daughter or grand kids I'll kill you." To me it was a scary comment at the time, but it sure didn't faze my dad. I'm sure he would have had her disposed of if he even thought for a second she was capable of carrying out her death threat. He was afraid of no one. Do you think he would've been afraid of chunky old grandma? Not likely.

So here she was knocking on the door. This was her Wednesday tradition; visit her daughter and grand kids. I don't remember a Wednesday in my lifetime that she wasn't at our house.

What was mom going to do? Seems mom had two options. Open the door? Negative, that poor over weight woman would've died of a heart attack right there on the porch if she had seen moms face. Or ignore her. Mom could walk to a pay phone later when it was dark outside, so no one in the neighborhood could see moms face, call grandma, and give her some jacked up excuse for not opening the door.

That didn't seem logical to me, even if mom tried to trick her as she had Mr. Magoo, grandma would not have fallen for that crap, she's a nurse, she would have insisted on nursing us all back to health. There was no alternative but for mom to ignore her.

Grandma knocked and knocked, she even tried jiggling the doorknob. Thank goodness she was never given a house key or she would have busted in like an angered cop on a drug bust.

Finally, completely frustrated, she took the five minute journey of waddling down our front stairs, avoiding the messed up stairs, mumbling obscenities as she got back in her car and left. Grandma was now forced to wait it out until mom or dad contacted her.

Mom had bought herself some time. But why go through all this to protect a monster? Why not just open the door and show the world what he had done to her, and have him arrested? End of her problems....

Why?

Because she knew damn good and well there would always

be that chance he would get out of jail, and then where would she run? She had her six little ducklings to worry about, not to mention if he would be angry enough to go after her mom, her brother, or her sisters. There was no way she would endanger everyone else just because she married the wrong man.

   Within five minutes of grandma leaving there was another knock on the door. If it had taken granny a few more minutes to get in her car, these two women would have met right on our front porch.
   Luck was on mom's side, for a second. The knock was a light tap, as if whoever it was knew we were inside, but also knew not to draw attention to our house. Another knock on the wood part of the door. Mom had put a piece of wood to replace the broken glass. Any one could have knocked that piece of wood out, put their hand in, and open the door themselves, if they really wanted in.
   Mom stood there a moment not knowing what to do. The woman knocked again this time saying, "Shirley, Shirley, let me in."
   I recognized her voice, the woman on the other side of the door was known to us as Auntie Bee. She had been friends with my parents for as long as they had been married, an unlucky thirteen years. Bee wasn't an actual blood relative, but she was a good friend and she loved all the kids to call her Auntie Bee, which we did.
   She was a busty woman in her mid forties, with the blondest hair. One look at her hair and you could tell she spent countless hours at the beauty salon. It was obvious that shade of blonde did not come out of a five-dollar bottle of hair dye.
   Bee also had a lazy eye. Anytime you spoke to her, it would be a bit uncomfortable, because her eye would wonder off while you were talking to her. I guess she just couldn't control that one particular eye. It was always confusing as to which eye to actually look at when speaking to her. Seems it was easier not to look at her at all.
   She was, or seemed to us, that she was desperately starving

for attention. No wonder, in her younger years she was a stripper.

Bee had three kids, ages similar to ours. She lived in one of those houses we created in our minds when we played rich house, only difference, hers was the real thing. She even had a swimming pool, which, none of us could actually swim so we were never allowed to get in it.

Each of her spoiled kids had their own room, a luxury we never knew. Damn we didn't even possess our own beds let alone our own rooms.

Two sons, and one even more spoiled ass daughter, which I couldn't stand because she was a whiney ass little girl demanding way too much attention. Maybe I was just jealous because she got it. Her voice drove me crazy, kinda nasal like.

Seemed like such abuse to take us to their gorgeous house, and then rip us from it to take us back to our shack of a house. Every time we left their house, I hated our house even more.

Auntie Bee, we called her, and her husband owned two strip clubs. Bee didn't strip anymore but was actively involved in managing both of them with her husband Ely.

Bee was a fun woman, always giving us cookies, snacks, and hugging us just as she did her own kids. We were always made to feel welcome in her home, though she was richer than we were by far, she never treated us inferior. (Ha! Ha! Inferior, a word I learned from her.)

Again, Bee tapped and tapped on the glass, waiting for some kind of response, finally, she spoke. "Please, let me in please. I know what happened; Johnny came by last night and told Ely what he did to you."

There was no way Bee guessed that one, seems to me she knew exactly what she was talking about.

Mom was hesitant at first, remembering dad's golden rule. *Never open the door.*

"I just dropped Ely and Johnny at the airport; they won't be back until tomorrow." Bee pleaded.

Without skipping a beat, without any further hesitation,

mom opened the door. I froze. What if Bee was lying? What if it was a trap?

Too late! Bee was in and locking the door behind herself.

Just one second of looking at my mom's battered face made Bee let out a faint scream.

"I'm so sorry, I'm so sorry Shirley." She kept saying.

She cried and hugged my mom over and over not wanting to let her go.

"This is all my fault. I'm so sorry." Bee insisted.

I was confused. How was this, her fault? It was my dad that beat mom, not Bee. I saw it myself. Bee wasn't there, just mom and dad. Why in the world would Aunt Bee want to take the blame for any of this?

We were all in the living room as Bee was hugging mom and crying. She gathered all us kids and hugged us over and over saying. "I'm going to take care of y'all, don't worry I'm going to take care of all of y'all." She cried loudly and was very emotional, going from one kid to the next, almost in a panic.

Watching her scurry around the room, I wondered how this stripper thought she was going to help. What did she possibly think she could do for us? I mean seriously, mom was risking another ass whooping just for allowing her in the house after dad specifically told her not to let anyone know of any of this.

I remembered the hateful look on his face when he had warned her to keep her mouth shut.

Mom instructed us kids to leave the room so she could talk with Bee. The little kids went back to playing their games while Sher went to make Kool-aid. Not me, I stood by the side of the door, and listened to what Bee had to say.

They sat on the sofa, Mom wiping her face with her hands. Bee repeated her self over and over.

"I'm sorry, this is my fault, if only youz guys, Bee called everyone, youz guys, hadn't come to my party."

Mom said nothing. Perhaps she too blamed Bee.

"What did he hit you with?" She asked.

There was silence for a few seconds, then mom told her

how dad beat her, threw her on the floor, pistol whipped her, choked her, and threatened to kill her.

Hearing mom talk of it, made me relive it all over again in my mind. I hated that miserable excuse of a father even more.

Bee cried, over and over insisting it was her fault, and then she said something that completely shocked me.

Bee said, "I'm sorry I tried to get y'all to join our orgy."

*Orgy? What the heck was an orgy?* I wondered.

I was so confused. I stood there a few seconds longer thinking again, what the heck is an orgy? So I did what I knew to do, I went directly to Sher.

Sher was in the kitchen; I walked in, went right up to her, and asked, "What's an orgy?"

She looked puzzled and asked, "Why?" As she continued making Kool-aid.

"Because Bee told mom they had an orgy." I blurted out.

Sher hesitated a moment, still adding sugar to her Kool-aid, not even looking up at me to answer my question. "It's where a bunch of people have sex together." She said matter of factly, as if she knew so much about it. She seemed annoyed but answered my question any way. I crept back to listen to mom and Bee talk.

Though Bee and Ely were like relatives to us all, dad was the one that spent the most time with them. Bee and mom were nothing alike. Mom a housekeeper, quiet, shy, mother of six. Bee was a loud mouth show off, always dancing around and pretending to strip, but never actually taking her clothes off.

Turns out Bee and Ely were swingers. They swapped partners, had sex with their friends, men and women, all together, at once, in front of each other, in the same room.

Absolutely sickening to me.

Apparently, mom never knew of all the disgusting things that actually went on at Bee's house, so when dad took her there four nights earlier, it was to be her first experience. Something mom had no intention of being a part of. When dad tried to force mom to participate in that disgusting act, she created a scene and stormed out of Bee's house, thus embarrassing my dad.

So, as it turns out, mom got an ass whooping because she wouldn't act like a whore and sleep with a house full of people. Mom also got her ass whopped because she embarrassed dad by storming out of Bee's house. She also got beat because she wouldn't act like a damn whore, like Bee.

I fucking couldn't believe this shit.

My mom wasn't a whore, Bee was. What the fuck was wrong with all these sickos? I wondered over and over in my mind.

I hated my dad at that moment more then I thought possible. So much went through my mind, so damn much hate. I remembered he made her put on those big old fake tits to make her look different, to make her look like someone she wasn't. He had no respect for his beautiful wife, beating her because she refused to act like Bee, a whore.

I hated him. I hated him so much, and now, I fucking hated that bitch Bee.

In my childish mind, I was thinking, this is too much for me. Why am I standing here listening to all this? These two grown women are speaking of things a normal twelve year old has no business listening to; but this was my mom. As disgusting as all this was to me, I simply had to know why mom was sitting on our sofa, her face so badly beaten, we kids imprisoned in our house for the next week, and why dad had gotten away with such a vicious beating?

Wasn't it a fact his hands were considered lethal weapons, because he was a so-called boxer. And isn't it a fact that by using those lethal weapons to beat his wife, couldn't that have landed his sorry ass in jail? So why the hell wasn't anyone calling the cops?

Why?

Because if anyone had, and he went to jail, and if, just if he ever got out, he just may as well kill us all.

Bee kept insisting to mom, "Come on, come with me, I'll help you get away from him."

No response from mom what so ever.

"I'll get you a place to stay. Ely and I will do everything we can for you and the kids think of the kids." She kept insisting.

Bitch! You should've thought of us kids, and you should've thought of your own fucking kids, I wanted to scream at her, while eaves dropping behind the door. You had a fucking orgy, there, in your home, where your kids live and play, with no concern for your own kids, much less any regard for us.

"You're a fucking disgusting bitch." I thought to myself.

Now, me finding out what an orgy was, seeing my mom beat, and hearing this skank of a woman talk, a woman until today was my aunt, my so-called aunt that I loved so much. I couldn't help but think in my mind, mom are you crazy? For sure, he will kill everyone, including Bee and Ely.

Hey! I thought to myself, that's a wonderful thought.

Dad would kill Bee and Ely, get caught, go to prison for the rest of his miserable life, then we could live happily ever after.

No such luck! Somehow, I already knew my mom would say no. So, Bee came up with another idea.

"Ok Shirley, Why don't you and the kids come spend the night at my house just for tonight. I'm the one that's going to pick Johnny and Ely up from the airport tomorrow afternoon; they'll never know you stayed with me." Bee said with the biggest smile.

Was this bitch serious? I wondered.

Ok, let's play this forward! I definitely was thinking like a little bitch myself.

Now stop me if I'm wrong...This hoe wants my beaten up mom to pack up her six kids and take them to the same house, not a week ago, Bee was hosting an orgy. The same house my mom stormed out of because she didn't want to participate in the humiliating ritual of fucking and being fucked by numerous people at one time. Furthermore, if I am correct, this is the same house, once mom did storm out of, and, if I know my dad, he began beating her ass in their front yard, in the car on the way home, and in our home.

All I could think was, "Fuck you Bee, you miserable whore."

I smiled to myself when I heard my mom say "no."

Besides, I thought to myself. You expected us kids to go spend the night at your house, sleep in a comfy bed, eat as much food as our bellies could hold, laugh, play, possibly sit in the swimming pool, stay up all night, be happy excited kids, sleep late, not wake up to my dad bitching about where's this, where's that.

Was this bitch kidding? Did she seriously think just spending the night in her fucking house would change all our lives, make our lives simpler? Get the hell outta here.

My mind was racing, re-living things in my childhood I had suppressed. Things I never wanted to think about or re live, now like opening the flood gates to a dam, the emotions, the pain, the horrific memories were all back. Emotions exploding in my brain, searching for a way to be brought back to life. Here I stood, conjuring them all to my present day psyche. In other words, I remembered something. Something that had not one damn thing to do with this bullshit about Bee, none the less something that just popped in my mind and I could not control my self from reminiscing.

# 9

For a split second my mind flashed back to the morning a few years earlier, who knows why, but my dad woke up early, or maybe he had just came home from a night of illegal hustling. Maybe he couldn't sleep, maybe he was fucked up on a different drug, or maybe he was still drunk from the night before, and just wanted to fuck with someone. So damn many maybes, it was mind boggling to try to figure it all out.

Whatever his problem was, he was bitching non-stop, of all things, for his comb. He just had to look good, but he had just got home why the hell did he need to look good?

This particular morning he couldn't find his comb.

"Where's my comb?" He hollered.

No one answered him, because, dumbass, everyone was still asleep.

"Juniorrrr where's my god damn comb?" He screamed loud enough to wake the dead at the cemetery half a block away.

Poor Jr! Hearing dad scream his name at the top of his lungs, he crawled out of bed to respond to dads hollering. I was already awake, had been, I just had no desire to get out of bed until I knew he was either asleep or gone.

"I don't know dad." J.J. squeamishly answered.

Dad was throwing things out of his dresser drawers. The more he looked for it, the more pissed off he got. You would have thought he lost his bankroll of illegal money, or worse his stash of illegal drugs. Not a fucking comb.

I hurried to dad's room as quickly as I could, knowing my little brother was being blamed for the disappearance of dads comb. Scared for my brother, I began looking for dad's damn comb, wanting desperately to say, "Where the hell did you leave it you stupid bastard?" Knowing damn good and well if I had been brave enough to speak my mind, by the time I would have gotten to the word "bastard" he would have been knocking my teeth out.

By then good ol' dad lost it. My poor brother J.J., who was standing near the dresser, trying to look for the comb, his little head barely taller than the top of the dresser, too scared to move, and just too tired and sleepy to even focus on what he was looking for. Attempting to rub his eyes, as if he cleared his sleepy eyes, he would magically see the damn comb, then he could go back to bed.

Out of nowhere dad back handed that poor little brother of mine and sent him crashing to the floor. J.J. grabbed his cheek, crying, too scared to move. Too scared to speak. I wondered for a second, where's my mom? Did she just get so used to the abuse that she drowned it all out? Why wasn't she there in the room begging dad to stop or at least comforting my lil brother?

Instantly I remembered dad had sent her to the store to buy milk and eggs. Unfortunately for J.J. mom wasn't there to pick up the pieces.

*Sher*, I wanted to yell out her name. Where was she? I wondered.

She was in the restroom taking a long hot bath. We would tease her she must be half mermaid; no one can sit in a tub that long unless they're part fish.

In a house with eight people and one restroom it seemed unfair to hog the restroom up just to take her princess baths. Even when we would have to piss, Sher would take her sweet time, not caring if any of us pissed all over ourselves or not.

So, laying in a tub and turning prune like, she missed it all. The other kids were still asleep.

I knelt down to comfort my brother, hugged him, and said.

"Don't cry, don't cry."

My brother and I sat there, too terrified to move an inch. I wanted to throw up, from fear and hate. The cries seemed to fade as I hugged my brother. Dad continued his rampage of throwing things around, mostly focusing on the dresser area.

Any time dad came home, he strategically placed his keys, wallet, handkerchief, comb and breath mints on his dresser. These were forbidden objects to us; we knew better than to ever touch anything that belonged to him or that was on his dresser.

As I sat there, cuddling my brother and trying to drown out all the hollering, simultaneously me and my brother looked up; through the reflection in the mirror, we both saw the look on dads face. It was the most horrid, sad, look of guilt I had ever seen.

While carrying on like a mad man he found his damn comb, right where he left it, folded in his fricken handkerchief, exactly where he put it every single day.

How the hell did he overlook it?

Idiot! You are a fucking idiot! I thought to myself.

He glanced over at us, through the mirror; saw me and my brother looking at him.

*Oh, shit!* I remember thinking. We're fixing to get the shit beat out of us, just because.

Dad froze, staring at us, his face turning white, and then a terrible, terrible feeling of sadness came over me. Not for me, not for my brother, but for dad. He had the most indescribable look of guilt on him, a look of such sorrow.

I knew what I felt at that moment. Years later, my brother would confirm that he himself had the same feelings I had. He felt so sorry for dad at the exact second I had...

Sorry, that he had backhanded this little five-year-old boy, a boy that tried so desperately to get approval from this monster. A child that wanted to be proudly called Jr. A child that wanted to be just like him.

We, as well as dad, did not know what to say or do. He stared, we stared, then he came toward us. Instinctively I covered my brother's head to protect him, thinking if this bastard is gonna hit him, he's also gonna hit me too.

Who was I kidding? He could knock us both out with just one slap.

Dad reached down and picked me up from the floor where I sat cuddling my terrified brother, hugged me and said. "I'm sorry Malina, go to your room."

One thing about this monster, he knew how to say he was sorry, especially when he was wrong.

He was a sick twisted individual that would slap, hit, beat and terrorize his family, yet turn around and be kind and loving...

Sick, I would think of his actions as simply sick. As much as I did not want to leave my brother behind I knew I had to. It was dad's orders, and one thing was certain, you never disobeyed his orders.

I went to the room I shared with my five brothers and sisters, trying desperately to hear what was said. All I could actually hear was. "Son, I'm sorry. I'm so sorry; I'll never do that again."

I wanted to laugh. That's a damn joke, I thought to myself.

Smooth talking bastard. You're a fucking smooth talking bastard.

Dad continued. "Son, I thought you took my comb and you were afraid to tell me." He apologized.

Bullshit, I thought.

Dad went on to tell my brother he was going to take him to the store and buy him whatever he wanted. I heard him tickling my brother and could hear my brother laughing.

All was seemingly forgiven, that quickly, that instantly. Moments of horror gone without consequences. It wasn't right, it didn't seem fair, but it was the only way we knew to forgive. Take the abuse and with one simple "I'm sorry," it would be over.

All this about my dad, and that damn comb shit went through my mind as I listened to mom and Bee talk.

My mind was running wild with memories. Maybe I was trying to block out everything Bee and mom were talking about. The memories flashing back had nothing to do with the shit I was listening to at the moment from mom and Bee. It was just more disgusting events in my life for me to think about.

Perhaps these were all suppressed thoughts, events my conscience had blocked. However, due to all the dramatics over the past few days, unfortunately I was being forced to remember them.

I tried to focus on the events that were present. Surely, mom really wouldn't be so cruel as to take us to spend the night at Bee's, then bring us back to our miserable house. Please say no; please say no, I repeated in my mind over and over.

Any other time I would have loved to spend the night at Bee's, but not now, not with all the hate I had in me for her. She was not a woman, she was not my aunt, she was the enemy now, and I never wanted to see her, Ely, her two sons, or her fucking bratty ass daughter ever again.

Mom said no and no it was.

Bee left our house for an hour or so. When she returned, she had snacks for us, maybe her way of trying to make it right, or make herself feel better for what had happened to mom. She didn't overdo it though, just enough for us to eat overnight while dad was away. Surely if she had bought a lot of things, when, and if dad came home he would have known mom opened the door, someone had been there, and he would react.

I was glad when Bee left. I knew she would never be welcomed in our house by mom ever again.

Yes, she left to go back to her rich house, her brat kids, and her nasty fucking orgy's.

Once again, my evil little mind said, "Fuck you Bee you damn bitch."

# 10

Funny how you can think you really know and love someone, but with one conversation, one eaves drop, you can begin to hate them.

Every time we went to Bee's house, she gave us whatever we wanted. We never had to ask for things like candy, cookies, ice cream, hot dogs, and all the things little kids like to eat. She just gave it to us.

There were pictures of Bee all over her house. She, as I said before, was the blondest of blondes. She wore long thick fake eyelashes and lots and lots of makeup. All the pictures of her were pictures of her dressed in skimpy outfits; probably the outfits she stripped out of back in the day.

Bee may have been beautiful in her day but the bar life definitely took its toll on her face and body. I never could figure why such a pretty woman, not beautiful like my mom, but pretty, saw in a chunky, balding, short man. I'm not sure what his nationality was, he wasn't Hispanic or African. He was dark skinned and had a different accent. Best I could figure, Ely was Bee's trick from her days of stripping. He undoubtedly spent the most money on her of all her other tricks so she took a liking to him.

Eventually he took her to work in one of his five strip clubs and made her his star performer flashing money, clothes, cars and a home at her, which eventually enticed her to marry him.

I lay in my shared room thinking of my newfound hate for Bee, my dad, and of my childhood. What a peaceful night it would be, knowing dad would not be coming home.

The night before, we weren't sure where he was, so we only half slept, you know like sleeping with one eye wide open.

But tonight, knowing for sure he would not come home, put a little peace in my mind. At least he wouldn't wake us up in the middle of the night to his drunken ass demanding my mom whip up a meal at a seconds notice at 3a.m., then falling into a drunken stupor before she could finish cooking, or to hear him bitch about any and everything just because he could and no one could stop him.

Yes, if Bee hadn't lied and he really was out of town, we had about twenty hours of peace and quiet.

Peace and quiet, something we knew very little about. I kept half thinking, I would not put it past this idiot to parachute out that damn airplane, walk his ass all the way from the airport to our house, slightly over forty miles, kick down the front door and yell, "I'm baaaack Mutha Fuckas!!!!" Just to ruin our peace and quiet time without him.

We ate our goodies, mom even managed to smile a few times. We all took our baths then said goodnight to mom. She tucked us all in, apologizing the entire time. It seemed we had just a tiny bit of happiness for a few seconds, if only it could have lasted.

I did not go to sleep right away. Several times I got up and tip toed to mom's room to check on her, wondering why she would sleep in his bed? What if he did come home? What if he started again? Finally, exhausted from the week's horrible ordeals, I fell asleep.

The next morning it was so nice to wake up to smiles and hugs, and not to a lot of cussing and bitching.

Apparently, that old bitch Bee must have snuck some eggs and milk in that grocery bag because mom had eggs and toast ready for us when we woke. I remember thinking, geez; this is how life is supposed to be. A good breakfast, smiles, and happiness, what could be better?

I wondered if other kids lived as we did. I wondered if any of the kids we went to school with had abusive fathers, ones that beat their moms. I wondered did any of our school friends hate their childhood. Did any of our friends live in fear? I would never know the answers to these questions, because I was too damn ashamed to ever ask anyone.

*Perhaps the plane had crashed !*No such luck.

We all helped mom straighten up that horrific house. You would have thought we were cleaning it in anticipation of a long lost father. One that would come in, all six kids and his wife would run to greet him at the door. He would have a bouquet of roses for mom, candy for his kids and a warm smile on his face.

I believe I saw that on TV once. "Father Knows Best?" "Leave it to Beaver?" Perhaps it was "The Twilight Zone?" It was a fantasy for my life anyway.

We were able to watch TV. but still couldn't go outside. Mom fixed us a good lunch and even prepared a decent supper.

Didn't seem any of us missed dad. What was there to miss? I watched as my two little sisters played jacks on the living room floor. They loved to play jacks and spent countless hours creating different names for the moves they created. They argued several times. One or the other moved the jack a millionth of a centimeter accidentally, which caused them to argue. Mom would quietly tell them to play nice. My brothers had some old beat up toy trucks pretending to be streetcar racers. Of course, J.J. let Danny win just so he wouldn't cry.

Sher was, guess? In her books. Well, she didn't get straight A's from not studying. She was smart and she knew a lot for a fourteen year old. It seems I could ask her almost any question and she knew the answer.

I watched her reading. I wondered, damn did she know how to speed-read or was she just looking at the pictures in the book pretending to read, because she was flipping through those pages like nobody's business?

She had the most beautiful green eyes, just like mom. They were greener than grass, and looked almost fake. She seemed too young to have grown up eyes, yet I already knew she would get a lot of attention with her eyes the older she got.

Sher always had her hair in a ponytail. As soon as she bathed, her hair went right to a ponytail. It seemed somewhat tomboyish but it made her look like a bookworm, which at the time she was. On a rare occasion she would wear it down but she would make such a fuss that it bothered her so much, she would put it right back up in a ponytail.

She had really long legs. I remember watching her in a race at school once; you know, one of those races where you pass the baton from one runner to another then run all around the track racing against other kids. She would be the last one to get her baton because the other runners on her team were so damn slow, but those long legs would kick into high gear, and she would haul ass around that track as if she were a million dollar racehorse at the Kentucky Derby. She would sail past all the other runners beating them by a mile. I would watch in awe, because not even the older boys could out run her.

"What are you reading?" I stupidly asked her.

"A book." She answered as if I already annoyed the hell out of her. She even held it up so I could see it really was a book.

"Yes grouchy, I see that, but what book?" I asked sarcastically.

"One to teach me how to beat the crap out of you if you don't stop annoying me!" She barked as she stood up and stormed out of the room. I laughed to myself for a second.

"You don't need a book for that; you have your precious father to teach you." I said to myself because she was just so easily annoyed.

Mom was tidying up our pigpen of a kitchen. It was old and I swear the stove must have had a gas leak. Anytime I was in kitchen for more than ten minutes, my head would hurt.

We were enjoying a nice calm peaceful day, then we heard it. We heard dad drive up, almost right to the front porch. Everyone froze.

Not even being told to, the kids gathered up their toys from the living room floor and ran to our room. Sher came back to the living room and looked out the window.

"My dad is here." Sher said without looking toward mom or me.

"Go to your room kids." Mom instructed us.

*Why?* I wondered. Do you really want to face him alone?

Mom repeated, "Go to your room kids."

Sher stuck her tongue at me as she walked past me, such a smart ass, then she smiled at me which damn near made me laugh. Mom stood there completely frozen not knowing whether to run for the hills, hide in the closet or open the door and let him in. He was back! We were scared, and we were defenseless.

# 11

We stood motionless, as if someone had instructed us to hold our pose to take a family picture. We obliged, each holding our breath. My eyes shot to mom's eyes. Hers looked as scared or even more scared than mine. It seemed like an hour passed, but it was a mere twenty seconds.

At first, he did not get out of his car. We knew we were at his mercy, nowhere to run, nowhere to hide.

Then I heard it…the sound of that old car door being shut. It would only be a matter of seconds before he stormed into the house, sending me into frenzy, causing me to piss on myself. I stood there shaking as if I was standing in a snowstorm in the middle of the North Pole.

*What was I going to do?*
*What was she going to do?*
*More so, what was he going to do?*

Sher rounded up all the kids and took them to our room. She looked at me sadly, though she didn't say a word, I couldn't help but think I read her mind.

*I know you will not come with me, so be careful!* Telepathy? Perhaps the look on her face, told her thoughts. Quite possible.

Mom didn't bother to tell me to go with Sher, and though I never defied her, this was one time I would, no matter what!

Mom seemed not to know what to do; sit down, stand up, cry, beg, or plead.

Oh! I think I would've hauled ass out the back door, jumped the fence as a Sprinter at the Olympic Games, and booked it to the nearest neighbors. But I knew she was not going to leave her kids alone to face the music with this monster. Again, it seemed she was frozen in time.

I was standing at the door, the same place I stood the day I eaves dropped on her and Bee. It seemed like mom was moving in slow motion, trying to get to me, but her legs weren't moving at all. Then a strange thing happened.

He knocked on the door!

He knocked? Like a regular person!

He didn't bang on the door, he didn't kick it open, he didn't demand to be let in!

He knocked, as a salesman knocks when they are trying to sell a newspaper subscription.

How incredibly odd?

He had a key! Why not use it?

I wondered why he didn't barge in, throw his anger fit, terrorize us all, then storm right back out!

He knocked again!

Mom opened the curtain to the front door. She was face to face with him, the only thing separating them was that thin square of broken glass, and the board mom had put in place of the broken glass.

I couldn't see her face, but I sure saw his. He had not shaven for days, although he always got that proverbial five o'clock shadow, this was different. If I didn't know first hand what a monster he was, I would've thought to myself, my dad is even more handsome than I remembered!

He looked through the glass directly at her face.

She stood motionless. "Come outside Shirley. I want to talk to you."

Oh sure, I thought. Talk my ass; you want to beat the shit out of her again.

She did not respond.

"Please, I need to talk to you. I promise I won't touch you!" He pleaded.

What the hell was there to talk about?

No, mom, say No! Tell him to leave! Tell him you have nothing to say to him! I wanted to scream at the top of my lungs.

"Please, just let me tell you what I need to say." He pleaded. "If you want, I will leave afterwards."

It's a trap, I kept thinking. He begged and pleaded.

God himself only knows why, without warning, she opened the door.

Every bone in my body shook with fear. My eyes swelled with tears. I was no longer hiding behind the door; I was standing in the doorway now; staring at the both of them. Dad never crossed the threshold. He took one-step toward the doorway and I screamed.

"No Mom!" I screamed as loud as I possibly could.

She looked at me with her beautiful beaten green eyes as I screamed, then turned back to look at dad and said, "Help me Johnny, she's afraid!"

He squatted down and held out his arms as if he had just returned from serving a tour of duty and hadn't seen me in years.

In the calmest of voices he said, "Come here baby. I won't hurt you." (It was a family joke that he called all the girls in the family "baby" and all the boys "son" because he could not remember any of our names). Baby, a term of endearment?

I wasn't budging. No matter how nice he was attempting to be, I knew if I took just one-step toward him I might piss myself, and that would anger him, losing this rare occasion of kindness.

Most of his torture toward us came after he had been drinking, or when he'd been out all night and would be so tired that he took it out on all of us.

He was a monster!

It was his way or the highway. When he would apologize, mostly when he was stoned, he would say. "Baby, I'm sorry, I love you so much." Then he would giggle, almost choking on his high.

So, here we stood, kind of like a western standoff, with pretend pistols pointed at one another, first of us to move would be shot. A scene straight out of a western.

I knew for sure I couldn't move, checkmate! It was up to one of them to make the first move.

Dad took one-step in the house, I screamed as if I had been shot with that fake pistol. Mom headed towards me, but dad got to me first. The moment he reached me, Sher and the other kids came running from the bedroom. Sher screamed as loud as she possibly could.

"Dad, no! Don't Daddy! Please don't!" Sher pleaded.

He always seemed to melt when she said "Daddy." We all called him Dad, but Sher called him "Daddy."

All the kids were crying, Sher was screaming at him, Mom was saying "No Johnny, no." Every one certain he was approaching me to slap me, or whatever he could to shut me up. He actually seemed scared, scared of his kids. He then reached me and threw his arms around me in an attempt to protect me.

"Johnny no, don't hit her!" Mom was yelling.

"Daddy, Daddy, no." Sher was crying as loudly as I was.

The other kids' cries seemed faint compared to Sher's.' She grabbed my arm and tried to pull me away from him, attempting to protect me as a mother bear protects her cub.

"Babies, babies, don't cry. I'm not gonna hurt anyone." Dad tried to explain. He actually looked like he was about to cry. He let my hand go, as Sher pulled me away from him and hugged me. Dad looked at mom then he looked at us, then at mom, then back at us, as if he had no idea who would trust or believe a word he said.

Mom consoled us by saying, "Shhhh kids, it's ok, everything is ok. Don't cry."

Her soothing voice knew just what to say, and when to say it.

"Come on let's go to your room." She said as she tried to scurry us out of the room.

"No wait." Dad said.

*Ok, here it comes, the Dr. Jekyll and Mr. Hyde routine.* I thought.

"Sit down kids. I want to talk to you."

*Huh? What did he say? Talk?* This was foreign to all of us.

Talk? We never talked! He would yell and we would freak out.

"Sit down, all of you. I want to talk to y'all." He repeated.

Seems he had a tear in his eye. Was it possible? The monster actually had a heart. I wondered.

Mom guided us to the sofas, without realizing, she sat us from tallest to shortest. We all looked at him, not knowing what was about to happen. We never experienced these "family talks." Ever!

"I messed up." He began. "I'm not worth a damn as a father or a husband."

He got that shit right!

"I'm sorry, and I beg forgiveness from each of you."

I didn't even hear the rest of his speech. I only remember thinking to myself. Who did he kill? Or rob while he had been gone during those two short days? And, where is my real Dad? This surely isn't him.

Then, my mind went back to his speech.

"I'm just going to sit on the porch and talk to your mama." (The word "mama" another term of endearment he only used when he was stoned.)

He continued. "I want to talk to your Mama, outside, on the front porch; alone."

I'm thinking, Oh no, here we go again.

"I give you kids my word, I will not harm your mom!"

Now, even a twelve-year-old daughter of a low life gangster knows that if a gangster gives his word, it is an oath, a sacred promise, one they always keep.

Sher stood up, took my two little brothers by their hands, and said, matter-of-factly. "If you hurt her one more time I will never forgive you!" She was so damn serious.

I don't know why, but I felt like laughing. Is that all it would take? For Sher to threaten him? Threaten to never forgive him? "IF" only that would work! She was definitely his favorite, the little sparkle in his eye.

My two little sisters followed her without skipping a beat.

It was a showdown, only dad, mom, and I remained in the living room.

Now, what? I thought.

Dad came and sat next to me. His breath did not stink as if he had been smoking marijuana, as it had so many times before. His clothes did not smell of that stinky herb. Could it be possible that he wasn't stoned?

He turned to me and said, "Baby, I promise you I am only going to talk to your Mama. Do you want to come outside with us?"

Now, that was a thought, me sit beside them, right in the line of fire should he get angry?

I'm a kid, but I'm not a dumb ass.

"No." I said, wiping my tears.

Mom said. "We'll leave the front door open so you can see us."

But what would I do if he started to hit her again? We had no phone. I couldn't scream loud enough for the neighbors a half a block away to hear. What good would all that do if I couldn't get help to her?

Reluctantly, I said. "Ok." Knowing damn good and well I was gonna eaves drop throughout their entire conversation. He hugged me again saying how sorry he was.

Walking out onto the front porch, they looked like a couple going out on their first date. The only difference was, she had a messed up face and he looked like a very handsome wino with his 5 o'clock shadow. I watched them as they sat on the top step. Within seconds I was on my feet standing by the door, drowning out all other sounds around me except their voices.

This is no life for a twelve year old I thought. Here I was again playing Sherlock Holmes, hiding behind the door, trying to protect the mom I loved so very much.

What could he possibly say to her now that would make a difference?

Do women actually forgive their men for such acts, or do

they burn their beds? My mom, would never stop, never stop trying to make some kind of life for her kids, but was forgiving him the right thing to do? Was this the way any mom wants her kids to live?

Something had to change.

# 12

I honestly could not hear anything mom was saying. She was just so soft spoken. I watched them sitting on the porch, remembering only a few nights before had been the last time I had seen them together, and it was so violent. Now, to see them together seemed as if the beating had never taken place. I could see her shaking her head yes then no. I could also see her lips moving, so I knew she was talking, I just couldn't hear her actual words.

His voice was deep enough that I could hear certain words he was saying, but he was not all over the place, yelling, cussing, and bitching as he normally was.

I focused my attention once again on mom. The only thing I could actually see was her side profile. He had beaten her, yet she still looked at him as he talked. I wondered if she looked at him out of respect, out of fear, or maybe she looked at him because, perhaps she really loved him.

She was a good mom; fun, happy and could do so many things other moms only dreamed of doing. As kids, we never were yelled at, but she would scold or punish us if we acted like brats, but never raised her voice, dad did enough of that for both of them.

When we would watch American Bandstand or Soul Train, she would step right up and dance around the room with us, never embarrassed or shy. If she missed a beat, she would laugh and try again always doing the latest dance steps, whether she did them right or wrong. She would get us by our hands, pull us up off the sofa, and make us dance with her. Even my little brothers would scream, "No! We don't wanna dance." Mom would tell us to sing the words to the songs, because it was obvious we knew them, so we would eventually give in singing and laughing with her, holding our pretend microphones.

If we were playing jacks on the front porch, she would sit

right down on that old porch and play with us. Sometimes she would cheat saying we were sore losers, laughing at us the entire time. If my brothers were playing catch in the front yard she would take one of their baseball gloves from them, play with the other brother, then switch off and play with the other. We all got the same amount of attention and love from her.

When it was time to go inside and cook, she would tell us girls to go in with her and watch her, not help her. She just wanted us to watch her so we could learn. "Come on girls y'all have to learn how to cook, I'm not going to live forever." There was not a better cook in the world, at least to us.

If we needed clothes she never bought them, rather, she would get out her old singer peddle sewing machine and whip us up a dress, effortlessly it seemed, and that was only if she had material to do so. She even made doll clothes for our dolls, always putting the tiniest detail on the dolls clothes, such as lace, tiny buttons, and trim. Mom had an excellent eye for detail, even sewing our names by hand, which couldn't be sewn on with that old machine.

Almost every Christmas all of us girls would get a new doll. Usually a month or two before Christmas she would be in her room making doll clothes .We could hear that old machine working hard to keep up with the speed at which she would peddle. She would say "Don't come in here girls, I'm busy right now." We would know she was working on our doll clothes so we never went in because we didn't want to spoil her surprise for us.

We never made a big deal of getting the dolls. The big deal we did make was when we opened the boxes full of doll clothes. She would wrap each box, of all things, in left over material. It was such a pleasant surprise to see the creative designs in which she made, without patterns, without sewing lessons, and with very little money or material.

I often wondered what all the hoopla was about, Miss Scarlet O'Hare making a dress out of that old green drape, it wasn't all that. Mom had taken down a red curtain once, washed it by hand, and made me a beautiful red dress for picture day at school. She knew our sizes without measuring.

She would just decide to make a dress, the next day it would be made and hanging on the outside of the closet for all to "ooohhh and aahh," wondering who she had made it for, each girl hoping to be the fortunate recipient. We would be so excited when she would say the lucky girls' name.

Yes, mom could have been the next Vera Wang or Carolina Herrera. She was so creative, spending many hours making our clothes as Picasso would have spent on one of his paintings or Michael Angelo on his Sistine Chapel. She had such precision and beauty. Wasted talent it seemed. I wonder if she ever dreamed of being a famous designer or did she know her chance had passed when she got married.

It seemed like a lifetime they were on those steps talking. Not once did he raise his voice, yell, curse, or even have a temper tantrum. He did most of the talking as she listened. I could hear such words as, "It will be good for us," and "I will do all I can." Blah, blah, blah…Was he leaving us? Could that be what he was suggesting that would be good for us? Was he walking away? Even I figured that was not a possibility.

I sat down on the sofa, my eyes heavy and I was tired, tired of everything. Here I was, standing guard, like the 7-foot guards that protect Buckingham Palace, trying to be a protector of my mom.

Simply, I would not have had the strength to help her if he would have hit her. We would have only been fortunate enough if the cops were to pass by at that very second, seeing him hit her, then arrest him.

I suppose they were sitting on the porch over an hour, when they decided to come inside. Dad went to the restroom while mom came to me and said. "Everything is ok; you can go to bed now Malina."

Just like that? I thought.

"But what's going to happen?" I asked.

"Tomorrow we are going to sit down with all you kids and

tell you of our plans." She tried to sound comforting, but she knew I was confused.

"Don't worry." She said smiling. "You will find out tomorrow."

I hugged her and did as I was told, there was no point in waiting to talk dad. What the heck would I have to say to him anyway? So I just went to our room.

Sher, the perfect one that she was, had already gotten the other kids to bed, and was still wide-awake when I got in bed.

"So, do we still have a father?" She asked.

Such a damn smart ass, I thought.

I wanted to blurt out something stupid like, "You do teacher's pet." But I didn't dare. From where she was laying in that miserable bed, I knew if I pissed her off her foot would, and could have smacked me right in my mouth with no effort what so ever. My better judgment guided me in the opposite direction.

"Yep, both parents and some kind of family talk tomorrow." I said.

"Gosh." She said as disgusted as she possibly could and even rolled her eyes.

I knew exactly why she was frustrated. It didn't take an Einstein to figure that one out. She wanted to be in school with her books, her friends, and everything positive she knew and loved.

"Do you hate him?" She asked me.

That question came out of nowhere. She was asking me, Malina, if I hated my dad. I looked behind me to see if possibly, someone had snuck up behind me and she was actually talking to them, because she, of all people had to expect the expected when asking me questions about dad. That question took a second for me to absorb.

Trying my best to sound a bit grown up I said. "I don't hate him; I hate what he does, especially to mom."

Since Sher was the one that apparently loved dad the most, well more than me anyway, I just couldn't say directly to her face, "Hell yeah I hate the rotten bastard." Because that is what my heart had been feeling since I was unfortunate enough to witness him beating the crap out of my mother.

"Do you hate mom?" I asked her.

She sat up in the bed. I didn't know if she was going to sock me right in my face or cry. I cringed.

"Why would you think I hate her?" Sher asked in a tone I had never heard from her before. Sort of a puzzled look, combined with a crackling voice.

"I don't know, it seems…" She stopped me.

"I love mom; I just don't understand why we don't leave him if he's going to treat us all so bad?"

This was my fourteen-year-old, going on twenty-year-old sister having a grown up conversation with me. I was her little sister and I felt honored to even be having this conversation.

"Really think about it, all these fights, over and over, I mean, do you really think this will go on until we grow up and move out?" She said, almost pleadingly.

My mind went blank.

*Move out? Move out?* What the hell are you talking about? Leave my mom behind? Was Sher out of her damn mind? Never! I thought. Never, ever will that happen?

I had to get out of that conversation; there was no way I would ever leave my mom alone with the likes of this crazy man. Nothing was said for a few minutes from either of us.

"I don't know," I said to her. "I'm glad you threatened him though."

Sher looked at me with a smile on her face "Yep I taught him a damn lesson huh?" She sure was talking brave considering dad was right in the next room. We giggled for a minute, thinking how sweet it would be to wake up tomorrow and Sher would be the boss, the real boss telling all of us what to do every minute of the day, even dad. Especially dad.

And by some freak of nature, dad would obey her. "Yep." She said, "Sher's the Boss, Sher's the boss." She made a little song jingle out of the words, moving her shoulders up and down as she half ass danced.

We both laughed something we hadn't been able to do in quite awhile.

Sher sort of kicked at me with her long ass legs. I kicked back barely tapping her leg. She kicked again, this time a little harder in a playful manner. I decided to stop while I was ahead. She seemed happy and playful, why push my luck. I knew that she could beat the shit out of me without even trying.

"Night." She said, as she lay back down.

"Night boss." I said as we laughed.

For the second time, again completely exhausted, we fell asleep.

# 13

    The first thing I heard the next morning was my two little brothers laughing. I was the last one to get out of bed. Like it or not it was time to hear the plan my dad had for us. I don't know if I was afraid to get up or just didn't want to be disappointed. One thing was certain; anything he said had to be better than how we were living at the time.

    Mom was in the kitchen, of course, whipping up a gourmet meal from scratch. How could the aroma of such good smelling food come out of such an old beat up kitchen? Even the dishes looked as if they were utensils cave men would have used back in the B.C era.

    I walked past the kitchen to the restroom to "wake up." It was a miracle Sher was not in the restroom relaxing, reading a book, or just annoyingly taking her time.

    I washed my face, brushed my teeth, and brushed my hair. Though I could hear my brothers laughing and running around as they did every morning, still had me wonder how much of this weeks past events these two little boys would remember, even later in life. I was glad they hadn't seen what I had, nor my sisters.

    As I continued thinking of all that had happened and wondered if mom would ever let dad know what I had seen. I thought about how he had come home the night before, like one of those traveling salesmen fathers that go away on a business trip, and stay away for days at a time. Instead, he stayed away due to his shame.

    I recalled not smelling marijuana all over him. He wasn't falling over drunk, and he wasn't mean. To be perfectly honest, in spite of all the bullshit we were going through, he was actually being nice.

    Times were not always fucked up in the Guetarro house. Dad actually was fun to be around at one time. He would laugh with us, tease us, play Monopoly with us, of course he had to be the banker, you know, rob the bank type of shit, let his "gangster side shine."

He would play baseball with J.J. and Danny, encouraging them every step of the way. He would purposely not catch the ball when Danny would attempt to make a home run, because he knew if he caught it and called "Out" on Danny, the big baby that he was, he'd cry, then they would have to stop playing, because Danny would quit. Dad would laugh at him as he ran around the bases, because he ran so funny. High or not, dad loved the way Danny ran.

But once J.J. would be up to bat, dad would get all-serious and shit, cause J.J. played as if he were on a professional team. J.J. would hit the ball literally across the street, while dad would yell, "Run Babe Ruth, run, getting J.J. so excited that he'd haul ass even faster. Yes, it was fun and exciting to watch the three of them together, doing father and son things. Mom and we girls would be the cheerleaders on the sidelines.

Then he would sit on the porch and supervise Becky and Carries' jack tournaments. He would purposely say. "Damn baby why you cheating? I saw you touch that jack." Which would cause Carrie to get pissed, and then she would jumble all the jacks up, signaling the end of that game and the beginning of another. Dad would laugh his ass of because he would know the jack really hadn't been moved, he just said it to start shit, then laugh at them for arguing.

Sometimes him and mom would go outside late at night and sit on the porch, long after we would go to bed, and talk. Yep, a lot of it was done while dad had them glassy eyes, but it got to the point we didn't even notice.

At times mom and dad would go out, sit in his car for hours, and listen to music on the radio. Jazz mostly, they both loved Jazz music.

Then there was my dad's love for the lake and picnics. He would get a whim and say, "Let's go kids." Out of nowhere and we'd be on our way to the lake. He would stare at the lake for hours, tell us scary stories, hug us all, and tell us how much he loved us.

I wondered what happened. Did he fall out of love with mom? With us kids? Was the gangster life too much for him? Just what happened, because he literally became a mad dog?

Strangely enough, my first memory of my parents was not a bad memory. Before I cried everyday in first grade mom put me in a kindergarten class. It was not in a regular public school it was a small old house that was converted into one big room for teachers to teach five year olds in an attempt to prepare them for real school.

Classes were part time, you either went from 9:00a.m to 12:00p.m or 12:30 p.m. to 3:30p.m. I did not like going, but it wasn't all day like first grade was, so thinking back, I wasn't so sad.

It was time for the Christmas program and the teachers asked my mom if I could play the role of the Blessed Virgin Mary in our school play. The teacher wanted all the little kids to perform for all the parents. It was going to be the nativity scene with Mary, Joseph, the Three Wise Men, and baby Jesus that was to be played by a doll, of course. Mom agreed that I could be in the play.

I was only 5 years old and did not know what a play was at that time. A few of the teachers tried to explain to each of the students exactly what our roles consisted of and what we were to do. I had no idea what they were talking about, but I knew I had to have a boy stand next to me and be my husband, which was Joseph. "Yuck." I thought.

I was dressed in a long white dress similar to what a nun would wear and my hair was long at the time. I was supposed to walk on stage holding the doll, which was supposed to be baby Jesus with Joseph by my side. The Three Wise Men were to follow us onstage. We were to approach the manger and I was to lay baby Jesus down, then cover him with a blanket, as the Three Wise Men adored him. Simple enough?

And to make it even easier these were all non-speaking roles, straight up acting only.

Keeping in mind we are all five year olds, we have no knowledge of acting. Actually, until that day I had no idea of baby Jesus, Mary, Joseph, The Wise Men, or what a Nativity scene was.

I was told what to do, how to do it, and when to do it. Geez, I was a little shy kid, I was scared to death to do any type of acting in front of a bunch of people. Yes, horrified is what I was the night of my acting debut.

We arrived early, mom, dad, and me. Mom took me back stage, which incidentally was not a stage. It was a sheet hanging from the ceiling to divide the stage from the back of the so-called stage. Mom stayed with me as long as she could then hugged me and went to sit with dad.

I realized I was the only girl, surrounded by a bunch of boys, with fake beards and dressed in long robes. They looked as scared, if not more scared than I did. I shook like a leaf, terrified to walk out on stage.

Showtime...

We walked out on stage, very slowly. Joseph by my side and the Wise Men followed us. We approached the manger, which was facing the audience. I had baby Jesus in my arms, the doll, I was standing right in front of the manger, and as I started to slowly place him in the manger, he rolled down my arms, directly to the floor.

I have no idea what happened, nerves I suppose. . It seemed to be in slow motion, I grabbed for baby Jesus, but I just couldn't stop the inevitable. BAM!" I dropped baby Jesus and he hit the floor, face down. He was a doll, yes to everyone, but to me he was a real baby.

What have I done? What have I done? Oh my dad is gonna be so mad at me. I was crying inside.

The audience roared with laughter, everyone was laughing and applauding. I on the other hand, was horrified, paralyzed, and scared. All I could see was my dad, everything in that place was a blur, except my dads face.

Then, I saw him laughing.

Like a dear in headlights, I froze again. Finally, I picked up baby Jesus and put him in the manger. I was just so nervous and scared and I knew I had already messed up, and I wanted to cry and run out of there, so when I put baby Jesus in the manger, I didn't realize at first, but I put him face down as to suffocate him. When I tried to turn baby Jesus back over, I dropped him again, causing further stress on me, more laughter for the audience.

People continued to laugh so much at that point, they were crying. I looked at my dad again and saw that he was crying and wiping away his tears of laughter. Mom was laughing also, because as she told me later that night, it happened so quickly, it was just so funny. I messed up so bad people thought it was funny. I remember wanting to cry but noticed that my dad was so happy, it made me laugh instead.

After the show, everyone came up to me, hugged me, and shook my dad's hand. He seemed proud that I made a mistake. All I could remember, he was laughing so much, and smiling that handsome smile, as if what I had done to that poor doll was a good thing.

This was my first real memory of my parents together, laughing. It was a good time in my life.

Back to reality!

# 14

It was just mom and us kids, dad was gone of course. I didn't dare ask, and I actually didn't want to know. Perhaps he lied about talking to us just to get back in the house. Maybe nothing was going to change at all.

We could go outside now since moms face was clearing. She sent the boys out to play with their cars on the front porch. My two younger sisters followed to play jacks. After she finished breakfast, she called us all in.

"Where's dad?" Sher curiously asked.

"He'll be back in a few hours." Mom said.

We sat in that raggedy kitchen and ate a normal breakfast not some half-ass oatmeal. This was a good, hot, home cooked breakfast. A normal breakfast I assumed kids ate every morning.

Once we finished eating Sher and I cleaned the dishes and tried to make the kitchen appear normal. After cleaning and straightening up our rooms, I went out to sit on the front porch while Sher stayed indoors with mom.

I watched my brothers throw the ball to one another, thinking how good J.J. actually was for being only six years old.

We continued to stay outside until lunchtime. Sher came out once to check on the boys as if she were their mother. She was holding a book in one hand, reading it as she walked down the five stairs leading from the porch to the ground. Not once did she look down to see where her feet were going, just kept her nose buried in that book.

I know it would have been painful if she had fallen, but I know it would have been funny if she had, which would have just pissed her off. She stood by the big old oak tree we had in the front yard, and continued reading her book.

So many years of cars being parked in the front yard had ruined the grass that we did have at one time. When it rained, it was a pavement of mud. Going from the car to the house on a rainy day was always pure hell. Our shoes would be full of mud, we would wipe them on the steps, but the next person entering the house would just step on the mud that was left behind, thus, causing one big muddy mess. The only thing all that mud was good for was to make mud pies...

Oh yes, we would pull down leaf after leaf from those two big trees, fill one leaf completely full with mud, then slap another leaf on top, hence the mud pie. Just what the hell we did with them beyond that, escapes my mind.

After having lunch, we did the same routine as always. We put up the dishes, and cleaned up after the little kids. There was still no sign of dad, and mom wasn't saying too much about him. Again, teachers pet asked, "Where's daddy?"

Mom replied, "He'll be here shortly."

I wondered why so much emphasis was put on "Where's daddy?"

Who cares? Is what I thought to myself? I was frustrated. It seemed we were all walking on pins and needles pretending nothing had ever happened.

Then like a dust storm from nowhere, he drove up. He parked that old car right in front of our house as if it had its own parking space.

He got out of the car smiling. *Bet he's high.* I thought to myself.

Mom was standing at the door, as she did so many times before, watching us, watching dad as he walked to the porch to climb the stairs he said. "Come inside kids I want to talk to y'all."

He went in first and actually kissed mom on her cheek as he walked inside. My brothers ran inside and flopped themselves down on the sofa as the two little girls followed behind. Sher went in and stood right next to her daddy; I then walked in and went right to my mom's side.

"Sit down girls, sit down." Dad said as he shuffled us to the other sofa, nearly exploding with excitement.

Here it is! Show time... He was going to tell us all his good news. I was scared, was it really good news? Or was he going to turn into Mr. Hyde? We all took our places on the sofa, as if we were watching a play. Mom, the director instructing each of us where to sit, even finding herself a spot as to be able to see dad perform!

Then there's dad, standing before his wife and kids (seemed more like he was standing in front of a firing squad) about to do his one-man show.

This terror of a man actually looked scared.

Really? I thought! You're scared of a bunch of kids and an even more scared wife. How ironic.

This was about to get good.

I looked directly into his eyes as he began. "Kids, I'm sorry for all the bad things I have done to all of you and your mom. I know I don't deserve any of you. I've done so much bad I just don't know where to begin. I messed up really bad and I guess I just didn't know how to do right by all of you. I look at your mom and I see what almost happened here, I know this is all my fault. She didn't deserve what I did to her, and for that, Mama I'm very sorry."

He said all this speech, looking at mom, then one of us kids, then back at mom, so on and so on, till he had actually looked each of us right in our eyes.

It seemed like a lot of sentence he was saying without stopping to catch his breath, which had me very curious.

I looked over at mom and saw tears in her eyes, which it was inevitable the tears were gonna flow out of my own eyes. I looked at my brothers, who weren't even paying attention to anything dad was saying, rather somewhat playing tag right there on the sofa. I guess because dad wasn't screaming and hollering at all of us, no one was interested.

Sher was staring at him as if he were the president of the United States, giving his inaugural speech. I was nauseous.

In our lifetime we never heard him do anything except yell if he were drunk, or giggle if he were stoned. This particular day, we must have caught him in between.

"I have a surprise for y'all." He bragged.

I wondered, he's staying. He's leaving? Confusing, very confusing.

I wasn't too sure if mom knew of this surprise; she looked a bit shocked herself, and still had tears in her eyes. Maybe she wanted to believe he was sorry, perhaps she wanted to believe this would be her last ass whooping. Maybe, just maybe she wanted to believe everything would be ok.

"Come on kids, get in the car, I want to take y'all somewhere."

Uh, oh I thought mass burial. Take us all for "A Ride." You know one of those infamous rides with no return. Now, stupid kid or not, I was educated in the fact I knew for sure if a gangsta takes someone for "A Ride" that means you're history, you ain't never coming back.

So to get in the car and go for "A Ride" was a bit creepy, to say the least.

I sure didn't like the sound of any of this.

But as a good wife and good kids, we obliged and piled in the car. Of course, Sher sitting up front right next to her precious father.

Me and the other four kids all crammed in the back seat of that old Oldsmobile. Dad with a slight smile on his face, sort of like the cat that swallowed the canary.

I swear, once again I thought mass murder…suicide. Then I rethought the suicide part, there was no way he would kill himself. Us yes, himself no, he loved his fucking self too much.

Our trip was short, maybe two blocks or so. It appeared we were going to that neighborhood bar dad visited daily. Oh hell no, I'm not going in there, I thought.

He did drive by, in our day drive by meant just that, drive by very slowly, but by no means did we do a drive by, in today's terms means everyone in the car shoots the place up, though when I saw Sal-E bar it would not have been a bad idea to shoot the place up. I had a vision of all of us, even Danny blasting the place.

Dad drove very slowly through the parking lot of the bar then drove maybe one hundred more feet to a neighboring business.

It was a gas station, the old school gas stations that you actually helped the customer by pumping the gas for them, wash their windshields, you know pamper the customer. Dad looked as proud as if he had won the lottery.

Seems he jumped out of the car before it even stopped. He went around the car and opened each of the car doors for all of us to get out.

As mom got out, she said, "What's this?" As she looked at the building.

"It's ours." he said.

"Ours?" she asked.

"Yes ours, well ours." And he said the name. No, not Ely and Bee, if he had said Bee and Ely's name I believe I would have gotten back in that car and run right over him for saying their names. I held my breath waiting to hear exactly what name he was attempting to say. I recognized the name "Sal."

Sal was the owner of Sal-E's bar right next door. Dad had the key to the front door so he let us in to tour our new "family business."

My brothers ran all over the place yelling and laughing making echo sounds. My sisters seemed bored. If they had remembered to carry their jacks with them, I'm sure they would've just flopped down on the cement floor and started playing.

There was a desk and a couple of chairs in the office area so dad and mom sat to talk of dad's plans for his new business.

Enormous wall to ceiling windows covered the front and sides of the building so we could see everything outside. It was a corner building with a traffic light forty feet from the front door. Anyone passing by could see in, we could see out. So many windows made the room feel warm, with brightness from the sunlight, it felt almost comfortable.

Dad said, "Sal and I are going to partner up. I'm gonna run it and Sal's gonna finance it."

Now, I know this was supposed to be a serious moment for him and for mom but I am sorry, I couldn't resist thinking Hhhhuuummmm?

Ok! You father, get a place to hang out all day, here at your new "business," which, coincidentally is right next door to the place you spend twenty three hours a day, doing all your illegal activities, and we're supposed to be happy?

Simply put, I didn't get it. How is this gonna be a win-win situation for anyone but dad?

Hey, this wasn't my call, this was his and moms, but I was willing to give him a chance. Everyone deserves a second chance right? Even a monster.

I watched him as he spoke. When he wasn't yelling and screaming dad actually was such a nice looking man. He had dark eyes and almost jet black hair. He had a very handsome face, I just never really noticed because I was always too afraid to look at him. It's hard to be real happy and excited, when not a week ago he had beat mom so severely.

He continued to tell mom of his plans. He would work eight or ten hours a day or as long as he needed to. He would do right this time, he promised over and over.

Mom looked at him as if this were the first time in their marriage she really had a chance to sit and discuss any future they may have together.

I looked at mom, the sun shining right through the windows directly onto her face. It made her beautiful green eyes even more beautiful. I looked past the now yellowish bruises and the slight swelling of her eyes and couldn't believe my beautiful mom could have died.

Dad took us all around the shop showing us every little detail. Talking about all his plans of getting a real mechanic to repair cars, and his plans to make this station a thriving business. It all sounded good in the end, but you're forgetting something, you have no money, I thought to myself.

Well that's where Sal came in. His so called bar next door was gonna bankroll this venture. So confusing for me, yet mom seemed to hang on to every word he said, as she had so much faith in him. A lesser woman would have booked ass. Not mom.

Maybe she just wanted to believe it was all possible. Stand by your man type of woman.

Dad seemed about to bust with excitement. Sher was glowing as if dad had just become partner in the biggest law firm in town.

I had been the one to wake up and see how brutal he could be, perhaps that made me so pessimistic about the entire thing.

Who was I to rain on his parade?

He seemed so excited and happy as if he didn't want to leave, maybe get some blankets and pillows and have us all spend the night right there on the cement floor, just because he was so happy.

I felt bad for him that maybe I was acting like a little bitch, but hey, no one could read my mind and I damn sure wasn't gonna voice my opinions.

Finally, he locked the door while we waited in the car. We drove back home and he kept saying, "This is gonna work mama, this is gonna work."

For once, there was no tension in the air, it seemed so normal. Yes, maybe this could work.

Seems dad realized, or someone made him realize, he messed up. He could be in jail at that very second eating bread and water, never seeing his kids or his beautiful wife again.

Yes, someone made this man turn his life around. It just seemed so different. We seemed like a real family, something new in our lives to be really happy about. If mom's heart could forgive, then I really had to try, so in spite of my fears I thanked God at that moment.

    I was thankful for whatever entity stepped in and made dad see the errors of his ways before it was too late…I hoped.

# 15

Mom and dad talked for hours. They even left so they could pick up a bit of much needed groceries. Dad wasn't one of those shop till you drop kinda guys, but I guess if your gonna turn over a new leaf, you sure gotta start somewhere.

We were designated sitters again, me and Sher, recalling the last time we watched the kids had been the night he beat mom. I put those thoughts in the back of my mind. Life looks so different when you're not crying, scared, and full of hate.

I spent the night once with my friend from school and her parents were all over the place with all the hugging and kissing, of each other. This is not normal, I thought. Moms kiss their kids; kids kiss their moms, but this? Moms and dads kissing and hugging in front of their kids, in front of their kid's friends? It just wasn't normal, at least not in my world. I'm sure my parents had their moments…yuck! Well they did have six kids! So I was aware of such behavior, but it just didn't seem normal to see grown-ups embracing.

Time drug by very slowly before they returned. With a trunk full of groceries, believe it or not, dad even helped unload the car and put the groceries away, without the use of any drug, without giving orders, and without talking shit to any of us.

With a belly full of delicious food mom had cooked, I was definitely gonna have a good night's sleep, except for those damn springs coming out of the mattress.

The next day was Friday and we knew by Monday we would be back at school. Sher was the most excited, talking about, "When I get back to school I'm going to have so much work to do." She actually couldn't stop talking about it. Surprisingly she was in a great mood; I mean why not, her precious father had become a changed man. She was going back to school in three days and didn't have to scurry the kids out of the room every five minutes to try to protect them.

Yes, it's fair to say Sher was on top of the world. Dad stayed gone all day Friday. Mom said he was busy making arrangements at the garage. She explained it would take a lot of work to get the station in shape and dad had a lot of things he needed to do with Sal and he probably would be gone a lot over the next few weeks.

"Good!" I thought. If he's sincere about changing his life then he would do whatever it takes to do the right thing.

Saturday, while the kids were outside playing catch, jacks, and hopscotch, me and Sher were inside helping mom do the laundry.

So many of us, so many loads of laundry seemed an endless flow of clothes, and when you have to do a lot of it by hand, it just seemed to never end.

Do the math Malina, seven pants, seven shirts, seven pair of socks, seven undergarments, chonnies and bras, seven wash rags, seven towels, sheets, pillow cases, over forty two items daily, times seven days, that a lot of damn laundry.

Of course, dad's clothes weren't included in this count, except for his lounging clothes and undergarments, all his things were sent directly to the cleaners. One must look tiptop in order to be a gangster.

Mom pushed that old machine beyond its limits. As old as it was, it still kept up with the demand of service she put on it.

If mom wasn't busy doing all of our laundry, she would be tirelessly washing or ironing clothes for others also. Since grandma worked so many hours at the nursing home, and didn't have time for much of anything else, she paid mom to do all the domestic things for her.

Mom took very special care to put that perfect crease in every pair of pants; every shirt was ironed with perfection, never a wrinkle. The second she finished ironing every item, she put the item on a hanger making it look nicer than it had when it was purchased from the department stores.

Mom did this three or four days a week, without a doubt, her skill of ironing would put even the most upscale cleaners out of business if they tried to compete with her perfection.

She didn't make much money compared to all the work she put into it, but it seemed a little bit of money was better than no money at all.

I always thought everyone took advantage of her kindness, because she spent so much time ironing, for what seemed like pennies, to ensure others looked nice.

She is an incredible woman, I thought as I helped her put clean washed sheets on all the old rotted mattresses. Yes, she's an incredible woman, and an even more incredible mom.

My brothers came running inside Danny yelling, "Mom, mom, there's a big, big twuck outside!" We both laughed at the way Danny said "Twuck."

Mom went to the front door expecting to see a pick-up truck. No, it was a big, big truck just as my brother had said.

There were two guys standing in the yard.

"Yes?" Mom asked.

One of the guys answered, "Are you Mrs. G?"

"Yes." Mom answered.

"Johnny's at the station and told us to bring these to you."

Being the over bearing husband dad was, mom knew darn good and well not to ever let a stranger in the house. First off, it was not safe. Secondly, being a gangster, one would never know who might try to get to him by getting to his family. One of the "Gangster's Life" rules.

With no phone to call and confirm these two guys were sent by dad, she had no way of knowing if this was true or not. Not many people knew about the station yet.

She asked. "What is it?"

At that very second dad turned the corner and pulled up behind the big truck. Just in time, I thought, saving mom from having to send them away.

One of the men jumped up to the back of the truck and lifted the back door, while the other guy climbed up and drug something out. It was a mattress set. Dad looked over at mom and winked.

My first thought was, oh my, more junk to put in this ugly house.

But no, these were new mattresses, wrapped in plastic, nice and pretty and from where I stood; they looked very, very comfy.

They brought one set into the house and put it in mom and dad's room. Then another set, identical to the one they put in moms room, was set up in our room for us girls. A third trip to the truck produced a new twin set for my brothers.

Surprisingly, another twin set was delivered to our room, for Sher, only for Sher. Well, when you think of it, Sher was the oldest and the smartest and she was dad's pet after all.

I didn't care; it made more free space on the bed for me, Carrie and Becky. No springs to gouge our backs anymore! I could not wait to go to bed that night.

Dad chatted with the guys for a few minutes. Seems he knew how to be chummy with everyone, even some hard working delivery guys.

Possibly, dad got embarrassed when they took the old mattresses out to their truck. I mean really. The old ones weren't fit to be called mattresses, only junk. Watching the delivery guys bring in the new mattresses, so clean and firm, almost standing on their own. Then when they took our old ones out, they seemed limp and almost so flimsy they could have rolled them up. There was even cotton falling all over the yard, another indication of the age of those rotted ass mattresses... I worried one of these guys would cut themselves on all those rusty wires. Fortunately, they did not.

Dad looked past the shame and smiled when he saw how nice the new ones looked in that ugly old house. Dad had done another good thing. I could really get to like this type of kindness.

Dad left with the delivery guys, but not before coming back into the house to announce he had another surprise for us. We were all excited, me, Sher, the kids, and even mom. Everyone screamed at once, "What is it?" Most kids got excited about toys, candy, and gifts. Not us! We were excited about simple things like new beds and food, the basic necessities.

He said, as proudly as he could. "Monday we are getting a home phone."

"What?" The boys said, sounding disgusted dad hadn't said new baseball gloves or baseball caps that would actually fit them. If it did not involve baseball, they could've cared less.

The little girls just turned around as to stomp away because he had just wasted their time on a surprise they knew nothing about and had absolutely no use for. I think mom and I thought alike, good, a phone to call the operator in an emergency. With small kids, you never know when you might need an ambulance or a police officer.

Mom, maybe thinking a phone for dad to call and make sure we were all ok, or just to say hi? Nice thoughts? Perhaps.

Sher had a sparkle in her eyes. A phone, a real phone. Contact with the outside world. A life beyond this house.

She was already a teenager and I figured she wanted to chat with her friends, the friends she loved to be with.

Monday was definitely gonna be a good day for Sher. Back to school, back to her books, and back with her friends. For me it was the exact opposite. Monday would mean mom would be alone, and I would worry if she were ok during the day.

What if dad started a fight with her? What if he hit her? What if she couldn't get away from him? What if she was hurt? What if my little brother saw everything? He was only four years old; he wouldn't know what to do. So many what ifs. This wasn't normal, I thought.

No, I was not looking forward to Monday at all. Why was I doing this to myself? Everything would be ok! Dad had promised us all. Sher had threatened him. Surely, he would not break his promise.

# 16

Sunday was just one of those beautiful days, so mom made plans to get us kids out of the house for a while, a surprise trip, a little family get together. Without hesitation, dad brought mom the car, so she could take us to the area park.

Driving was not something mom particularly cared about, but dad told her he would be busy all day and just wouldn't have time to go with us. We hadn't been to the park since before Danny had been born.

Mom packed some sandwiches, chips, and Kool-Aid, even a blanket for us to sit on so we could have a little picnic.

There were times dad would love to do family things, then the next he would be on a rampage. The times we would go to the lake, he would have us girls sing songs from the radio or we would make songs up ourselves. We would practice the songs a few times and then present them to him and mom. He would smile a great big smile and say, "Mama one day our girls are going to be rich and take care of us."

He would brag we were geniuses the way we could just make songs up and harmonize.

Rare occasions other friends of his would accompany us to the lake and dad would tell them. "Listen to my daughters beautiful voices." And we would spend hours singing to his friends and their wives. Dad would be so proud he would make us sing the same song over and over because he said our singing relaxed him.

We never complained that we were tired or didn't feel like singing. If singing kept him in a good mood, we were more than happy to oblige. Moments that we shared with him, that put a smile on his face, sometimes a bit of a tear in his eyes, helped us forget when times were bad.

I wondered so often, what had happened to him? Why did he seem to be a person with a split personality? Why would he be so nice one minute, and so damn mean without warning?

After being cooped up for two weeks the kids needed to let it all out. We stayed at the park for about two hours. The kids played on the swings, took turns sliding down the slide, and just ran all over the place letting out some of the frustration from being locked up. After we ate our picnic lunch, we headed home.

Since the station was so near our house, mom decided to stop by and say hi to dad.

The two men that had brought the mattresses were there with dad, and there were two other men. They had completely transformed the outside of that place, now a nice warm shade of green. These four men were busy painting and cleaning windows, one guy sweeping out the garage area, one painting, and another picking up all the mess that was left behind. Each seemed to be deep in thought as they worked hard to get the station presentable.

And there was dad, giving orders, telling each guy what to do, as a contractor would. Not getting a drop of paint on his hands or the casual clothes he was wearing. I thought he would get mad when he saw us drive up, the old dad would have, but this new dad waved us in so we could see all the changes.

All four of the men cleared out of the way so we could go in, while dad, smiling as proud as he could, instructing each of us not to touch the paint so we didn't get it on our clothes.

I have to admit, I figured dad would not do any of the physical labor himself, hell I didn't think he knew how to do any of it, just look at our house, look how we lived. However, I have to say he sure put that place together in a few short days.

We all admired the transformation, Sher the most. She was proud of what her daddy was doing, and I saw a little twinkle in mom's eye over the new and improved dad. She had waited a long time for this, and now, if ever she dreamed of a good life, quite possibly this was it.

Dad gloated, which was actually quite becoming on him,

and though he offered us to stay as long as we wanted, mom told him she wanted to get home to start supper.

As we were leaving, I saw some of those nasty women going into the bar next-door.

How the heck was dad gonna stay away from that place? It was just so close, and I'm not sure how much he could resist going there. He practically lived in that bar; it was like a real home for him. Seemed our house was just where he laid his head at the end of each night.

# 17

Ever once in awhile I would see mom glancing in the mirror at her face, which was clearing nicely. If she had put a touch of make up on, you would never know her face had met the butt of a pistol.

The next day we would be back in school, so Sher was the first to get her necessities ready, as though it were her very first day of school. I felt bad for her because I knew she really missed being there.

We were both in the same school, a junior high. She was in eighth grade, I was in seventh. I felt sorry for Danny because he wasn't gonna have anyone to play with until we got home. Becky and Carrie were in elementary; I know they liked school enough to be excited to return.

It was getting late, I'm not sure what time dad came in, when we awoke the next day he was walking out the door, so mom kept the car so she could take us to school after breakfast.

I kissed mom on the cheek as I got out of the car, horrified as I watched her drive off with my little brother. Not knowing what would happen to her. God please keep them safe.

School drug on that first day back. I saw Sher several times in the hallway, completely excited and laughing with her friends. The teachers all knew Sher by name and they all loved her. All the boys liked her, as did all the girls. Sometimes girls are jealous and might not like you for whatever reason, not so with Sher, everyone liked her.

At home, she seemed so annoyed by all of us, but at school she smiled, laughed, and talked loudly and freely, almost a different person. It was just the way dad was at the bar with all those fake people. Why couldn't I be like her? She was more like dad than she knew; she was just a nice version of him, a happy popular teen.

   Finally, the end of the school day arrived. Sher and I met at a certain spot every day. If mom or dad wasn't there to pick us up we knew to walk home, yet we always took the same route every day just in case mom or dad showed up to get us. We never ever took a different route. Mom knew the exact moment we would walk through the door, and like clockwork, we walked in. She had already picked up the other kids, but didn't have the car to pick up me and Sher because dad had errands he needed to run.

   Danny ran to us and hugged us as we walked in, talking and talking about something. We didn't realize he was trying to tell us we now had a phone.

   Mom explained to us that dad called and Danny talked to him, which made Danny's eyes even bigger. He was so excited to hear dads voice coming out of this machine, which he had never seen before... It was so adorable to see him pick up the phone and say "Daddy, daddy, hi daddy." We all laughed at him because he was simply adorable.

   We pretty much did the same routine all week. Just as he had all our lives, dad wasn't at home, we were used to that, but this time he was doing something constructive. Something for his family. I didn't realize at the time because we kids all went to bed by ten, but dad wasn't coming home until real late at night again.

   I guess I called it right, that bar was just too close for comfort.

   How could he avoid it, he was still the man. He hadn't resigned from his gangster duties. He still dealt his drugs, stayed out until all hours of the night; he still did everything he had done right in front of me and my sister the time we were there at the bar with him. That hadn't changed, how could it?

   You don't just walk away from that life. You either owe, or are owed something. But you don't just walk away. Once a gangster always a gangster, right?

   If he was still doing all the illegal things he had done

forever, if he were still an assumed murderer, and a drug dealer and if he still had his little crew of gangsters doing any and everything he told him to, then what had changed? Why was it so different now?

Why did we have to be so terrified of him? Why did he have to be so mean? And, why did we all have to sacrifice things in life, so he could be a gangster? What was so different? Could it be his ass was on the line and someone higher up wanted him to straighten his life up for appearance sake. Was dad such a snake in the grass to change his ways only for appearance sake? Was he that devious? You bet like hell he was.

# 18

Some things got easier with a house phone, especially where granny was concerned.

Seems the day she showed up right after mom got beat, she had left town, and apparently, her sister had become very sick and was hospitalized.

It was Aunt Pat that had been hospitalized, a skinny version of grandma with the same smile. She loved to give hugs, just like grandma and had a lot of wrinkles on her face, that she tried to cover up with a lot of make-up, which only caked up in her face wrinkles, making her look a bit odd. She was very kind to all of us, everyone but dad. She hated him with a passion, and she really didn't know anything about the way he treated mom.

She visited us maybe twice a year, always unannounced. She never came inside our house, instead sitting in her car to visit with mom. I didn't know if she just hated the dump we lived in and was ashamed for mom, or a combination of her hate for dad and our house. Maybe she just wanted to make a clean get away if dad showed up, and sitting in her car was safer than sitting in our living room and try to escape him.

Dislike for dad or not, we loved when she visited because she always had some kind of treats for us when she was visiting.

One day during the first week we had to stay home due to dad beating mom, our closest, neighbor Mr. Sandy came over to check on us. Grandma had Sandy's phone number and anytime grandma really needed mom; she would call Mr. Sandy or his wife Mrs. Jewel, to ask one of them to give mom messages from her.

Mr. Sandy, an old skinny man who drug his foot when he walked, sort of like Frankenstein, would come over and tell mom she was to call her mom. Always relaying any messages, day or night.

When he got the call from granny that week he admitted he hadn't seen any of us playing outside, going, or coming past his house from the store or school. Concerned about us, he drug himself to our house but it was impossible for him to climb the five big stairs to our porch. So he knocked on the side of the house until someone came out side.

"Hello." He yelled then banged on the side of the house.

"Helloooo." He yelled again.

Of course mom wouldn't go out for him to see her battered face, so she answered him through the closed door.

"Yes Sandy." She almost had to yell at him in order for him to hear her.

"Your mama called, she wants to know if y'all are ok? She said she is worried because you haven't called her and she's leaving town." Mom didn't want to ask too many questions so she just said, "We're all sick with a stomach virus. I don't want to use your phone to call her and then get you and Mrs. Jewel sick. Would you please tell her we're ok and I'll call her in a few days?" She yelled.

"Ok ok." He said sort of mumbling as he turned and walked away dragging his foot leaving drag marks in the dirt.

It was hard to understand Mr. Sandy when he talked, see Mr. Sandy didn't have a nose, straight up no nose. Just a big hole in his face where his nose was supposed to be. He kept a big bandage over it ninety percent of the time, but the rare occasion we caught him without it, it would scare the shit out of us, because you could see the bones through the gaping hole in his face... It looked like a mask, it was frightful.

He had explained to mom, when he was a younger man he had a construction accident and it simply ripped off his nose.

In spite of everything wrong with him, he was a very kind man and loved kids because he and Ms. Jewel never had any. It seemed quite a bit of a bother for old Mr. Sandy to drag himself to our house to relay messages to mom from grandma, so the first person mom called when we got the house phone was grandma.

She was so excited knowing now she could call daily, which she sure the heck did.

Every day, numerous times throughout the day, and night for that matter, which I'm sure would have annoyed the shit out of dad, had he ever been home.

It was strange to hear the phone ring in our house. It was a sound we were not accustomed too. So when it did ring we would all rush to answer it, usually it was dad calling, I guess just to chat with mom for a few seconds.

The conversations usually went something like this, "yes, yes, no, ok, I know." Something along those lines, is what mom's side of the conversation would be, we never heard dads side. Always short, brief conversations.

Sher was allowed to give out the number to her friends because she was the oldest and she had the most friends. I was told I could give it to two friends if I wanted. But really, I couldn't think of anyone I wanted to chat with. The other kids were still so young they could have cared less about a phone.

It might just as well have been a space ship sitting on that dresser; they had absolutely no use for it.

As happy as the phone made Sher, she was about to get her first lesson in phone etiquette, and her ass chewed out for the first time.

She was chatting on the phone with one of her friends. The phone was in mom's room, mostly because mom would be the main one using it. I was in the living room watching TV, while the little kids were playing outside. Mom was cooking.

Sher was trying to whisper while chatting on the phone, but I could still hear her...

"I know he is sooo cute isn't he?" I could only hear her end of the conversation of course.

"Yes I want to tell him that." She continued to whisper so I couldn't hear her, or so she thought.

She would giggle then she would say stupid stuff like, "I'll meet you in the hallway and we'll give him the note."

I was more interested in watching the Three Stooges. I didn't care about her crush on some boy or her plans for the next day. She knew there was no way on this planet dad would allow her to have a boyfriend, much less chat with one on the phone even if she was his favorite.

All of a sudden, she got this really strange look on her face. "Mom, mom the operator is on here." She yelled to get moms attention. Mom came as quickly as she could and took the receiver from Sher.

"Hello, hello." Mom said looking puzzled.

"There is an emergency call from Johnny." The operator said. Mom was repeating to Sher, everything the operator said.

What the heck is that I wondered?

Apparently, with the line being busy dad was trying to call, he couldn't get through so he made an emergency interruption.

Mom said. "Yes" to the operator when she asked mom if she wanted to accept the emergency call. Remembering this is all new to us, so I'm just sitting there wondering, what's next?

Then I heard mom say "Hello." She tried to explain to dad, not meaning to throw Sher under the bus. "Sher was on the phone with…" Mom was interrupted by a lot of dad's yelling.

Sher got tears in her eyes since she was standing right next to mom and was able to hear dads voice. I believe Sher thought "emergency" meant something had happened to dad and she got scared. Not… emergency, hang up the damn phone your "Daddy" is trying to call, and he's frickin pissed cause he can't get through.

Seems they both panicked, mom not really realizing how long Sher had been on the phone and Sher half-scared for dad and half-scared she was in trouble. Mom did a few more minutes of trying to explain the situation, but I don't believe it worked. She had a bit of fear look in her eyes when she hung up, then looked at us, and said. "It's ok; he just wanted to say he wouldn't be home for dinner."

That's it? He never was anyway. So why all the yelling and cussing just to tell her that?

Nope, as far as I was concerned this phone business was not going to be a good idea after all. At least before the phone we didn't have to deal with his shit until he got home. Now we had to deal with it at any given moment twenty-four hours a day. I wanted to rip that damn phone right out of the wall.

We now had another problem to deal with. Dad could terrorize us any time he damn well pleased, and there was no way to avoid it. Seems life slowly turned back to the way it was.

No, at the moment he wasn't hitting anyone, but mentally and emotionally, it was back to square one. Seems he would try for a few days then any little thing would set him off.

It was almost a pleasure when he would come home, eyes all glassy with his stinky smelling clothes and breath. Why couldn't he be happy like this all the time? It's sad to think someone has to use an illegal drug to be normal, but then I guess that's just how it was.

If I knew for a fact that I could've grown marijuana in our back yard just so he would never run out, I sure the hell would've done it, just to keep him in a good mood. I would take that chance of being busted for growing illegal drugs, for some type of peace in our house.

I often wondered if mom smoked with him when we weren't looking or when they would go off somewhere alone. She never stunk like him nor had glassy eyes like him but the thought still crossed my mind. I believe she was just so high on the fact there was a way for him to be kind even illegally, that it made dealing with dad and all his fucked up bull shit bearable and had her teary eyed from time to time.

If it weren't for mom being so good to us, trying her best to make us kids happy, I'm not sure we kids could have coped with our lives. She tried very hard not to show her fears to us, but she knew I would never forget what I had seen that night. How could she possibly help me forget?

# 19

Slowly but surely dad and his guys got that old station looking pretty damn good. It was the day before his grand opening, of course we weren't invited but dad came and picked us all up, so we could see the new and improved "JOHNNY G's STATION."

His guys had planted flowers and grass along the side of the station, scrubbed down the pavement, and cleaned the big windows to a clear shine. Everything looked perfect, especially dad's smile. Mom got kinda teary eyed, so did I but not because of the station, I was teary eyed because I thought, you fixed up this old heap of a building, yet we lived in a dump. It just made no sense, but then nothing my dad ever did made sense.

Mom was pretty much back to being mother and father to all of us. One day about two weeks after his so called grand opening, which by the way, turned into grand opening/ dad get drunk and come home at 5 a.m. Absolutely no surprise to me.

We went to see dad at the garage, to pick up money so mom could go grocery shopping. Dad was dressed in his mechanics uniform, which consisted of a light brown shirt with his name embroidered above his shirt pocket, dark brown pants, and a brown belt with his perfectly shined shoes, and no, these were no shiny Stacy Adams.

Something about a man and his shoes, more so a gangster and his shoes. Every day he would pick a pair of shoes from his closet, out of a possible thirty pairs; call out one of our names and say, "Spit shine these please."

While he would be showering, we would have the miserable task of shining his shoes. He never went anywhere without first having his shoes shined. He marveled on, "The shinier the better," so we would put all our strength into getting the perfect shine, hating every second of it because this was not something we could do in sixty seconds. We couldn't just get a rag, wipe off the dust, then say to him.

"Here, here's your shoes."

He taught us the military way, or his military way. First, wipe off the dust. Step two, get the wax polish, and spread it all over the shoes. Step three; with one brush begin the vigorous task of making them shoes shine. Steps four get a second brush, making them shine even more so we could see our reflection in them. And trust me, we could never skip step two, three or four, because he could tell the difference.

All that hard work we would put into them, breaking out in a sweat, just to get a five-second compliment. He would come out of the restroom with his Bermuda shorts on, look down at whichever one of us had the misfortune of having to shine his shoes for the day, pat us on the head and say. "Good job, good job."

He was a very handsome mechanic, although, he wasn't really a mechanic, he was just the front man. He had two other men that were actually working on cars.

As soon as a car ran over the dinger, indicating someone was waiting to get gas, he would run outside to pump gas, and clean his or her windshield. He would half jog out to greet the customer, with a big smile on his face, and with perfect manners, he would say "Good morning," or "Good afternoon," whatever the case may be. The customers would smile back; tell him what they needed. While he would be washing their windshield, dad would start up a conversation with them, laughing and joking with his customers as they sat in their car. Seems he could get every customer to join in on friendly conversations with him. Most customers, by the time he had finished servicing their car, would look at his nametag and say, "Thanks Johnny."

If it were a friend of dads or someone from the neighborhood, dad would carry the conversation even longer, laugh louder, and carry on as if they were in their backyard with him having a Sunday barbecue.

Seems the entire world loved him. He knew just how to charm people and make them feel good about themselves. It's safe to say dad was a character. Everyone knew him. I believe more people knew his name before they knew the name of our City's Mayor, which incidentally, I cannot remember either.

If we said we're "Johnny's kids," no one ever asked Johnny who? They already knew. If someone didn't know who dad was then they weren't from North side. You must have come from another planet not to know who "Johnny" was or what he was.

Someone once told me maybe dad led a double life. This was his poor life and he secretly had another life, an entire family somewhere else, with a big nice home, nice cars, and some more kids. Being with us was his undercover life so no one, the cops, or F.B.I. would think he was up to no good, had any money, or was involved in anything illegal.

I was certain it was a myth; no one in their right mind would purposely live like us just to throw off any government entity. This was not a life you chose to have; this was one you were forced to have and had no way out. If dad had another life, then he had a way out, and there is no way he would have chosen to keep this one. No, this was his life; it was bad for us, but obviously not too bad for him.

Our main purpose that day was for mom to get money for groceries. The mechanics were working on a car and the owner of the car was sitting in the office area with dad. We could see her through all the glass windows that surrounded the office.

When we ran over the dinger, he didn't immediately come out as he normally did for all the other customers. He was just sitting there, talking to this woman for several minutes and didn't even budge to come out to talk to mom. Surely, he did not want mom to send six screaming kids into his office.

Finally, he stood up and came out to the car. He reached for his wallet as he walked toward the driver door, where mom sat just staring at him. I'm sure every bone in her body wanted to ask "Who, what, when, and where was that woman?" Because of the woman mom was, she never said a word about her. She asked dad if there was anything in particular he wanted from the store. He did have some requests, which seemed unusual.

However, it was his hard earned money she was about to spend. He asked if she was taking all us kids with her to the store. She looked at him like, "Are you kidding?" How impossible would it be to take six kids to a store at once?

Usually when she was going to buy groceries she would take two of us, but would never take my little brother. Seems he just wanted too many things that caught his eye and she would have to constantly say, "No baby, you can't have that."

We older kids knew better than to even ask. I believe she chose to take Becky and Carrie with her on that day.

Sometime during our childhood, after mom had all the kids she planned to have, we were paired off. It was easier that way. It was Sher and Danny, the oldest and youngest, then there was me and J.J., second oldest and next to last, and finally, Carrie and Becky, the two middle kids together. Being paired off gave us status quo.

Each of the oldest was responsible for the youngest from each of the pairs. Sher and I called our two brothers "our babies." Carrie and Becky just called each other "sista."

We remained paired off like this all our lives. I enjoyed J.J. as my baby because he was so cute and funny, and obeyed mostly anything I would tell him to do. Danny, on the other hand, took full advantage of his second mother Sher. Being the youngest, even with murderous Sher, he acted like a baby all the time.

It crossed my mind going home from the garage, "Who was that woman? Why was dad so focused on their conversation? And did it make mom jealous to see him so engaged with her?" I hope she wasn't a girlfriend. She seemed to pretty to be a bar tramp, but I wouldn't dare ask my mom.

Mom left to go to the store taking Becky and Carrie, usually rotating who she took with her. She hardly ever took Sher and Danny with her. Sher was the responsible one and mom trusted her to watch over all of us. It wouldn't have made any sense to take Sher and leave everyone else behind.

Sher didn't care; she just wanted to be at home now, chatting on the phone with her friends. She learned a valuable lesson that day. Talk quick and don't stay on the phone too long. That way dad would never have to make an emergency break and cause unnecessary conflicts. Being at home didn't bother her. Better to be home where she could at least communicate with the outside world, then to push a buggy cart around while mom looked for bargains.

Seems to me, since there were so many of us and dad had no provable income, we would have been on food stamps so we could buy some things we liked rather than only necessities.

One of my Aunts asked mom once, "Why don't you apply for food stamps to help you buy groceries?"

"Oh no, I wouldn't want to lie on an application and possibly go to jail." Knowing damn good and well she would really have to lie on the application because dad had no provable income before the garage situation.

Hold up! My poor innocent mom was worried about lying on an application because she would run the risk of going to jail? Yet my dad shot someone and never worried about spending one night in jail.

There surely was something wrong with this life, if a woman can go to jail for possibly lying on an application to feed her kids, yet a man could straight up shoot someone and never worry he could go to jail? This made absolutely no sense to me.

Grocery shopping for mom always seemed to take a long time, not because she ever had a lot of money, but because she bargain hunted. She could find sales and mark downs that others barely cared about. You had to enjoy being in the store if you went with her, because she rushed for no one. She was like that with everything she did. She took her time. "Do it right." She always said. She could cook, she could clean, she took care of his six kids, and dealt with an abusive husband. How in the world did she do it?

Dad now had his garage to deal with; mom had her kids and her funky old house.

## 20

Getting those new mattresses seemed to make the old house feel a little nicer. And, with the new mattresses, our backs began to heal from all the cuts and scratches we seemed to get on a nightly basis.

As raggedy as the all the furniture was and as old and shabby the rooms were, I wondered if the few relatives that did dare come inside think to themselves, what a frickin dump. I mean how good could mom make it look. But one thing about mom, she spent countless hours, sweeping, moping, scrubbing, and any and everything it took to make it a livable home for us.

Never once complaining that she didn't have the nicest home in town, focusing more on the fact that we were all together, and she didn't care that it was a dump as I called it, but that it was a home because it was full of love.

It made sense; maybe it was just me because even when the top-notch gangsters would visit, no one seemed to notice. Perhaps their business with dad made our house irrelevant. Did any of them live as badly as we did?

Someone gave mom some old lilac paint once and she went to work painting our house all by her self. She painted the living room lilac, her room lilac, the big room lilac. It wasn't the most beautiful color in the world but it sure was better than rot and funk.

In all honesty, no matter what color she used, it was a million times better, than the dirty, dingy, funky, spotted walls that were there before she painted it. She worked so hard every day doing the very best she could to make it half-nice.

Mom's sisters and brothers seemed to instinctively know just when we needed things, so like clockwork two or three times a year we would receive big boxes of clothes and nick-knacks. It would be hand me downs from their kids to us.

Some odds and end things for around the house, which mom would clean up, and proudly display them in the appropriate place around the house.

It's funny how an old picture in an old frame can be cleaned up with a little baby oil and made to look brand new. We actually loved getting those boxes.

The relatives knew exactly what to send and when to send it. We would receive clothes, shoes, sweaters, jackets, just about every item of clothing we might need. Among other things, they would send bras for us girls. Auntie would say she bought them only for a nickel and you damn sure could tell.

They were not your normal form fitting bras; these were some crappy old things that looked like they actually did cost a nickel. Some discards from an old discount store maybe, but nonetheless they were bras, and to us they were new. They looked funny because they were real pointed, giving our boobs the appearance of cones. Dad called them titty holders not bras. He would laugh at us when we would put these odd-looking bras on.

We did the best we could with whatever was sent to us. Remember, beggars can't be choosers, we were taught. Why did we have to be beggars any way? What a terrible saying, especially since our dad was supposed to be this famous gangster.

Regardless of how we felt about hand me downs, we already knew mom would simply alter anything that was too big with her sewing machine. Then she would wash it; starch it, and Walla, something new.

Starching our clothes did not come out of a spray can; rather this was powder stuff she would pour out of a box into the washing machine. We would hang the clothes outside on the cloth line to dry, so by the time they dried they would be hard as a rock.

Once mom accidentally starched dad's boxers and he could not stop laughing. He literally stood them up on the floor laughing and saying "damn mamma, that shit gonna hurt if I try to wear them."

It was just a few weeks before school would be out for summer. Sher volunteered for everything she possibly could, rather than stay home bored.

She woke up in a foul mood one morning saying, "I wish I could live at school."

I wasn't in a practically happy mood myself, so I snapped back. "Why don't you then?"

She looked at me as if she wanted to punch me in the face.

"Maybe I will, and then you can stay here all day and babysit instead of me." She yelled.

I wondered why she was bitching about babysitting. Mom never asked either of us to watch any of the kids, unless she was going to the grocery store or somewhere with dad.

"Good then go." I yelled back.

*Grouch.* I mumbled but dared not let her hear me.

"Who cares, go live at your stupid school." I snapped back.

I really did care but I guess I felt brave talking to her like that because mom and dad were in the next room.

With her summer schedule approved by mom and dad, Sher carried on how she would only come home to eat and sleep.

"Whatever." I thought. No way dad's gonna let you stay gone all day. She seemed as spoiled as Danny.

None of us ever went to or even had to go to summer school. It seems that our grades were always good enough to pass us on to the next grade. Extend school beyond the normal nine months, no way. I'd rather repeat the grade, then go an extra month or six weeks. I already hated school, but to extend it, no damn way.

Mom got a phone call from an organization that sponsored kids to go to summer camp. The woman told mom they were looking for girls my age group. She said they would furnish everything. The cost of the camp, my clothes, my transportation, food, anything I needed, all expenses paid. It would be for one week in July. Mom told the woman if I wanted to go I could, but she would have to ask dad and also make sure it was something I wanted to do.

"You will receive a letter in the mail informing you of all the arrangements." The woman told mom.

Sher was pissed, because she wanted to go. She wanted to get out of the house and away from all of us for an entire week. However, the organization wasn't offering it to Sher. They were offering it to me. Turns out one of my teachers at school gave my name as a potential candidate for this particular program.

"Why can't I go?" She insisted, almost like a spoiled two year old.

"It's for Malina's age group, Sher, it's not for teens." Mom tried to explain.

I really wasn't sure how I felt about leaving home for an entire week. Leave this house, yes, to get away from all dads griping, goes without saying. Of course, all that sounded pretty enticing but to leave mom for a week, all day all night. Not to see or talk to her, I don't think so. But I still had a few months to think about it.

Sher, though she was pissed that I was the one the organization was inviting, tried to convince me by eagerly saying, "It will be fun for you; you will make new friends go hiking, camp fires, and swimming."

Hold up, hold up… swimming? That word right there ruined the thought of even going on this trip for me!!! Swimming? Was she kidding?

## 21

Just last year on one of dads, "Let's do a family thing," had Sher really not remembered? How could anyone forget that day?

Dad, for whatever reason, decided to take us all to the lake. Mom made her famous fried chicken, Kool-aid, potato salad, cookies, packed up a nice little picnic basket and loaded us all into the car, and drove to the local lake. It was summer time, it was hot, and there were a lot of people there.

Dad drove around the lake until he found a nice spot, with swings, a picnic table, and lots of beach area so we would have plenty of space to run around.

Mom and dad took all the things out of the car, set out the blankets and basket and even left the car radio on so we could enjoy music. Mom began setting things out so every thing would be ready when we got hungry enough to eat. The kids were running around, screaming, and laughing at one another on the beach. Danny and J.J. had had their little toy trucks to play with in the sand. Carrie and Becky brought their volleyball and began playing.

Sher and I slowly started toward the water. None of us knew how to swim. We had never been in a pool or in the lake before. The times dad would bring us to the lake, we were never allowed to go near the water.

We were standing on the beach, not knowing what to do, while the kids got on the swings and began kicking sand at each other.

Dad said. "Come on girls, I am going to teach you how to swim."

Great! I thought. I didn't know anyone at this point that actually knew how to swim except them damn brats of Bee and Ely's. I figured it would be exciting to learn.

Sher and I grabbed our towels, took off our flip-flops, and started towards the water.

We didn't own bathing suits, so we were going to swim in our shorts, then sundry before getting in the car to go home.

Sher and I, standing patiently at the shoreline when dad took off his T-shirt and ran past us screaming. "Come on slow pokes." We laughed and ran into the lake just till the water got to our chest and then we stopped. We froze for a second or two not knowing what to do next. We stood there staring at dad, then staring at each other, again waiting on some type of instructions for this "swimming lesson." Dad was a bit further out and repeated, "Come on chickens."

Hold up a second, I thought. "Did you forget we don't how to swim?" I wanted to say but did not. He came towards us shaking his head as if to say; come on, I ain't got all day.

He looked both of us dead in our eyes and said.

"Swimming lesson number one."

I honestly believed he was going to show us how to duck our heads under water, hold our breath, hold our noses closed with our fingers, show us how to float, back stroke, something along the lines of an actual educational swimming lesson.

Nope, not dad!

He picked me up, without any kind of warning, just picked me up, threw me up in the air, and bam... right into the water.

I never saw it coming.

No warning what so ever!

He never said, hold your nose Malina, take a deep breath Malina, take a deep breath, and hold it Malina.

No this bastard just picked me up, threw me up in the air, and just like that, he stood there like I was supposed to know instinctively what the hell to do next.

It happened so damn fast, just like that. All I could see was dirty water. When I did realize what had happened, I completely panicked.

It seemed like an hour past, but in reality, it was only five seconds.

Water filled my lungs, my ears, my eyes, and my fricken mouth. Damn….What the hell… I was drowning.

In the distance, I heard Sher scream and in the even further distance, I heard mom scream. Surprisingly, I did not float right to the top as one is supposed to. There was no time to hold my breath because I had no idea what this mad man was doing.

One minute I was above the water and the next I was supposed to become a fish and swim downstream as nature had intended.

You fucking nut!!! You almost killed me! These exact words I wanted to yell, but with all the mud and dirty water and God knows what in my mouth, I could not utter a word.

All I could remember was, I was a flopping my hands, kicking my feet, but going nowhere. I had a vision of myself, flipping and flopping, like a fish out of water, only I was a kid in the water.

I was choking to death and trying to scream all under water, a horrific pain in my chest. Everything was dark, darker than night. I couldn't hear or see anything. Water and or mud were jammed into my ears and eyes. All I remember was I started to see day light or the preverbal light at the end of the tunnel.

Suddenly, someone had me by my hair pulling me straight up out of that dirty, filthy, muddy water. I could not hear or breathe. I panicked again. Of course, I panicked. I had never been in any water except a damn bathtub.

The person that pulled me out was not my dad. I had no idea who it was, some fortunate swimmer that just so happen to be swimming by. He was there just in time to save a terrified kids life, the daughter of a gangster that was thrown out into a lake and instructed to "SWIM."

Mom was half way in the water, when I could finally focus my eyes, leaving the little kids on the beach. She grabbed me from the rescue swimmer thanking him.

I was chocking and spitting water. She wrapped a towel around me and laid me on the sand.

She kept saying, "Are you ok? Are you ok?" She was horrified; almost crying herself.

Well, I knew for a fact I didn't die and go to heaven because when I did stop choking on mud, and when I was finally able to open and focus my eyes, dad was standing above me looking down at me shaking his head in disgust.

Mom asked, "Is she okay Johnny? Why would you do that? You know they don't know how to swim."

"She does." He said as he turned with the biggest fucking smirk on his face and pointed at his pride and joy. Sher was actually swimming. I suppose he must have thrown her in the lake a split second after he threw me in.

She had survived the near drowning and was still in the water not even bothering to check on me. Of course, maybe, she had read "how to swim" in one of her books, knowing exactly what to do on impact of being thrust into the water.

Once I quit choking on all that crap that was forced into my lungs, I felt a little bit better. Mom gave me water to drink and told me to stay on the beach, so I could rest.

Rest? Are you kidding? There was no way to rest with all this water around me. How could I not relive that experience when I was three feet from the millions and millions of gallons of water? I will never get in the water again. I don't care if Tarzan himself tried to teach me to swim. I will never ever do that again.

People accidentally drown all the time and they know how to swim. Some swim for years and they still drown.

I thought briefly of the saying "Cement Shoes" Wondering if dad did this sort of thing on a regular basis.

Just toss some poor idiot out in the lake with the famous "Cement Shoes" on, and dare them to float to the top. My mind was racing with horrible thoughts.

My dad must not collectively be all there, or maybe he wanted me to drown, one less mouth for him to feed, I thought as I sat on the beach, wishing he would accidentally go under for a few seconds and see how the hell he liked it.

Swimming lessons my mother fuckin foot, I wanted to yell.

It wasn't funny at the time but later on as we were driving home dad tried to re-enact my near drowning episode. He would make screaming noises and choking sounds as to mock me, making everyone in the car laugh, everyone, except mom and me.

He knew I was sensitive and eventually would cry from being made fun of; which I did. Then he would say. "Ok baby, I guess you don't want to go to the lake anymore."

Ya think, fucker? I thought. You wouldn't be laughing so much if I had drowned, or would you?

I never hit it off with lakes and pools after that horrifying experience. Some lessons in life are hard learned. This lesson I learned quick and easy. Safe to say I never learned to swim. I never even tried. To this very day I cannot swim, I can't even face the showerhead when I take a shower. Traumatized? I tell ya, completely traumatized

Life's valuable lessons; swimming lessons, check that shit off my list. Thanks dad.

## 22

Sher and I walked home from school together every day unless it was raining, then of course mom or dad would pick us up. If Sher had an event after school or volunteer session mom would pick me up. I was never allowed to walk by myself; dad said it wasn't safe for a girl to walk alone.

This particular day Sher had no such events, so we walked home together. Seems Sher walked slowly as to not get home too quickly. I, on the other hand, wanted to always hurry to see mom, and the kids.

When we arrived that particular day, the kids were outside playing in the front yard. Mom was on the front porch talking to someone, for a second I wasn't sure who it was, but I could tell it was a kid about our age.

He had his back to us so I was unable to see his face but I could hear him talking.

"I'll put the newspaper right here on the edge of the porch." He said, as he pointed to the top step.

"Especially on Sundays." He continued.

"Sunday's paper is very heavy and I wouldn't want it to get all over your yard." He looked down at the ground, squinting his eyes trying to see at least one blade of grass somewhere amongst all the rocks and dirt. I wasn't sure if he was being a smart ass or not, by that gesture.

At that very moment, he looked up and saw me and Sher approaching the porch. He tried not to make eye contact with us.

"What's your name?" Mom asked him. He seemed a bit shy. Not at all the way he was at school.

"Ahhhhh Louis, Ma'am, my name is Louis." He said as he fumbled with the pencil and tablet that he had in his hand.

"Well Louis, if Johnny sent you, then I guess we have us a paper boy." Mom said as she smiled that calm beautiful smile.

Apparently, he had met dad at the station and convinced

him to subscribe to the newspaper.

Sher walked past him without saying a word, but I stood next to mom and watched him try to squirm his way past me.

Louis my foot. I wanted to scream to embarrass him.

You're not Louis, your Screwy Louie, everyone knows you. Who did he think he was kidding? I thought to myself. He smiled at mom a sort of cute smile then turned to walk away.

"When do we get our first paper?" Mom asked.

"Right now." He answered, as he ran to his bike, which was ten feet from where he was standing, grabbed a newspaper out of his bag, then handed it to mom, trying desperately not to smile or look at me. He couldn't even look at mom, he was so embarrassed. Then he took his little writing tablet that had all of our info like our name, address, phone number, nervously putting it in his back pocket and sped off on his bike.

Louis my foot! I repeated my thought. He's Screwy Louie. All the girls at school call him that. I wasn't sure if it was because everyone thought he was crazy, or if he was called Screwy Louie just because screwy rhymed with Louie.

Anytime we passed him in the hall at school, or on the playground, or even at a neighborhood store, every girl said the same thing. 'Screwy Louie, Screwy Louie, watch out he might try to screw me."

Only thing was, at twelve years old, I had no idea what screw meant. Someone had made it up and it stuck with him. We all said it jokingly to him, the more we said it the more hyped up he would get.

He got a lot of attention from that name and he enjoyed it.

He would huddle up with his friends at school and talk nonsense to us. Sometimes we laughed, sometimes we were annoyed, but always he enjoyed joking and playing around with everyone.

I believe he was the class clown. I used to see him in the Principals office on a regular basis, thinking to myself, I wonder what Screwy Louie did this time. For sure he was gonna get a paddling.

Because he was the paperboy, he had to rush home every day after school to deliver the newspaper to all the neighborhood homes. He had his own route, which normally wasn't given to guys quite as young as him. Routes were usually given to the older teenagers or people that had vehicles. I suppose he was given his own route because he had proven himself to be loyal and a good paperboy.

People depended on him to get their newspaper to them by the time they sat down for supper.

So everyday, suppertime, our paper was delivered to our top step, just as Screwy had promised mom. Sunday morning, the heavy newspaper would be there bright and early, same spot. Seems Screwy Louie was quite a paperboy.

Me, Sher, and two of our neighborhood friends were walking home from school, we weren't walking our usual route, which was a big no no anyway for us! If mom or dad had gone to pick us up and we weren't walking the way we had been instructed to, we would get a whooping, deservingly so. But Sher, Miss bossy insisted, and hey, I'm not gonna walk alone.

Turns out one of the girls had a little bit of change, and wanted to go in the store and buy candy. She said if we went with her, she would split it with us. There was no way we were gonna pass up that offer.

We were only in the store maybe three minutes, buying what candies each of us wanted, then stood in the parking lot for a few moments, when screwy Louie and three of his friends ran past us saying some stupid obscenities. We assumed they were obscenities, they blurted out the words so quickly, we really couldn't make out what they said.

They were half a block in front of us, when, out of no where, as if the only place on the planet this rock belonged, it hit me right on my lip! Perfect aim, if they were aiming for my lip. If not, lucky shot.

Lucky for them, not so lucky for me. I screamed the instant

the rock hit my lip. As quickly as I screamed, blood gushed from my lip.

My lip was cut. I was bleeding, and we were going to have to explain what had happened and what we were doing on a street we had no business being on.

I saw who threw the rock. I know exactly which one of those boys threw it. He was the one that looked the most scared. Those boys hauled ass as fast as they could, completely out of sight.

I'm sure Screwy knew what was going to happen next. Tattle tell Malina, would tell on him and my dad would be on his doorstep within an hour.

We ran home, I mean hauled ass. Mom was picking up toys off the front porch when she heard us screaming and saw blood all over me. I'm sure she thought the absolute worst when she saw me.

I was crying, mom ran off the porch to assist me. "What happened? What happened?" She yelled!

Sher tried to explain to mom that a group of boys had thrown a rock and hit me right on the lip.

"What boys?" Mom wanted to know. Sher and I looked at each other, simultaneously said. "I don't know."

That sounded like a lie, even to us. Mom took me inside and washed my face and lip. Seems the bark was louder than the bite. It was a small tiny bump on my lip, and a small cut. Mom instructed me to stop crying, hold the washcloth on my lip, and tell her what happened.

When Sher realized I wasn't going to die, she abandoned ship. Left me there to tell, or not tell, what happened?

"Malina, don't lie to me. Tell me what happened." Mom said.

I explained we went to the store with the neighbors and when we came out of the store four boys ran passed us and one of them threw a rock.

"Who threw the rock?" She insisted.

Now, I knew the way of the world, at lease the way of the

school. You do not snitch…ever. You can make a lot of enemies at school if you tell on anyone. And, being the daughter of a gangster, dad always told us, never, ever rat on anyone. You take the fall yourself if you have to, but never ever rat them out.

"I can't mom; all the kids will pick on me." I cried to her.

"You can tell me, I won't tell dad."

Dad? Oh no, I hadn't even thought of him yet. Over react, beat someone up. He would do whatever he wanted to do. I was horrified at the thought of him finding out. Mom was no fool though, she knew if she told dad he would go directly to Screwy's house, probably give him, his mom, and his dad a fat lip too. She definitely didn't want that.

I told her everything and she agreed she would not mention any of it to dad, but I knew he would see my lip a bit swollen, and demand an explanation.

"I'll tell him I was throwing the ball to the boys outside and you walked in the path of the ball." Mom explained to me. Simple enough!

Mom called Sher in the room and told her of our plan. Sher seemed annoyed by the entire thing. Mom reminded us we would probably be in more trouble than screwy because we were somewhere we were not supposed to be. Sher looked at me as to say, Oh my goodness you are a damn pest. All this frickin' trouble just for a hairy twerp. I believe I could always tell when she was thinking evil thoughts. .

Did she prefer we get our asses whooped? Then Sher did something she never had done before, she winked at me as if to say, "life or longer."

# 23

The next day we were all outside with mom as she watched Becky and Carrie play hopscotch, Danny and J.J. play tag. Sher and I were sitting on the porch with mom, talking, mostly small talk. Laughing, mom could make us laugh over the silliest things. She loved to laugh.

It was a few weeks shy of the beginning of summer and it was starting to get hot outside. Our neighbors Sandy and Jewel came out of their house and waved hello to us.

They were standing in their yard when we saw a big truck backing up towards their house. They didn't have a driveway, as we didn't, so the truck driver had plenty of space to back the truck in.

At first, we thought they were moving, but that wasn't the case. The driver backed it to the far side of their house, opposite ours. We watched, wondering what the heck they were doing.

Jewel was a big woman and had to use crutches to get around. I'm not sure if it was because she weighed over four hundred pounds, or her legs just gave out from hauling all that weight around. Her armpits appeared to be raw from the years of walking with the crutches.

One-day mom suggested to Sandy to put a rag underneath her arms so she wouldn't be in so much pain from all that rubbing.

Sandy didn't work; instead, he took care of Jewel. It was sad to watch them try and climb their stairs together, sad but funny. He would help her climb one stair at a time, while dragging his left foot behind him, then pull his left foot up to the next step. He would be right behind Jewel, which always seemed he was trying to protect her from falling backwards.

Truth is, if she ever would have fallen, she would have crushed him to death.

Once this thing was backed up to the house and the driver left, Sandy motioned mom to meet him half way between both houses, Jewel stayed by the porch.

"Mrs. Shirley, how are you and all the kids doing?" Sandy asked.

"We're just fine Mr. Sandy. And what is all that?" She pointed to the silver thing that had just been parked on the side of his house.

"Well Mrs. Shirley, I went and bought a snow cone stand." He had a big smile on his face. The little kids started screaming with joy.

"You know I don't work anymore, and, well, me and Jewel are going through some really tough times." He seemed ashamed that he couldn't "make it," and there were only two of them.

"My brother was selling it." Sandy continued. "And we talked about it, and well, now we own this monster thing." He said.

"What a great idea, a snow cone stand, right next door to us." Mom seemed almost as excited as Sandy. How exciting for the entire neighborhood. I had a vision in my mind. How the heck was Jewel gonna climb up into the snow cone stand?

"It's going to take us a few weeks to get syrup and ice, but when we do, the first one will be on the house." Sandy said as kindly as he possibly could.

Now that would make the extremely hot summer days almost bearable. At least we would be able to cool down some, instead of depending on that sticky water cooler. Only thing, we never had any money. We were too young to get jobs, we didn't get an allowance, and for sure, there was no loose change in all the rocks and dirt. The goose with the golden egg had landed right next door, and we had no means to scrape up any kind of change for a snow cone.

Sandy showed mom the inside of the snow cone stand, while we kids waited outside.

Mom told him how nice it was, and if they needed any help to let her know. It was even better than I thought. A job at a snow cone stand. We could eat all we wanted all day long. I was getting ahead of myself. I don't know if technically a twelve-year-old girl can legally get a job... `

Oh well, we had a few weeks to figure it out. One thing was certain, cold snow cones on a hot summer day, was definitely the way to spend the summer.

I spent the entire night thinking of the snow cone stand. The rock incident had happened on Friday. I didn't see Screwy all weekend. He delivered the paper in the early morning hours while we were still asleep. It was scary, thinking of a young guy being out there in the dark delivering newspapers alone. I wondered if one of his brothers helped him.

Well at least dad hadn't seen my lip, if he had I think dad would've scared me so much with his interrogating ways, I might have been forced to tell on Screwy.

Fortunately, dad never saw my busted up lip, I mean think about it, in order for him to see it, he would actually have to be home to see me, which he wasn't. Therefore, it pretty much saved me and Sher from getting a whooping.

When I went to school that following Monday, Screwy Louie did his clumsy attempt of an apology. Seems boys that age just don't know how to say they're sorry, besides that, he had to save face with his jerk friends.

I accepted his apology.

He asked, "What did your dad say?"

"Don't worry Louis you still have a job." I assured him.

He sort of laughed it off. Then he asked.

"What about your mom? Does she know it was me?" He asked.

I let him know my mom was the one that saved me and Sher from an ass whooping.

"She knows." I said. He threw a look at me like, damn girl, why did you tell?

"I had to, I don't lie to her." I was quick to defend myself.

"Now my dad, that's a different story." I continued.

Dad hated liars. He would bust our ass if he caught us in a lie. He would rather we tell the truth, and take the chance, than to tell a bold face lie. Seems not telling him where we were that day would just have been a cover up lie. My busted lip, and mom not telling him any of it, all of us covering it all up, would have caused him to blow a fuse, you know, beat the shit out of everyone, just because we lied and it would have made him feel like a damn idiot..

I told screwy, "And don't go to the station and tell my dad what really happened."

Screwy looked relieved. "Ok." He said. A bit of relief in his voice.

"I'm sure you would much rather deal with my mom than my dad wouldn't you?"

He sort of smiled. "That's for sure, and thanks girl, I really didn't mean for the rock to hit you."

I laughed to myself, thinking how some boys are such show offs.

While delivering the afternoon paper at our house that afternoon, mom cornered him.

"Ok Mr. Louis. Let me hear your side of the story." Even when mom tried to sound tough, we all knew she just couldn't be mean to anyone.

Screwy was scared, a little, but not as scared, as he would have been, had dad confronted him.

"It was an accident; I didn't mean to hit her." He said, too embarrassed to look at mom.

"Why did you throw the rock?" She asked.

He hesitated before answering. "Acting stupid." He said as he finally looked at her. Mom was not yelling at him, not cussing, she was talking very kindly to him, as she did with everyone. She called me out on the porch.

"My concern is that you could have put out her eye or cut her forehead, had the rock landed anywhere beside her lip." He looked over at me like, Geez girl!

"Yes ma'am." He rather whispered, as if perhaps he really was sorry.

"He apologized to me at school today mom." I got him off the hook

"You did?" Mom asked him.

"Yes ma'am. I really didn't mean to hit anyone. I just threw it acting stupid with my friends."

"Well, since you have apologized and you say you didn't mean to hit her, I think every thing will be fine." Mom said.

Mom smiled at him as if to say. "You just got a reprieve young man."

Screwy thanked her, said bye to me, and hauled ass on his bike. It was a good thing dad had not showed up. He would have wanted to get in on the conversation. Who knows what would have happened. I was ok, no permanent damage. No need for anyone else to know what had really happened to me.

# 24

The last day of school was approaching; the kids were excited because now they didn't have to wake up early. Danny was happy because he would have his brother home to play with. When you think about it, I guess it would be lonely for a little kid to be home all day with no one to hang out with.

Becky and Carrie had their days planned. Jacks, jacks, and more jacks.

Sher already knew she would be up early at least three days a week to volunteer at the elementary school, helping the teachers, and the teacher aides. I think she would've also volunteered for the janitorial duties, just to have something to do at the school.

Finally, it was the last day of school. The younger kids went only half day, so mom picked them up at noon. Sher and I were to get out of school one hour early.

We began walking our normal path, when a girl approached us. She was a freshman in high school that had also gotten out of school early.

"Sher!" She yelled, and ran to catch up with us. She was a friend of Sher's' that used to volunteer right along side Sher at school. Her name was Patty.

"Where y'all going?" She asked. Seemed like a stupid question considering it was the last day of school, and everyone got out early and headed home.

"Home." Sher said.

"Oh come on; please come to my house with me. I want to show you what my parents bought me."

Her house was not a house we would pass on our way home. It was a bit of a walk in a different direction than we were accustomed to.

"Naw we can't." Sher said.

"Oooohh please, just for a few minutes pleeeeaaase." Patty begged.

"No." I told Sher. "Mom will be waiting."

"Come on Sher, y'all can run home once you see my gift."

She continued to beg.

Seems Patty talked Sher into it with very little effort. Well, I couldn't very well walk home alone so, there we go, walking through streets we had absolutely no business being on.

I was horrified. We had just escaped ass whoopings a few weeks prior, now we were taking the risk all over again. What the heck were we doing?

Sher told Patty, "Let's hurry." So we sorta jogged the extra few blocks to get there more quickly.

When we arrived, no one was there just us. Her parents weren't home, and we knew that would be another reason to get the shit beat out of us.

One of dads rules, you never enter a house unchaperoned. No parents at home only meant trouble. You never know what kind of trouble kids can get into.

Patty opened the front door and said, "Come on in." We stood there a minute, and then Sher went in. Well, I wasn't gonna stand there alone, so I went in too.

Then I heard it, her surprise. The cutest, tiniest, little brown puppy ever. It was so hyper from being home alone, I'm supposing all day. She took it out on the front yard so it could pee.

Once it relieved itself, it began chasing us and jumping all over us, then we sat on the grass and played with it for a while.

It was barking and trying to bite us with its little bitty teeth. Patty went inside and got some dog food and water so we could feed it. It was the most adorable puppy we had ever seen. We were sitting on the grass, passing the puppy back and forth, laughing, and enjoying how excited the puppy was getting all the attention all three of us were giving to it.

We simply lost track of time. A look of total terror, Sher realized we messed up.

"Come on Malina let's go." Sher yelled.

We had been there for two whole hours. Horrified, we knew we were in trouble for sure. We ran and ran, with almost ten blocks ahead of us. Sher was almost an entire block ahead of me; I guess she thought if she got there sixty seconds ahead of me, we wouldn't be in as much trouble.

As we approached our house, we could see mom outside, walking back and forth, pacing, and pacing. I could see she was crying.

The second she saw us she screamed. Apparently, she called the cops and dad.

She tried asking us questions, but really, she couldn't get the words out, she was so upset and crying and just so happy to see us, she could barely speak. She didn't really have time to ask us anything because just as she started to ask, the cops arrived. Even before dad.

They began to question us about our whereabouts. They seemed annoyed at our lack of respect, especially for our mom because she looked so pitifully sad, not to mention disrespecting our father, though I could hear the cop lecturing us, I seemed to go a little deaf thinking, *we disrespected our dad? It was more like we inconvenienced him.* I guess I was just trying to convince myself what we had done wasn't that big of a deal. However, one look at my moms face, told me we fucked up. She looked pale as a ghost, sick with worry, and I knew Sher and I did that to her.

Whatever ass whooping I was gonna get, I was ready for it. Never in my life did I want to hurt my mom, I never wanted her to be sad over something I did.

Mentally I welcomed the ass whoopin I was about to get. The cops explained to us that we should never do anything like that again.

"Your mom was worried sick." One of the police officers said as the other police officer left to check out our story. It took all of three minutes for the cop to radio back that we were telling the truth.

Just then dad pulled up, jumped out of his car, and I'm sure would of slapped the shit out of me and Sher, but there was a uniformed policemen standing right in front of him.

He was not a frickin idiot after all. Mom tried to calm him, but we already knew. The cop told dad that our story checked out and where we had been. Dad thanked the cops, one of only a few rare times he had any kind words for a cop or them to him.

The cops left, but not before warning me and Sher to never do this again, and also to remind mom and dad this one had a happy ending, we were safe.

Happy ending my frickin' foot, that's what you think, I couldn't help but think. He sure didn't know our dad very well, if he had he wouldn't have left us there with him, instead he would've arrested me and Sher for what ever he could have, being dumb ass kids maybe?.....

There was no way to stop what was about to happen. Should we just take off running, as fast as we possibly can? Maybe two teenage girls could out run the main gangster in north side.

I started crying the second I got in the house. Dad was in Sher's face yelling at her, then for the first time ever, he smacked Sher right across her face and then he took off his belt and hit her with it, over and over.

Mom jumped in and blocked the hits, I was screaming, "No dad, no don't hit her." I hated seeing any of my brothers or sisters being hit, I would much rather dad hit me then to watch one of them get beat.

Dad was telling her "How stupid can you be? Your mama was worried sick. The fucking cops were everywhere looking for you." He was enraged. Instead of hugging us and thanking God, we were safe, he beat on Sher. All the anger he had

bottled inside, for whatever reason, he was taking it out on Sher.
  Mom was hit a few times in the crossfire, finally he stopped. He didn't stop cussing but he did stop hitting her.

  He never laid a hand on me.
  I felt so bad for Sher, I think she thought I got hit, I mean she was actually getting the butt of all the hits. I guess through all the commotion she didn't realize that he never actually hit me.
  Once he stopped hitting her and calmed down Sher went to our room crying. She hugged me and said, "I'm sorry."
  "Sorry for what?" I asked.
  "I'm sorry I got you in trouble." Sher said.
  I hugged her. My poor big sister. She was taking the blame and taking the punishment dad was dishing out. I suppose Sher understood why only she was whooped. I didn't.
  Mom told us to get ready for bed. She made us some sandwiches and told us to go in the kitchen and eat. I really didn't have an appetite after what I had just witnessed.
  Of course, we were going to be punished.
  Dad was sitting on the front porch when Sher and I started to go to bed. He called us outside.
  Dad was good on apologizes. He hugged us both and said he was sorry.
  "Do you know why I didn't whoop you?" He asked me.
  "No." I said
  "Because Sher is your older sister and she knew better."
  "Sher I'm sorry." He told her. "But you had your mom sick with worry."
  "I did what I had to do." He said.
  "I know daddy, I'm sorry." Sher said.
  He melted. She melted his heart. He had whooped his favorite and he whooped her good, and though he felt he had to, you could tell it was something he hated doing.
  Sher apologized to mom, which started everyone crying. Sher apologized to everyone, and then she went to bed.

She had made a grown up decision that cost her a whooping and even worse, she lost dad's trust for the moment. She had taken the whooping, and accepted it.

Tonight Sher was my big sister. I loved her, I felt bad for her, and I never wanted to see her get hit again.

Over the next few nights, once supper was done, the dishes put away, and kids down for the night, mom would sit with me and Sher and have those mom and daughter talks with us. You know, where your mom tells you the dos and don'ts of life, being a girl, having a boyfriend, and just growing up in general.

"Sooner or later," She began. "You're both gonna begin to like boys, and want to have a boyfriend." She continued. "You know you aren't allowed to have boyfriends just yet."

Really, at age twelve I could have cared less about boys. I knew after the conversation I overheard Sher having on the phone, that one particular day, Sher, for the most part had a small interest in boys or at least one boy in particular.

Mom told us without hesitation, "If any boy ever touches either of you girls in an inappropriate manner, you must tell me so I can tell dad."

Tell dad? I questioned in my own mind. Oh, that definitely would mean trouble.

We understood everything she was saying, even the part about dad. He was supposed to be our protector.

Sher and I looked at each other somewhat embarrassed, that our mom was telling us such things. We knew what she meant, we heard girls talk about this and that at school. Some girls talk like they really know about boys and personal things, when in fact, they know absolutely nothing. We did not know anything beyond what mom had just told us.

Mom also let us know how terribly worried she was when we didn't come straight home from school. She told us of her fears.

"You girls very well could have been kidnapped." She said. Her voice cracking.

"Someone could have taken you both." She said, in her kind tone and comforting manner. She explained to us what rape was, and that it was possible for someone to kidnap us, rape us, and even kill us.

Mom cried as she explained all the possibilities and scenarios of the things that could happen to girls.

Possibly those were things Sher and I never even thought about. Mom attempted to tell us just how easy two girls could be swooped up, thrown into a car, and horrible things could happen.

She continued, "Always walk facing traffic, so you can see if someone is going to try and grab you. If, God forbid, that were to ever happen, you are to scream! Scream as if someone is trying to kill you. If one of you were to get grabbed the other one should scream and try your best to run away, scream, scream, scream," she said.

"Fight, scratch, kick, and bite, anything and everything you can possibly do to try and get away."

We knew that exact second just how frightened mom had been that day. She scared us, we had no idea what a parent felt. We had no way of knowing, but we knew we were scared.

I guess we never thought anything like that could happen to us, we were the daughters of a gangster, who would dare attempt such a thing? She also told us because of who dad was it could be even more reason for someone to hurt us.

"Be aware." She said. "Always be aware."

We were growing up and she wanted to teach us how to take care of ourselves. I suppose she wanted to have this talk with us now, instead of waiting until something bad happened and it may have been too late.

We grew up a lot that night. Mom made us aware of things we had only heard about; never thinking we could be the victims of such horrific acts. Dad never said another word to us about that day. Maybe he was so stressed thinking what could have happened to us. I was sure it wasn't easy to be a dad, even our dad.

# 25

Dad was working now six days a week at the garage. Working or supervising? He did not have the hands of a mechanic; he didn't come home all greasy and dirty. He came home exactly as he had left the house, clean and smelling of cologne and after-shave, whatever it was that made him smell so good.

He would talk about changing oil, fixing brakes, easy simple car repairs, but never serious repairs like rebuilding a motor or transmission. As we witnessed the times we were there, he sure knew how to make a customer feel special, through his exciting conversations. He made the customers want to come back, if for no other reason than to get back into the conversation they had experienced the first time they were there.

He would come home usually after we had all eaten supper. Most nights mom tried to get us to wait for him hoping to have a sit down dinner with all of us, but more nights than not, it was just too hard to keep six unfed kids till he got home.

Most night's dad would come home, take a bite of food, shower, get dressed, and leave.

He would convince mom the money he made at the garage wasn't enough to support us all.

"I just have to go baby, we need the money." He would try his best to convince her. Mom would tell him she didn't think he had to go out every night. But really, he was already going out seven nights a week before he inherited the garage from Sal. Why would she think he would stop now?

The bar was like a magnet to him. He would spend ten to twelve hours a day one hundred feet from the bar. Hell he probably went to the bar while he was supposed to be at the garage. Mom would never have known if he did or not.

Watching people come and go all day from the bar as dad sat at the garage was, I assume too much for him. So at the end of his so-called legit day, he would end up at the bar anyway doing his illegal crimes. It was just too much temptation for him.

A nice cold beer, a game of pool, a bunch of skanky women around him, all the gangster wannabes that idolized him, and even a back room to smoke his weed, and do whatever the hell he wanted.

Nope not mom, or his kids, or God himself could have kept dad from Sal-E's bar.

He was a hustler, a con man. The one he pulled the biggest con on was mom.

Perhaps she just put on a big show hoping that maybe he would stay home. I think she knew it was a big waste of time. Being out in the streets was what he did, seems he knew nothing else. So mom did what she liked. Everything she could to please her kids.

Mom spent all her time with us kids, playing games, watching TV, laughing. She wasn't shy at all; she loved doing things we liked to do. Once we were all down for the night she would get on her old sewing machine and make clothes. She would make things for my two little brothers and us girls.

It was summer time and within just a few hours, she could make four of us girls a pair of shorts and a matching top. I could only imagine what she could of done if she had money to buy a bulk of material.

She would make the outfits; iron them with perfectly ironed creases, never a wrinkle anywhere. It would not look like some old crappy outfit she threw together; it would be perfectly made, as the finer clothes sold in the high-end department stores.

Little kids didn't normally have that kind of care put into their clothes just to sit around an old house, but she took such care to make every inch of every outfit to appear like a masterpiece. If she had any material left, she would make headbands to match each outfit. Though we never got to go to the department stores to buy new clothes, and lot of times we depended on the hand me down from the families, when mom made our clothes they looked better than any thing from the department store. And we were proud of what she did.

# 26

Dad working, whatever? I always thought, six days a week, hustling six nights a week seemed to be a very busy schedule for any man, except dad. All those hours at the garage and even more hours at the bar, somehow he still managed to find the time to play on a local baseball team.

Some Sundays we would go to the ballpark and watch him and his ban of gangster baseball teammates.

I really did not understand the rules of the game, but it was fun to watch dad and all the other gangsters get so excited each time they won. Which, just so happened to be every week. Once they won, they sat around and drank twelve pack after twelve pack of beers, commenting on how good they played and how terrible the other team was.

Get real guys, y'all are gangsters playing against regular men, of course y'all are gonna win.

The other teams were not stupid enough to beat y'all, especially on your own turf.

For sure, a win for the opposing team warranted looking under the hoods of their cars, every day for the rest of their lives.

I could only cringe thinking, one day the other team is gonna beat y'all on your own turf, in front of your wives and kids, then humiliate y'all gangsters by drinking cold beer in front of you, then gloat and laugh while y'all pack up your humiliated asses and families into your cars and drive away.

Not in this lifetime I thought. Dad's team knew before each game ever started they were gonna win. I have no idea who made the schedules for these Sunday games, which were always played at Rockwood Park, every single Sunday, 6 p.m., but you could bet your right arm it would be a gangster team against a "real" team. I mean even we kids knew before we got to the park it would be a sure win, but it was entertaining to say the least.

All the cussing and bitching dad's team would do to the opposing teams. They humiliated and embarrassed them, and pushed them around, not in a mean way really, it was actually funny, or maybe I was just so used to watching grown ass men pick on other grown ass men, it just seemed funny to me...

It never was violent or physical, just funny. Even the regular guys would try to talk smack and leave the park laughing at all the name-calling and swearing.

I remember hearing dad tell one of his teammates "Hey, if that mother fucker, (referring to the guy up to bat from the opposing team), if that mother fucker makes a home run, go to the trunk of my car and get my machine gun. I'm gonna blast his mother fuckin ass all over this park."

As you would guess the poor guy struck out, fear of a massacre at the park. Dad and his team laughing their asses off just minutes after the team packed up and left.

The wives did the same thing every Sunday also. Brought their famous picnic lunches, sat around and gossiped, and took turns watching after each other's kids.

Maybe the Sunday games were a way for the housewives to get to relax a bit.

As dirty as all these men's uniforms would get by the end of the night you would have thought they played eighteen innings at the World Series.

Men and sports?

Gangsters and sports, there is no comparison.

Because they were so good, or they muscled their way to the top, dad's team was going to a playoff game in San Antonio. They were that good, so it seemed.

Every man, player, gangster was going to take their wives and stay three days and two nights in a hotel.

At first mom wasn't going because of us kids. She couldn't take us all with them; expenses were being paid by sponsors. (Bank rolled by the head of the gangsters) which was funding each player, and his spouse, hotel rooms, and three meals a day. Players had to take their own spending money. It would be a great escape from mom's life.

Finding a babysitter was going to prove a difficult task. No one would of dared stayed in our creepy old house and baby sit us all. Mom didn't know anyone that would take the responsibility of watching six kids in their own home. Mom tossed ideas of who could watch us all, but it seemed impossible.

Then dad came up with a brainstorm of an idea. Pair us off in our usual big kid little kid style, that way it took the pressure off just one person to watch all six of us.

Only thing, now they were going to impose on three separate families instead of just one family.

Mom and dad were going to be gone from Friday afternoon until Sunday evening. The playoff game was going to be Saturday afternoon. I remember it was San Antonio because dad kept bragging to mom they would be able to visit the Alamo, and since mom never got to go anywhere, she was excited.

Mom and dad set out to see which relatives from either side of the family would agree to take a pair of kids for the weekend. Actually, it seemed dad was calling in favors from some relatives.

Mom had two weeks to prepare us for our first time ever away from her. She had only left us long enough to give birth to one of our siblings. She wasn't one of these moms that would get rid of her kids so she could go here and there.

The plan was for Sher and Danny to go to my Aunt Mary's on dad side. Aunt Mary had two sons and one daughter. Danny was close in age to one of her sons. But of all the kids, dads' side and moms' side, Danny was the baby of all.

Possibly, Danny would be ok there, but no one there was near Shers' age, so she would not have fun with a bunch of boys and a little girl. Aunt Mary had a phone and was more than happy to suggest Sher could stay on it as long as she desired. This would turn out to be a good thing for Sher. Aunt

Mary was married to Uncle George. He was an automobile painter by trade. He worked for a large company, but did a lot of jobs from his own garage. He often bragged how he wanted to have his own paint and body shop one day.

Becky and Carrie were going to stay at Aunt Gloria's house. Aunt Gloria's house was the house everyone on dads' side of the family went to for holidays. She had seven kids, three boys, and four girls. We were all close in age. Their house was the complete opposite of ours. Aunt Gloria had a big living room with a piano.

Pianos were foreign to us. We loved going there if for no other reason just to play the piano.

We didn't know any songs to play so one of our cousins taught us one particular song. Everyone learned the same song and it was played over and over.

Aunt Gloria's husband Uncle David was a seemingly strict man. He was kind and had a nice smile. He didn't talk much, at least in front of us kids. His voice was calm, when he did talk. I wondered if he ever yelled, considering that's all my dad did, I suppose I just wondered if all dad's did. I had never even seen him get mad at anyone. He was very good at being a host in his home.

Having such a big house, it was obvious to be the gathering place for all our family and his side of the family as well. Guess he figured if he had to have all dads side of the family, then he would have his side there also. Needless to say, there were always a lot of people there, not only for Thanksgiving but Christmas also, birthdays, and even funerals.

It was the only house that could accommodate so many people at once. It had a large front porch with a big swing, which we would spend countless hours swinging on that swing. Their front porch was cement not wood like ours. They had a perfectly manicured lawn; all grass no dirt and rocks. Beautiful colored flowers everywhere and lots of perfectly cut bushes.

They had three bedrooms down stairs, and a big dining room that had a table large enough to seat twelve. There was a big beautiful kitchen with a breakfast area.

Uncle was constantly remodeling parts of the kitchen to accommodate his growing family. Their washer and dryer were in the basement, which seemed so scary to us all.

Who the heck wanted to go down in a basement to do laundry? They even had a den where everyone gathered to watch football games.

Upstairs was one big bedroom. There were two sets of bunk beds, which Uncle David had taken down from bunk beds and made four single beds out of them. Each of the four girl cousins had their own bed, their own small chest of drawers to hold their personal items. They each had space for themselves, lots of it, something we didn't know anything about.

On rare occasions, we would spend the night with them, usually because we had no electricity or gas at our house.

Mom and Aunt Gloria would put three or four blankets on the floor in the large upstairs bedroom to make us a comfortable place to sleep on. Mom, dad, and the two boys would sleep in their den, which had a fold out sofa that made into a bed.

Uncle David had all their kids in the church choir. Going to church for them was as normal as our Sunday baseball games with dad. They had no choice, it was a given, so when we would spend the night with them we would spend hours singing. All eight of us girls. I believe we all sounded pretty good.

Dad and Uncle David would stand at the bottom of the stairs and listen. I know for a fact dad loved the sound of our music, just as Uncle David loved the sound of his daughters singing. When it would be time to go to sleep Uncle David would say "Lights out" and without missing a beat, his oldest daughter Celia would instantly turn out the lights. We didn't need lights to sing, so we would still stay up sitting in a circle singing the newest song on the radio.

Sure enough Uncle David would snap, snap his fingers, which would be his warning sign. His warning sign for all of us to be quiet and go to sleep or else. But being hyped up we would continue, maybe just daring to press our luck. We would giggle and act up.

Like a prison guard he would stand at the bottom of the steps, snap that finger just a little bit louder as the final warning. We instinctively knew it would be our final warning.

You did not get three strikes in their house. The snap of his finger was the calling card.

No one, and I mean no one would ever pushed their luck to see just what would happen if he had to snap a third time. I think he would stand at the bottom of the stairs with a smile on his face, knowing he would never be pushed to the limits of climbing those stairs. We never ever pushed his buttons to test him; we just knew enough was enough. However, he was fun and kind to us always. Possibly, he was aware we had it pretty tough at our home, and though he wasn't gonna let us get one over on him, I believed he loved us and treated us all very special.

Me and J.J. were going to stay with mom's brother, Uncle Bill, his wife, and their three kids.

Uncle Bill lived on what appeared to be a small farm. They lived out in the country with their closest neighbors three blocks away.

Uncle Bill had blue eyes and light brown hair, he was not handsome like dad, but he was nice looking. He was a painter by a trade, a house painter.

Him and my Grandpa, who we called Papa painted houses together. Papa was the boss but had taught Uncle Bill everything he possibly could on how to paint a house perfectly and make money.

Uncle Bill was not strict with his kids at all; they pretty much walked all over him.

Aunt Lily was a nerdy type of woman, that wore red thick pointed glasses and all she did was read. If she were cooking she had a book in her hand, if she was watching TV, she had a book in her hand, if she went to the restroom, a book was in her hand. She absolutely loved books; her kids on the other hand hated them.

They had two daughters, one son. Their house was very clean, mostly because their oldest daughter always kept it that way. She complained constantly that Aunt Lily was going to go blind because she never put the books down. She wouldn't even put the books down to go to sleep; she would read till the wee hours of the night, then just fall asleep, waking in the morning with the book still on her chest from the night before. She would fall asleep reading, yet we assumed she never turned over in her sleep, for the book to remain on her chest the next morning.

In her dining room, Aunt Lily had an ivy plant that started in one corner of the ceiling and traveled around the entire house. It looked like a vine Tarzan would swing on in the jungle. It was everywhere. She loved her ivy's and forbid everyone, kid, husband or visitor to ever dare cutting a leaf off for a starter.

This was going to be mine and J.J.'s home for the next three days, I dreaded it.

Any house was definitely nicer than ours was, cleaner and more modern than ours was, but none was a home if mom wasn't there.

# 27

Mom spent a couple of days preparing overnight bags for all of us. She had to pack three days of clothes for each kid, not to mention packing for herself and dad. What should've been exciting for everyone seemed a dreaded event, especially for me. I admit I hated our old shabby house, but in spite of its condition and my fear of dad, that old house was my comfort zone. It was the place my heart called home, mostly because of mom.

Friday came too quickly for me. Dad managed to help mom with the rest of the packing. He even loaded all the bags in the trunk of his car himself. Surprisingly, without the use of any cuss words or arguing, separating each pair of kid's bags so he and mom could make a hasty departure once arriving at each relative's house.

Sher and Danny were the first set of kids dropped off. Sher took Danny by the hand, while mom and dad unloaded their things. We all went in Aunt Mary's house for a few minutes to say goodbye. Mom and dad hugged them both. Sher even hugged all of us. She wasn't gonna be bossing us around for three whole days. I sorta felt sorry for my cousins because I already knew Sher sure was gonna boss them poor lil kids around.

Next, we dropped off Becky and Carrie. They had no problem running inside that nice big two-story house the second they got out of the car. They didn't even look back to say bye or to wave or anything. They just took off, like two bottle rockets, bam, gone in a second.

Me and J.J. were to be dropped off last, because Uncle Bill lived the farthest away. It took about twenty minutes to get to his farm.

I remember how different it felt sitting in the back seat of our car, not being crammed up against the car door, because everyone was gone now except me and J.J.

We always sat five in the back seat, Sher in the front seat with mom and dad.

I glanced over at my brother as he sat there. He looked so small with all that wide-open space around him. Mom and dad talked about the four hour drive they were about to take. Seems they decided to ride with one of the other team members and his wife. Split the gas and such. Once they dropped us off, they were going to pick them up.

I remember thinking, *Ok tough guys. You muscled your way to a championship game, now what?* I wondered if the players in San Antonio were gonna be regular hard working baseball guys, or other gangsters.

Who cares? I thought.

It was sinking in now, this stupid American past time was about to rip my mom away from me for the next three days and I hated it. Dad actually seemed excited to go somewhere, anywhere, with mom.

Well, why not? He would have his beautiful wife with him, his gangster friends playing ball with him, and he wouldn't have to worry about his kids for three days. Damn! He had it made.

Mom looked a little sad as we pulled up to Uncle Bills' house. For some strange reason their house looked as creepy as ours. Maybe it looked like that to me because I really didn't want to stay there. Wonder if it were possible, even a little possible, for them to take me and J.J. with them? Oh, how desperately I wanted to suggest it. But four adults in a car, for four hours, I knew darn good and well they wouldn't want to cram two kids in between all of them.

Dad got out of the car, opened the trunk, and got our bags out. Uncle Bill and Aunt Lily came out to greet us.

*Hey! No book in her hand. What? Had Uncle Bill burned them all?*

Lily hugged J.J. saying, "Oh my goodness he looks just like his daddy." Smiling the entire time she said it.

Mom took me by the hand as Aunt Lily took J.J. by his hand and began to walk us into the house.

Dad and Uncle Bill were bringing in our bags, talking about dad's trip, baseball and what ever it was men talk about.

Like clockwork, I started crying.

"Why are you crying Malina, don't you want to stay here with us?" Aunt Lily pleaded.

I wanted to scream, "Hell no, I don't want to stay here with you! I wanna go with my mommy!"

Mom knelt down beside me and said. "Malina, it will be ok, I promise I'll call you every night."

That wasn't enough, I thought. I want to go with you!

She smiled and said. "I promise I'll be back in three days."

She didn't say "I promise we'll be back in three days." She said "I."

Then she hugged, and hugged and hugged me and J.J... I didn't even look at my dad. I only concentrated on my moms face.

She was so beautiful. Then I caught a glimpse of Aunt Lily. She was so nerdy. I almost laughed.

Uncle Bill interrupted and said. "Come on Malina, don't cry, the kids can't wait for y'all to play with them."

What? That was supposed to make me feel better? Was he kidding? The only thing that would make me feel better is to go home with my mom, or for dad to drive off without mom and go on his stupid baseball trip by himself. None of this was likely.

It was a few minutes of tears, the only consolation being that mom would call me every night. I instantly began counting down the minutes before they would be back, and they hadn't even left yet. I stood at the door and watched them drive off. I hated dad for winning the stupid games.

I couldn't help but think to myself. Why couldn't they just loose? Why did they have to win?

Why, idiot? You know why? Because if they had lost there probably would have been a few blown up cars all over town. For mom's sake, I guess I had to try to make the most of it. Thank god there was a phone at that creepy house.

Aunt Lily showed us where to put our things and where we would sleep. J.J. was to sleep with their only son, Billy, of course and I was to sleep in their oldest daughter Candy's room, what a name Well, at least I wasn't sleeping three to a bed for the next two nights.

Within an hour, Aunt Lily had already made lunch for us. It was good; she even served ice cream for dessert. She had everyone sit together and eat, even Uncle Bill, which was a rare event in my house.

Uncle Bill was a funny man, always making jokes, even though some of them weren't funny or they didn't make any sense at all. But because he laughed at them himself, made them seem funnier.

Aunt Lily said, "Quit making them laugh Bill, you're going to make them choke on their food." He continued anyway.

After lunch, Uncle Bill took Billy and J.J. outside to play ball.

Auntie had already picked up a book and sat on the sofa to read while her daughters and I cleaned the dishes. This seemed normal to me, but these cousins of mine had horrible attitudes and cussed their mom behind her back. I didn't understand how these kids could use such language directed towards their own mother. And why would Aunt Lily just sit there and allow such behavior. Was she deaf? Was she afraid to say anything to her own kids, or did she not give a damn.

Once the dishes were put away, I went outside to check on J.J. Then, something happened that...well something I could not believe... As I stepped off the porch J.J. saw me, he ran to me, and hugged me. He was teary eyed and I kissed his cheek and told him not to cry. He looked so sad and I knew he was already missing mom. I was hugging him trying to comfort him when Uncle Bill said.

"Come here J.J."

At first J.J. did not budge, then in a stern voice, Uncle Bill said, "Come here J.J.…NOW."

I thought to myself, my parents have only been gone a few hours and you seem to be raising your voice at my lil brother.

J.J. held on to me as Uncle Bill said, "Come here Malina."
I did as I was told. As I walked toward him, J.J. held on to my leg.

"Here J.J., catch the ball." Uncle Bill commanded. J.J. ignored him and held on to me.

Again, Uncle Bill said, "Here Malina, run after the ball." For a third time I did as I was told. I tried to run to catch the ball, but J.J. held on to my leg even tighter. It seemed Uncle Bill got mad.

"Let her go J.J., I want her to get the ball." I did as Uncle Bill instructed. As I ran, J.J. ran after me, crying. I stopped to hug him and Uncle Bill screamed at the top of his lungs.

"Noooooo!" Stop, let her go J.J.! You mind what I'm saying Malina," he said as he pointed at the ball.

"Get the ball Malina…. J.J., you stand right there." Such demanding tones in his voice, he was screaming and carrying on as if we were in a World Series play off game, and we had just fucked up a Grand Slam. Uncle Bill, the bastard, was almost hysterical with all his damn commands and orders.

J.J. stood there crying, as Uncle Bill threw the ball clear across the yard and yelled at me to get it.

I was scared to do it, and I was even more scared not to. So I ran to the other side of the yard to get the ball, as I did, J.J. came screaming behind me.

"Malina, Malina!" He cried, with his arms stretched out for me to hug him. I stopped in my path, turned around to see Uncle Bill laughing, just laughing. He did it again, ordered me to run so J.J. could chase after me crying.

This hateful bastard was enjoying making me run and J.J. chase after me crying. This was not right. We were both missing our mom and this terrible bastard of a man was torturing us.

He was no longer Uncle Bill in my eyes, he was just Bill. He was enjoying watching us suffer and cry, almost as if he was getting some cheap thrill out of hurting two kids. I wanted to scream I hate you, fuckin jerk!

I could not believe my mother's brother was a monster just like my dad, only difference, Bill wasn't torturing his own kids, and he was torturing Johnny Guetarro's' kids.

I had no idea how J.J. and I were going to survive the next two and a half days.

Aunt Lily came out and rescued us, saying, "Oh Bill, quit teasing them."

Teasing? Teasing? What are you talking about lady? This is not teasing. This is abuse.

I might have to take abuse from my own dad, but from you, Uncle Jerk, no way.

We avoided Bill the rest of the night. We stuck by Aunt Lily as much as we could. After dinner, Bill left to go to a bar or somewhere for the rest of the evening. Auntie buried herself in her books once again, her kids running ramped. J.J. and I just sat in the living room watching TV until bedtime. Just as I was about to fall asleep, mom called.

I cried and cried for her to come home, but she said she couldn't until Sunday. J.J. was already asleep so she didn't get to talk to him, but she promised to call the next night. Aunt Lily took the phone from me. I believe she knew I was about to tell mom of Bill's abuse.

She told mom, "Oh don't worry about them, they're fine. Bill was playing ball outside with them running around having a good time."

*You lying bitch*! I thought. I wasn't allowed to speak such words, but no one could control any of my thoughts. What was wrong with these people? Bill was not any better than my own dad, only difference, he was being a monster to someone else's kids. I hated all of them.

My so-called uncle, for his abuse, Lily (from this point on she was no longer Aunt Lily, she was just Lily) for not stepping in and helping us.

Their kids made me sick because they acted like wild animals.

I envisioned taking her damn ivy and wrapping it around all their fricken necks as they slept, then just walking out of that house, me and my little brother. I knew damn good and well that was impossible. Being forced to watch someone other than my dad mistreat my little brother made me realize I had an obligation to protect him. I was going to do that, no matter what.

The next two days were pure hell with Uncle Bill. He was a monster sober, which made it seem even worse. At least drunk you could give him a messed up excuse for being a fucking idiot. But this, there was no explanation for this. It wasn't the beer that caused him to act like that. Uncle Bill took every opportunity he could to make J.J. cry. Seems like he just couldn't stop torturing him.

Finally, Sunday arrived, I couldn't eat. I couldn't sit still. I literally had all mine and J.J.'s things sitting on the front porch, waiting, just waiting to get away from these people.

I was so sick of this good for nothing family. Relatives or not, I was just sick and tired of them and the cruel ways of my so-called uncle.

I put it in my mind, Lily wasn't reading a book, the lazy bitch was pretending to, so her older kid could be the parent, do all the housework, and watch the smaller kids so she didn't have to do shit but sit on her lazy ass all day.

Argument would say Bill just inhaled too much house paint he had fucked up his brain. It could be the reason he tortured us and didn't even blink an eye over it. I wondered if he treated his own kids like this or was he just so afraid of his kids, once given the opportunity, he took full advantage of us.

No idiot in their right mind messes with another man's kids. Unless you want an ass whooping or you're messed up on drugs or something. I mean get real dude, if I tell my dad what you did to me and J.J., he would kick your ass, at least I really hoped he would. I never really wanted my dad to hurt anyone, but after what Bill had done to J.J., I would have welcomed the monster to do his gangster thing.

Bill was mom's brother after all. I don't know, and I don't care. I just wanted to see my mom. I cared less about everyone else. I wanted to go back to that rattrap; I wanted Sher to beat me up, or whatever. Almost anything was better than this.

Finally, I saw our old car rolling up the street. I could see mom, smiling, I even welcomed dads half ass smile.

Mom hardly let the car stop when she jumped out and ran to me and J.J., hugging and kissing us. Me and J.J. were crying, mostly because we missed her, partly because her brother was a damn jerk.

Dad, of course wanted to sit around and brag about the trophy's they had won, or should it be known, they had stolen from the other team. The die-hard baseball players, like so many more before, had lost, yet, walked away with their lives, which gave bragging rights to the real gangsters until next year.

Mom reminded dad we had to go for the other kids. Mom and dad said their goodbyes, me and J.J. just got in the car. Not looking back at these, relatives?

I wondered if Lily would tell mom how Bill really treated her kids, or would Bill open his big mouth himself.

I hadn't decided what might be the right thing to do yet. If I told on Bill, dad would turn the car around and confront him, possibly, a fight would break out, thus forcing mom to pick between her husband and her brother, her only brother. Which, it was surely a given she had to pick her husband.

Or my other option, I could say nothing. Let that idiot Bill get away with not one word being told to him, or I could just forget about it all. What was I to do? At that very moment, I chose to keep quiet.

We went to pick up all the kids, slowly but surely, the car got more and more crowded and louder, everyone talking at once.

We had never been away from each other, it was different. We definitely all missed one another. Even Sher couldn't keep her hands off the little kids. No, she wasn't hitting anyone she was actually hugging everyone, even her lovable dad. And everything was turning back to normal.

When we arrived home, we all helped unload the car. The kids ran to our room and began their normal routine of playing.

Danny had a few new toys Uncle George had given to him, which he was instructed to give two of them to J.J. and two for himself. They were as excited as if it was Christmas.

Becky and Carrie had new jacks. Seems Aunt Gloria had taken them to a little neighborhood store and bought them some new jacks, and even bought them a little velvet bag to carry the jacks in.

Obviously, me and J.J. had stayed with the worst relative babysitters of all time, not because we didn't get a gift, but because we were treated so poorly. I wanted to tell on them but I just wasn't sure.

We hadn't been home an hour and dad left. Suppose all the so-called players were gonna meet up at the bar and brag on winning a defenseless team.

I wondered what they would do if they ever played another gangster team, or a team that simply would not let muscle them out of a trophy.

Oh well, this would be the talk of the neighborhood for months and months, and we would have to hear about it every time we went somewhere with dad.

Mom fed us a light meal then told us to get ready for bed. I could tell she was a bit tired and stressed I'm sure, it had to be tough for her to just leave her kids at three different homes for three days. She had never done that before.

. We watched TV for a bit with her then we all went to bed. Even mom turned in early. I was glad to be home, we may not have the best lives, but where J.J. and I had been, at the moment, there really was "No place like home."

# 28

It had been a few weeks since Sandy and Jewel bought their snow cone trailer and parked it in their yard. They made a big ol' fuss about it and for sure, it was going to make them a lot of money.

Money, now that was going to be a difficult one to come up with, we had none. So how the heck were we gonna bankroll enough change for all six of us kids to get at lease one snow cone a day.

Me and Sher put our heads together and came up with a brainstorm of an idea. We would draw pictures, lots, and lots of pictures. Then we would go to all the older folks in the neighborhood and try to sell them. Though we only had Sandy and Jewel as our closest neighbors, there were two blocks full of folks just past their house.

We vigorously drew pictures of houses and landscapes and anything we could think of. We had this one thing we did, we got a sheet of paper and colored different areas different colors, just sort of mingled the colors any which way. When the entire sheet of white paper was filled with different colors, we took a black crayon and colored the entire picture black.

Once we were finished, we would get the edge of the scissors and lightly scrape out lines, shapes, forms, just any random design, forming a kaleidoscope of colors.

Even Carrie, the future Picasso, got her skills and drew a few pictures for us, pictures of houses and landscapes, she was the genius here... We loved them all. Combined we made about twenty-five different pictures hoping to sell them all and make some spending money. Once we were done, we put them away until the next day.

After breakfast, me and Sher set out to sell our masterpieces. We weren't allowed to go too far from our house. "Only two blocks away." Mom would insist. "Don't go any further or I won't be able to keep an eye on y'all."

Just at the corner of our house was a fire station. After living on that block as long as we did we were on a first name basis with the firemen. They knew all of us kids very well, they knew mom, and they definitely knew dad.

I didn't realize it at the time, but that fire station was the closest thing to a police department or in my eyes, it was. I never would have dreamed to go to them for help. Since we were the closest family to the fire station, the firemen took a special interest in us, especially my brothers. They knew of dad's reputation, and they knew we were sternly guarded by him. If they knew more than that, they never mentioned it to any of us.

Sher and I went to try to sell some of our drawings to them. Argument would have it that these firemen didn't particularly need or want our pictures, but they understood why we were doing it. They knew we were dirt poor, and they too saw the snow cone stand about to open, so they were more than kind when they purchased five of our pictures. Perhaps they pitied us; perhaps they understood the business end of what we were doing.

One thing is certain, they had kind hearts. I never really thought it was out of pity they would buy our pictures. I believed then, they did it because they saw two young girls trying, really trying to do something positive, and they admired our attempt. It was mom that encouraged us to do things, stay occupied.

The first actual house we came to was old lady Miss Kitty.

Miss Kitty was a dead ringer for Betty Davis. She had big, big eyes and wore way too much makeup. She was very old and didn't put her makeup on properly so when she opened the door she looked a mess. Possibly, she had no idea how awful she looked because her house was so dimly lit.

She always wore a pillbox hat that had lace covering her face, as if she were going to or coming from a funeral. She was scary looking, even in the daylight.

It took her a few minutes to open her door but once she

recognized who we were she said, "Yes pretty girls, can I help you?" Her voice was crackly sounding as if she was about to cry.

"Hello Miss Kitty, me and my sister Malina would like to know if you would like to buy one of the pictures we drew."

Sher had all the pictures in her hand and handed them to Miss Kitty, whose glasses were hanging around her neck with an old faded eyeglass chain. She slowly lifted her glasses to her eyes, squinting as she looked over each pictures. She was standing in her doorway, holding her door open with her foot.

Obviously, it was difficult for her, holding the door with her foot, and holding twenty pictures and flipping through the pictures to find the perfect one to hang on her wall.

"Come in girls so I can get a better look." She suggested. Now going into any house, even an old lady's house was forbidden. Not even for the sale of a picture would we go in.

"No ma'am." Sher explained. "We aren't allowed."

"I see." She said looking up at us, her glasses on the tip of her nose.

"I see, I see, well very good girls, your mama raised you well, but I pose no threat to you." She lectured.

"No ma'am you don't, but we just can't." Sher explained.

"Ok, if you would give me a moment, I will return as quickly as I can." She said.

She slowly came out on the porch and handed all the pictures back to us except two. She took the two inside with her, and instructed us to wait a minute.

That minute turned into ten minutes. We weren't sure if she fell asleep, forgot about us, or just left us there because we didn't follow her into her house. We joked maybe she wasn't gonna come back out to pay us, we were giggling about her when she finally opened her front door.

She handed us a five-dollar bill.

*What?* We thought as we looked at each other.

"I will give you girls one dollar if you run to the corner store and buy me a Milky Wave."

I wanted to laugh, but didn't because she didn't pronounce it properly. She said Milky Wave not Milky Way.

"I need a Milky Wave and a loaf of bread and some kitty food for my "Precious."

We looked down toward Miss Kitty's feet and there, snuggling against ol Miss Kitty's leg was her, way to fat cat, purring, with its eyes closed.

Sher and I didn't know what to say or do. We hit the gold mine here. We told her we had to run ask our mom, and if mom said yes, we would be back for the money.

We could not run home fast enough, pictures flopping in the wind as we ran. We got home, ran up the porch, and almost out of breath explained to mom. "Miss Kitty is going to give us one dollar just to go to the store for her."

Mom said, "Yes" when she saw just how excited we both were.

We raced back to Miss Kitty's.

Again, we waited what seemed like forever for her to open the door. So excited we happily told her we would go to the store for her. She gave us the money and reminded us what she wanted from the store, as if we had forgotten.

We ran faster than lightening, got to the store, filled her order, and were back at her house in less than five minutes. We handed her the change from the five-dollar bill and just as she had promised, she gave us a dollar, an entire dollar. Plus the fifty cents for the two portraits she was purchasing.

We thanked her and as we were walking off the porch, Sher told Miss Kitty. "If you ever need us to go to the store again for you, all you have to do is tell us."

"As a matter of fact." Miss Kitty blurted out. "If you come three times a week and go to the store for me I will give you girls a dollar each time."

*What? How lucky did we get?*

There were other kids in the neighborhood. Miss Kitty could have easily chosen any of them, but she didn't, she chose us.

We actually had a job now. Me and Sher together were

going to possibly make a few dollars a week, just to go to the store.

How excited we were, how excited mom would be for us.

"Thank you Miss Kitty." We both said. Wondering if she would ever know just how happy she had just made two young girls.

We drew pictures, we colored, we ran errands for Miss Kitty, we did everything we could in anticipation of the snow cone stand. We were determined to stay nice and cool for the summer. We definitely were going to get to buy snow cones, possibly every day. How exciting!

# 29

    Mom would watch us while we played outside. Sometimes she would stand at the front door and watch; sometimes she'd sit on the old metal chairs that had been there ever since the house was built. Other times she joined us in everything we did.

    She came out and looked around the yard; I watched her wondering what was she looking for. She looked down at the ground, without saying a word. Then she looked around again.

    Because of the lack of grass in our front yard, there really wasn't a good spot for Danny and J.J. to play, so mom told my brothers to follow her. To the left of our house, even with the porch, ran a fence. It separated the front yard from the back yard.

    Sometimes dad would park his car right up to the fence, sometimes he would park right in front of the house, right up to the front steps. On other occasions, he would park horizontally right between the two big trees. We never knew where he would park so it was difficult to know where to play, jump rope, play foursquare or the occasional hopscotch. No matter where we were in the front yard, if dad came racing around the corner, he would just slam into whichever of the three spots he chose.

    Why not have a designated area to park, so that we wouldn't have to scurry out of his way like ants about to be sprayed with ant spray.

    If we had hopscotch game going and he drove up, half the numbers would be erased with the slamming of his brakes. If we had a kickball game going, it ended abruptly because we knew better than to kick a ball anywhere near his car, for fear of kicking that ball hard enough to break a window. If my brothers were playing on the ground with their toys, we would have to scream at them "watch out" or dad would've completely run over them.

Why couldn't he park that old heap in the street? I mean really. Not even the stupidest of car thieves would have taken that piece of shit car, not only because it was ugly, but also look who it belonged to! Was some car thief stupid enough to take Johnny G's car right from under his nose? Not likely.

At any given time dad could have designated himself a parking space, but no. He wanted to keep us on our toes even in our own front yard. Talk about control.

I suppose mom knew he would never give us the respect of having a kid space. Many times when my little brothers wanted to play in a nice yard, with grass, or we wanted to ride on a skateboard, not ours, not our neighbors, but it was the firemen that were more than kind enough to offer to let us play in the grass at the fire station. There were many times mom didn't want us to bother the firemen, so she decided to designate us our own play area.

Any yard space north of the fence was ours, that space wasn't all that either. Just north of the fence was about a fifteen feet by fifteen feet area of nothing but dirt. It was impossible for dad to fit his old heap in that space, unless of course he rammed the fence, so mom decided it was to become our play area.

Beyond that fifteen by fifteen area was grass, but not your normal Saint Augustine beautiful grass, are you kidding? This was more like weeds, tall dried up weeds with stickers and chiggers.

With broom in hand mom stood one foot north of the fence.

"Ok kiddos." She began. "Pick up all the big rocks from this area." She pointed to the fifteen by fifteen area, meaning the area with dirt. Without even thinking about it, or asking why, we began picking up all the rocks. This was like an Easter egg hunt only it wasn't nice colorful eggs, and it wasn't a dozen or so as in an Easter egg hunt. It was hundreds and hundreds of rocks. Some big, some small, nonetheless a trillion or so rocks, or so it seemed.

It seemed like a game to us because she made it fun and exciting. We were on a mission.

Mom instructed us to pick the rocks up and put them on the far left side of the yard. We did exactly as we were told, then she began sweeping to clean the area, but she didn't calculate how much dust she was stirring around, so as we were picking up rocks we started chocking on the dust. I mean really choking.

Mom realized what had happened and she ran and got the water hose. She had us all drink from the hose, no time for her to run inside, make lemonade and serve it to us. We didn't have lemons anyway. She reacted quickly, as if she had done this a thousand times.

Once all six of us stopped choking, herself also, she lightly watered down the ground she had been sweeping.

Wondering why she didn't use a rake?

Beginners, we didn't own one, never bought one because we had no grass. Only alternative was to sweep the ground. Within twenty minutes, she had that sectioned off area looking nice and clean.

In the far backside of our back yard, was a small little shed, which we called "the shack." It was old and weather beaten like our house; actually, I honestly think it was the original out house that must've been built right along with the "mansion" we called home.

It was about an eight by eight area, old, and it appears it had never been painted, just old sun beaten, rotted wood. It was high enough that we kids could stand up in it, but I'm not sure if it was tall enough for an adult, but then I never saw any adults go inside it. There was a doorway but no door. The floor was dirt, so when it rained the floor got sloppy with mud.

It had some junk inside it, but not so much that you couldn't go in there at all. We kids would use it when we played hide and seek. Ok sure no one would find us!

Really, it was the only place to hide. It would have been a nice playhouse for us girls, but then where would she have put all the junk, in the yard of course, to match the junky house.

Mom went into the old shed; when she came out, she was carrying an old basket with small pieces of lumber in it. Not large pieces, pieces about the size of your hand some smaller some longer.

We followed her back to the now cleaned out area of the yard.

"Becky, go inside and get all of your crayons, J.J. you and Danny go get all your little trucks and cars." Mom instructed them all. Everyone did as they were told.

Mom sat down, right on the ground, sitting cross-legged, and placed the basket in front of herself. Becky came out with the colors and Danny and J.J. came running with all their cars and trucks.

We all sat in a circle and just watched as mom took one of the pieces of lumber and began to color black squares on one, and then she drew what appeared to be a door. She instructed each of us to get a piece of wood and draw windows and doors on each, then she began to draw what appeared to be shingles on the tops of the wood, she then wrote names on each such as library, grocery store, school.

Some she left with no names on them, some she drew horizontally some she drew vertically. As we were all drawing on our own piece of board, which were more square and thick like blocks rather than boards.

Mom stood up, took one of the blocks of wood, placed it horizontally on the dirt, and began making lines in the dirt here and there. Then she took the blocks of wood with the name on them and stood them up, some were short some were tall.

Oh my goodness, I couldn't believe what she had just created. She was making a small city. The lines in the dirt were streets. She was making a little small city so my brothers could have a designated area to play with their old trucks and cars.

Once Danny and J.J. realized what mom was doing, they started screaming with excitement. They had their own play area. A fantastic little city.

Mom picked up some of the bigger rocks and placed them in various areas around the little city as if they were boulders. She pulled off some tiny little twigs from the trees and buried them as to have just planted real trees for this little city.

Mom's eyes glowed with pride as she stepped back to look, just as dad drove up. Surely, he wondered what we all were doing outside on the side of the house. He smiled when he saw what we had done. He actually liked it.

Mom and dad went inside, but within a few minutes he left and mom was back outside with us. We all continued to make streets in the dirt. Becky ran inside and came back with a small bag. "Look." She said, then opened it, and began taking out my brothers little army men, placing them in various spots around their new little city.

It was exciting to see everyone so happy. We had made a million dollar play area for my little brothers. It cost nothing but time, some old junk lumber and lots of love. This was a very prideful moment for us. Mom knew exactly how to make her kids happy. And once again, she had.

Every morning, bright and early, my brothers were outside playing in their little city. They would stay outside all day and half the night. Playing around in the dirt left them dirty from head to toe, but it didn't matter, nothing a little soap and water couldn't take care of.

When it rained, the little streets would be washed away, leaving a muddy mess, but as soon as the sun dried up all the mud, mom and all of us would repeat the routine of recreating the city. It seemed to get easier to rebuild each time. Every few days mom would add another street and a couple more buildings or houses. We all absolutely loved the city. Even the neighborhood kids would come over and play with my brothers. It was different, it was exciting, and our mom had made it just for her kids. My brothers could not get enough of their little city. Even Sandy and Jewel came over to admire what mom had created. At one point Danny and J.J. brought two of the fireman to show off their new play area. Seems the entire neighborhood was fascinated by what mom had done, but none more proud than her six kids.

# 30

The day had arrived, which I completely forgot was coming. The lady that signed me up for the summer camp showed up unannounced. Mom was talking to her outside, then mom sent Sher in the house to get me.

"Hi Malina." The lady began.

"This is Miss Rhodes, Malina." Mom introduced us.

"Hi." I said.

"Come to my car Malina, I'd like to show you all the things we have bought for your trip." Miss Rhodes said with a smile.

I went tone deaf. I saw her lips moving, I saw her smiling and reaching into the car to show me everything she had bought for my trip, but I didn't hear a word she or mom said.

My mind was racing. Should I throw up now? Hold my breath to faint? Hit this bitch with a rock to make her think I was crazy so she wouldn't want me near any of the other camp kids? What should I do? I couldn't think. My mind was drawing a blank. I had to get out of this situation.

Sher ran up to the car at the very second I was going to smack that lady in her face and said. "Oh my Malina, how exciting. Look at all these nice things." Sher was so damn excited.

Oh, shut the hell up, big mouth. I screamed in my own mind.

"New clothes, new shoes…" Sher went on and on. The woman began telling mom they would be by early Friday morning to pick me up in the bus. Too much was being said too quickly, which obviously I was lost in all the words. I must have turned as pale as a ghost, because I actually heard these words coming out of my mom's mouth.

"Well Miss, (whatever her name was.) We didn't know until this week, but my family has planned a family reunion, beginning this Friday and I'm afraid Malina may not be able to go camping after all, yet of course, she would rather go camping instead of a family reunion."

"Well, Mrs. Guetarro, I wish you had called me sooner." Miss Rhodes began to say.

Mom went on to tell her a big ol' story of why I may not be able to go. Mom was my hero. She was getting me off the hook without even consulting me.

What a mom! What a wonderful mom!

Mom gave Miss, whatever her damn name was, our new phone number and assured her she would call her if I had a change of heart.

There is no way I was gonna change my mind, or my heart. Not for any new clothes or shoes or campfire or swimming lessons. There was no way I was leaving my mom. Ever!!!!!!

Mom knew it. I knew it. That's why she convinced that woman I couldn't go. Being away from my mom for three days was way, way, way, too much for me. Now, to go away for a week, no phones, no contact with my mom, no goodnights. No damn way. Mom knew I wouldn't go, why even try to convince me.

All the things they had bought for me could easily be taken back to the stores for a full refund, even if they couldn't get their money back, too bad. If I had to forfeit my picture money and my share of the money for going to the store for "Hush Hush Sweet Charlotte" Miss Kitty, I damn sure would. The thought of being away from my mom for one day let alone one week was just too much for me.

Mom tried to talk to me. "It really would be a good learning experience for you." She said. "Maybe you could learn how to swim, the right way. And maybe you would have a good time."

She looked at me knowing darn good and well not even she could convince me to go. Not even if she insisted, would I go. The thought of being away from home was just too lonely for me. No way was I going!

In my mind, end of it, case closed no more discussion.

Or so I thought.

Dad hit the frickin ceiling the second mom told him. It was a given I knew she had to tell him, but he went off the deep end.

Seriously father? You're never home anyway to miss me, so why should you care?

All he cared about was that I made our family look stupid. Well, if we looked stupid it surely wasn't because of me. And if it were true, I damn sure didn't care. My heart couldn't handle it. If you weren't such a fucking jerk to my mother, I wouldn't be afraid to leave her, so hey, Al Capone wannabe, this is on you, not me. I screamed in my mind.

Dad carried on, just to carry on. Bitching non-stop at mom saying, "You should have insisted she go. Whoop her ass and make her go."

What the hell was he talking about? What was wrong with him? You don't just whoop someone's ass because they don't want to be away from home. What the fuck is wrong with this moron. Whoop my ass? Someone should whoop his ass.

I knew exactly what this pitiful excuse of a man was doing. He was picking a fight, giving himself a reason to leave. But why I wondered? He didn't need a reason to leave; he did it all the time anyway.

What now? I thought. Does the shit ever stop with him?

I wanted to jump in and save the day for my mom.

Stop mom, please stop. You don't have to defend me. Don't even say a word to him. Let him piss himself off and leave. I wanted to scream just to stop what I thought was about to happen.

"I can't believe your going to let these brat kids walk all over you." He hollered at her. Who the hell was walking all over her? I wondered. I simply did not want to leave my mom. What was the big fucking deal? I wondered.

Completely out of nowhere, Sher walked into their room just at the moment I thought it was going to go south for mom.

"Daddy." Sher began. "Do I have your permission to join the girls' softball team that the summer school is sponsoring next week?"

Whaaaaaaaat? I thought. Sher had not said anything to mom that I knew of, or at least I hadn't heard about it.

Dads face completely changed from anger to pride. He looked at Sher just as she held up a piece of paper, waving it pretty much in his face, even mom looked shocked.

"Yes daddy. Right here. I need you to sign your name and check yes or no., if you will give me permission to join."
She pointed to the dotted line where he was to sign his name and the box he was to check yes or no.

I didn't get it! Why? How? How did she manage to bring the subject up just at the right moment, seconds before dad either whooped me for being a sissy, or seconds before he went on a rampage?

Sher handed dad the paper somewhat gloatingly.

Mom said nothing.

"Did you know about this?" He asked mom.

"No." Mom answered, but not in a shocked tone, more like,

"No, she mentioned it but it slipped my mind."

"Well," Sher began, as she sat next to dad.

"I have had it for two days, but I figured I couldn't join if Malina were gonna be gone for a week, so actually, Malina I'm very glad you are not gonna go camping because I know I wouldn't be able to go if you were gone, and, daddy, I really would like to learn how to play softball properly because when I start high school I want to get a letter on the jacket I will get for playing sports in high school your old high school, daddy.." The bitch was literally flapping her eyelashes like the actresses did in the old silent movies.

Now, was this some fuckin bullshit or what? I thought watching Sher give the performance of her life. I felt like slapping the shit out of her for kissing dad's ass, except for the fact she was doing this to save me.

Wow, who the heck was this young lady, I thought to myself. Actress or spoiled daddy's girl. She spoke as if she had memorized a script from a play, barely stopping between sentences to breathe. She should have received an academy award for that performance. I sat in shock. Mom sat in shock, Dad was in shock, but only for a second.

"Well sure baby, you can go, since this chicken shit," he looked my way, "doesn't want to leave home for a week." He growled.

He had called me chicken shit several other times in my life. It was the times I would fake being sick so I didn't have to go to school. He would call me chicken shit and whip me, but he didn't whip me on this day.

Sher, with all her daddy this, and daddy that. Producing a parent consent form and jumping in the conversation just in time, had saved the day, and saved my ass.

Dad took a pen from his shirt pocket and signed it without hesitation.

"And daddy, you don't have to buy anything for me, no uniforms, no shoes, no bat, and no ball. The school is providing it all." She gloated.

Dad was speechless. Mom was speechless, I was speechless.

"Thank you daddy." She said as she passed by me with the parent consent form she had taken from dad, rolled up into a seeming bat, and smacked me on the head with it as she walked past me to go to her room.

This sister of mine was something else.

I was gonna owe her possibly for the rest of my life. She had stepped in and saved what could have gotten nasty only because dad was so easy to fly off the handle and become Mr. Hyde.

Yes, Sher did a very, very good thing just at the right moment. I guess I didn't need to explain anything to Sher, she knew how I felt about mom. We both felt the same only she had a bigger heart for dad. She had not seen the horrible things I had that night. She only saw the after effects.

Sher kept her heart open to everyone, something I couldn't bring myself to do.

She was allowed to join her softball team, which met two times a week. With her volunteering for the schools and now her softball games, she was pretty much gone all day.

# 31

It was summertime now, and it was very hot. Mom had bought some material with her ironing money and what little she got for washing her moms clothes. She was making each of us girls a beautiful sundress. Bright pinks and yellows in the material, with tiny spaghetti straps. As with everything mom made, once she made it she then ironed it, and hung it for all to see. One would've thought she bought it at Macys or one of the higher end Department Stores. She even made a beautiful dress for herself.

I don't believe dad appreciated how beautiful she was. No one I knew had a more beautiful mom than ours. It seemed all the kids loved her. Whenever she would take us to school, everyone would wave at her and say hi, she would smile and wave. She wasn't able to volunteer at the P.T.A. she just didn't have the time.

Anytime the principal at the elementary school would see her at the school he would always stop her and tell her she was welcomed any time to help out at the school.

It had been a few months now and her wounds had all healed.

She was talking to a woman on the phone one day, a woman whom she had been friends with since elementary school. Her name was Lavon, they had grown up together, the very best of friends. Sometimes I think she was closer to Lavon than to her own sisters. They had been friends all moms life. They were inseparable, until mom started dating, then married dad.

"I don't like her, and I don't want her around here." Dad would argue and fight with mom about Lavon.

"But she's my friend, she always has been." Mom would plead.

"Well she's trouble and I don't want her around here."

It seemed so final. I believe Lavon hated dad as much as he hated her.

One-day dad came home unexpectedly and before words were spoken by either of them, Lavon left. Any time Lavon was at our house her and mom would sit around, drink coffee and laugh. Oh, it seemed they loved to laugh.

They may have drunk an entire pot of coffee each time she visited. The more they drank coffee, the more they would laugh.

I wondered if coffee could make two women act so funny. Perhaps Lavon was slipping some refreshments in the coffee, or maybe mom was.

Naw, I think they just loved being around one another so much, that they expressed themselves with laughter.

We called her Aunt Lavon. Sometimes her visits were brief, but always she showed us love just as if we really were related to her.

Honestly, other than mom's sisters, two of which lived out of state, Lavon was her only real friend.

One day I heard mom on the phone with Lavon and mom began to cry. It seemed like mom had just lost her best friend. Sad to say, she had. I never was sure if dad told Lavon to never come back, or was it Lavon's husband telling her to stay away from mom.

Two incredible women, childhood friends, who had a bond, maybe stronger than sisters, with years and years of memories between them, broken in the blink of an eye.

Mom never explained to us, why Lavon wouldn't be coming over ever again. How could she explain to us if it was dads dislike for mom having a friend, or Lavon's husband demanding she abandon her friendship with mom because of his dislike of dads' lifestyle?

What gave either man the right or both men at that? Who had the right to end their lifelong friendship, their lifelong love for one another?

These were not two women having an argument of their own and deciding to end their friendship, it was in fact, one, or both men stepping in and saying it's over, just like that. Who ever was at fault, mom's heart was broken.

What right did either man have to dismiss the other? Whoever, whatever, and for whatever reason, as I recall, mom's lifelong friendship with Aunt Lavon was over.

I won't swear on it, though I never saw Lavon again, I believe periodically, mom would sneak a phone call to her here and there just to say hi, or whatever conversation could be held in ninety seconds the allotted time mom assumed she had to spend on a phone call, knowing damn good and well if dad called and the line was busy, mom might just get caught up in a lie about who she was talking to.

Oh yes he was just the type of man to say, "Who are you talking to?" Then turn around and call that person just to see if mom was lying to him or not.

Lavon couldn't call our house because they never knew when dad would be lurking about.

Lavon's husband had a nine to five job, so I believe mom took ninety seconds a couple of times a week to chat briefly with Lavon knowing her husband would not walk in on them and hang the phone up. I was sad for my mom, knowing she had to give up her dear friend because of two men and their hateful ways.

Giving up her friend just because dad insisted was one thing, but mom's love for her own mom and dad, even if dad tried, mom would never give them up.

Grandma's weekly visits still remained on Wednesdays. I believe mom loved her own mom as I loved her. Rain, sleet, hail, or whatever. Nine a.m. sharp. She was like the mailman, on time and dependable. Mom always had coffee and toast ready when Grandma came over.

Grandma would tell mom of all her patients, the ones that were very ill and the ones that died. She was a good nurse. In general everyone loved grandma especially all the patients at the nursing home.

After grandpa died, she traveled and spent more time visiting her family. Many times Grandma would cry about how much she missed papa. Though grandma was a nurse, even she couldn't prevent papa's death.

Papa was a big man, not tall, but big because he had a big beer belly. We kids would make fun of him because he had an enormous nose, just as the truant officer, Mr. Johnson. Behind his back, we would call him Mr. Magoo in a joking manner, just as we all did Mr. Johnson. Papa and Mr. Johnson could very well have been related.

A painter by trade I never understood why Papa and Uncle Bill never painted our house for mom. I wondered if it was Papa that gave mom that ugly lilac paint she used to paint almost every room in our house.

When papa was alive, he and grandma lived in a second story apartment. It was an apartment I assumed you would see in a nice area in New York. The front door was street level, that had a buzzer, not a doorbell, which you would have to buzz to be let in their apartment. It also had a speaker you could talk into to let them know who you were and what you wanted.

Once buzzed in, you had to climb about fifteen stairs to get to the top. Once at the top step there was no door to enter, you were already in. In a foyer, that led to this magnificent two-bedroom apartment. I wondered if my grandparents were rich. No, they were not. They were just better off then we were.

Since grandpa was up in age, and didn't work anymore, he was the family chef. Grandma went home everyday to a home cooked meal specially prepared for her.

Being that she was the supervisor at the nursing home, she was on call 24/7. There was no time for cooking; she was always just so busy. Seeing grandma working multiple hours without any rest, grandpa loved to cook for her, and he especially enjoyed that she appreciated him so much.

Papas' specialty, other than a perfect meal, was his delicious homemade biscuits. The second you entered their apartment you could smell the biscuits. These weren't biscuits from a can, Papa always made them from scratch. We absolutely loved his biscuits and we loved to go to their apartment. No rats, no roaches, and hundreds of miniature porcelain figurines for us to play with, while mom and dad would play cards with grandma and Papa.

Sometimes, it would be women against men. Sometimes mom and dad against papa and grandma. Sometimes papa and mom would go up against dad and grandma. It was a place mom and dad would take us on the rare occasion dad would spend with his family rather than the bars. We did this maybe twice a month.

Always, always, there was lots of beer. Dad would drink one beer after another, while Papa would drink three to dads one. Mom and grandma wouldn't drink because grandma never knew when she might be called to go back to work.

She wasn't a heavy drinker, she drank maybe a half of a beer, just to relax she would say. Mom on the other hand would never drink.

Poor papa, he became an alcoholic. He drank and drank and drank. Maybe because there was no one home all day with him to stop him from drinking. Maybe he had been an alcoholic all his life, I never was really sure, because anytime I saw him, he was drinking. However, I'm certain once he quit painting; he drank all day every day.

He was not a mean drunk like dad. He was a happy drunk. Once he got a buzz going he would begin to sing, sing loudly.

Then when he would get to another level of drinking, he would tell stories to us kids, all while never missing a beat in the card game.

It seemed so strange to me, dad was so mean and cruel when he was drinking, except when he was around papa.

Perhaps it was a respect thing, you know father-in-law influence. Not even dad would hit his wife in front of her own father. Around papa, dad knew his limit. He would stop drinking at a certain time insisting he couldn't drink anymore because he had to drive.

Not papa, he drank and drank and drank, and like clockwork, grandma always had his bucket right next to him, because once his big fat belly got full of alcohol he would stand up, say "bull shit," burp, lean over the bucket, and throw it all up.

The second we heard him burp we already knew he was gonna throw up, so we covered our ears and looked away, so not to see him get sick and get sick ourselves. He would stumble his way to his room, fall on the bed and go to sleep leaving mom and grandma to clean the mess.

I heard mom say once it was all beer. Like he just swelled up on beer and instead of pissing it out, he took the easy way out and threw it up.

I never ever understood the concept of getting that drunk. He drank himself to death, ruined his liver. Mom was very sad when he died, because he suffered in the end. Grandma being the great nurse she was, stayed with him every second of the day until he passed. She loved telling stories about him. We all loved him, and never have we ever eaten any biscuits that could even compare to his.

When Wednesday rolled around grandma showed for her weekly visit, this time she brought aunt Dolly, whom was moms' youngest sister.

Dolly, a few years younger than mom, but looked so much older. Actually, she looked as if she was grandmas' younger sister, rather than her youngest daughter. Dolly didn't work, so she was able to come and go wherever and whenever she pleased.

I heard talk once that aunt Dolly liked dad before mom did, but being that Dolly was so young, grandma forbid her to have a relationship with him, not even a friendship with him, or any other boy for that matter.

Dad argued he never liked Dolly it was mom he always loved. He would say *Dolly is just a little girl with a big crush on me.* Actually, every girl in school had a crush on dad; he was the baseball, football, and basketball star athlete. Everyone loved him especially in high school.

He brought more sports trophy's and awards to his high school than all the other players combined, seems mom cared less for all the sport stuff. Mom had been the one to fall in love with dad and had his six kids.

Mom loved having her mom and brother and sisters over for coffee anytime they were able to stop by. It was fun to see them all together, and hear them all laughing.

Seems like all everyone did was drink coffee. What was the big deal with drinking coffee anyway? I mean, really. Cup after cup, after cup, and it was hot, even on hot summer days they drank hot coffee non-stop. I would've thought they would have wanted ice-cold sweet tea, or cold lemonade, not hot coffee. I just didn't understand a bunch of people sitting around talking and drinking hot coffee. It wasn't liquor or beer after all. Something to get high from?

I stupidly drank half my moms left over coffee when she walked grandma and Dolly to the front door. Within fifteen minutes, I found out what the big deal was.

I could not sit still. I walked seemingly in faster motion then my legs could not keep up with where I was trying to go. My heart was pounding. It felt like it was pounding right out of my chest. I got scared, very scared wondering *Oh no what have I done to myself?*

I saw mom look at me a few times with a look on her face like *what the heck is wrong with you Malina*, but since I had already washed all the dishes she wasn't sure how much coffee I had consumed. I felt as though I was awake non-stop for three days, but actually it was just one long scary, creepy day.

This, I thought was what these people did for hours a day, drink this crap and get a rush of speed in their veins. This to me was a form of drug, a high, just like the stinky weed my dad smoked, only this was in a cup, it was legal, and it was limitless.

# 32

Coffee drinking, I believed was a morning ritual until Helena and Ray started showing up on a regular evening basis.

Helena was a very quiet woman, with long dark hair that was always in a braid, never down. Actually, her and her four daughters wore their hair exactly alike.

Helena had big white teeth, which looked like the "Chiclets" teeth Mr. Wilson wore on "Dennis the Menace."

Her lips were extremely dark, which made her teeth look even whiter and bigger. She never had on make-up, not even when she visited people. She seemed like a very shy woman, until she heard Ray's voice. Then she would light up, get a twinkle in her eye, and a big smile on her face. At times, she would try to cover her big teeth with her hand, indicating she was ashamed of them.

Helena loved to drink coffee. As soon as the last cup was poured, she would instinctively make a fresh pot.

Ray was a tall man, who wore a cowboy hat, but by no means was he a cowboy. His skin was more wrinkled than any normal thirty five year old mans' should be. I wondered was it because he was so darkly tanned, it caused his face to wrinkle at an early age.

He was a loud sort of guy that loved to joke around and make people laugh. The second he entered our house he would let out a loud yell. "Heeeey everyone, Uncle Ray is here." Then proceed to grab each of us and hug and kiss us, even my brothers, especially my brothers, because Ray wanted a son more than anything. But, due to the fact that Helena had gotten very ill after giving birth to their fourth daughter, they decided not to have any more kids.

Ray loved Helena so much; just the thought of losing her would have him in tears. He loved his four daughters as much as he loved Helena. Ray seemed to always be happy, in a good mood. He smiled and laughed at everything, even if he was getting his ass chewed out by my dad, he still smiled.

No matter what he was doing, he always asked Helena.

"Are you ok baby? Do you need anything baby? Are you happy baby?" It seemed his main priority in his personal life was pleasing his wife.

Dad called them Indians, because Ray would actually yell like he was an Indian just before a tribal war. He would entertain us with his rendition of an Indian Pow Wow, which was so damn funny to watch. Helena would sit back and just laugh and smile at him.

Ray was the affectionate one, always loving on his family; he was never ashamed to show how much he loved them.

When they would visit, they would be there maybe fifteen minutes and dad and Ray would take off, just get up and leave. They would not tell mom or Helena where they were going, one minute they would be outside talking and laughing, the next they would just be gone. We would know they were gone because we no longer could hear Ray's loud mouth.

Sometimes dad and Ray would be out side, I'm sure passing a joint back and forth. I would watch them, both laughing their asses off at usually nothing at all. It was funny to watch because they would laugh, then they would take a big hit off their joint, and try to hold it in their lungs as long as they could, to get the biggest high possible. They would not be able to hold it in, rather damn near choking to death on the smoke and the laughter. I thought at one point one or the other or both for that matter would simply pass out right where they stood. Loss of oxygen to their damn brains I would assume.

Mom would already have the coffee brewing for Helena and herself, knowing when dad and Ray left, it was usually for quite awhile.

Again, cup after cup of coffee mom and Helena would drink. They never waited up for dad and Ray, because they always knew they'd be gone most of the night.

Helena would just gather her daughters, go to the sofa, and fall asleep. We never knew when dad and Ray would come home, but one thing was for sure, you could hear Ray talking long before they even pulled up in our yard. His voice carried, especially late at night.

He wouldn't have to wake Helena and the kids, because the instant she heard his voice she would start smiling. He would come in the house and say, "Rise and shine baby, daddy's home." And Helena and the kids would just get up and go.

Ray was always in dad's life, as long as I can remember. He wasn't a relative, but it seemed he was. I believe he was the closest thing dad would ever have to a brother.

Anytime day or night, if dad called Ray came running. All dad had to say was "It's time." And Ray would be there.

At first, I wasn't sure who or what Ray was, then I realized he was dad's right hand man. As big and loud of a mouth Ray had, you would never guess Ray was the triggerman.

When I realized what a triggerman was I thought, no way that fun loving, kind, hyper man is a killer. How the hell did he ever creep up on his intended victims with that big ass mouth he had?

I over heard dad say once. "Shut the fuck up Ray, you almost blew it, next time I'm gonna have to shoot you instead, with your big mother fucking mouth. This could've gone bad Ray, really bad."

Best I could figure Ray must have talked right up to the very second of whatever crucial crime they were planning and because of Ray's loud mouth he could have gotten dad and himself killed, instead of vice versa.

It was hard to imagine Uncle Ray doing anything bad, he wasn't a bad ass, he wasn't a mean man, and he loved his family so much. There was no way he would risk losing them. I was wrong. I was as wrong as I could be. Turns out, Ray was the best, he was the highest paid killer, and he worked for dad.

# 33

Dad's old car had about had it. It was old, wore out, and the motor was about to give out. Not really sure who helped him, what it cost, or where he got it, but he drove up with a beautiful gold Cadillac.

At first, we weren't sure who was outside in the front yard honking their horn like a mad man, but the second he stepped out of that car, we could see the ear-to-ear smile on his face.

It's strange how a beautiful car can bring out the happiness, the glow in a person. Not only was dad smiling more than I had ever seen him smile in my life, but he seemed to be glowing, as a little kid lost in a toy store. He looked even more handsome standing right next to his new car. He sure would attract a lot of attention with that car I remember thinking. With his dark black hair and his dark sunglasses, for a second he appeared to be a movie star that had just received a new Cadillac for an Oscar winning performance in a number one movie from a movie production company.

Mom went out side first to see the car, and then we kids followed, everyone giggling and laughing with excitement.

Four door Cadillac, spotlessly clean interior, automatic windows, the smell of a brand new pair of shoes, I had never seen such a beautiful car, much less ever been in one. We all piled in our designated spots in the new car as we did in the old car.

"Goodness, we have room for more kids." Dad teased.

That was a scary thought!

Dad was proud of his new transportation.

He told mom to lock up the house, he was gonna to take us for "A ride."

Another scary thought.

Dad drove around our neighborhood, proudly waving at Sandy and Jewel, the firemen and any other neighbors that just so happened to be outside.

Smiling with his beautiful white teeth and handsome smile, just as the Governor or even President would do if they were in a parade.

We drove passed Aunt Gloria's house, but we didn't stop, just honked as we passed. We did the same as we passed Aunt Mary's, honk, smile, and drive on.

Actually, we all were waving by this time, at every person we saw in their own front yards, either walking on the sidewalks, or getting out of their cars at the grocery store. It was a game now, dad was honking at everyone, and all of us kids were waving and smiling at everyone we saw.

How we must have looked to everyone we came in contact with, a car full of kids, a handsome driver and his beautiful wife passenger, honking, waving, and smiling, without a care in the world.

Yes, I could see us being dropped off in front of the school proudly, instead of trying to hide our faces in the old car.

Having a new car didn't change who we were, I knew that, but it sure would change how people looked at us.

I didn't know how much it was going to cost, but I did know it would be worth it, no matter what the cost.

Dad drove around with us for a bit then took us home and he left. I guess he wanted to show the car off to his friends at the bar. It would be nice to have a new ride once school started again.

Seems having a new car kept dad gone more than normal, if that were possible. Mom didn't get to keep the car as much now, as she did with the old car. I suppose that was expected.

One night dad called and said to have us ready, he was gonna pick us up and take us somewhere. We were excited, of course, so as he requested, we all sat on the porch waiting. We waited ten, twenty, then thirty minutes.

Possibly, we stupidly waited an hour for him, he was a no show. We went back in the house, disappointed of course.

Mom told us he must have gotten busy at the garage and just couldn't make it.

It was nine thirty at night. The garage usually closed at eight, so I knew darn good and well he wasn't at the garage. We continued waiting in the living room for another hour, still no show for dad. Mom knew we were disappointed, but she really didn't know what to say. He could have at least called…no, not our dad.

The next few days dad stayed out pretty late. Seems everything was as it was before he beat mom, only now he had a new car.

The snow cone stand didn't thrive as Sandy and Jewel had hoped. Maybe there just weren't enough people in the neighborhood interested, other than us kids.

Sher and I continued to sell our pictures, but we realized we did not need to buy six cones a day, we only needed three, which we split to feed six. It was just as good as buying six, besides the idea for us in the beginning was to buy the cones to give us a break from the heat and keep us cool, which we were still able to do with only three cones.

One day it was hotter than normal so I went to go buy our daily cones and when I began to eat one, I noticed it had a funny taste. I couldn't eat it, it tasted horrible. Mom took a bite and instantly recognized what it was.

It tasted like cigarette ashes. Mom went over to talk to Jewel who was in the snow cone stand at the time, and sure enough, she was smoking a cigarette as she made a snow cone for one of the firemen.

Mom told her what had happened, even giving her the remaining cones. Jewel could not apologize enough. She insisted on making us all new cones, but mom wouldn't hear of it, though, she did want to make sure it didn't happen again. Jewel assured mom it would never happen again.

We got a call from dad, again wanting us to get ready so he could take us somewhere. It was already eight thirty at night, though there was no school the next day, mom liked to start getting the younger kids ready for bed by nine.

Dad said he had shut the garage down for the night, and he would be home in ten minutes. Again, I thought, here we go again. We kids, like fools, sat on the porch waiting for dad, mom sitting in the living room, everybody just waiting. It could have been thirty minutes, who knows, wasting time waiting on anyone seems timeless.

Then, out of nowhere, Becky stood up and said. "The next car on this street better be dad or else I'll scream." We all looked at her like, what the hell is she talking about?

We lived on a street that wasn't busy with traffic at all; actually, it was more like a fork in the road. Our fork not busily traveled. Other than the neighbors passing through, we got an occasional car now and then. Maybe ten minutes passed and we could see a car heading in our direction. We weren't sure if it was dad or not, so we watched as it approached the fork in the road. When we saw that the car wasn't dad, Becky stood up and screamed at the top of her lungs, just as she had said she would do if the next car wasn't dad.

It was so unexpected, we all began to laugh. We literally could not stop laughing.

Perhaps twenty more minutes passed another car came by, it too did not stop. This time we all stood up and screamed, loud.

We could hear mom laughing from inside the house. We now had a new game to play, "Next car on this street better be dad or else I'll scream." For a second time we waited as long as we could outside, but somehow we knew. We just knew.

One by one, we slowly started to trickle into the house knowing darn good and well he wasn't going to show up. Two more cars passed, Becky screaming each time. Finally, she too got tired and followed us into the house.

I suppose mom just didn't like to see us get our hopes up, so when dad came in that night, she let in to him. Really, the very least he could've done was called. But again, everything was dad's way. He owed no one, not even his wife and kids, an explanation of anything.

I was still awake and was so afraid he was going to hit her, but he wasn't drunk he was high, and being high, it wasn't very likely dad would hit anyone. Actually, I think he was afraid of all of us when he was high.

He tried to plead his case, sounding more like a little kid trying to talk his way out of an ass whoopin.

"We do have a phone Johnny! I mean really now, this is the second time this week you told me to get the kids ready and each time you don't show up and you don't call. The kids get very disappointed sitting here waiting on you."

"Oh, I'm sorry mama, I just got real busy." He said in a very calm voice.

"A ten second phone call to let us know you're not coming is all it takes." She said.

He apologized more times then I could count. I wondered if his high was going to wear off and then he would start barking at mom. However, he didn't, he just fell asleep.

He did this a couple of more times throughout the week. We would wait, dad wouldn't show or call as mom had asked of him, and we would be disappointed.

Now, whatever it was he was up to, we simply didn't care anymore. Disappointment was in fact disappointment. So it was a complete shock when he called Friday night said, "I'm on my way." And before we could drag ourselves out to the front porch, he drove up, honking and smiling.

Mom grabbed her purse, and locked the door as we kids piled in the car, completely in shock because we literally didn't expect him to show up.

He was smiling so I knew he wasn't drunk. I couldn't smell that funky smell of weed, so I wasn't sure if he was high or not.

Mom asked, "Where are we going?"

"It's a surprise." Dad declared.

He was driving in a direction we were not familiar with, though we knew the route to grandmas and all dads' sisters' houses, this was an area none of us had ever been before. When we entered the neighborhood dad was taking us to, I noticed every house was at least two stories tall. Some had white pillars on either side of the front porch; others had enormous picture windows, with postcard perfect lawns, and long winding driveways.

These were not the rich houses as we created at home, with odds and end junk from our house, no, these were not rich houses at all, these were real mansions.

We drove slowly, very slowly through the neighborhood "ooohhh and aaaahhhing" as we passed each beautiful mansion.

Dad would point and say, "Look at this one mama, or look at that one kids." He seemed as excited as we were.

We traveled five blocks or so, reached the end of the fascinating neighborhood, turned around and went back the way we came, driving even more slowly then we had on our first drive through that beautiful neighborhood. Being there in that neighborhood, driving in our new car, we almost fit in like maybe we belonged in that neighborhood...

When we got to the third block dad slowed down, then, without warning dad turned into a driveway.

I looked around; none of these houses had curtains hanging over their windows, enabling us to look right into these beautiful homes. Every house was lit up, and glowing, like a beautifully over decorated Christmas tree.

Massive picture windows allowed me to see into these homes, noticing elegant chandeliers, lavish furniture. Every house seemed warm and inviting. I stared at each house, wondering to myself, "I wonder who lives in this house? What family lives in that beautiful mansion?' My mind wandered as I stared into these picture windows from the car window. Mesmerized at the beauty of a real home.

Wondering at that very second, would there ever be a time in my life I might be fortunate enough to live in such a home.

When we pulled into this particular driveway, I noticed there was no lights on in this house, no porch light, nothing, just pitch dark. All the other houses in the neighborhood were lit up, beautiful, warm, and inviting.

So many times I would dream of a house like this, now, I was in the driveway of one of them.

Dad got out of the car and told us all to follow him.

What the heck was dad doing? I couldn't help but wonder.

Dad got a big flashlight from the trunk of his new car. Mom gathered us all together and watched as dad walked up to the porch, got a key out of his pocket, unlocked the door, opened it, and said, "Come on in."

We all stood frozen for a few seconds then dad repeated.

"Come in baby. Come on kids."

It was a big wood double front door. Just as we entered, the front door there was a massive staircase, like the ones you actually see in the movies. We couldn't see the entire room because dad had only one flashlight, but we could see enough.

Enough to know this was one very beautiful home.

First thing he showed us was the gigantic living room, which appeared larger than our entire house. Then he took us to the kitchen, which had every appliance you could imagine.

The dining room seemed large enough to serve a banquet for a royal family. He showed us a library that had hundreds and hundreds of books. There was no furniture in this house, it was completely empty, but I could only imagine how beautiful it would be if I could conjure up what some real, expensive furniture would look like in such a beautiful enormous mansion.

After touring the library, he took us to the basement. The basement? I was always afraid a basement would be filled with water and rats. Not this one.

It had one big room which dad said was a game room and laundry room. Where you put real washers and dryers, not the ringer style washer crap we had.

Then he took us up the massive stairs case. It was like climbing to heaven. When we got to the top of the stairs, he showed us a room for my brothers to share, one for Becky and Carrie to share, a room for Sher of course, and then he showed us a room for me, a room just for me, all to myself. I could not even imagine the luxury of such a thing.

A room just for Malina. Dad's voice echoed in my mind. He actually said my name. He actually wanted me, Malina to have my own room. It seemed a cruel joke, but I was there, I saw for myself. My own private room. Then we saw a master bedroom with its own restroom for mom and dad.

There were two and a half bathrooms on the second floor, and two on the first floor. Each bathroom had a double vanity sink, and separate showers. These were things I only imagined I would ever see.

Hold up, hold up. A room for me, for me, for me, for me, was all I could think about, was all I wanted to think about.

I lost focus of everything I had already seen; nothing was relevant to me anymore. I only saw Malina's room, nothing else. I would actually have my very own room, which would mean my very own bed. One that I would sleep in all alone, no one kicking me in my mouth every night. I could roll over in my sleep and not feel sticky sweaty bodies all about me.

Was he serious? Was dad really serious? How was any of this possible? How the heck could we go from "Rats Ville," to absolute luxury?

Then dad went on to say, "This is going to be our house one day."

'Fingernails on a fricken chalkboard.'

One day? What do you mean one day? I thought this was our house now. I felt my face get red, the heat that was building up in me. I went from excitement to discouragement in a heartbeat.

"One day I am going to buy this house." He smiled with pride.

Slowly, I floated back down to earth. Back to the reality of where I really lived, how I really lived. It was like buying a lottery ticket, and wanting so desperately to win, envisioning all the things you could do with the money, all your dreams coming true, and then realizing you didn't even hit one number, let alone six. Complete devastation.

I instantly got a headache thinking of our stupid rich house we always created, comparing the cheap nasty props we used to create our rich house, now having something to compare it to.

That stupid, meaningless game. Thinking of Bee and Ely's house, now realizing theirs was a dump also, compared to this real mansion. Now I hated Bee again, because she thought she lived like a queen, when in reality she was just a cheap, nasty bitch.

I looked at dad, thinking, 'Why? Why would you bring us here? Where the hell did he get the key to this place? Whose house was it anyway? Was this one of his illegal adventures and he was including us in all his bullshit?'

How cruel of him to bring us out here to see how real people live, not the trash we were raised to live like.

It was a mean, cruel, hateful thing to do.

Or was it?

As much as I wanted to hate him for dragging us to this beautiful mansion, tease us with, this is your room Sher, this is yours Malina, so on and so on. As much as I wanted to hate him for having us wait day after day for him to finally bring us here on the pretense of, this will be all ours one day, then loading us up and driving off, leaving all our hopes and dreams locked up behind us in that mansion, to become cob webs of dreams.

Could I hate him any more then I thought I already did?

No, as much as I wanted to, I couldn't even hate him for this. This wasn't a cruel hateful prank, this was reality.

This was how any one could live if they wanted to, if they worked hard and tried. No one really had to live the way we did, gangster or not dad could have done right by his family. The key words here were "could have," but he chose not to.

Such a damn shame.

Our problem was, we never stood a chance. Dad had ruined his life by going from military to gangster status. Yet, I knew from the movies, gangsters could live like this, did live like this. At that second, I really didn't care how much dope dad had to deal, how many whores he prostituted off, how many contracts he took out, I wanted to live like this. I knew in my heart, it probably wasn't right, but it definitely was possible.

No, I did not hate my dad for what some may conceive as a cruel unnecessary joke. I actually thanked him for this adventure. It gave me a reason to dream beautiful pleasant dreams, not terrifying nightmares every night. Lessons were being thrust on me, seemingly every day. Lessons of life, lessons I didn't want to learn, lessons I knew I had to learn.

Perhaps when my dad was a child, he had high hopes for his life. Maybe he also dreamed of entering a house as fine as the one we had just left. Perhaps this would be the closest he would ever get to being in a real mansion, perhaps he dreamed as I did.

I was quiet on our drive home. Everyone else was talking and carrying on about the mansion. Not me. I wasn't sure to hate everyone for their excitement, or laugh at them because they actually thought dad might buy that house one day.

Me, what I did, was I created. I created in my mind, a life. I created a life in all probability I would never live, but it would not stop me from dreaming. I had something to focus on, whether or not I could ever live like that wasn't important at the moment.

What was important to me was that I could envision it; I could make my mind believe it could be real. For me, one day it would be real. Somehow, some day this here little scared kid was gonna be someone, not just anyone. The joke was going to be on every one else, not on Malina.

# 34

I couldn't concentrate for a few days. The mansion. The mansion was all I could think of. I found myself going back to the mansion in my mind, going to my own room, which by now, in my mind was filled with the nicest furniture, the softest bed, and the richest clothes hanging in my very own closet. I wanted to be in that house, I wanted to live a good life, but eventually I had to come back to reality.

There were just a few weeks left of the summer and we would all be going back to school. Sher would be first year in high school, me in eighth grade in junior high, Becky in sixth grade, Carrie in fourth grade, and J.J. in second grade. Danny would still be home with mom.

Mom had already begun making our clothes for school. She made all our dresses, blouses, slacks, skirts, and even my brothers' shirts. No one ever suspected our clothes were not store bought. I wouldn't have cared if they knew mom made them anyway. I actually would've been proud for them to know. I don't believe any of our friend's moms were as creative as our mom.

Dad was beginning to make some money at the station, and starting to spend a bit of time at home. Of course, he was stoned most of the time, but I guess it was take him like that or don't take him at all.

Mom was trying to prepare Danny for the fact he was gonna be home alone again several hours a day while we were all in school. Last year maybe he didn't understand we were in school, because he was so young.

Now, I think Danny understood very well what school was, and it meant he had no playmates for the entire day again.

Bill and Aunt Dolly were visiting quite a lot these days. I

never spoke to Bill when he was there.

One day, after Bill and Dolly left, mom asked me why I didn't say hello to him.

I responded, "Because."

"Because is not an answer." She said.

"Malina what's wrong?" Mom asked.

I really didn't want to tell her. I didn't want problems with him and I sure didn't want dad to find out.

Mom said, "You have never kept anything from me."

And I hadn't. I wasn't going to start just to help him out, so I told her how he made me run from J.J. and how J.J. cried for me and how I cried because I didn't want to be mean to J.J., but uncle Bill insisted.

She got very upset and I started crying. I was pleading with her not to tell dad. She promised she would not tell him, but she did pick up the phone and call Lily.

Lily tried her best to defend Bill saying, "Oh Shirley, he was only playing with them, he meant no harm."

Mom went on to tell Lily that she did not appreciate Bills' behavior, and why would Lily, a woman and a mother, sit back and let that happen. Before she hung up on her, she told Lily, "Have Bill call me or I'll have Johnny call Bill." Mom slammed the phone down.

I knew she wouldn't tell dad because of the war it would cause between the families.

Thirty minutes later Bill showed up at our house. "Oh my." I thought. This is gonna get very ugly. My biggest fear was dad would show up and both men would duke it out right in the front yard.

When Bill arrived, mom went out to talk to him on the porch. He had no idea how to talk his way out of this. At first he tried to say he was just playing with us, then I guess he just knew there was no way out of it, so he admitted he thought it funny that J.J. would cry so quickly just because I would run from him. He had no concept of us missing mom and the pain of being away from her. He admitted it was wrong of him and he even cried to mom that he was so sorry and he wanted to talk to me and J.J...

"No." Mom said. "You cannot talk to them. You traumatized them. What kind of beast are you? I'm telling mom what you did and you're lucky as hell I don't tell Johnny."

Mom never ever cussed. I knew for sure she was pissed now.

"Those are my babies in there." She screamed.

"How dare you betray my trust in you? I trusted you and Lily to be good to my kids while I was gone." She was crying and she was very upset.

Bill just kept saying how sorry he was and what could he do to make it up to all of us?

"I can never trust you or your wife with my kids ever." She yelled.

This was her older brother, he was supposed to be on her side in life, not devastate her kids just for kicks. He was almost as big a monster as dad.

At first, she told Bill to leave and never come back, but she knew that would only destroy their relationship forever, because once dad found out, dad would whoop his ass and she wouldn't blame him. She knew the bitching out she was giving him would never get past the porch they were standing on.

Bill had never seen an angry side of mom. He had never seen her yell or become that upset. He knew then, just as I knew, that weekend we stayed with him, he fucked up. He had mistreated his sister's kids and he lost his sisters trust. It would be very difficult for him to get an ounce of that trust back again.

They talked all of thirty minutes. Bill was crying when he left because he knew he really hurt his sister and he did not want to lose her. When mom came in she stopped crying, she explained to me how sorry Bill was, and that it was up to me if I ever wanted to speak to him again or to forgive him or not.

I never meant to hurt her or him for that matter. I had put

the incident behind me and left it there on his farm the day I left his house and vowed never to go back. I wished I had never said anything about it to mom. I didn't want her to dislike her brother because of me. I didn't want dad to ever find out, but I really didn't want to lie to mom just to save Bill's ass.

I had just witnessed the downfall of a man for messing up. I had just witnessed the pain of Bill losing moms trust, brother, or no brother.

Not for Bill, not for anyone, was I going to lie to my mother.

I never ever wanted that feeling of guilt, the pain of hurting her. Bill had been the one to mess up, not me. I had to tell her.

I was sorry for what he had done because he thought he had gotten away with it, but never would I have wanted to hurt mom like Bill had.

It would be a few weeks before I saw Bill again. He showed up with his proverbial tail between his legs one morning. Always the laughing man, the clown, the jokester. He wasn't like that the last week before school started.

He had convinced mom how sorry he was, grandma chewed his ass out, even Lily called crying to mom, asking for mom's forgiveness, for her own actions, mostly for Bill's actions.

I think all were afraid dad would find out and beat the shit out of all of them.

I walked in the kitchen; Bill and mom were drinking coffee.

"Can I talk to her?" He asked mom.

"If she wants to." Mom said.

"Malina, can I talk to you, please." Bill asked me.

I looked at mom.

"If you want Malina, it's ok." She said to me in her soft voice.

He began, "Malina I am so sorry that I hurt you and J.J. I'm ashamed of myself. It was something I will never ever do again. Please, please forgive me, I love you kids and I'm so sorry for what I did."

He started to cry. I had never seen a grown man cry before. I didn't like to see anyone cry, even this man that had been so cruel to me and my brother just a month or so ago.

He held my hand. "I'm so sorry, will you please forgive me?" He pleaded.

I wasn't sure if I really could actually forgive him. J.J. was my little brother, the one mom had paired me off with, trusting me to always look after him, take care of him.

Though Bill had been the monster that hurt J.J., I felt it was my responsibility to protect him

Forgive Bill? I wasn't sure how to, but I knew for mom's sake I had to try. One thing I didn't want to deal with was dad and Bill getting into a fight over something I said. I felt sick, thinking I would rather see my dad hit a man for something he did wrong, than to see my mom get hit for something she didn't want to do.

I felt like I just had to say, "Yes, Uncle Bill I forgive you." Just to keep the peace. My heart didn't feel like I could forgive Bill, but for mom and everyone concerned I told him I forgave him.

He smiled, that friendly Uncle Bill smile. I guess he believed me. He seemed desperate to make it all right, he seemed desperate to make mom understand he didn't mean to do all the terrible things he had done. I really never knew if mom completely forgave Bill or not.

Maybe like me, she felt she had to say she forgave him. I mean does a mother ever forgive anyone that hurts her kids. I don't believe they do. For now, for so many complicated reasons, it just had to be ok.

I made him and mom happy. I didn't want to be the one to destroy a family. Other than us kids, all mom had were her mom, her brother, and her sisters. Keeping my mom happy was all I ever wanted.

# 35

It was now the Friday before school started. Dad was at the garage doing his mechanical thing. We kids were all at home with mom. I guess she figured we had a boring summer and she wanted to do something about it. She called dad at the garage.

"Johnny G's." Dad answered.

Mom said, "Johnny, can you bring me the car?"

I wondered why he even needed a car at the garage. He didn't go anywhere, and if he did have to go somewhere, all he needed to do was walk less than one hundred feet to his second home, "Sal-E's bar."

I think dad just liked having control of everything mom did, where she went, how long she was gone.

Some men, it is a term of endearment to show concern and love as to where their wives are at any given moment. To others it is a control thing, to know how long the wife is gone, where she is going, with whom she is going, how many miles were put on the car, how much gas was used?

Oh, yes these were things my dad calculated. To me it was just normal. I was tempted once, to look under the car to see if there was a tracking device. I mean really, all the questions. Who? Where? How long? Did you take a left? Did you take a right? How fast did you go?

Come on father, she wasn't messing around on you! Yes, she was beautiful, but no man was stupid enough to approach her, not only with six kids on her hip, but really, she was married to the infamous Johnny G. after all. Who would be so stupid to make a move on her?

So on the Friday before school was to start; mom decided she wanted to take us kids to the local zoo. I believe I had been there once on a field trip with the elementary school, but as a family, we had never gone. I was excited to go, especially excited for the little kids.

Dad began with all the hundreds of questions. She gave him every answer correctly. She even asked him several times if he wanted to go with us, he insisted he couldn't go. Mom planned a picnic lunch knowing darn good and well she wouldn't get any money out of dad to buy snacks. She wanted to make a long field trip sort of day out of it. This was not an event she was going to come and go in less than an hour as she did the grocery shopping, which by the way was usually timed.

Of course, he questioned her motives. "Why didn't you plan this earlier?" He questioned.

"Why all of a sudden?" He asked in a harsh voice.

"It's the last weekend before school starts. I just want to have some fun with the kids." She answered.

Did he feel left out?

Dude you're the boss! Let your mechanics take over for the rest of the day, jump your ass in the car, and go with us. I wanted to scream.

Close shop for the rest of the day or shut the hell up and get in the car. I sure wanted to scream, because I knew exactly what the hell he was up to. If dad could've ever read my mind, he would've whooped my ass every day of my life.

My goodness such a fuss! Perhaps mom felt like saying.

"Just forget it, were not going."

And I'm very sure dad would've said "Ok." With a big ol smile on his face, but there was no way she was going to disappoint us. Whether he liked it or not.

Part of me was scared for mom the other part sad. We prepared for our trip and just as we were about to leave, dad shows up, and takes the keys to the car off the dresser.

He needed to go buy parts for a car the mechanics were working on.

Now wait a minute. Wait a fricken minute.

One of his mechanics just dropped him off to get his car, why didn't the mechanic just take him to buy the part for the car at the auto supply.

I'm not a very well educated kid but I saw right through this shit. What was wrong with this man? Was he just that mean?

Why not buy a thousand foot chain, wrap it around the entire house several times, put a big pad lock on the outside of the front door, plywood up all the windows, place a bowl of water in the front door for drinking water and call it a day.

You talk about being a fucking jerk. If he wanted to go with us why not just come along? If he didn't want mom to go without him, why not just say so. But, to strong arm us with such a stupid unnecessary performance, just further confirmed what he was. A monster! A fucking hateful monster!

Of course, he ruined the day. Why couldn't he just be a normal man? What was he so afraid of?

Mom wasn't about to let him ruin the day though.

After he left, as if she were on a mission, mom got the food she had fixed for our trip to the zoo, sandwiches, her famous Kool-Aid, chips, pork and beans; she even sent Sher and Danny to the neighborhood store for cookies and candy.

Mom went to the back yard, set up a little picnic area, got an old sheet, and built a canopy to block the sun. She put out an extension cord from a back window, brought out an old radio, and had music on for us.

However, we didn't have a zoo full of animals we had each other, to joke around with, to have fun with.

We stayed outside for hours lying on blankets talking and laughing. When it got dark outside mom brought out that old nineteen inch black and white TV, set it up on a chair and we watched TV outside as if we were at a drive in theatre.

Mom was creative; she knew just what to do when it seemed everything was ruined.

Dad came home while we were outside watching TV and eating cookies. Of course, he was stoned and did a miserable attempt to make the rest of the night fun. Fun for himself I guess. He lay back on the blanket, looked at mom and asked.

"Whose idea to bring the TV outside?"

"Mine of course." She said as if it didn't matter if he were trying to be nice or not.

"Good idea." he said.

He lay back on the blanket and watched TV until he fell asleep.

Meanwhile we gathered everything up and took it inside, everything except dad.

Sometime later mom woke him up. He went inside, lay on his bed, and fell asleep all night long. Wow, he was actually home on a Friday night, only thing it was barely 10 o'clock, on a Friday night.

Mom reminded us we were going to have to start going to bed early, because school was about to start.

It was before midnight when I went to lay on the "big bead." Sher was still awake lying on her twin bed. She still had the light on, reading of course.

"Are you excited about staring school?" I stupidly asked old bossy. Sher lowered the book she was reading, didn't say one word to me, just raised her eyebrow like "little kid, what the hell is wrong with you?"

I covered my face with my hands, as to say, "Please don't let this bossy ass girl still be staring at me when I uncover my face."

She still was.

"Ok, ok." I said. "I know you are."

"Well one thing is for sure, I will miss seeing you at school every day." Sher said trying to sound sincere.

'Yikes.' I thought. That's right, she was moving to bigger and better things.

I laughed, "Yeah right." I said because I sure didn't believe her.

"I'm serious." She said in such a serious tone. "I'm really gonna miss seeing you and all your ugly friends in the hallways." She said so damn seriously. We laughed.

"By the way," she said. "If anyone ever picks on you, I

want to know about it. I mean it. I will beat the crap out of whoever even thinks about messing with you." Sher said in such a tone.

I got scared just thinking of some idiot attempting to pick on me, Sher finding out, and straight up beating the crap out of them.

What? This bossy ass sister of mine was actually defending me.

"I may not be able to protect you here." Looking around our room in total disgust. "But at school, well, just watch."

Gosh, she sounded just like her dad. She wanted to beat up any stupid little girl that might pick on me.

"And if I find out someone picks on you and you don't tell me, I'll beat the shit out of you instead." She whispered so no one could hear her cussing.

She got out of her bed, and with two steps, well it only took two steps with them big long legs, kind of body slammed herself on me, as to beat me up.

"Ouch, ouch." I pretended it hurt, well, actually it did.

"That's just an example of what I can do to you or whoever might mess with you. I'd rather hit someone else, not you, but just let me find out you lie to me." Something she learned from dad, hating liars.

She grabbed a tiny strand of my hair and tugged at it, pretending she was going to yank it out of my head. That shit really did hurt, what the hell was wrong with this girl, I wondered.

Then she half ran, well took two more long steps and flopped herself on her bed, with her long legs and ponytail.

How funny she was, how scary she could be if she wanted to be. She turned off the light that was near her bed. Grabbed her pillow and covered her head with it. I had forgotten that is how Sher slept every night. Pillow covering her head so she could drown out any noises and any light that may bother her while she slept.

I then realized that was why she didn't wake up the night dad had beat mom. Her pillow covered her head the entire night, every night. I guess her pillow over her head was the same as a security blanket is to a small child. She heard nothing at all with that pillow over her head.

How very fortunate for her.

# 36

The weekend was over. It was Sunday night; time to get ready for bed so we could wake up bright and early for school the next day. I hated the thought of going back already, but knew for sure I was going to have to go.

We all hugged and kissed mom goodnight. I could hear Danny telling J.J. as they lay in their twin bed.

"Will you hurry up and come home from school?" Danny pleaded with him. .

"Huh?" Danny asked again.

J.J. assured him he would hurry home. I think Danny was a little character. I often got the idea he bossed J.J. around, just because he could. Maybe J.J. enjoyed looking after Danny, but quite often ol crybaby Danny got the best of J.J.

Everyone fell asleep, even the super excited Sher. I lay awake, just hating the thought that I had to go to school in just a few hours. I think I was too old now to fake being sick. Dad would see right through my fakeness for sure, especially on the first day of school.

Who knows what time dad came in, but he was there when I woke up, griping, of course about needing the car.

The initial plan was for mom to take us all to school, dad stay with Danny so mom didn't have to wake him, take us all to school, go home, dad go to work then take the car back to mom when it was time for all of us to get out of school. Upon which, mom would take the car back to dad later in the afternoon. I wonder if he pre meditated any or all of his actions that morning.

Game change!

Heeeeee would take us all to school, mom would stay home with Danny, and we would either walk home from school, or heeeee would pick us up. Either way my day was ruined. Completely ruined!

What the heck could he possibly need the car for? We were leaving for school at 7:40 am; mom would've had us all at school before 8:00. Dad didn't even open the garage until 8:30 or 9:00, which, when you think of it, he really should open the garage at 6:00am just to catch the people going to work early in the morning. But it was impossible for him to stay at the bar until 2:00am, get three hours sleep, then open the garage at 6:00 a.m.

So he dilly dawdled around every day till 9:00 am or slept till just before 9:00 to open the garage.

Now, out of nowhere he wanted to open bright and early. Seriously, what a jerk. If I had a choice to have him take me to school or walk, hands down I would rather walk.

Why did he ruin our plans? He knew exactly what mom wanted to do on the first day of school, even the first week or two of school was planned out weeks in advance.

Lesson here, never ever make plans, at least not in this family. Somehow, they will be ruined.

Mom fixed us breakfast and got herself ready, then she woke Danny and got him dressed.

"What are you doing? Dad asked her.

"I'm going with y'all." She said.

"Why?" He asked. Looking pissed off, and in his normal bad mood.

I wish I had a joint to shove in his mouth and say, "Here jerk off, stay home and get high and quit fucking everything up."

"I can't just let the little kids go to school, not knowing what class they are going to be in." Mom tried to explain.

We had all been going to these schools all our lives. Yes, Sher would go alone to high school, me and Becky would go to middle school, but you couldn't send a second grader all alone with his fourth grade sister, with no mom by his side. He would be horrified.

Mom was annoyed that dad wanted to just send them like a couple of orphans with no family.

"Me and Danny can walk home. Just drop us off." She said to dad. Mom was very well accustomed to walking. There would be times our car would be broke or flat or not there at all. She was no stranger to walking where she needed to go. Dad had no shame letting her either. I believe she enjoyed walking on cool autumn days, or breezy spring mornings. Dad wouldn't hear of it this time. In control, he always had to control every thing any of us did.

Danny was excited to get to go with us on the first day. At first, I thought dad was going to take Sher first and embarrass the hell out of her with all of us in the car. All though it was a beautiful car, there was no way she wanted to be seen with all of us.

Perhaps Sher thought it would be just her and mom riding together in the beautiful new car, once they dropped the rest of us off. Sher must have visualized mom would pull up right in front of the school, Sher would depart the car and happily wave goodbye to mom. Such a nice thought!

Every one of us was in total shock when dad pulled out of the makeshift driveway and took a right instead of left towards the schools. I shook my head without him seeing me. What was it with him? Did he just love fucking our days up or was he a mental case?

Now answer me something! Why not wake up, kiss your wife and kids good morning, sit down at the breakfast table, and wish us all a wonderful day. Then ask mom to drop you off at your place of employment, (garage) or better yet, go with mom to drop all of us off at school, say to each of us as you drop us at each of our own schools, "Have a wonderful first day of school kiddos, I'm gonna miss all of you." Then take mom and Danny home, go work your ass off to support your family and live happily ever after?

Instead! He had us all walking on eggshells. Nope, that's an understatement because there were not enough egg shells in the largest egg farm in the great U.S. of A. to cover the amount of shells we needed to walk on to satisfy him.

I know if he would've seen me shaking my head, he would have turned around, while driving, reach his boxing arm clean across the back seat and knock the hell out of me, which if I'm correct, were lethal weapons. For this reason, I never sat behind him. I didn't want to see those piercing eyes looking at me through the rearview mirror. If I had it my way, I would've sat next to my mom in the front seat, but then that would mean I had to fight with old bossy Sher, because she always wanted to sit next to her daddy. So I sat behind my mom.

Just as I figured, there were no workers at the garage when we got there, only pigeons. These jerks probably wouldn't even show up till 9:00am the allotted time anyway. Dad played it off, got out of the car, in a hurry as if there were fifty cars waiting for him to fill up their tanks. Who knows, he was an hour and a half early, maybe he would get fifty cars or so. Whatever!

He got out of the car as mom got out of the passenger side and into the driver side. Dad started to walk off without saying a word, like some grouchy old fart of a man, then he turned around, reached into moms' window, and gave her a kiss.

"Sorry kids." He said.

My eyes filled with tears, I literally wanted to cry. I didn't get it. Did he really want to be nice but he was just so accustomed to being a jerk, that he didn't know how to be nice especially to his wife and kids. This was rare; this was one of those rare moments I just wanted to hug my dad and say. "It's ok dad."

"Are you sure you don't want to come with us?" Mom asked just as he said. "Bye kids. Have fun today."

I know for a fact that I was teary eyed now. He looked so sad, and so alone.

He said. "No mama, I gotta open up here, I'll call you later."

I swear I wanted to cry. I felt so bad for him, but then I caught myself. I felt sorry for him, but nowhere near the sorrow I felt for mom the day he pistol-whipped her. I hope I didn't grow up to be as messed up of a woman, as he was a messed up man.

It was almost like a sigh of relief that he did not go with us. At least mom could take her time and get J.J. settled in his new class without being rushed.

Every mom wants to join their little kids on the first day of school. Mom knew me, Sher, and Becky would be ok, maybe even Carrie didn't need to be walked directly into her class, but J.J., no, she couldn't just drop him off curbside in front of the school and let him fin for himself. Mom needed to go with him, find out who his teacher was and where his classroom was.

You need to have a plan where to pick them up, where to park so on and so on. Mom knew that, and I'm proud she stood her ground.

She dropped me and Becky off first, as to not embarrass Sher with a bunch of kids sitting in the back seat. I wasn't ashamed at all, especially that we had a new car. As mom pulled up in front of my school, I reached over and kissed her cheek.

"I love you." She said.

"I love you to mama." Then Becky did exactly as I did.

"I'll pick you girls up today." Mom said.

We knew we had to get the hang of all the new schedules. Who gets off school at what time, first, second so on and so on? It would be a very busy day for mom. I knew I would miss her.

"Bye, little sistas." Bossy yelled as she waved with her long ass arms out the window.

"Bye bossy." Becky and I said at the same time.

I looked in the backseat, where Carrie, Danny, and J.J. were waving. I waved back and blew them a kiss. Danny actually tried to grab the kiss out of thin air. He was so cute and loving.

It was definitely going to be a long day for me. Long day was an understatement. At times, being in school was fun. I did make new friends, though I was very quiet, seems a lot of other kids were also.

It's funny, when you're in elementary school you go through five years with the same kids, year after year, then once you are in middle school, five or six elementary schools merge together, and all the old friends get lost among the crowd.

I thought about mom throughout the day, wondering if she were ok. I thought of Danny catching the kiss I blew to him. I wondered how Carrie and my J.J. were doing.

I had seen Becky two times at school in the hallways. Being loud and walking fast in the hallways, you could hear her in the before you ever saw her. And oddly enough, I wondered how Sher was.

She was big league now. She was among all the football players and the cheerleaders, and the freedom to go outside at lunch. For some kids in high school to leave campus in their cars for lunch was a big deal.

Sher was definitely in her element, she was older, by far than her fourteen years. I knew when we got home she would be blabbing about it all day and night.

Lunch came and went then it was time to go home. Becky and I met at our designated areas and within ten minutes, I saw our car turn the corner.

Mom already had the little kids and Danny with her. Danny could not stop talking to J.J. He wanted so much attention from everyone. Seems Danny would start one sentence before even finishing the other. We laughed at Danny because it was so funny that he was so hyped and excited.

Mom took us home because the wait for Sher was thirty minutes, instead of us just waiting on Sher outside parked in the heat. I was to stay with the kids while she went to get Sher.

Mom had snacks waiting on us when we got home. When mom left for Sher, I remember thinking how nice it was to come home to her, and a nice snack.

I had friends that went home, either to an empty house because both their parents worked, or friends that had to wait after school up to an hour because they lived too far to walk and their parents couldn't get off work to get them any earlier.

Though I hated our house, I loved that mom was there, doing all she could to make us happy.

Oh yes, old bossy couldn't quit talking when she got home. She talked for two hours about her new friends, her classes, her teachers, her lunchroom, her life outside our house. I think she even told me the custodian's names, the secretary's names, and the monitor's names. She already knew everyone and everything. She was just too smart for her own good.

We got through the first week of school, the second then before you knew it we had been in school a month. Same routine every day.

Dad managed to stop trying to interfere with the morning routine. We were seven against one, he couldn't fight that.

Oh yes he could! He could have us all knocked off, but I think even he realized he had been a total fucking jerk that first day, bitching for absolutely nothing.

# 37

The leaves were beginning to fall from the trees, indicating Halloween was near. School was rolling right along and I was going to be in a school program.

I had no idea the concept of this, but it was a jump rope routine. Me and eleven other girls were going to jump rope in sync to a predetermined song chosen by the music teacher.

We were to wear burlap bags, which are the bags twenty-pound potatoes come in. It's sort of like a woven material, which is itchy and very uncomfortable. My goodness, these bags are intended for bulky potatoes, not to be worn like clothing by eighth grade girls. This material is not silky by any means.

Each of us was to decorate our burlap bag with some type of American design or an American emblem of some sorts... How mom came up with the idea of the American Bald Eagle beats the heck out of me.

Later I realized there were twelve different decorations to choose from, mom picked the eagle for me. I have no idea how she did it, but she drew a beautiful bald eagle on the front of my burlap bag, with watercolors. She cut out holes for my arms, and a hole at the top of it to slip over my head. She fixed my hair in a long braid.

There were three dress rehearsals for all twelve of us girls to practice our routine. Once our P.E. teacher taught us the routine and after our rehearsals, we knew we were ready.

I was not a talented kid, I was very shy, and I did not like a lot of attention placed on me. I did not like the idea of performing in front of anyone, let alone in front of the entire school.

Oh yes this was to be performed for the parents and student body at parent night. I mean, I could sing with my other three sisters and not be embarrassed, only because it was what dad insisted we do. But to actually get up in front of an entire school, I was not anxious for this to happen what so ever. It did cross my mind to fake being sick, but I knew I couldn't let the other eleven girls down.

We had fifteen-second duets and my partner would have kicked my ass if I didn't show up. So, I knew I couldn't bail.

It was the night of the event; Sher was going to stay home with the kids. Only me, mom and, yes dad, were going to attend this event at school. I got ready, putting on my clothes, black shirt, and black shorts underneath my burlap bag. Mom fixed my hair in a braid and she even put a touch of red lipstick on me and a tiny bit of blush.

"It will make your face stand out." She said with pride as she touched up my make-up. When dad saw the lipstick on me, at first he just stared, of course I looked away. Here we go I thought.

"Look at Johnny Belinda." He said, even with a smile.

Now, for those who don't know who Johnny Belinda is, it is a movie about a deaf girl that can't talk and can't hear, but she could see. Something bad happens to her in the movie.

The reason dad called me Johnny Belinda was because all my life I was so shy and quiet, same as Johnny Belinda was. Maybe he meant it as an insult, but once I saw the movie and appreciated it, I loved the name. Joke was on his ass.

So here we go. Mom, dad, and me. For some reason my mind went back to kindergarten, baby Jesus being dropped, then smothered.

Oh lord, please don't let me get tangled in the ropes and fall off the stage and get knocked completely out. I was a nervous wreck.

Mom and dad walked me to the class where I was to meet the other girls and our teacher.

Dads' instructions. "We will pick you up right here." Easy enough I thought.

After fifteen minutes me and the other girls lined up on stage, the music began and our routine was on. I made eye contact with absolutely no one, for fear I would lose concentration and my premonition earlier about falling off the stage would come true. Four minutes of deep concentration.

Music, jump, stop, jump, go jump, I had this routine down pat, no way was I gonna mess it up. Hey, if one of these other girls flubbed it up to bad so sad for them, but I had this. All I could hear was the audience applauding and yelling encore.

We went back on stage. Took a bow, then back to the classroom where I was to wait for mom and dad. Easy, right?

Well as bad luck goes; it didn't turn out the way I had planned.

For some reason, must have been a demon seed planted, the teacher detoured us to another classroom, seven or eight classrooms down the hall. I told my teacher I was to meet my parents at the other class, but she was too concerned with all the patting on the back she was getting for an excellent performance to care about my predicament…

I began to panic. I knew, I just knew my dad was gonna be looking for me. How did I know he would be pissed? What do I do? They won't know where to find me. Would they leave me behind?

I busted out of that room like an escaped convict being chased by a pack of bloodhounds, and went directly to the original classroom down the hall.

Now, of course there were a lot of parents in the hallway looking for their kids also, so I wasn't the only one lost and confused.

I'm desperately looking for my mom, and even more surprised I didn't hear dad's big mouth screaming out my name. I was in a straight up panic. I got to the room where we were to meet, no one there.

I started to go out the side door of the building just ten feet from where I was standing, but my better judgment got the best of me. I started getting teary eyed, thinking.

"Oh my, I'm lost, dads pissed, moms scared, I can't find them, they can't find me. Dads gonna beat the crap out of mom cause they can't find me." My mind was going crazy, then, a slight tap on my shoulder.

It was my mom. As an angel sent from heaven, she grabbed my hand. What an incredibly safe feeling. Dad threw one of them looks at me like '*you just wait.*'

We were out the side door. By this time dad was walking twenty paces to our one, as if he were being chased by popo.

I could hear him saying, above all the parents and kids and commotion.

"I told you where to meet us. Why can't you do what you're told?"

Mom held my hand as we walked to the car. I must've looked like a big old baby, an eighth grader holding her mommies hand.

So what? I didn't give a damn what any one thought.

I tried to explain to mom how the teacher made us go to the other classroom.

"It's ok." She said. "Don't worry, don't worry."

Don't worry? Mom are you serious, this is "No patience Johnny" we're talking about. He shoots people for stupider shit than this.

Dad was fuckin yakking nonstop. I got tears in my eyes. Oh my goodness here we go.

He kept saying. "Didn't I tell you to wait for us? We were looking everywhere."

I tried to explain that the teacher moved us to another classroom, but he didn't care. I disobeyed. I cringed at the thought he was gonna hit me, but better me than mom.

It seemed like an hour drive to our house, which was actually less than five minutes from the school. I contemplated opening the car door and jumping out just to avoid the inevitable, but I don't think he would've even noticed till he got home and realized I wasn't in the back seat. Then he would've bitched because he had to go back and look for me.

The minute we got home, he shut up. Instead of giving me a pat on the back for a job well done, he sought out the one thing I did wrong.

What the hell is the use? I thought. What's the use of even

trying to explain, he never listened anyway.

We weren't home but ten minutes and he left.

Good, I thought. At least the rest of our night would be peaceful.

I wondered if I had been the one that screwed up, maybe everything was my fault. Maybe it was, but he had no patience to listen to an explanation, then take the time explain to me what he thought I did wrong.

With dad, you were guilty till proven innocent, which to him was never, plain and simple.

I had a bad feeling in me. I was experiencing guilt. I felt guilty for mom when she got beat because I did nothing to help her, but this was a different feeling of guilt. This was a feeling that maybe, just maybe I had done something wrong and it really was my fault.

Damn I didn't like this feeling at all. However, he wasn't your normal father. He wasn't a father that could talk through things, listen to your side, and try to figure a solution, in case there was a next time. He just blew up and ran his mouth right there so everyone could hear.

He left me and mom almost an entire block behind, instead of walking with us to the car. No matter how I felt, I wasn't taking the blame for this one. I just wished he knew how to be a dad, a real dad, not a gangster that had to be in control of everyone and everything.

He would never ever shut up on this. I figure I'd hear about this till I was old and gray. I already knew everything was always his way, in his home life and in his gangster life. This was just a school program gone wrong, gone wrong for me, unfortunately. I could only imagine how he would react to a real catastrophe.

# 38

Nothing was ever said to me about the jump rope incident. Maybe mom handled it, maybe dad reconsidered, thinking I might hang myself with that damn rope if he brought it up again. One more reason for me to hate school, nonetheless it was behind us.

It was now Halloween. Sandy and Jewel shut down the snow cone stand for the winter. No one was buying, since some of the snow cones tasted like cigarette ashes.

The cooler weather was upon us now; the house wasn't hot and sweaty anymore. Actually, it was a bit comfy in spite of the roaches and rats. We never actually saw the rats in our house but we definitely could hear Susie our cat tearing them up. Disgusting.

Every year for Halloween, mom would make or fix us all some kind of Halloween costume. You know the usual ghost, princess, and witch. The only reason I ever liked Halloween was for the candy.

Sure mom took it all and checked it for whatever some nut case may put in it, poison, blades you know the usual psycho shit. Then she would hand us a handful for the night, and put the rest away, giving us one or two candies a day. Seriously, six kids trick or treating, we got hundreds of candies and mom made them last for months. She was careful so we didn't rot our teeth.

This year mom was going to be creative. None of us kids had noticed what she had been sewing on for over a month. We knew it was Halloween costumes, but she wanted to surprise each of us, so we stayed out of her way while she created her masterpieces.

Finally, on Halloween she presented each of us with our

costume. She dressed us all differently, only this time I was very different. I wasn't sure what she was up to though, wondering why the heck she needed soot from the hot water heater and put it on my face to look like I had the five o'clock shadow dad would have if he didn't shave before 5:00 p.m.

She then put my long hair up and put one of dads' gangster hats on me. She had me put on a white long sleeve shirt, and through all the sewing she had done for the past month, she had made me a suit, one just like dads with a tie and all. Oh my, I'm not sure what she was up to but by the time she was through with me, I was my dad.

To me I looked like a hobo, but the instant the kids saw me they started laughing, dad, dad, dad.

Oh my! That was the last person in the world I wanted to look like, or was it. She had us all dressed and waiting for dad's arrival.

He was going to chaperone us along with mom, for our trick or treating adventure. I thought possibly me and Sher were too old for such a thing, but not in our family. Mom loved doing it, and we loved making her happy.

Rather than all of us showing dad our costumes at once, she was going to call us out of our room, one by one, as she presented us to dad.

Mom had fixed dad his plate of food, and he was sitting with his back to the wall, you know the gangster position.

Mom had worked everything out, our costumes, what each of us was to do when she called out our names. It was more as if we were performing for dad, and this was to be our curtain call.

Dad sat and looked in amazement as mom said. "Welcome to tonight's presentation of the Guetarro kid's Halloween Night." She was pretending to be an M.C. She smiled at dad.

Mom looked at dad's hands, indicating that she expected him to clap as she began the night program. Dad looked at his hands wondering, what is she looking at? Mom clapped her own hands, suggesting to dad he do the same. He got it, so he clapped and laughed.

Dad continued to eat his food, smiling at mom as she announced the first up. "Marshall Danny" short for Marshall Dillon, and out came Danny in his little cowboy outfit, his white cowboy hat, with his little pistols, and his bright shiny sheriff badge.

He was smiling and shooting his little pistols right towards dad, the closest the poor kid would ever get to actually killing him, I thought. Danny popped every last cap in the cap gun, before mom moved on to the next act.

Dad began the first of many many laughs he would have that night.

Then mom introduced J.J. who she called. "Babe Ruth Junior."

J.J. came out from behind mom's make shift curtain, which she had prepared from an old sheet. Dad's eyes lit up. He had on an old white shirt, which mom had put the name Guetarro and the number seven, dad's baseball number, and one of dad's baseball caps. J.J. was an imitation of dad as a baseball player, only smaller. J.J. was swinging his bat in every direction, almost knocking dad right in his teeth. Even dad had to say, "Watch it son." fearing J.J. would really knock out those pearly whites of his.

Dad gloating with pride as J.J. took his place standing right next to Danny, which mom had instructed each child to stand side by side until the end of our performance.

Then Carrie came out as "Carrie, Bozo the Clown" mom said. Mom had painted Carrie a big red nose, made her some big shoes, some old ones of dad's and strapped them to her feet so she wouldn't trip and fall.

She made Carrie some big floppy pants, and gave her three balls to juggle and gave her a honk honk horn to honk rather than talk. Carrie began attempting to juggle the balls which went flying every where, almost landing in dad's food, and without hesitation, she honked the horn right in dad's ear, which, for a second mom and Carrie froze wondering if dad was gonna throw them both out of the kitchen, instead he almost choked on his food from laughter. Carrie then, took her spot next to Danny and J.J.

The show continued. We kids' could be heard laughing our asses off from behind the curtain. Mom got back into character, once she realized dad wasn't going to choke to death on his food.

Next, we have Becky Cottontail, named after Peter Cottontail.

Now my mom did not have a malicious bone in her body, and we all know she did not dress Becky as a rabbit to hurt her feelings, even Becky knew it, so as the court jester Becky was, she hopped, not walked, but hopped from behind the curtain, with her little hands propped as a bunny. With big rabbit ears mom had made especially for her. Dad looked at mom, almost like "Shirley, are you sure you want to dress Becky, of all people, as a bunny?" Then Becky bucked her teeth out even more as if attempting to nibble on something. Dad was crying by this time. She hopped right up to dad's face, thus creating another five-minute laughter session. We were all hysterical by now. Now we had, a bunny, a clown, a baseball player and a cowboy lined up five feet from dad.

Then mom called Sher out, not me, we were going in order, but she wanted me to come out last. "The future Old Maid," mom introduced Sher.

Sher, normally miss beauty queen, was dressed as an old lady. Mom had put flour in Sher's' hair and made it all white. She put Sher's hair up in a sort of bun; she had on a long skirt and a white shirt, which was buttoned right to the top button.

Sher had glasses, with no lenses, on the tip of her nose, and a shawl around her shoulders. Mom had drawn wrinkles on Sher's face with her eyebrow pencil; to give the illusion Sher was over a hundred years old.

Mom had picked a stick out of the yard for Sher to use as a cane. When mom called Sher out, she came out in character. She hunched her back, sucked in her lips as if her false teeth were missing, then she walked very slow, and shaky, as she walked in the room she said to dad, "Hey sonny," in an old lady shaky voice.

Dad could not stop laughing. He was literally crying. Mom gave dad a few seconds to catch his breath. Now, there were all five of the kids lined up, dad wiping away his tears of laughter. Mom trying to keep her composure, wanting to laugh but didn't.

Then she called me out. I'm not sure why I had to go last; the kids had stole the show. While I was behind the so-called curtain, I wondered what I could do to make this fool laugh. I got stage fright suddenly.

The second I walked out my dad stopped laughing and his jaw fell to the ground. At that instant he saw a twelve-year-old son, he saw himself. He knew then what my two brothers might look like at my age, an almost gloating look came over him. I felt sick.

My hands in pocket, sunglasses on, one of dad's gangster hats on my head, I sort of swagged my way towards him. I didn't even have to speak; he was beyond hysterical by this point.

Mom smiled with pride as she called each of us back for our encore presentation. Dad hugged each of us and thanked us for an excellent show.

"Mama, you out did yourself this year." As he gave her a big hug.

I was imitating this man, one I had spent months hating, but if for a second I got approval for pretending to be him, then all the humiliation in the world was worth it.

He, for a second was proud of all his kids. He was proud to take us out for the world to see. Maybe by instinct or just because we were talented kids, the second we stepped off our front porch we all got into character. Danny shooting his fake guns, J.J. swinging his bat, Carrie honking her clown honker, Becky jumping like a rabbit, instead of walking. Sher taking her time walking like an old hunch back old lady, and me with hands in pocket, walking with a little swag, acting like a gangster, all I needed was a real pistol.

Yes, it was a good night for us. Dad did not complain about anything. He had all us kids acting like fools and he loved it.

And, of course being stoned made everything that much funnier to him. So we laid it on him, intentionally over doing our roles.

We walked forever and got lots of candy. When we got home mom got the little kids ready for bed. Before she started going through the candy, dad called me and Sher into his room.

He told mom he wanted to take us to the bar to show our costumes to all the jokers at the bar. I did not want to go but dad insisted. Of course, Sher wanted to go, anything to please her daddy. So off we went. Dad, the old lady, and his twin, me.

When we entered that stinky disgusting bar there were people dressed in costumes. Mostly there were whores looking like uglier whores.

Dad introduced us pretty much the way mom had introduced us to dad. Getting applause, laughter, and pats on the back. Little Johnny I was called. I wanted to rip that hat off my head and let my butt length hair fall to my butt, but I didn't dare.

Dad could not have been more proud with all the compliments and back patting.

Then a song came on the jukebox that Sher and I were familiar with. Now remembering I was very, very shy. I had just survived the jump rope incident and barely escaped the baby Jesus thing seven years earlier.

But this was different. I was incognito, I was disguised, and I didn't care. So as an old lady and my father, Sher and I began to dance to the song.

A little old lady dancing like these fools had never seen before and me, shy me, trying to dance like a cool gangster. The gangsters and whores went crazy. Dad was almost on the floor with laughter. We had the attention of everyone there,

Sher nor I planned it. Sher never said come on Malina let's dance, she just got that old cane and started shaking her ass, I kinda leaned back and let the gangster in me take over. It was funny even to me and Sher.

We got about one hundred and twenty five dollars as tips and appreciation that night.

Of course, we didn't get to keep the money.

It was ok, we had pleased dad unexpectedly and we had gained his respect. For one night, he was a real dad, and we were proud to be his kids.

Being at dads second home, Sal-E bar was going to be the talk of the town for quite a while. Dad talked about it nonstop, of course, it wasn't as funny without all the costumes, but overall it was an occasion that we all won't soon forget.

# 39

School seemed to drag on, but by the end of every day, I was so happy to go home and see my mom and all the kids.

The leaves had all fallen from the trees indicating the holidays were approaching.

Now, J.J. and Danny had piles and piles of leaves to play in, rather than all the dirt and rocks.

Mom and dad were planning our Thanksgiving holiday. We usually always spent it at Aunt Gloria and Uncle David house. Theirs was the largest house and more than accommodated everyone that would be there.

Seems all the women got together and decided who would bring what, how much to bring so there would be enough for every one and so it wouldn't be a pain in the pocket book for just one family.

Thanksgiving was just one of the holidays you could not wait for. Aunt Gloria always had so much for all us kids to do. She planned events as if it were a birthday party. Actually, it seemed more like a birthday party, with all the kids running around and having fun. The boys would all play football outside, the girls would all gather upstairs in my cousins' room and talk and laugh and giggle.

Aunt Gloria always had two large long tables set up in the dining room. One table for the men and one for the women. Seemed easier to put the men together and let them talk all their macho bullshit at one table so they were easily accessed to re-serve them second helpings. Without a doubt, all the men, not just the gangsters in the room, depended on their wives to serve them first and second helpings of food.

The older cousins would all sit together at a table in the kitchen where we could continue our conversation pretty much in private. There was also a smaller table set up in the kitchen for all the little kids like Danny and J.J...

There was always a table for the wives, which rarely had them sitting. It wasn't just mom either, it was all the wives, I mean from getting second helpings for their husbands, serving all the little kids and serving beer after beer to the loud husbands. Seems the wives had to eat on the run or just wait until everyone had finished.

Every year I half-expected Sher to stand up and say, "Damn you lazy bastards, get up and get the shit your damn selves!" But it wasn't her place, unfortunately. Sher would've been the only kid any of the gangsters would have accepted such language from without putting a contract on her life.

We were out of school the entire week of Thanksgiving, so the night before; mom began cooking what she needed to take to Aunt Gloria's. She would cook a turkey overnight so it would be just perfect by the time we were ready to celebrate at Aunt Gloria's. Seems no matter how much food there was on the tables, I always knew just which food mom cooked and which she had not.

I would wake during the night because the smell of cooked turkey filled our house. I could not wait to be at Aunt Gloria's house and enjoy the elaborate feast.

Mom spent countless hours cooking the turkey and checking on it, peeling the potatoes, and making cakes and pies. It was obvious she loved doing it, so I often wondered why we didn't stay home, just our family and celebrate, but dad would insist he wanted to spend it with everyone.

Dad was the main attraction at just about every function we went to. Not only did everyone enjoy listening to him talk his talk, it seemed all the women adored him, as did all the kids.

For sure all the men wanted to be like him. He would sit all the kids down on Aunt Gloria's' living room floor and tell scary stories. Nine times out of ten it would be the same stories we had already heard, the year before at Thanksgiving and Christmas and the year before that. Though we had heard the same stories over and over, seems we never tired of them.

He was a fantastic storyteller, and he was also a pretty

damn good magician. He could seemingly make quarters appear and disappear out of our ears. He was so fast we could never figure out how the heck he did it. He would have all the kids so excited because he was funny when he needed to be, he was serious when he would be telling one of his numerous scary stories. He could literally entertain everyone for hours.

The plan was to be there at noon. We arrived fifteen till. The families that were there came out to help dad unload the car. Mom went right in to help Aunt Gloria with whatever she needed in the kitchen.

We paired off with our babies so mom could do what she needed to do in the kitchen. Barely 12:30 dad and some of the men were already drinking beer. Seemed to me, beer would ruin the taste of a turkey dinner. Obviously not for these guys.

Everyone had arrived just as they all had every year. Thanksgiving dinner was being served by 1:30. The tradition never changed. It was an event that took about two hours, once every one had been seated and served.

The food was delicious as it was every year. Seems I just couldn't get enough no matter how much I ate... No one said that's enough; don't eat anymore; the food was not rationed, so I took full advantage. I wished so badly we could eat like this every day of the year. It was a once a year event and I certainly appreciated it. Mom, though exhausted from being up so many hours, continued to serve dad, any kid that was still hungry and herself. So many people, so much food, an endless stream of second and third plates of food each. I wondered how it was possible for all these women to be on the go for so many hours. Not to mention, it was dessert time. Cakes, pies, ice cream, cookies, candy, more sweets than we would have all year. Every person there complimented the women on the best meal they had all year. Dad was smiling the most. A belly full of food, dessert, beer and quite possibly, he snuck off and hit a joint for a second, but hey, he was happy, we all were at that.

We were home by 8:00 pm. I knew mom was about to collapse, because she had been on the go for over 36 hours now. Once home we received a call from grandma; she didn't go out of town for Thanksgiving as she had planned.

Apparently, grandma had been calling all day, trying to get us to go to her apartment. When she finally did reach us, she insisted we go to her place for a second helping of turkey dinner.

There was no school of course the next day, so we loaded back in our car and went to grandmas. Dad asked mom several times if she were sure she was up to it. Of course she was, she loved visiting her mom.

From what I understand, grandma had worked until three at the nursing home. When she got home around 4:00, she had a wonderful surprise. We found out what that surprise was when we arrived at grandmas' apartment.

As soon as we walked into grandmas' apartment, there were all grandmas kids, even the ones that lived out of town and their husbands and wives and all their kids.

Uncle Bill was there, of course with Lily and his monstrous kids. I believed my grandma had chewed his ass out and he really felt bad for being a jerk. There were cousins I hadn't seen in years, because it had been a long time since any of them came to Fort Worth for the holidays.

Seems all my aunts had cooked for grandma, while she was at work. Apparently, Uncle Bill had a key to her apartment, so everyone from out of town waited until grandma left for work then they all got busy cooking. She had no idea any of them were in town until she got home and was surprised.

They said she cried and was so excited but refused to eat until mom was there. Since we didn't get home until 8:00, poor lady hadn't eaten because she waited on us. I'm not sure but I do believe mom was grandmas' favorite.

There were way too many people in grandma's apartment, but it was cozy and fun. Mom hadn't seen two of her sisters in over two years, so they had a lot of catching up to do. I do believe we stayed until dawn, everyone chatting and catching up.

The plan was to meet back up at grandmas about 6:00 pm for seconds and thirds if we desired. But of course we would desire.

Yes, this was a great thanksgiving this year. Both sides of both families together. It was nice.

I can't remember if we ever had been to both sides of the family for Thanksgiving. This year I had a lot to be thankful for. And I was.

We spent a lot of time at grandmas over the next two days. One of my older cousins was to be graduating from high school in May of the coming year. She begged mom and dad to take all of us to Albuquerque to be there for her graduation. Dad said he promised he would try.

We had a new car so, transportation wise, we could get there. But, her graduation was to be the last week of our own school year.

With all the testing and such, there was no way Sher would agree. Freshman in high school, she wasn't going to flunk just to go to our cousins' graduation… I knew that would never happen.

The good-byes with moms' family were pretty sad. Who knows how many more years would go by without seeing one another? Mom cried a lot. It was her two older sisters that lived out of town, yes, they talked on the phone a lot now that we had a phone, but really, it wasn't the same. I guess when families move away, emotions change.

Mom saw grandma, Uncle Bill and aunt Dolly on a regular basis, but it wasn't the same. Grandma was in tears as everyone left, it was mom that comforted her own mom.

I know grandma was grateful mom was there for her. It was mom who stayed by grandmas side when grandpa died. Grandma had a special spot in her heart for mom, not just because she was her daughter, but also because mom was just such a special loving woman, everyone knew that, and everyone loved her.

# 40

I remember the year I found out the truth about Santa Claus, I was completely devastated.

No Santa? What were these words coming out of my mom's mouth? Mom and dad were Santa? I could believe mom could have been, but dad? No way!

Christmas would never ever be the same for me. Though we were dirt poor, it seemed something good always happened at Christmas time. I honestly don't know how they managed to pull it off every year, but we always had a good Christmas.

Our old house was so cold in the wintertime; we were forced to literally live with sweaters and sometimes our jackets on while inside the house. We kept them on all day, even slept in them at times because it was just too cold to take them off. But, I actually loved that feeling.

When we were younger, dad always personally invited Santa to our house. I wasn't positive at the time, but I knew it was probably one of his gangster friends, because his beard was always slipping off, and as you would suspect, ours had the aroma of marijuana. Jolly ol Saint Nick my foot, that jerk was as high as my dad was.

Every year the fake Santa would always show up at midnight, with bells in hand, convincing us his reindeers were up on our roof waiting for him while he made his cameo appearance just for Johnny G's kids...

It was both exciting and scary.

This old Santa, that dad just so happen to find every year, would come into our house and try his best to get us to talk to him and ask us what we wanted for Christmas.

Now, I assure you it's one thing to see Santa in the department stores with hundreds of people around, it's a completely different thing to have him actually come to your house to talk to you. It was just unheard of.

As soon as we would hear him ringing his bells, and laughing Ho, Ho, Ho, Merry Christmas, we would all take off running to the back room from fear.

Dad, from embarrassment, would entice us back to the living room, with the threat if we didn't talk to Santa there would be no Christmas for any of us, or the customary ass whoopin...

So, reluctantly, we would blurt out what we wanted, knowing darn good and well if he really were Santa he should have already known what we wanted. After several minutes of shock, we would get use to the fact that the real Santa was actually in our living room, visiting, and promising us if we had been good kids we would get exactly what we wanted.

Bah, Humbug! Even I had to raise an eyebrow on that one.

Christmas vacation had already begun. We would have fourteen days off from school and it was now two days before Christmas. Needless to say, we were the family that did the last minute shopping. I wondered now, if Sher had gone shopping last year with mom, since it was apparent Sher already knew the horrible truth about Santa.

This year would be different though, as far as shopping for gifts and such. Since I had been made aware of the truth about Santa, I was to join mom on her "Christmas Shopping Extravaganza"

Dad brought the car for me and mom to go shopping. He couldn't or wouldn't leave the garage to go with us.

I honestly don't know what I expected, or how much money I thought he would give mom to buy gifts. I didn't know the value of a dollar in those days so I believe it shocked me when I saw him give her fifty dollars. Yes fifty. I believe he spent more than that on one roll of the dice when he played dice in the back room of Sal-E's.

Now, I had no idea how many gifts mom could purchase with fifty dollars, but I know one thing, it just didn't seem like enough money, but of course, she didn't complain. I suppose two days before Christmas she appreciated anything, than nothing at all.

When we entered the department store there were literally hundreds and hundreds of toys. I had never been to this particular store and had never experienced Christmas shopping, but I was more than excited to be there. I wasn't sure if mom planned what to buy or was she just gonna play it by ear.

She got a shopping cart and started down the first aisle. Now, being the Catholic family we were supposed to be, each of us had our very own god parents, you know the designated couple that is supposed to step in and take care of you, if ever needed, or be a designated…heck I really never understood what they were for. I just knew there were six couples, dad's friends, and relatives that stepped up to the plate and, "baptized" us in the Catholic Church. "Padrinos," they were called.

Therefore, it was customary for these godparents, to "hook us up" at Christmas time, and on our birthdays.

Becky's godparents always out did the other godparents getting more for Becky than the rest of our godparents combined. Seems the gifts were very well appreciated, but anything from mom was always from the heart.

"You don't have to worry about me mom." I told her as we looked at item after item.

"Why do you say that Malina?" She asked.

"I'd rather see the little kids get things than for you to worry about getting things for me." I said.

"All grown up?" Mom asked with a smile.

"Something like that." I said. That, and of course my devastation of learning about Santa. I think I was traumatized, not because there was no Santa, and not because my parents were really Santa, but it was the fact that they hid it so well from all of us. I mean really, I knew about gangster shit long before I knew about Santa. Somehow, I felt a bit sad. Mom was right. I was feeling a bit grown now.

Now, I really was having the feeling of, "it's better to give then to receive."

I was daydreaming about Christmas when I heard my mom say. "Don't worry baby, I would never dream of not surprising you." She hugged me as she said it.

We slowly went through every aisle, mom carefully getting the best for her dollar. We were in the store for hours, it seemed. Knowing now that there was no Santa, I understood why it always took them so long when they were gone for hours during the Christmas holidays. I guess all those years I really thought that they were "talking to Santa."

Geez, I was a big ol baby. I thought.

I honestly did not pay attention to what gifts and for whom she had picked them for. I was in awe of all the toys. I fell in love with everything on every shelf, wanting desperately to grab as much as I could from the shelves and take it all home for my brothers and sisters, knowing darn good and well it was impossible.

When we got to the check out counter mom had the buggy filled with gifts. The sparkle in her eye, knowing she had done her absolute best for her kids. I looked around at all the toys and all the people with smiles on their faces, my own mother with her beautiful smile, the excitement of Christmas, and if I hadn't known better would've thought she had spent five hundred dollars, not fifty. Seeing her so happy made my heart fill with joy.

Decorating the tree, hanging ornament after ornament, some store bought, some we kids had made in school. Each of us hanging shiny silver icicles on every branch of our beautiful tree. The wonderful smell of pines, the beautiful shiny lights, the chill in the air, all the excitement, because Christmas was only a day away.

Christmas Eve was always spent at Aunt Gloria's, same as Thanksgiving. Every year we had the same tradition. We always arrived at 9 pm. We never took gifts for anyone, we just didn't have the money, but it didn't matter, there were so many people there, no one could afford to give everyone a gift anyway.

It was freezing cold outside, cold enough for a white Christmas, if it had snowed. I remember walking into Aunt Gloria's house and feeling the warmth. It wasn't freezing cold in their house as ours was, also there were so many people in Aunt Gloria's house it was almost too warm, so we had to immediately take off our coats and sweaters.

Once everyone arrived, we all ate. It was not the big "Thanksgiving" type dinner that we had at Thanksgiving, instead it was home made soups and corn bread, and gravy and biscuits. Though there were as many people there as there were on Thanksgiving, it just wasn't the long process that it was at Thanksgiving. After we ate all the cousins sang Christmas Carols while dad entertained us all with his usual magic acts and story telling rituals...

Just before midnight, Aunt Gloria's kids went to midnight mass, with Uncle David a tradition they did every year. Also, since they were all in the church choir it was expected they be there to sing. It usually lasted an hour, so we would all wait for their return. Some of the family would accompany them to mass, some would stay at Gloria's' and wait for their return.

Once they all returned from mass Aunt Gloria would begin handing out gifts, to everyone. Those that had brought gifts began exchanging them with one another. Good ol Aunt Gloria, with seven kids of her own, still managed to get everyone a little something. I remember when she handed a gift to me I was so excited.

When I opened the gift, it was a beautiful heart pin that I was to wear on my shirt. It was shiny, with different colored fake diamonds; I couldn't stop staring at it. Most everyone was opening gifts, talking, laughing, and having a good time.

Then, out of nowhere, my dad called everyone into the living room.

Once everyone gathered, he called upon my mom. We had no idea what he was up to, then he began.

"I love you so much, and I know I'm not the best man in the world, but." As he knelt down on one knee and got moms hand, while putting a ring on her finger!

"Will you please, please marry me, again baby?"

Now.... hold up, they were already married weren't they? I wondered.

I was so confused. Aunt Gloria began crying, even before mom and the rest of us were able to sink in what was happening...

It was Aunt Gloria that constantly told dad, "Until you get married in the church before God, you will always have troubles, go before god, and do it the right way."

I suppose dad finally wanted his life right. Or was convinced, in order to have a good life you must do the right thing. The right thing being, marry in the church.

Before mom could say yes, everyone was crying. Of course, she said yes and began crying as dad stood up and hugged her.

Here was this mean gangster monster, on bended knee proposing, in front of an entire house full of people, and all he could focus on was mom.

Never in my life did I ever see them happier than that moment. Mom, so it seemed, had absolutely no idea how dad had planned such a proposal or when and where they were to be re-married, she just knew this was an entirely different man than she had married the first time fourteen yrs ago. At that moment, he was the ideal man.

After all the hugging and bragging and thank you and I love you, we went home, with mom and dad smiling as if they had just met. Once we all went to bed, I could hear mom and dad wrapping presents and laughing. Finally, it was lights out.

The next morning bright and early, Danny was the first to wake up. Within seconds, he was screaming with excitement.

"Santa came, Santa came." Danny yelled loud enough to wake us all.

Mom and dad jumped out of bed the second they heard Danny yelling. Within moments, all eight of us were in the living room, with our sweaters and robes on, shivering because it was so cold. We each sat in our designated spots to open our gifts.

Dad played Santa and handed out gifts, slowly, one by one, smiling his rare but very handsome smile. Seems like every other gift he handed out went to Becky because her godparents had bought so many for her.

I got one gift from my godparents it was a purse, a strap purse actually, for me to carry all my personal things in. Then I got another gift from my godparents, it was a wallet, which matched the purse. How pretty I thought, because I had never owned a purse or a wallet. Then mom told me to open the wallet, I did, and to my complete surprise, there were twenty-one dollar bills in it. I felt like a millionaire.

Now, considering four months ago I was selling hand drawn pictures for change in my neighborhood, I felt I literally hit the jackpot. I could not even count the dollar bills properly because there were just so many.

Then I was handed two more boxes. I opened the first and in it was a beautiful watch. I had never owned a watch either. This one was so beautiful, I wanted to cry. It was from mom and dad. Then I open the second box, it had a heart diamond necklace. On the back of the necklace was an inscription.

*'We love you, mom, and dad'*... I started crying because I was so excited and happy. All these gifts were firsts for me.

I really hadn't expected any gifts from mom and dad because I knew they didn't have much money, but some how, for me, they pulled off the best Christmas we had ever had.

Being so excited I couldn't remember what each of the kids had received because I was just so excited for myself, but I was also happy for everyone. We all seemed so excited and happy, even mom and dad.

It had been a very tough sad year for me for all I had seen and heard, and though I had so much hate in me for all the bad events, for my mom I was happy.

Maybe just maybe everything was gonna be ok. I loved my life that day... Not because of the material things but because it seemed finally things were going to be ok for us. For all of us.

# 41

It was now New Year's Eve. A new year, a new start. Every year for new years at the exact stroke of midnight dad brought out his arsenal of weapons and blasted the sky. As illegal as it was, it didn't matter to Johnny G. or his henchman Ray.

Now, yes, I'm a kid, but I know for sure what goes up must come down, and I knew darn good and well those hundreds of bullets had to land somewhere.

Living next to a fire station had its advantages but there was no way dad would talk his way out of going to jail if one of the bullets landed on our heads.

I noticed how dad and Ray would shoot their guns; they didn't shoot straight up in the air. I guess knowing the bullet could wind up right back on their heads.

It had to be Ray, the killer, that knew the perfect technique in which to shoot the guns and spread the bullets everywhere else. Neither Ray, nor dad gave a shit less if those bullets landed on anyone else miles away; actually, they aimed right for the cemetery...

Their guns were loud and scary, but these two men got an absolute thrill out of shooting them. What was normally a five-minute thrill to most pistol owners on New Year's Eve was a thirty-minute joy ride for dad and Ray.

I would, at times wish they would, one… run out of bullets, or, two… get caught by the police. Yes, it was exciting the first few shots, but to go on and on and on, seemed a nuisance. Nonetheless, the New Year was upon us.

Mom and dad seemed to be getting along very well. Aunt Gloria was going to help mom plan her little wedding, which was going to be at the church we went to when we did attend church. Aunt Gloria and Uncle David would attend, but not any of us kids. There would be a little reception afterwards at Aunt Gloria's house to celebrate the newlyweds' wedding. I heard them talking about a March date for this second marriage.

We were back in school from the Holidays, it was freezing cold outside. Every morning when we would leave for school Danny would be right there sitting on the floor in front of the heater trying to keep warm talking and talking to all of us. Knowing he would be so lonely throughout the day.

Dad had agreed months ago to stay home with Danny in the mornings while mom took us all to school. As much as I didn't like school, it seemed all the other kids just loved it. Even Danny couldn't stop talking about "When I go to school."

Sher had activity after activity at school, that is all she talked about, this class, and that class, talk about the cheerleaders, and the football players, and the class rooms and how old and beautiful her school was. She did her homework the second she entered the house, not even stopping to eat a snack mom always had prepared.

"Don't you ever have homework?" She asked me while she was busy writing something called an essay.

"No." I answered.

She never looked up at me. "What kind of grades do you get on your report card?"

"All A's." I answered as smart-ass as I could, knowing damn good and well I was lying but, I also knew I would get a reaction out of her.

"Whatever, you little liar." She growled.

"What do you get?" I asked, though I already knew the answer to that one because I heard mom and dad bragging about her for the past six months.

"Straight A's baby, what you think?" She gloated and smiled.

Oh my goodness, a nerd, a damn nerd. I thought with out daring to say it. Nah, she was to pretty to be a nerd.

"I already know. Mom told me." I said.

"Oh yeah." She said. "Ha-ha don't you want to grow up to be like your big sista?" She bragged.

"No." I said as quickly as I could.

"Liar." she said again and laughed.

"No really Malina, what kind of grades do you make?"

Now, I thought, she was just being cruel and making fun of me because she knew darn good and well my grades couldn't compare to hers.

D's and F's bitch. I wanted to say, but knew better. She would've beaten the shit out of me just for saying D's and F's, much less bitch.

I was annoyed at this time. I wasn't sure if she was trying to give me a pep talk to help me, or humiliate me because I was a dummy compared to her.

I got up off the bed and started to leave the room, but she stopped me.

"I want to tutor you, if you need help."

Why? I thought. This girl has absolutely no patience. The first time I mess up she will put me in a headlock and if I scream for moms help, she will probably stuff her sock in my mouth to shut me up.

This was, in my eyes, a trick question.

No thanks. I wanted to say. I'll stay dumb. Just to save my ass.

"I don't like school. I never have since first grade." I said.

"But why?" She asked, with actual concern in her voice.

"School is so fun." She sounded so happy just to say the words.

"For you maybe" I said. "Not for me."

"It's exciting." She went on.

"Again, maybe for you, not for me. I have hated school since first grade."

I began wondering if she really wanted to know, or was she just messing with me.

"Why? Did someone pick on you?" She asked.

"Yep," I said. Before she could even ask who I blurted out,

"The principal."

"What did he do? Did you get a paddling?" She asked her eyes just staring at me.

"No." I said. Then I told her of the incident in the first grade when I cried every day. She said she never knew of that.

"But why did you cry?"

I believe she was enjoying this.

"Because, I wanted to be here with mom." I said in defense of myself.

"But why?" She asked again.

Ok bossy, I'm getting tired of all these "why" questions, I wanted to blurt out. But, it seemed this was the very first grown up conversation we had in awhile.

"I just want to be here with mom." I almost cried just thinking of it.

"But Malina, mom will be here when you come home." Sher said.

Well, I knew that, but I just hated the thought of her being alone. I thought to myself.

"But every kid has to go to school." She reminded me.

"Maybe so." I said. "But every kid does not have to like it."

"True, but maybe you'll like it when you go to high school next year." She said, looking at me kinda sad.

Hold up, was she giving me the third degree because she was so pretty and popular. Maybe she was embarrassed that I might show up and be the stupidest one in my class. Or make her ashamed of me. I didn't dare ask her what I was thinking because I knew she would get annoyed and either hit me or run me out of our room. So, I played along.

"I just feel that if you ever need my help all you gotta do is ask."

I'd rather walk on hot coals. I thought.

I got the fact that she was in high school and she had a good reputation and kids loved her and teachers loved her and all the boys were noticing her, and she was beautiful, but come on.

"I am not a reject. I do have some class to me." I blurted

out. I knew the second I said it, it was a mistake.

"Oh yeah." She laughed with her very visible white teeth.

"Yep." I said. "Just wait till next year when I'm there, you and all your stupid friends are going to want to be hanging around me." I almost wanted to cry.

She laughed. "I'm so sure. I just don't want you to be in the office every day getting a paddling."

What he hell was I saying, even I knew how stupid my side of the conversation sounded, but I couldn't stop myself. Foot in ones mouth? That was me at that second.

Just at that moment I thought of screwy, sitting in the office every day in school waiting to get his butt whooped by the principal for whatever mischievous thing he had done. I cringed. Poor guy, I thought.

Now, I really didn't want to be in the office. If I ever had the misfortune of getting a paddling, I think I would've just run away.

Sher obviously was trying to prepare me for high school, which I would be attending in about six months. She had no one to prepare her for the ups and downs of high school, she was learning all her own, but Sher was smart, she knew how to handle herself.

I realized then I had Sher to guide me, through her mean bossy ways she was trying to prepare me for things she learned on her own. I realized I had for myself, a built in tutor that was going to teach me and teach me the right way. Not only would she tutor me for my classes, but also she would tutor me about being popular, and having fun and not being so afraid, if it were possible. I was the proverbial ugly duckling. Sher was the swan. I guess you could say I was very, very lucky. I just didn't know it yet.

# 42

I was making passing grades in school when spring break came around. It was March, and it was still slightly cold outside. We had an entire week off school, and nothing planned.

Danny had been sick with a cold so mom made him stay in. It was the weekend mom and dad were to be married in the church, mom seeming a bit nervous, dad more than mom.

Aunt Gloria was excited because she had always wanted this for mom and dad. She and Uncle David had raised all their kids pretty much by the hands of the catholic religion.

All seven of their kids went to catholic school which I'm sure cost my uncle a pretty penny. He just didn't approve of the public schools. He and all his older kids were in the church choir and his three sons were altar boys.

Anytime we went to visit Aunt Gloria, whether it was just a visit or a family get-together, she blessed us before we left her house. You know the sign of the cross right there where you stood and she said "God be with you." It was her way of saying, Should anything happen to you once you leave my house, you're covered, religiously.

She was a beautiful woman, always soft spoken and quiet, like mom, never did I hear her or Uncle David ever say a foul word, as a matter of fact, I never heard them even yell at one another. Aunt Gloria loved everyone, always talking kindly to all the kids, adults equally. Sometimes she would come to our house unexpectedly and bring her kids to visit us.

Her seven, and six of us, were pretty much all the same ages, so we all got along pretty good. Dad used to tease mom and Aunt Gloria, "Damn are y'all racing to see who can have the most?" Because mom and Aunt Gloria were always pregnant at the same time. Some of us born weeks apart from Aunt Gloria's' kids, some only days apart.

Whenever we visited them, we had plenty to do at their

house. They had a piano, games, TVs, toys, basketball hoop, you name it they had it. They really wanted for nothing, at least nothing I could think of.

Uncle David did very well for his family, working ten to twelve hours a day, I often heard. As quiet as he was, he was equally as strict. He kept his kids on their toes.

Visiting them was like going to another planet, everything so different from our lifestyle. The occasions they would visit us, we definitely couldn't have fun playing in the dirt and rocks. Oh, my two brothers and the three guy cousins spent hours playing in the city mom had built. Their yard was full of grass, bushes, and flowers so they did not experience the fun of playing in the dirt until they played at our house.

We didn't have a piano, or girly things for the four girl cousins to play with at our house, so when they did visit, me and my sisters would entertain them.

Now it would have been ridiculous to play rich house with them. They would not have understood the concept, their house was already nice. So what we did, we made up plays to perform in front of them. Every time they visited, it was a different play. All four of them would sit on the floor of our big room, crossed legged and just wait to see what was the act of the day.

We would be so funny they would applaud and cry at the same time. I don't think they saw us as poor per say, I think they saw us just not having the things they had.

What we lacked in material things, we made up in talent. It was fun for us to make them laugh; I honestly don't think they ever got bored when they visited us. We were never ashamed of what we didn't have because mom told us on many occasions, "Never be sad for what you don't have, be grateful for what you do have."

After we would entertain them, all eight of us girls would harmonize as we had so many times when we spent the night at their house. Singing just came naturally for them as well as us... Mostly them because they did it every week in church.

We did it because we liked it, more so because dad liked it.

All the preparations for mom and dad's church wedding were all planned out. Sunday arrived, dad so handsome in his black suit and black tie. Mom wore a beautiful beige dress that made her green eyes seem to turn a beautiful color of hazel.

Mom was as nervous as if it were her first time to marry.

Aunt Gloria and Uncle David accompanied mom and dad to the ceremony, which was to be held in their church. We all stayed at Aunt Gloria's house because that is where the reception was to be.

They were gone maybe an hour and a half, when they returned; looking happier than any other couple I had ever seen. Perhaps Aunt Gloria glowed as much as mom that day, it just seemed she wanted this so bad for them.

The reception lasted a few hours, then we were told we would stay the night with Aunt Gloria so mom and dad could go on their so-called honeymoon. Dad was really going all out to make mom happy.

. What a difference a few months had been for him. He actually seemed happy, with his beautiful smile and dimples.

They were gone about twenty-four hours, Aunt Gloria more than happy to have us stay with them. When they came to pick us up, they seemed like two entirely different people. Life was good, really good for us.

It was one day in early April mom had used the car to pay some bills and run some errands and we were all with her. We went to the garage to visit dad, and sitting there was the same woman that had been there before. Sitting just as she had the last time I saw her. I was unsure now what to make of this woman. Surely, mom had to be curious, or did she already know who she was?

I was so confused. Again, dad came to the car and once again, nothing was said about the woman.

I guess if curiosity didn't get the best of mom who was I to say anything. It just seemed odd seeing her again. I wondered how often she was there, I mean this was my second time to see her, sitting there staring at dad as he talked. Did she go there often I wondered? Surely, her car was not breaking down that often, and generally, if a customer needed gas, they did not get out of their car and visit with dad.

That night when dad came home I heard mom and dad talking somewhat loudly. They really hadn't had a fight since he beat her; they had arguments but nothing violent. Whatever the problem was with this woman, I didn't believe mom was going to get to the bottom of it any time soon.

# 43

A few weeks passed, and one day when we came home from school I could tell mom had been crying. I was horrified to ask, but I just had to know.

"Are you ok mama?" I asked.

"Yes, I'm ok. Call all the kids inside I need to tell all of you something." She barely whispered it to me.

I did as I was told. We all sat in the living room as mom began.

"Dad had to leave town, he won't be back for a few days." She started.

"What?" Sher asked, "He couldn't say good bye to us?" She was pissed.

"No." Mom said. "This wasn't a planned trip." She said.

"He's"… She didn't want to say it but she had to.

"He's in jail."

Sher instantly started crying. "Why, what did he do?"

One thing was for sure, mom was not about to tell us kids one more thing than she absolutely had to.

"Let's not worry, Ray is getting the money to bond dad out. It may take a few days. Everything will be ok." Mom tried to be so calm.

"No it won't." Sher cried. She really did love her daddy. The little kids could've cared less, so mom sent them to play outside, while she sat with Sher and tried to explain what had happened.

Sher was not satisfied, she wanted details, details mom was not about to disclose to Sher. She may have been fourteen years old, but to mom Sher was still a kid. Sher pissed off at the world, just stormed out of the room.

My mind went racing wanting desperately to confront Sher, what the hell do you want mom to do Sher; she just said Ray was getting the money to get him out. Damn he wasn't facing a firing squad, he was in jail. Probably for a night or so, give it some time. Let Ray and mom work together on this.

It took a few hours but mom calmed Sher down. Ray came by and said he had the money and it would be another twenty four to forty eight hours before dad would be home.

Ok Sher, you can handle that. I thought to myself.

It was the weekend and I figured dad would get out at least by Monday. Mom did all she could to take care of us. Sal took care of the garage and gave mom money for grocery's and whatever we needed. I wondered if dad had done something for Sal or the gangsters or had he done something stupid on his own.

Mom was already stressed enough as it was. It wasn't my place to ask a bunch of kid questions. Seems just when things start to do good, something happens to mess everything up.

I really don't believe Sal or Ray told mom the truth behind dads lock up.

When he got out of jail Monday, he looked like crap. Ray brought dad home just as we were leaving for school. Sher cried when she saw him and asked if she could stay home that day. Ah ha! Now she wanted to be home with her daddy, how ironic, all the times I cried to be with my mom.

"No." Dad said. "You need to go to school."

This is what jail does to you? I thought as he hugged us all as we left for school.

Mom seemed very bothered by the entire jail thing. She was very quiet the day's dad had been gone, though she got collect calls from jail, and calls from Ray and some of the gangsters. I would hear her talking, and she just seemed annoyed, rather than frightened or worried.

It would be another long, long day at school for me. Worrying about everyone and everything. I wonder, do kids get ulcers. It was a miracle I didn't have a million of them, or what ever you get from stressing and worrying.

Mom was there to pick us up after school; I could tell she had been crying all day. Dad was home, with Ray and two other men. I didn't recognize the men but I heard them say.

"Don't worry Johnny; we'll take care of it."

Dad had a very strange look on his face. This wasn't the gangster... "Oh I got away with another one." This was different. I knew for sure no one was gonna tell us kids anything. Dad at home in the middle of the day, not at work or at Sal-E's. This really had to be bad, really bad for dad.

Always my concern was my mom. Dad was a gangster he could handle himself, he chose his life style, or didn't, either which way he was a grown ass man and knew the consequences of his actions, good or bad.

I mean, men that choose construction as a career, know the consequences of being out in the hot sun all day long. Men who work in liquor stores know the risks of being robbed, yet they choose that career. It's the same being a gangster, you know what your up against pretty much twenty four seven, so if you choose that life you bear the responsibility that goes with it. Right?

Somehow, this jail thing just didn't seem right. If it had been a gangster related issue, dad would not have gone to jail. In all fairness, I think Ray would have, he was the right hand gunman, unless he squealed on dad. However, really, it was Ray pushing the hardest get dad out of jail.

What did it matter to me? This wasn't my fault, my burden, my problem. I mean really now, they don't lock up innocent men do they?

Sure they do, but dad wasn't innocent. He had done many things in his life and never had to pay the price for his actions. Beating my mom was one of them, but mom hadn't squealed on him, none of her family even knew of the beating, all her bruises were gone.

Besides, there was no proof he had beat her, no one knew about it except me, and he didn't even know that I had witnessed it. Only other person that knew of mom's beating was Bee, and surely, she loved her husband and brat kids too much to try and snitch dad off, besides there were no pictures of mom's beaten face. I wasn't gonna tell.

Mom definitely wouldn't, she loved dad to much and Bee wasn't about to risk her family just to see dad locked up, she still would have to worry about Ray getting even if it had been Bee.

I'm not really sure why I thought dad had been locked up for beating the shit out of my mom. Possibly, it was because that was the only thing I had ever seen him do that was bad. I knew of the bad things he did, but to actually be a witness to his violence, this was the first time.

This was different. Sal-E or none of the other gangsters would've let dad take the fall for anything gangster related, so that only leaves something personal.

I had learned to be a good spy the last time Bee was at our house. But I couldn't hide behind the door every time.

Some men I had never seen before were at our house within thirty minutes of us getting home from school. Part of me wanted to say, oh to hell with this, I don't care, the part that kept me wanting to know so bad what was going on, was my mom.

She didn't deserve what ever was happening. How much shit does one woman have to endure in a lifetime. I listened for a while, and then I thought of the kids I went to school with. I wondered what their lives were like. Did they go home to a bunch of fighting and cussing and moms' being hit, and whoopings and arguing? Or did they go home to a loving warm home.

No one ever talked about it at school. I mean really, who the hell would say, "Hey my dad beat the shit out of my mom last night." Or who would say. "Hey everyone I'm scared to death of my dad and we have no food in our house." Who would volunteer such words? No one, that's who.

I suddenly felt sad for many of the kids at our school, not really knowing how they lived, but if they lived anything like us, then my heart hurt for them. If anyone lived as we did, they sure as hell never bragged about it in school. I thought of our classmates often. I mean, really; these kids were the ones we spent nine months out of the year with.

They, in a sense, were family. I would look at my classmates and wonder, just wonder what their home lives were like. I wondered did they have mean dads, nice moms. Nice dads mean moms. Did they have food in their iceboxes, did they get hand me down clothes, did they sometimes cry themselves to sleep. I'm not sure, but I'll bet, I'll seriously bet a lot of them lived like us. I felt sad, sad for everyone. Another bad chapter in our lives.

In spite of all this jail crap, our routines still continued, kids still ran all over the place, Sher still the smart-ass boss, me still stuck like glue to my mom, dad still running all over the place, garage, gangster, garage, gangster. He seemed anxious, and nervous, not as bitchy as usual he just seemed to be worried...

Mom still went about doing the things she always did, cook clean, drive us to and from school. She did it just as she had before dad was locked up, only she was very quiet now, almost sad. I wanted to know so bad what was wrong, why she just didn't seem herself, but mom wouldn't say a word about it..

Me of all people, because she had seen my face, my fears when dad beat her, she was not about to fill me in on any of this.

A few days passed, dad had to leave town, but this time it was only overnight. More than likely, this really was gangster related.

It was a Friday night we were watching TV. Mom was preparing supper for us when there was a knock on the door. Mom went to see who it was. It was Helena. She was alone, no kids no Ray, which seemed so unusual because I didn't even know she knew how to drive.

Helena seemed very scared. When mom let her in, they went directly to the kitchen to talk, and I assume, drink the pot of coffee they loved so much.

Mom was still preparing our supper; Helena helped her, as if she wanted to hurry the meal preparation so she could have moms' full-undivided attention. There was no way I could follow and listen in on the conversation so I stayed put, in the living room with all the other kids watching TV.

After about fifteen minutes, I needed to go to the restroom, which, I really didn't even think about it, but the restroom was right next to the kitchen. When I got to the restroom I realized I could hear them talking, only thing was, I couldn't hear the exact conversations, only muffled words, such as, lady, old, hospital, jail.

Not even a real spy could figure this one out. So, I gave up. Mom and Helena fed us supper, then went to the living room to continue their conversation. I wondered where Helena's kids were and for that matter, where was Ray? Maybe Ray had gone out of town with dad, it just seemed so strange all the secrets and whispering. Helena stayed talking quietly with mom.

Just before ten o'clock, though we kids had already gone to bed, I heard mom and Helena go outside. I could barely hear them talking on the front porch, then I heard them talking at the side of the house. Within a few minutes, Helena left and mom came inside and locked the door behind her. It was so strange Ray hadn't called looking for Helena, and dad hadn't called his normal twenty times to talk to mom.

I fell asleep for a few minutes I guess, then I heard mom on the phone with dad. She wasn't saying much only listening. I did hear her say, "I don't know how much more I can take." She was crying by then. I'm glad dad wasn't there, at least at a distance he couldn't hit mom if this were something he would've reacted to. .

She came in the bedroom to check on us kids before she went to bed, she saw that I was still awake.

"Mom did dad do something bad?" I just had to ask, putting her on the spot.

She could easily lie to me if she had wanted, but she hesitated for a long time.

"He did something bad to a bad person."

"Did he kill someone?" I asked.

If she had said yes it would not have surprised me at all, why shield me from anything now.

"No." She said very quickly. "No he did not."

"Then why did he go to jail?" I insisted on knowing.

"It's so complicated Malina, lets just wait till dad comes home, if he wants you kids to know, then he can tell you."

My mind was racing; I couldn't figure this one out. I believed her when she said he hadn't killed anyone, even I was aware he had hired gunmen for such acts. But mom had confirmed he wasn't an innocent bystander wrongly accused and falsely locked up, he had done something with or without Ray by his side.

Maybe Ray was in jail. All the maybe, maybe, maybes, I was exhausted just thinking of it all.

"What was I doing? I was just a kid, I couldn't correct the mistakes of a bunch of gangsters, I couldn't force my dad to be a good man, he was who he was, none of that concerned or bothered me at this exact moment. As always, all I cared was about my mom. Something just wasn't right.

After Helena left mom seemed to have a ton of bricks lifted from her shoulders, then she talked with dad for a few moments on the phone, and she cried.

All I got out of it was mom was getting tired of everything, and she had every right to be, she had been through more hell than any other woman alive, and she still stood strong with her kids, and by her gangster husband side.

There was no monetary gain for her in any of this. She did not live in a mansion like the one we had visited that one day. She did not wear mink coats; she did not possess a maid or a chauffer. She was a mom, a wife. She had been drug to hell and back, yet handled it all with pride and love.

What was there for her to be proud of? She had to lie to protect the man she loved, she had to lie to protect her kids, and she had to lie to survive. Yes, she was one of a kind woman. But, every person has his or her breaking point.

Was mom about to reach hers?

Some would argue mom stood by dad's side because she feared him, others would argue she did it out of love.

Only God knew.

## 44

Dad was home the next day as promised. He and mom had a lot of serious talks that we kids weren't allowed to listen to of course... They would even go sit out in their car to talk in private.

Several men came and went throughout the day, as if they were attorneys, or some type of legal advisors, perhaps they were. Mom didn't seem as upset as she had been the previous week, maybe dad had sweet talked her, maybe he convinced her of his innocence for whatever crime he had gone to jail for, maybe she just came to the reality there was nothing she could do about any of it, but stand by her man.

It was near the end of April, with about a month left of school to go. Sher had already began making all her summer plans, not asking mom or dad, just telling them how it was going to be.

Mom listened to Sher's' plans, not saying yes, not saying no. Whatever plans Sher was making, she was still the child not the adult in the family. Sher was actually going to try out for cheerleader in her sophomore year, which really would've given her a reason to stay away from home even more, if she made the team. Really, one look at her and you already knew she was a winner.

Danny would be starting school the next year also. He and J.J. sat around for hours talking about the things they would do together in school. Danny was so excited he couldn't sit still at times, just carrying on about all the plans they had made. He would now be one of us, with a lunch box, and schoolbooks, and crayons, and friends of his own.

One night when dad came in from work, or the bar, or wherever he had been, he told mom to go to the store, and insisted she take J.J. and Danny with her, which seemed strange to me because we usually went in our designated pairs.

After mom left for the store and dad knew she wouldn't walk in on him, he called all four of us girls into his room.

"I want to talk to you girls." Dad said, with a very kind smile on his face. Becky and Carrie were still a bit young, but not so young that they couldn't understand the things he was going to say to us.

"I have two things to tell y'all." He began.

"First off, I got my self in a bit of trouble and I'm not sure yet, but I may be going to jail." He said it just that bluntly.

I thought this was odd for him to be telling us this without mom there for moral support.

"In about three weeks I will have a trial, and if everything goes well I will not go to jail, but if things go against me I will go to jail for awhile. Just the thought of her daddy being in jail had tears flowing down Sher's' cheeks.

"What did you do?" Sher insisted, staring directly into his dark eyes.

Dad didn't answer her. He purposely did not look at his favorite, Sher. Possibly, he knew if he did, he would break down and cry. Gangsters don't cry.

"How long will you be gone?" Sher insisted again.

Once again, he did not answer her questions.

"Let's just put it this way." He went on.

"I did something I felt I had to do, whether it was right or whether it was wrong, I can't change that it happened." He looked scared for a brief second.

"But as of today, we are not going to worry about it at all."

"Ok?" And with that, he ended part one of his conversation.

"Now." He said with an enormous smile on his face. The expression on his face went from night to day. Just like that.

"I have to tell you girls something else."

We listened, wondering what now. Was it a good thing or another bad thing he was gonna tell us?

"Next week is mama's birthday, as y'all know she will be thirty three years old. I have planned a big surprise party for her, which she has no idea about it. This is a big secret, so I am counting on you girls to take care of your brothers while I take her out. I have planned this big party for her with all our friends and gifts and, well, it's something she has never had and I want to surprise her. But you girls have to promise not to tell her."

"Next Saturday I'm going to call here and tell her to get ready. I'm gonna tell her we're going to dinner for her birthday. So, I'm leaving it up to you girls to help her pick out some thing very nice to wear, but just keep it a secret. Can y'all help me with this?"

"Yes, yes." We all said at once and with a lot of excitement.

Looking at him as he told us of his plans, was like watching him tell his famous scary stories at the family get together's during the holidays.

Dad was talking with such excitement, the same excitement he gets in his voice when he's telling the stories and about to scare the crap out of all of us, even though we already know the ending to his story.

"And, can y'all promise not to tell her anything about the party? Please." He smiled.

"Yes." We all agreed.

Honestly, we were so excited about the party we forgot about dad's trial. Seems the weekend came really quickly. Saturday was here, and just as dad promised, he called at six o'clock telling mom to get ready.

As predicted she began looking for something to wear, and just as we had been instructed by dad, we each suggested what we thought she should wear. By the time dad was home at eight, she was dressed looking more beautiful than ever.

Dad showered, got dressed, and as always, put on his good smelling cologne. Mom had already fed us kids and instructed the younger kids to go to bed by eleven. Dad said he wasn't sure what time they would be in, if we wanted, Sher and I could wait up until they got home.

I watched them leave, mom having no idea dad was about to surprise her. Such a beautiful couple, and they actually looked to be the happiest couple in the world.

We were still awake when they returned home, mom so happy and excited, it was obvious she had been crying, but these were happy tears. She had never had a party and it was a complete surprise. Everyone had managed to keep dads secret. What a wonderful feeling she must be feeling I thought as I watched her. For once, my mom seemed happy, really really happy.

Dad brought in her gifts from the car while mom told me and Sher of her party. She was like a small child bragging about her very first birthday party, she even brought home half the cake for us to enjoy.

Then dad came in, carrying the last of mom's gifts, also there was something in a box and before he could present it to mom, it barked. We screamed with excitement.

Mom looked at dad like, "you son of a gun," which was a very good term of endearment. He placed the box on moms lap and in that box was the tiniest, littlest, brownest big-eyed Chihuahua I had ever seen.

Tears filled moms eyes, "Johnny, I can't believe you did this." She had wanted a puppy for as long as we could remember, never daring to ask, knowing we could not afford one.

We had a family cat but she always wanted a tiny, tiny puppy and now her dream came true.

It goes without saying; we all fell in love with this little puppy. Dad even woke all the kids to come meet our new family edition...

It was a little boy puppy. Though everyone was sleepy, the second they saw the puppy they were wide-awake. More so was Danny. So little himself, so cute, so happy. Danny's big eyes bugging out with excitement. Mom handed Danny the puppy to hold, and at that very second she came up with a name for the puppy.

Mom called him Babytoo, as Danny's nickname was baby, because he acted like such a baby all the time. The puppy had big eyes like Danny, brown hair like Danny, the perfect name for an adorable little puppy looking just like the youngest member of our family.

Babytoo. We all loved the name she selected. We all fell in love with the puppy, and dad, well; he actually did something very very good for mom, again.

He was beginning to be the dad we only dreamed we could have. Babytoo was more joy than we ever could have imagined. The next few days we kids could not get enough of Babytoo at all. The second we came home from school, until we went to bed we focused all our attention on our new puppy.

Danny was so attached to Babytoo now, when we tried to play with Babytoo, Danny would cry. Mom tried to explain to Danny that he had to share with all of us. He would cry and say no, Babytoo was his friend. It was adorable to see Danny carry on so.

He finally had him a little play mate, someone to keep him company on the days we were in school

It seemed it would be difficult to get Danny to go to school next year; he surely would not want to leave Babytoo alone.

We barely had a few days to get use to Babytoo when dad showed up with a new surprise.

Much too all our surprise dad brought home a bigger dog, this time it was a German Shepherd, nothing at all like Babytoo. It seemed strange to me that dad would want a second dog. Turns out it had belonged to a friend of dads that was sick and couldn't care for it anymore.

The dogs name was Gee-gee, and though she was a big dog, she apparently had been raised around kids because she was no different from Babytoo. She was playful, and excited and happy, only difference she was just about ten times the size of Babytoo.

"What are we possibly going to do with two dogs now?" Mom asked. "I can't train a big dog Johnny." Mom said. "I wouldn't even know how to begin." She was worried a big dog would scare or bite us.

"Gee-gee is a well trained dog." Dad said, "You don't have to train her to do anything. She will stay outside, and I'll be getting her a dog house tomorrow." He explained.

Sher especially fell in love with Gee-gee. Mom was concerned for us, our safety, but not so worried that she would send Gee-gee away. Once mom saw how good Gee-gee played with the kids, she had no objections to us having another dog.

Later dad confided to mom that should he go to jail he wanted a dog to protect us in case we had intruders.

It made sense. It would be difficult for mom to be eyes and ears twenty-four seven, if she had to be left alone taking care of us all. It was a very wise choice.

We couldn't get enough of both the new dogs. Danny was more excited than any of us because he now had two new friends to spend his time with.

Outside he had Gee-gee, inside he had Babytoo. He was a very happy child now.

# 45

We were near the end of school. Monday would begin the last week of school for the year. Sher bragged about all the exams she had to take and all the upcoming events she had planned for the summer. Though dad had promised to try, it was impossible for us to travel to Albuquerque for our cousins' graduation. We just had so much to do with our own schools.

It was Friday night so we stayed up late watching movies. Mom was on and off the phone all night with dad possibly an argument ensued, I honestly believe she hung up on him. When I went to bed, dad still wasn't home.

I woke later that night. Mom was crying, I instantly got a sick feeling in my stomach, a déjà vu feeling. Dad was there in the room with Mom, but they weren't fighting, he was actually comforting her. She was very upset. Then I heard her say something very strange.

"I might as well be dead." She cried.

"Don't say that mama." Dad sounded so sad.

"Why? The kids don't need me." She cried.

Dad just kept saying "No mama, no mama." Mom couldn't stop crying. It wasn't the same type of cry I heard the night he beat her, this seemed like the type one cries when they are just so hurt over something.

I lay awake crying myself, wondering why Mom was so upset. Why she was so sad? And why she thought for one second that we did not need her? What had dad done that hurt her so badly?

When I woke the next day, dad was gone but grandma and aunt Dolly were there drinking coffee. I went in to hug grandma, and I heard mom telling them of a dream she had.

Mom explained that she dreamed she had died, and as she was going to be with god, she cried out to god.

"No God please, I can't leave, what about my kids? I can't leave my kids."

Every one in the room got teary eyed, me more so. Grandma assured her it was only a dream and God would never take her away from her babies. I looked over at my mom just as grandma said that, and she looked so sad, so lost.

Once everyone left I asked mom about her conversation with dad the night before.

"Oh baby, I was just sad." She tried to sound comforting.

"But why would you think we don't need you?" I began to cry.

"It was a bad thing for me to say." She began crying. "I'm sorry I said it and even sorrier that you heard it." Mom hugged me, apologized, and promised never to talk like that again.

It was certain now dads' trial was going to begin June first. He was nervous, yet still I had no idea what he had done and what the charges were. Mom seemed worried but tried so hard not to let us see just how worried she actually was.

It was Sunday night, before the last week of school. Since the kids were already in bed, Mom called me and Sher into the living room.

Mom always kept a big bible on the coffee table that had a lot of pictures in it. We kids would periodically look through the pages though very seldom did we read the pages. It was a beautiful book with a burgundy leather cover with big gold letters that said "Holy Bible."

Mom opened the book and read a few lines from it. I saw how beautiful she looked as she read. Just as quickly as she read a few lines, she closed the book and sent us to bed. It seemed odd for her to read from the bible, because she had never done that before. We were not an overly religious family.

When we did go to church we always went with relatives or the local church would send a bus to take us. I suppose in dad's eyes it really didn't seem appropriate to go to church and ask for forgiveness, then turn right around and sin all week. Kind of, hypocritical, even for dad.

Mom had already begun plans for our summer vacation, insisting to dad that with or without him we were going to go to the zoo and the Children's Museum and any other fun spot she could think of to take us.. She even talked of going to Corpus Christie or Galveston, somewhere to just get away. Mom told dad she wanted us to all have fun, especially Danny because now all her kids would be in school all day and she would be alone.

"No baby, it will be me and you, while the kids are in school."

Dad insisted this summer that he would include himself on every venture we took. It would seem strange thinking of mom all alone, everyday while we would be in school. So much time for herself, I'm sure she would appreciate, but after fifteen years of having kids around her all day, I couldn't help but wonder if she would be lonely.

I wondered would she take Mr. Mann's offer and volunteer at the elementary school, so she could be near the kids all day.

Dad allow her to volunteer herself everyday? It didn't seem possible. But then again with this new dad, anything could happen. I mean seriously, what do women do once their kids are finally all in school? Do they lounge around all day? Do they get a job?

Yikes, do they have to go to work with their husbands? Anything seemed possible at this point, but with this new Johnny G., it was quite possible he would let mom just be mom. Whatever she needed to do to make herself happy. Knowing mom, her happiness was her kids; she would want to be with her kids...

# 46

Once mom put the bible away, Sher and I hugged her goodnight and went to bed. Dad wasn't home when I finally fell asleep.

I'm not sure of the time, I'm not even sure what I heard, being awakened from my sleep. I woke to what I thought was mom crying again. I could only hear dads voice saying, "Shhhh mama, its ok, don't cry mama." Then I heard nothing at all.

Just those few short sentences. Everything went quiet, I fell back asleep.

The next morning I was the first to wake. On my way to the restroom I looked toward moms' room, I saw mom laying on her side of the bed, which was nearest the kitchen, dads back to her. Usually she was up starting breakfast, but this was a few minutes earlier than we usually got up.

Once I got out of the restroom, washed my face, and brushed my hair and teeth I went to get the clothes I was going to wear to school that day. The night before I remembered my skirt was too wrinkled to wear so I tip toed in moms' room to get the iron and ironing board. I tried to be quiet not to wake anyone just yet. I tiptoed over to mom and tapped her shoulder. "Mom, wake up mom." Actually, I wasn't trying to wake dad, mom was the one who always got up with us for school.

I plugged the iron and began ironing my skirt, but I noticed something. Mom was still in the same position she had been when I went to the restroom. Which I wondered why, usually with the slightest of noises she would turn over and or get up all together.

I finished my skirt and went over to shake her again. This time I shook a little harder and said her name a little louder.

"Mom, Mom, wake up." Still no movement from her or dad. I tried again, shaking her again, a little harder, saying her name even louder. Then, out of nowhere, I screamed.

"Mommmmm!"

Dad rolled over. "What?" He yelled.

"Mom, mom. She won't wake up!" I was screaming and pointing at my mom.

Within a few seconds, Sher ran into the room. She stood at the foot of mom's bed, yelling "What Malina? What happened?"

Before Sher could finish asking me what happened, dad was turning mom over, at that second saying "Mama, mama wake up! Wake up baby!" As he turned her over, I saw it, the most horrifying thing I would ever see in my life. Moms eyes were shut, but her lips were blue, purple, her face completely drained of color.

I screamed as loud as I could scream. "Mama, mama!" I was already hysterical.

Dad jumped out of their bed screaming, "Shirley! Shirley! Mama wake up! Wake up!" Baby please wake up!" Dad was panicked. He had no idea what to do. He was shaking her limp body.

Mom lay there, lifeless, no color to her face, eyes shut and her purple blue lips, I could only stare in complete shock. I continued screaming and crying "Mom, mom! Please mom wake up, please wake up mommy."

Dad was shaking her and trying to wake her, but there was no life in her.

Sher screamed "Daddy!"

Dad yelled, "Call the operator Sher, call the operator!" Instinct had to have set in with Sher, I heard her saying our address, telling the operator all she could, through her tears, my screaming, and dad calling out for mom to please, please wake up. Dad was yelling "Mama, mama!"

I was crying out of control. "Mama please, mama please wake up."

Panic, there was complete and utter panic. All the kids were in mom and dads room now screaming and yelling, possibly not really understanding what was happening.

At this point, I think poor Danny was screaming just because everyone else was, and he was just so scared. Dad had no idea what to do, I just recall watching him go from the bed to try and wake mom to walking in circles, lost, literally going in circles, yelling

"Mama, mama wake up, please wake up! Shirley baby please wake up!" While shaking her and hugging her.

I have no idea how many minutes passed before the ambulance arrived. Sher had called our friends mom that lived across the street. She came running, still in her pajamas and rollers in her hair, already crying and hysterical when she climbed the steps to enter our house. Not really knowing what to do her self, she did the first thing she thought to do, she ushered all of us kids outside just as the ambulance arrived.

Sher was the only one allowed to stay inside, seems she could stay a bit in control, compared to me and dad. I heard screaming and crying from inside the house, dad, Sher, and our friend's mom.

The police arrived at the same moment the ambulance did. Every adult that showed up ordered us kids stay to outside except Sher. Sher stayed on the phone calling grandma and relative after relative. Within minutes dads sisters arrived crying and screaming. Dad kept walking out on the porch with the most horrid look on his face, yet made no eye contact with any of us as if he didn't see us at all. Almost like we were invisible.

Me, J.J., Danny, Becky, and Carrie cried uncontrollably. I could not stop crying.

"I want my mama, I want my mama!" I said to every adult going into or coming out of our house. The paramedics were in there, what seemed like hours. I just kept thinking she is going to wake up and say "I'm ok kids, don't cry."

I was hysterical, I was in shock. I felt like pulling my hair out, scratching off all my skin.

I didn't know what to do. Walking back and forth on the porch crying, desperately trying to get back in the house several times, only to be stopped by a police officer. I could see dad in his room looking toward their bed, looking on as the paramedics worked on mom. I couldn't see mom at all, from where I stood. I could only see the paramedics, the cops, and Sher on the phone.

Dad kept saying, "Shirley, wake up baby, please wake up."

I screamed as loud as I possibly could "Mom, mom!"

Then for reasons I did not understand, the paramedics started to leave. Without mom! "What? What happened?" I pleaded with them. "Is my mama ok?" I pushed past them and tried to run inside but the cop stopped me again. "Baby you can't go in there." The cop hugged me.

Sher and dad were in the room with mom alone with a cop. I could see Sher's' face, she looked horrified. Dad, I believe was in shock.

"Mama, Mama." He just kept saying.

I tried to get in the house to see my mom.

"I want my mama, I want my mama, please let me go to my mom." I begged and begged, but no one would listen to me.

Sher walked outside to check on the kids. Such a panicked look on her face. She was moving like a robot. They kids were all on the porch crying. Sher tried her best to comfort all of them, but there was no way to do that. Sher was also in shock. We had no idea what was going on.

I was on the porch while the cops talked to dad.

What was wrong with everyone? Why was my mom just laying there on the bed and no one was helping her? Why wouldn't anyone help her?

Just then, aunt Dolly and Uncle Bill drove up. Seemed he didn't even put the car in park, he was just out of the car and up the steps in seconds. Aunt Dolly stayed in the car, but she knew by all of us crying it was bad. She was too scared to get out of the car. Uncle Bill ran in the house but was also stopped by the police officer.

"She's my sister!" He yelled at the cop.

"Shirley, Shirley!" He screamed mom's name.

Dad came out of the room.

"What happened Johnny? What happened?" He screamed at dad in disbelief.

"I don't know Bill, we just woke up and she wouldn't wake up." Dad's eyes were already swollen from crying. Dad tried to explain through tears, crying, and hysteria.

"What happened to my sister?" Bill screamed in my dads face.

"I don't know. I swear I don't know." My dad cried back.

The look on Uncle Bill's face, the hate in his eyes, dad was already being judged. Already... Not even seeing moms lifeless body, the fact that there was not one scratch on her, no knife wound, no gun shots, Bill already assumed dad killed her.

The cop made uncle Bill leave the house. Brother or not, he had no right to be there yelling. He got back in the car with aunt Dolly.

I could hear him saying, "We need to get to mama before she gets here!"

What were they going to do? What were they gonna tell grandma, no one knew anything at this point, only that mom was dead, the cops gave no details. I didn't care about any of them, I cared about no one. All I wanted was my mom.

I could not stop crying. I was hysterical; we all were for that matter. People were coming, going, crying, and asking questions and shouting.

Then I saw a car drive up, a car that made it definite. It was a car that was to take her to the morgue. Now I knew for sure my mom had died. But how could she be dead? She was young, she was beautiful, and she was healthy. How could this even be possible?

Why would a car from the morgue be here? Why wasn't someone, anyone taking my mom to the hospital, hook her up to a breathing machine, anything, just do something to help her? Why wasn't someone, anyone helping her? Why wasn't dad, of all people, making them help her? Why would all these people just leave her on that bed and not help her?

I honestly blocked out everyone and every thing. I couldn't see anyone, dad, Sher or any of the kids. Everyone was now a blur. Images, coming and going of no particular interest to me.

I wanted desperately to go to my mom's bed, kneel down beside her bed, and beg her to wake up. Maybe if she hears my voice, hears me beg she will wake up. I visualized being by her bedside, kneeling down, holding her hand, whispering to her, 'Wake up mama, please, if you don't they are going to take you away, and I will never see you again.'

I knew what death was, though I was not allowed to attend my grandpas funeral, I did know when people die, life was over for them. I also know the pain thrust upon the survivors. I had seen my own mom agonize over her own father's death, but she at least had time to deal with his death. As much as he suffered and the pain mom endured watching him suffer, she at least got to say good-bye. But this! No dear God this could not be happening. WHYYYYYYYYY??? I screamed.

Watching all these blurs come and go, I literally wanted to hit all of them as they passed by me. . I contemplated running into that old house I hated so much, grab my dads' machine gun and shoot every bastard that walked into our house that wouldn't help mom.

I was suffocating. I was choking to death. I couldn't breathe. My mind went completely blank…

# 47

The next thing I knew I was alone, on a bunk bed. I didn't recognize where I was, whose bed, or whose house, but I was on the top bed of someone's bunk bed.

When I opened my eyes, it appeared the ceiling was a few inches from my face, giving me the feeling that the ceiling had collapsed on me. I was Closter phobic for an instant. I literally had to roll off the bed to avoid hitting my head on the ceiling.

As I stood up, I could hear his voice. It was Uncle Bill's voice but this wasn't his house. I had no clue as to where I was, or how I got there. Walking quietly through each room, I could hear people talking outside on the front porch. It was my Grandma, Aunt Dolly, Uncle Bill, and Aunt Lily.

Grandma was crying, and then I heard someone say my dads' name. Grandma was the first to see me standing in the doorway. She instantly jumped up from the chair she was sitting on.

"Oh my baby!" Grandma cried, as she grabbed me and hugged me, squeezing me so tight, trying her best to comfort me, comfort herself.

I began, once again, to cry.

"Grandma, I want my mom, I want to go home."

They all began to cry even louder of the thought of me wanting to go home to my mom. The pain they must have felt knowing that was never gonna happen.

"No baby, you stay here with us for now." Grandma said in between her cries and her cracking voice.

"Grandma please take me to my mom, please grandma." I yelled.

Grandma looked at me, horrified of the reaction I was having, not really knowing what to do.

"Dolly here, take her inside." Grandma said as she passed me to Dolly.

"No!" I pushed Dolly as she tried to comfort me.

"I don't want to go inside, I want to go home."

Dolly forced me back in the house as if I had done something wrong. She tried to be kind to me by bringing me food to eat and something to drink. I had no desire for food; I wanted nothing from any of them. I just left it on the table, ignoring her instructions that I needed to eat.

I went back to the bedroom and sat on the bottom bunk crying.

Why was I here? Why wasn't I with my brothers and sisters? Why was I alone without any of them?

I was shaking, scared and miserably sad. I could hear people talking and asking each other questions.

I literally just sat there. I don't want to be here in this room alone. I want to go home.

For once in my life, I wanted to be in that rat-infested house, I wanted my brothers and sisters, I even wanted my dad, and mostly I wanted my mom...

I screamed "Heeeeellp me, someone please help me."

The next thing I realized, every one of them was in the room with me, all around me asking me a lot of questions.

"Were your mom and dad fighting last night?"

"Did you hear any thing?"

"Tell us exactly what happened."

So many questions, so many different voices, I didn't even recognize who was asking which question. One question would begin before the first one was answered. Over and over the same questions.

I was scared, tired, and all alone. I hated everyone for asking me things I could not answer. I didn't know what to say, whose question to answer first, and I surely didn't want to make up a story, so I told the truth.

I told them I heard what sounded like mom crying, then I heard dad say don't cry mama, then I heard nothing, nothing at all.

No one said a word, each just staring at me. I believe Grandma fainted, next thing I know there was an ambulance taking her to the hospital. Even after grandma was hauled off in the ambulance, I was still bombarded with questions. I answered everything I possibly could, not understanding why they were still asking so many questions.

Then as if to save me, the phone rang, it was dad.

"Yes, we have her here." Uncle Bill said.

I suppose dad must have asked, "Why did you take her?"

"Because," Uncle Bill said. "She was just so upset; we didn't want her to see her mom being taken out of there."

Then Uncle Bill said "Hold on."

He looked at me and said. "Your dad wants to talk to you."

I was crying before I ever got to the phone.

"Hello." I cried.

"Malina are you ok?" He asked in such a kind voice. I could only cry. I didn't answer him, I couldn't answer him.

"Do you want to come to Aunt Gloria's house with your brothers and sisters?

"Yes." I was hysterical again.

"Put Bill on the phone baby." I handed Bill the phone without looking at him.

I heard dad scream. "Ten minutes Bill, ten mother fucking minutes."

Bill, Dolly, nor Grandma had asked dad if they could take me with them, I guess dad felt they had kidnapped me.

Without saying a word to me, Uncle Bill instructed Lily to take me to my Aunts house.

Not a word was spoken between us while we drove to Aunt Gloria's'. All I did was cry.

Uncle Bill and Dolly were too afraid of what may happen if they went with me, so they sent me with the neutral relative, Lilly.

When we arrived at Aunt Gloria's, everyone was there, just as it always was during the holidays, only everyone was crying. Dad wasn't there, but Sher was the first to greet me and hug me and hold on to me. Hugs, hugs and more hugs from everyone, everywhere. I hated it. All these relatives hugging me non stop.

I was suffocating once again. Unable to catch my breath. I knew everyone meant well, but I didn't want to be touched by anyone.

Aunt Gloria came to me and took me inside where all the kids were. She prepared me a plate of food and told me I had to eat. I hadn't eaten all day; actually, I hadn't eaten since the night before when mom had made pork and beans and wieners. But I wasn't hungry, I wasn't thirsty, my heart was literally in my throat. My head was pounding, about to explode. All I wanted was my mom. .

Aunt Mary came in the kitchen and said. "Malina you have to eat, you must eat something, just one bite of food at least, please."

I saw the concerned look on her face for me, so I took one bite of food, and even that bite had me sick to my stomach.

Becky was sitting next to me, her eyes swollen from crying so much.

All dads' sisters were in the kitchen now, their husbands and even dads mom, standing there staring at me. Someone handed me a glass of water, but I couldn't drink it. My throat was dry feeling as if someone had poured sand down my throat and said. "Here drink this."

I reached for a napkin and blew my nose then tried to take another bite of food, but it was impossible.

Then, just as it had happened at Bill's it began, the thousands of questions of, what, if anything had happened to mom the night before.

I was surrounded again, nowhere to run, no one to help me. The only person who could've helped was my mom, but I knew she wasn't there. I looked around for Sher, she was the only other person that would be brave enough to stand up and say, "Leave her alone." But she too wasn't there.

Already drained from the previous million questions I told them that I heard mom crying and dad comforting her telling her not to cry.

"Is that all you heard?" Someone asked me.

"Yes." I said.

Then out of nowhere, Becky said. "I heard her choking for air." As Becky did a mock gasping sound...

Everyone froze where they were standing... Some had to turn away.

"I didn't hear that." I assured them all I heard was mom crying. Becky said. "No, I heard her trying to breathe."

It was obvious by Becky's comments they all thought the same thing, dad smothered mom.

Aunt Gloria started crying so loud Uncle David had to take her out of the room. This was dad's family we were talking to now, not moms. I cringed thinking if Becky had been with me at Bill's and Becky told them mom was gasping for air, I do believe Bill would have gotten his gun and went looking for dad, though I don't believe he would have gotten close enough to shoot him, because Ray simply would have blown Bill away.

Mom's family was asking questions trying to find out what happened to her. Dad's family was trying to get answers also, but in reality, everyone came up with the same conclusion, dad killed her. The accusations would eventually start flying. It was just a matter of time. But by whom, no one dared.

Every thing was a blur for me the rest of the night. I hated everyone within 100 miles of me. I just wanted to go home, be with my mama.

Please mama, walk through the door, and take me out of here. Pleaseeeee. I cried, cried, and begged her to come get me. Please. Please Please mama.

# 48

We were still at Aunt Gloria's house. Dad was nowhere to be found; I assumed he was home alone.

I really knew nothing about funerals, death, and the whole process of it all, but one thing was certain, its true, the empty, horribly sad depressed feelings you have when someone dies. But this wasn't just anyone, this was my mom. The only reason I was even alive.

I wanted desperately to wake up in my bed, with my sisters, mom in the kitchen cooking breakfast, dad out trying to score....

When I opened my eyes, it dawned on me where I was, and what had happened... I didn't have the strength to get out of the bed. The instant an adult saw me they began asking questions. Though I was a kid, I knew everyone was curious about what had happened.

How did mom, just die? Just like that? Everyone knew dad's reputation, he was abusive towards mom, he was jealous, and she was pretty much a prisoner in our home. However, what everyone wondered was "Could he actually kill Shirley." Was he that much of a monster to kill his wife, take her from her six kids? Everyone was over anxious wanting answers.

Aunt Mary tried her best to protect me from all the questions and comments that were gonna be thrust at me once I was awake.

My cousins were also curious, but not to the extent that the adults were, mostly they wanted to know if I were ok? Did I feel like talking? Was I hungry?

I was in a daze, a lost soul. I did nothing that day but cry and cry. My dad finally showed up, an entourage of men around him everywhere he went. Ray no more than two feet from dad's side the entire time. Dad looked horrible. His always-handsome face was now undeniably worse for the wear. He hadn't eaten or shaved in over twenty-four hours.

Once he removed his sunglasses, his eyes were swollen from crying, as if he had been in a fight.

Each one of us he saw made him cry even more. He did not know what to say to any of us, he couldn't comfort us the way that we needed to be comforted. We couldn't comfort him at all...

He cried and cried, talking to all the men that had re-gathered at Aunt Gloria's. His mom and sisters trying their absolute best to comfort him. Each trying to ask him what happened without seeming suspicious. He paced back and forth he cried, he paced, he cried.

Time stood still it seemed. Not certain what day it was, what time it was, or even how, but somehow we all wound up at the funeral home. This was the night before mom's actual funeral.

So many people were there, crying, hugging one another, talking, every one it seemed was in shock, everyone in disbelief.

It was just so much confusion. Sit here, come here, go there, do this, what happened? Who did what? Where was she? Who found her? What did you do? What did your dad do? Who called the operator?

The questions were endless. Again, one question started before I got the answers out to the previous questions. The exact way it had been at Uncle Bill's house and Aunt Gloria's.

My brothers sat quietly, normally the two loudest kids in the room, now just sitting, not knowing what to do, same as Carrie and Becky. They all just sat side by side motionless, looking up as people walked past them.

Then Aunt Mary came and got me, not all six of moms kids, just me.

"Come on Malina you have to see your mom."

For just a split second, I thought mom was sitting in the next room, waiting for me to come get her.

Aunt Mary took me by the hand. I could hardly see, every face a blur. I heard my dad crying, as Mary led me down a hallway. Suddenly she stopped in the doorway, what seemed like one hundred feet away was a bronze coffin. I couldn't see who was in it.

Someone had made a mistake, my mom wasn't dead?

Aunt Mary guided me into the room. As we got close to the coffin, I saw my mom.

First, I saw her hair, which wasn't the way mom wore it. I expected to see her hair in a French twist or even a ponytail, but her eyes…

This isn't my mom, my moms eyes are green, beautiful, beautiful green, I can't see her eyes.

Very few times in my life did I see my mom asleep, she was always the first to wake in the mornings, the last to go to sleep at night.

I always wondered when did she ever slept, always so busy taking care of us she never had the time. The rare occasion I did see her sleep was when she would come from the hospital after having another baby and pass out of pure exhaustion.

"I can't see my moms eyes, wake up mommy please wake up mom." I screamed as loud as I possibly could. Dad went crazy. He ordered Mary to take me to the front lobby.

I saw nothing or no one after that. I woke and I was at Aunt Gloria house again, did an identical routine that I had done for forty-eight hours. One bite of food, no sleep, question after question. People in my face non-stop wanting to know details I wasn't able to supply them.

These were relatives, dads' relatives and they just couldn't stop. They asked more questions than a detective might have. Oh no, what if I had to answer questions to a detective. God please this can't be real.

I was awakened the next day to someone handing me a blue dress to put on. Moving now like a robot. Every bit of energy was draining from me. Always a skinny child, I could feel my bones piercing through my skin. Having not eaten but two bites of food in three days, I was weak and shaking.

"Hurry kids, we must be at the funeral home by ten." Aunt Gloria was doing her best to get us ready.

Someone, not quite sure who, but someone took it upon themselves to suggest Danny, Carrie, and J.J. not be allowed to attend mom's funeral. Convincing dad it would be too stressful for the three youngest kids. Should they be allowed to say one last good bye to their mom or that they should remember her as she was? How does any one make such a decision?

Now it was just me, Sher and Becky, sitting in the hallway of the funeral home. For some reason no one was allowed in the room where moms body was. Through tear-filled eyes, a shaking sick body and an explosive headache, I spoke to no one.

What I gathered, through all the whispering and the comments from the funeral home staff, the medical examiner was rechecking moms' body even though they had already performed an autopsy... Not quite sure what they were looking for. However, autopsies normally occurred when foul play was suspected. Mom was after all, a young, beautiful, healthy woman, and her husband was on his way to a trial that pretty much could've landed him in prison for a very long time.

Suspicious? Sure it was.

Dad the suspect? Without a doubt.

It's terrible how people will whisper, talk, and gossip at a funeral right under your nose... Did they think I couldn't hear the things they were saying?

So that's what was going on? Finally some kind of reason for all this. Some medical team was checking mom's body for bruises, cuts, missing hair, dad's fingerprint around her neck, anything they could point the finger at dad and say, "You killed her." Everyone was there just staring, mostly at dad, wanting to comfort him, but being standoffish just in case he had actually killed her. Ray, the loyal soldier, right by dad's side whether he killed my mom or not.

Dad looking so sad, so terribly sad, and guilty. Not guilty for killing her, but rather guilty for being so damn mean to her, guilty for not being a good husband.

At that moment, in spite of my hate for him beating her, I didn't think he killed her, but I knew he was a horrible husband to her, and that was the guilt he had to live with.

The more questions people asked me, the more my mind wandered.

Everyone wanted to know the position I found her body.

"She was laying on her right side." I said over and over, to everyone that asked. As though she was asleep, I remembered so clearly.

If anyone was suspecting dad smothered my mom, I could tell them she wasn't lying as if she had fought off strangulation or suffocation.

If anyone thought she was gasping for air, I didn't find her body in a position to suggest she was trying to catch her breath.

She was asleep, in a deep peaceful sleep.

I only realized something was terribly wrong when I saw her blue purple lips and the fact she never opened her eyes. Even with all her kids screaming and crying mom never woke up.

Since, by order of the medical examiner, no one was allowed in the viewing room, every one waited in the hallway and lobby. People were gathered in small groups talking amongst themselves, some people stopped and hugged us, some people went outside to smoke. Once in a while I could hear someone laugh, wondering at the time, what was so funny?

Out of nowhere, I heard a horrible scream. The funeral director ran into the room next to the room mom was in.

I heard screaming and yelling, and people running all over the place trying to figure out what happened.

I was sitting down, staring at the floor, only half hearing the commotion around me, not really caring about anything.

No longer looking up as people scurried past me. Some one tapped me on the shoulder, I looked up, and it was screwy. Screwy and one of his brothers.

He looked at me really sad and said, "I'm sorry about your mom, she was a really nice lady."

I believe I thanked him and his brother, and then they just disappeared through the crowded hallway. Before they got out of the building, but as he and his brother tried, at least it seemed to me they tried to get out of there very quickly, I heard the secretary say.

"It was two young boys, two of them."

There were many kids there, from our school and relatives' kids, all she could say was. "It was two young men." Which, in all fairness could've been anyone.

I really had no idea, or what to think about any of this. Just then I looked down the hallway with people running every where and walking up and down the hallway, Screwy and his brother looked back in my direction, not looking at me per say, just looking, then disappeared out the side door just as I heard someone say. "Oh my goodness, someone put a cigarette in his mouth."

Whose mouth? I wondered.

Turns out, when the family members of the deceased man in the room next to mom, walked in to view him, they screamed because someone had placed a cigarette in his mouth.

It was a disgraceful, horrible, disrespectful thing for anyone to do. Who could do such a terrible thing, at such a sad time?

I would not have bet my life on it, but something tells me old screwy or his brother could very well have been the culprits.

They just had a glare in their eyes as they walked out the side door. I would never have accused him or his brother for that matter, after all, he had come to pay respects to my mom, and if it were him or his brother that did that unthinkable act, he or his brother had disrespected another family.

No one really knew who did it, there were literally hundreds of teens in the funeral home at that time, no names were ever mentioned, but it's just something in me that said, 'Yes, that class clown did it. That crazy boy!

Years and years later, I heard that the video tape was played from that day, and I was wrong. Poor screwy, he just looked guilty but was as innocent as he could be.

Gossip told me dads men found out who the culprits were and let's just say, they didn't get away with shit.

# 49

Finally, we were allowed back in the room with mom. People were everywhere, walking up to mom, and praying, crying saying goodbye to her.

We were all escorted to the church area of the funeral home. I had no idea what was being said, who was where, who was saying what... I was sick.

Aunt Mary sat with me, holding my hand as my mom always had. I believe Sher and Becky were sitting with dad. I really couldn't see them. There was just so much going on, and it seemed so rushed, as the funeral director may run out of time before another funeral was to begin.

There were so many people, hundreds of them. How do you organize so many people? Everyone, of course, wants to pay their last respects, they shake your hand, they hug you, they tell you just how sorry they are, everyone in one long line waiting. I know this is how it is supposed to be, but my short life seemed too frail to handle all this.

I looked up for a brief moment and saw people walking past moms body, people kissing her, people hugging dad, people hugging Sher and Becky.

Just people everywhere. I had no idea what was going on, no one explained any of this to me, they just told me what to do and when to do it.

In my heart, I guess I knew this was how it was supposed to be. I knew everyone loved her, and would miss her, and was sad, and shocked by her death because she was so beautiful and so young. Everyone instinctively wanted to show their respects to mom, to dad, to us kids, but nothing at all mattered to me. Mom was not going to come back. I did not want to be there.

Aunt Mary said. "Come on Malina, we must say goodbye to your mom."

Goodbye ? Goodbye? No I did not want to say goodbye to my mom.

This was so final, and at that moment, I realized this was the last time I would ever see her face again. I would never get a hug from her; I would never hear her voice. I would never see her smile, or laugh, or play with the kids or dance with us, or even worse, she would never tell me she loved me again.

"No I can't." I whispered to Aunt Mary.

"You must." She said.

"No." I cried out. "I can't, I can't say good bye."

She took me by my hand, not quite dragging me, but definitely making me go to my mom's coffin. I objected the entire time.

There I was, standing one foot from my mom's coffin, looking down at her as she lay, asleep, never to wake again. I stood there, just staring at the most beautiful mother in the world.

I screamed, "Wake up mommy, they are going to put you in the ground, you will not be able to get out, you will be all alone, please, please wake up. Why won't you wake up mommy?"

I was hysterical; everyone in the church was hysterical. Dad could not take it anymore. Sal took dad outside with Ray.

I was out of control crying. Mary got my hand and told me to go with her.

"No." I yelled. "I want my mom." As I pulled away from her.

Sher and Becky were also hysterical. I guess watching me was just too hard for them. As Mary took me away from my moms coffin I looked toward the over crowded church and noticed moms side of the family on one side of the chapel, dads on the other side, and the gangsters standing in the back of the chapel. What was this? Why was everyone separated? She was every ones family. Mom loved everyone, everyone loved her.

Mary took me out side. I sat in a car and cried and waited and cried.

Finally, everyone came out, one by one, with their tears and their sad faces and their hugs and their kisses. I didn't want to look at anyone. I didn't want anyone to look at me.

Mary came, got me, and put me in the funeral car. She sat in the car beside me, Sher, Becky, and dad.

Honestly, poor, poor dad, he had no idea what he was up against. He never looked more scared in his life.

During the drive to the cemetery Mary asked dad if he was sure he wanted us kids to attend the burial.

He looked at each of us, didn't say a word at first, then he asked each of us if we wanted to go to the burial. Sher and Becky said yes right away.

He looked at me, but I didn't say a word. He told Mary.

"Just stay with her."

Once at the cemetery we remained in the family car for a few minutes, then we were escorted from the car to the burial site.

Standing there in front of our designated seats, waiting for all the people to gather, the pallbearers brought moms casket out of the car. Six men placed her coffin on the stand that was supporting the coffin before it would be lowered into the ground.

Twenty minutes, Thirty minutes I have no idea how long the actual ceremony lasted. Before I knew, everyone was lining up again to say their last goodbyes. Then without any warning at all dad says, "wait." He whispered to the funeral director for a moment. Shaking his head yes, the funeral director takes something from dads hands, he and another man dressed in a black suit, opened moms coffin and placed her wedding ring on her finger.

I believe that was unheard of. To actually open the coffin at the cemetery. There I was looking right at mom. Mom lying in this beautiful coffin. One foot from being lowered into the ground. The beautiful green gown she was being buried in, that would have matched her beautiful green eyes if she could've only opened them.

Her beautiful face, her beautiful model hands, now with her wedding ring on, the one dad had just given her in March when they re-married.

It was just too much. Too much for everyone. I screamed and I screamed and I screamed.

Someone fainted; I think it was old Aunt Franny...

I had a pain in me; the type of pain you feel inside you that you know will never ever go away. It was just all so real now. This was the spot, the exact spot my mom was going to be for eternity.

There was no begging, praying, pleading, asking her to come back. It was definite now, she was gone. All my love for my mommy was right there, all the love she had, all the love I had. All the hugs, all the kisses, all the future I would ever dream about, all the love she would ever show me was there in that coffin. I was going out of my mind.

I do not know how to live without her. Dear God I want to die. How do I ever live without all that love?

Then I saw it, the most unexpected thing I thought I would ever witness. With all the confusion, crying, and hysteria the cemetery employees started lowering mom's coffin into the ground, right there with all of us watching.

Dad went crazy screaming at the cemetery employees that were lowering her coffin.

"My god." Dad screamed, "Her kids are here, what is wrong with you?"

Dad started toward the two employees, possibly to shoot them, or knock the shit out of them, but Ray stopped him. Complete hysteria at this point.

I have no idea what possessed those men to do such a thing, such a disrespectful thing. They froze where they were, realizing just who dad, Ray and over one hundred other men just might be.

Dad instructed my aunts to get us to the car.

"No. I don't want to go." I screamed and ran to the coffin.

"Mom, mom please wake up, please don't leave me, please mom."

I was hugging the coffin, pounding on it, and pounding on it, trying to bust it open to get my mom out.

I could not stop pounding...

"Mommmmmy"...I screamed. 'Please mommy, I'm sorry, I'm sorry you were so sad. I'm sorry if we didn't mind you. Please. Please don't leave me here, I can't..."

Dad interrupted me by trying to get me from the coffin, but he couldn't. Dad, Mary, Gloria, everyone was screaming and crying trying to get me from the coffin.

I believe they were afraid I was going to fall into the six-foot pre-dug hole or die of a heart attack. If I were going to die, it would have been from a broken heart.

"No, no I want my mom, I want my mom, dad, please bring her back, please dad, I want my mom." I was looking directly into my dads eyes. Dad was just crying too much to help me.

"Malina I can't baby, she's gone, I'm so sorry, I'm so sorry."

Ray was trying to get dad, who was trying to get me. Everyone, even the cemetery employees, were crying.

"Mom, mom." I screamed so loud it echoed throughout the entire cemetery.

Some of the family members walked away, they just couldn't handle what they were witnessing.

Relatives were holding one other crying, almost as loud as me. It seemed everyone was hysterical. I was in shock.

"Dad I want my mom, I want my mom." That's all I remembered. All I could remember... I couldn't go on.

# 50

The family car waited and waited for dad. It was obvious no one was going to rush him. I mean really, how can you take a man away from his wife's coffin?

Dad just stared and stared, possibly not believing what had happened, possibly wondering what to do next.

I know he was talking to her; I could see his lips moving but couldn't make out what he was saying. I watched him, everyone watched him. Everyone may be suspicious of him, but only dad knew the truth.

Ray tried his best to get dad to leave but he wouldn't budge.

"Come on Johnny, let's go." Ray tried persuading him.

Dad wouldn't move. He stood just like a statue made of cement. He did not move. He wasn't even blinking his eyes. He was just staring at mom's coffin.

I tried to get out of the car but Aunt Mary wouldn't let me.

Ray finally came to the funeral car that we were sitting in.

"Take the kids to your house please Gloria; I'll get Johnny there as soon as I can." He said.

"Ok." Aunt Gloria said. "Watch after him Ray." Gloria said through teary eyes.

As the limousine driver attempted to leave the cemetery, I started screaming. I desperately tried to open the car door so I could jump out and run back to my mom. I couldn't get out of that car or past my aunts. They had no idea how to control me, what to do or say to help me through all this.

The driver stopped the car for a brief second, not knowing weather to stop the car, drive the car, or throw us all out of the car. I screamed and screamed for my mom. I was out of control again; everyone in the car was crying and trying to comfort me. I kept telling everyone to leave me alone. I literally hated anyone to touch me. Don't talk to me, don't touch me, and don't ask me questions I can not answer.

Why was my beautiful mother dead? She was young she was beautiful. There were no gun shot wounds, there were no knife cuts, there were no bruises, there was nothing that I could see to tell me how, I went to sleep at night then wake the next morning to go to school, and she's gone, just like that, gone. No signs of trauma, or beatings, she's just gone. Please somebody, explain to me why? What happened? How did she die? Why did she die?

Somehow, the driver managed to get us to Aunt Gloria's, safely, where hundreds of people were waiting outside on her front lawn. Relatives, gangsters, kids, teachers of ours, school friends. I really didn't even want to get out of the car. I wanted to just sit there. I wanted to be alone, I wanted to be alone, or with my mom, I knew I would get neither.

Someone, maybe Sher, tried to get me out of the funeral car. Ol' bossy, I would have fought her too, right there. All her years of bossing us around, I was willing to take her on, not because I hated her or anything, I just wanted to take my pain out on someone else. I was just so damn angry at the world.

Eventually, reluctantly I got out of the car, knowing what I was up against.

Hugs, hugs, kisses, hugs. I'm sure I should have been grateful everyone cared enough to try to comfort me, but none of these hugs was my moms. It wasn't the same for me. It just wasn't the same.

I went in to the house, not wanting to eat or drink anything. There were literally hundreds of different types of food people had brought to feed the hundreds of people there. I sat in the dining room, not wanting to look at any one or talk to anyone.

One of my aunts brought me some food and insisted I had to eat. "You must eat Malina, you are going to get sick if you don't eat honey." Food would have no taste for me; I just couldn't stomach the thought of eating. I sipped on a glass of soda, and almost threw it up because it was so sweet.

I wanted some of mom's Kool-aid. I wanted some of mom's food, I wanted her to call us kids into the kitchen to eat, but it wasn't going to happen, ever again.

Everything in me wanted to get up out of that house and run as fast and as far as I possibly could and never look back, ever.

Instead, I sat there looking at people going through the motions of a funeral routine, I just didn't know what came next, what was to be expected.

What was supposed to happen next, sit and let everyone stare at me, talk about what they think happened? My head was pounding. This was the most horrible pain in the world.

Not the pain in my head, but the pain in my heart. The worst pain was my loss, the mother I loved so much. Now she was gone, gone forever, with so many questions I myself wanted to ask, and answers I wanted to hear. Like, why? How? What did happen? Why didn't dad know she was dead? Why didn't I get out of bed when I heard her crying? I had promised her I would never let him hurt her. Why am I doing this to myself?

I never would ever get over this pain. I just knew there was no cure for this. How could there be?

I got up from the table and went to the restroom, if for no other reason than for some kind of privacy. While in there, I actually looked in the medicine cabinets for a razor blade to slice my wrist. .

I stayed in there so long a line began to form outside the restroom door of kids and adults waiting to get in there. I took my time anyway, I just didn't care.

Finally, when I thought someone was gonna kick the door down of fear I had sliced my wrist, I opened the door and walked past all of them. I heard a few sighs of relief that I hadn't actually killed myself.

While outside, my brothers were half playing with the other kids. I wondered if they really understood what was happening. How in the world would anyone ever make these two little boys understand what they had lost?

I stared at them, admiring how cute and innocent they were, wondering why?

Then dad arrived with Ray right by his side... Dad was so tired; he could hardly get out of the car. He stood by Ray's car for a few moments, looking around, just looking.

For some reason I believe he was looking for mom amongst all the faces of friends and relatives. I believe he forgot for a second why we were all there, and he was looking for her smiling face to pop out of the crowd and say.

"Here I am Johnny, don't look so scared."

Then the look on his face told me he realized mom wasn't there at all. He had left her alone, at the cemetery, in a coffin, all alone, nobody there to take care of her, as she had taken care of all of us.

He must have realized where he was when J.J. and Danny ran to him. He hugged them and he cried. One by one we all went to him, hugged him, he cried even more.

What was he going to do?

Someone, maybe Uncle David called him into the house, to eat, or to talk, or to just sit down before he collapsed. It was obvious someone and or everyone wanted to hear his version of what had happened that night.

It goes without saying, over the past three days no one had told him mine and Becky's version of the night mom died.

This was all his family here; surely, they were going to question him. Maybe he would tell everyone what happened. He owed everyone an explanation, I mean it's not everyday you lay next to your wife at night and the next morning she is dead.

Who did he owe an explanation to? Would he even give an explanation? He was Johnny G; he could do as he pleased.

Everyone had already heard mine and Becky's version. It seemed now they were going to want to hear his.

So much commotion. People eating, people talking, some even laughed here and there again. Maybe again discussing the good memories of mom. .

Why were all these people here? Were they here just to be near the gangster Johnny G? Were they here to see six kids crying for their mom? Were they here for the food? Did they have nowhere else to be on a weekday?

I was deliberately being mean and hateful and I knew it and I hated myself for being like that... Something was happening to me. It seemed my childhood innocence was gone. Honestly, how could I be nice to anyone? The mother I loved so much was gone now, forever. I did not understand because I was just a child, and I was filled with so much hate. Hate for everyone I came in contact with, and I didn't know why I was so angry with everyone.

A snow cone truck passed while we were all outside, with its joyful music blasting the neighborhood. All the little kids were yelling, "I want one, I want one." And of course the gangster men pulled out their bank rolls and bought a snow cone for any and everyone that wanted one. I hated the snow cone driver, because he was happy and smiling, of course he was smiling, he just hit a gold mine with all these little kids. I hated his smile and the fact that he was happy. I wanted to yell, "Get out of here you disrespectful bastard, my mom just died."

*Malina, Malina, stop Malina!* Even hearing my own voice talking to me in my head, I began hating myself.

I was outside, just staring at all these people, and wishing everyone was gone, away from there, away from Gloria's house, away to another town, away to another planet for all I cared. Actually I didn't care, I just wanted everyone out of my sight. I looked around at Aunt Gloria's big porch and there was the big swing we would swing on for hours anytime we visited her... All the little kids were running around, getting their favorite flavor of snow cones, laughing and having fun. I guess they really didn't understand what had happened.

Adults were going and coming, some were smoking cigarettes, some were walking up and down Aunt Gloria's big long driveway, and others were standing around gossiping. I say gossiping because I could hear some saying "I wonder what happened? She was so young, how did she die?" On and on.

I was sitting alone on the swing, rethinking all the events of the past few days. I had a vision of everything, mom, dad, my brothers and sisters, all the people, the divided chapel, for a second I thought of screwy, causing such a ruckus in the funeral home, and for just a brief second my mind felt cleared.

I was lost in all my thoughts then I realized of all the people here, none was my mom's side of the family. This was my moms funeral, why wasn't my moms family here? What was it with these people?

While I was sitting there, one of my cousins came and sat beside me on the swing.

Marcy was Aunt Gloria's third daughter. She was the one I had always been the closest too. Marcy was the cousin that laughed the loudest and appreciated our talent nights anytime Aunt Gloria brought them to visit. Marcy was the cousin that smiled the most, and always made me feel welcome. I suppose Marcy appreciated what she was blessed with, and tended to always want to share with us girls, especially me.

She would be the first to give me her slightly used clothes, saying "Oh Malina that will look so pretty on you." She never bragged that she had more, she just didn't ever point out I had less. She was like a sister to me.

"Do you need anything?" She asked.

"My mom." I said to her, not meaning to sound like a smart ass.

"Are you hungry?" She asked.

"No." I answered

I really wasn't wanting to conversate with anyone, perhaps she sensed it. She sat there a few more minutes then she asked if I wanted to go upstairs to her room and rest.

"No I'm not tired." I told her.

"Do you feel like talking about it?" She asked.

Marcy was the first person who didn't seem to be prying in my life, wanting to know every detail. She didn't ask what happened. She asked if I wanted to talk about it, giving me the choice, not drilling me for answers like every one else, asking, who? what? where?

The thousands of questions I had been asked over and over. I was aware people just wanted to know, but some people asked me the same questions over and over as if I might have lied and they were trying to catch me in a lie. Or so I felt.

Marcy honestly seemed concerned about me, not the gossip, or the fact that there might be a possibility dad killed my mom. She wanted to hear what I had to say. Somehow it seemed right to talk to her, at that point I felt like I just had to talk, so I told her everything I remembered.

Everything, from mom crying, to the bible, to my moms purple lips, to me waking up on a bunk bed, to me wanting to bust open the coffin with my fists when I was pounding on it to get my mom out. Everything I could remember, I shared it all with her.

Everything, except dad beating mom. I just didn't think I could get those words out of my mouth.

She was crying I was crying, but I felt there was now someone to confide in. Someone who wasn't gonna gossip, or assume, or judge, or be mean or talk shit. Marcy was my cousin, but she was also a friend. My friend I wanted to tell all my feelings to. We sat on that swing for hours talking about mom, her parents, her brothers and sisters, we even compared notes on how Sher, and Marcy's older sister Celia that were exactly alike, so bossy, so strong, yet the sisters that would protect us no matter what. I'm sure the people that walked past us as we sat on the swing could hear the things we said, but I said nothing I was ashamed of.

We kids had been informed we were going to stay at Aunt Gloria's for a day or two because I heard dad tell Aunt Gloria he wasn't ready for us to go home yet. Honestly, all I wanted right now was to go home and sleep in my bed, but dad wouldn't hear of it.

I can't remember what time it was, I only knew it was very late. Finally, everyone left and dad went home.

Aunt Gloria was exhausted but she did manage to sit with all six of us and tell us, if we wanted to stay with her for a few days we could, if we needed to talk she would listen, if we needed anything just ask her.

She was kind and she was trying to help, but there really wasn't any way to help me, maybe the little kids could be helped, but no one, not my cousin Marcy, my aunt or my dad could help me. Only my mom.

The next day after we woke and aunt Gloria fixed breakfast, I went through the motions of eating, getting dressed, bushing my hair, but everything seemed like such a waste of time.

I was doing what was expected of me, but I had no heart for any of it. Robot, you had better believe it. Just a mechanical person, with no feelings at all, but pure sadness, and emptiness.

Late that day dad came to pick us up and take us home. Seems every time he saw us he cried more and more. I guess it was expected... I didn't even know a person could shed as many tears as I had. So much pain in me.

Dad was about to take us home after almost a week since mom had died. It seemed a million years had passed, yet it was barely a week. All the emotions, the fears, the pain, the love I wanted, the mom I wanted to see, to talk to, and it had only been a week. Then it hit me. I had the rest of my life to deal with this. It just seemed it was impossible to go on.

Home, the house I hated so much. The place I wanted to burn to the ground, now it was the only place I would or could feel close to my mom.

He was taking us back there for the first time since mom had died. I wanted so bad to go home, see my mom, have my life back. It was never going to happen but I could not accept it.

He loaded us all in the car, the closer we got to our house the more I cried. As we turned the corner of our block, and pulled up in the yard, the first thing I saw was the little city mom had built for my brothers, still, exactly the way she had made it.

For a split second, I actually saw her sitting there, on the ground laughing and smiling and glowing with happiness, as we kids squealed with joy over the little city. I could see her, I could actually hear her laughing.

I cried and cried. Everyone in the car just starred at me.

"It's ok Malina." Dad said.

Ok? Ok? What are you talking about it, it's ok? It will never ever be ok with out my mom.

I hate you.

# 51

These are the things I wanted so badly to scream at him. He was crying because he was hurting so badly, but I was hurting more than he was. You're the bastard that beat her; you're the one that hurt her, not me. I'm the one that woke up and saw how violent you were with her. No one else knew what you had done to her, only me.

Now I had to go inside this house, the one that my mom spent so many years trying to make into a home for us, go inside with a monster and pretend everything would be ok.

Yes, I felt bad for my dad during the funeral, but now, seeing the house, the little city, it all came back to me.

Danny and J.J. got out of the car first and ran up the stairs, dad behind them to unlock the door. I thought to myself. 'Why do you even lock the front door?' There is nothing in this dump anyone would ever want to steal.

Dad unlocked the door and went in, the boys behind him, Becky and Carrie next, then Sher.

I slowly got out of the car, standing there, looking at that old piece of shit house, wondering how my legs would ever be able to get me up the five stairs.

Slowly I inched myself away from the car, inch by horrifying inch I climbed the stairs. I mean, who was I kidding? I definitely couldn't live outside.

I stood in the doorway.

Not even completely in the house yet, I could already smell my moms perfumes, her hair, her minty breath, her shampoo, her hairspray, her powder, everything that smelled of mom.

I saw no one as I walked past the front door, and had no idea where everyone went. It was like being the last person alone on earth. I literally just stood there waiting, and waiting, but what was I waiting for?

To get to our room I had to pass moms room, to get through mom's room I would have to pass her bed, the exact spot I had last seen her in this old house.

I couldn't do it. I just could not do it.

Dad walked in the living room, looked at me for a second.

"Come on Malina." He said as to persuade me to just walk through one time and it will be a synch the next time.

I began to slowly walk. Taking only baby steps. Halfway through the living room my legs would not move, as if someone had nailed my shoes to the nasty old linoleum floor. I was stuck, couldn't go forward, couldn't go back.

Sher was the one I remember getting me and helping me walk the rest of the way through the living room, eventually stopping in the doorway that separated mom's room from the living room.

"I can't Sher, I can't." My voice a mere whisper.

"Yes you can Malina. Come on I'll help you." She took one-step inside moms room and got my hand and said "Come on."

I just couldn't move... How was I ever gonna get from one room to the next? I couldn't even get one-step in the doorway of mom's room, let alone walk through every room in the house.

Then I saw it. Right in front of me, clear across mom's room, hanging on a door, hanging on a hanger, I saw it.

The dress mom had on the night she read the bible to me and Sher. The dress she had on the last night she was alive. I could not get to the dress quick enough; I almost fell over my own two feet trying to get to it. It was a dress with dark blue and dark green stripes, with solid green at the lower part of the dress.

Mom always looked so beautiful when she wore it. I grabbed the dress and hugged it and there was the smell of her perfume, her shampoo her hairspray her powder, all the things I smelled the second I walked in the house. For one tenth of a second she was there, there in the room with me, there in that dress, as if she had never taken it off. I was again crying uncontrollably. Dad attempted to hug me; he attempted to take the dress down from where it hung on the door of mom's closet.

"No dad no." I screamed.

He didn't know what to do, take it down or leave it hanging right there where I could see it. The horrible look on my face, knowing he might just consider taking it down, he re-hung it where all of us could see it.

There I was face to face with a dress, a dress, if I looked hard enough I could see my mom still wearing it, still smiling in it , brushing her hair in it, cooking in it, sitting with us kids watching TV in it, talking on the phone to dad in it.

Could he possibly be so cruel as to take it down? Would that be my punishment?

Shut up Malina, stop being a pain in the ass or I'll take your mom's dress down and you'll never see it again, I imagined hearing him say those hateful words to me.

No not even the meanest man in the world, the one I hated so much for beating mom, the one I felt so sad for when he acted like a complete jerk on the first day of school. The same man my heart was breaking for at mom's funeral. Not even he would punish me by taking her dress down.

Then I made the mistake of turning and facing her bed. Just as she had lay, on her right side, looking so sound asleep, so peaceful, just sleeping, I saw her, there on her bed, as if the past eight days had never happened.

Standing in the exact spot I had the day she had died. Screaming for her when dad turned her over and I saw her blue purple lips. Here it was all over again.

I screamed, and I screamed and I screamed, but this time I did not stop...

# 52

When I woke, I was in a hospital. Dad and Aunt Gloria were sitting in the room with me. Aunt Gloria was the first to get to me and said she was going to take me home with her.

"No, I want to go home." I cried.

Dad said, "Malina you have to go with Gloria."

"No dad I won't." I said as mean and stubborn as I possibly could, thinking to myself, did I really think it would be my choice?

What could anyone do to me now? Nothing any one would ever do could possibly hurt me more than I hurt at this very second.

Before dad could open his mouth to enforce his authority, the doctor walked in, papers in hand, papers to release me from the hospital.

Dad asked the doctor, "Should she stay with my sister? What do I do?"

The doctor sat down beside me and asked. "How do you feel Malina?"

Serious?" I thought. Of course, I did not respond to that question, that question did not deserve a response. The doctor looked at me for a few seconds then he looked at dad.

Again, dad asked, "What do we do?"

The doctor stood, then walked toward dad. "She will re-live this over and over, more than likely every time she enters the house until she is able to accept her mom's death."

"Actually going to your sister's house would only prolong the inevitable. She needs a tremendous amount of emotional support. Are there other children in the home?" The doctor asked.

"Yes." Aunt Gloria said. "Five more."

"It will take a lot of counseling and support for these children to understand, to be able to grieve properly, I strongly suggest you have them all speak with a therapist, and Mr. Guetarro, you need to emotionally support your children."

In other words "Gangster boy, you are now the designated mother and father, like it or not. Which I already knew the answer to that one. He wouldn't like it at all.

The doctor instructed dad to give me an aspirin for my headache. Was he as stupid as dad? Did this doctor think an aspirin would take all this pain away? Perhaps the entire bottle would.

The doctor did some hog wash, mumbo jumbo talk about how these things take time, blah blah blah.

I heard nothing else the doctor said. This quack couldn't feel my loss; he had no idea this charming bastard father of mine had beat my mom with a pistol. He had no idea my dad was mean to us kids, he had no idea of all the times my mom cried, or of all the times I pissed on myself just because he spoke.

I'm sure it was easy for an outsider to have a lot of sympathy for any man that had just buried his wife and was now forced to raise six kids alone.

He was looking into the eyes of a charming monster and he didn't even know it.

Dr. Frankenstein, I believe his damn name was, without a doubt, was being conned by a con artist. Johnny G. the con.

I refused to listen to anything else anyone said, thinking only of my mom.

I wanted to go home. I didn't want to go home.

If I go with Gloria then I won't be able to see any of the things that reminded me of mom. If I go home, it would be the constant reminder of my mom. Which would be harder?

Endure the sorrow every day that old house had, all the memories of mom, all the love, the pain, and sadness, or go with Gloria?

To what? No memories, no smell of moms perfume, no memories of moms laughter, nothing, just move on as if my mom never existed. I knew at that very second what I had to do.

I, a dumb ass kid, had to suck up all that heartbreak, all that unendurable pain of loss, all the crying, praying and begging for my mom's return and tuck it all away as if I felt nothing, just to please a monster. .

I had to put on a mask, pretend it was easy, as it seemed to me everyone else had done. Move on, so to speak. I had to move on as if this never ever happened, just so I wouldn't be ripped from the memories of the mother I loved so much, just to please this fucked up man I call my dad.

Why was I being punished? Was it me? Was it something I did? Was I being punished for all dad's mistakes in his gangster life? Was I being punished because my mom picked the wrong man to marry? Was it God punishing me? Because he certainly wasn't there for me.

I knew exactly what needed to be done, because really, no one knew what to do with me. None of these grown ups were in my skin, they were not in my brain and they damn sure were not in my heart. But to keep them from having to deal with their inadequacies, I would have to pretend, like a soul lost, as if I were wandering in a field of lilies, all alone in a maze, with no way out. This, I kept thinking, is not right.

I would have to cry to my self from now on, keep my feelings to myself, not let anyone see how much I hurt, just so I wouldn't be forced away, into a life of uncertainty. I knew dad wouldn't be the one taking care of me; he wouldn't take care of any of us for that matter.

I felt I wasn't going to be allowed to mourn, to remember, to miss my mom without the threat of losing everything that belonged to her, that reminded me of her, taken away.

Why did it have to be mom that left me? Why did it have to be mom that died? Why my mom?

## 53

Aunt Gloria did everything she possibly could to comfort me, even insisting if I went home with her, I would have her four daughters to talk with if I wanted, and she would have one of her daughters give up their bed just so I could have space for myself... But I had my own sisters to talk to. And though I hated sleeping three and four in a bed, I actually missed our bed and everything about our house. I just wanted to go home.

When we arrived from the hospital, the kids were watching TV just as they always had. My body shook as I walked into the house, trying not to look toward my mom's bed, trying so hard to be strong.

I glanced at mom's dress still on the hanger, hanging from her closet door, wanting so desperately to get it and hug it. I saw Sher, with a pale scared look on her face.

How was I ever going to do this? It just seemed so impossible. I could hear Aunt Gloria saying something to dad, seemed she was mumbling for him to take me to her, if he couldn't handle me. I wasn't going anywhere with her or anyone for that matter.

I stared at moms dressed, trying to walk quickly so I could get to our room. I wanted to be alone. Just as I passed through mom's room, the phone rang.

Dad reached over and answered it. Someone on moms side of the family, not really sure who, was calling to ask us to go to grandmas. Mom's two sisters that lived out of town would be leaving first thing in the morning, and whoever was calling, asked us to go say our good byes.

Though I remember all the separated people at the funeral, I knew they were all there. And whether any of mom's family, or mom's entire family thought dad killed her, they were, in fact, still our relatives. And whether they hated dad, or dad hated them, there was still common ground, six of us.

Dad did give us a choice asking each of us if we wanted to go, though I hadn't been out of the hospital an hour, I too wanted to say good-bye to my aunts. They were, after all, my mom's sisters, and since they lived out of town, I really had no idea, when I would ever see them again. I reluctantly agreed with everyone else.

The drive to grandmas was very quiet. Dad tried to conversate with us, but dad usually wasn't the one doing all the talking, it was mom. She's the one that would sing with the radio, she's the one that would see one of us staring off in space, and say, "What are you thinking about?" As though she already knew our deepest thoughts.

Mom's the one that would see a car broke down on the side of the road and say. "Ooohhh, poor thing." It would be mom that would make us all laugh at once, then say "Shhhh, not too loud, dad needs to concentrate on his driving." Knowing darn good and well we would laugh even louder. It's safe to say dad was not the conversationalist in the car. He was the one, while driving would find something, anything to bitch about.

He would look at one of us and say. "Did you brush your teeth today?"

"Did you feed the dogs?" Or, why do your fingernails look dirty?" Though there was no dirt under them at all."

Always a negative comment, never praise, or a pat on the back.

"Sit up straight. Don't run, slow down, eat all your food."

Ok, ok, so do a lot of other parents, huh? However, some parents also say good job, I'm proud of you, thanks for helping.

Not this man, he was so used to controlling and talking shit to his "men," he didn't know how to be nice, talk nice to kids. It was the first time we would be with dad without the guidance of our mom.

We arrived; it was grandma that opened the door. The second she saw all of us, she exploded with tears. It was going to happen, inevitable, no matter who I saw that reminded me in the slightest bit of mom. Of course, I cried and cried.

No one could take anything that reminded me of mom, away from me at grandmas, because everything and everyone reminded me of her.

Grandma shuffled us through the front door then I noticed a strange thing happened. All three of mom's sisters and Uncle Bill hugged us kids, but not one word was said to dad, nothing at all.

No one said "Hello Johnny....Do you want to sit down Johnny? Are you hungry Johnny? How do you feel, how are the kids?" Nothing. He was asked not one single question. Actually, they ignored him completely.

It was a horribly awkward situation. I didn't know, or realize what all the tension was about. I know everything they had been told about the night mom died, I mean Geez, I'm the one that told them all, but by no means did I mean to insinuate dad had killed my mom, and that, is exactly what I knew they were thinking.

Guilty, without a trial. I already knew. But as far as I knew, dad didn't know I had told them the events that night. Or did he?

I wondered why are we here? Why, or who called us to come over here? How in the world would I ever explain to my dad the things I had told them at Uncle Bill's house the day I was interrogated? I told the truth, that day. I didn't fabricate and I didn't lie, knowing in dad's book, was a serious crime.

Snitch...he would think I was a fricken snitch...

I'm really not sure if everyone was afraid to ask us questions with dad standing right here, or if they just already assumed his guilt. Whatever the reason everyone more or less just stood there, looking at us, wondering....

Dad took ten minutes of this silent treatment and said.

"Let's go."

Just like that. Nothing else, no good byes, no hugs, only the words, "Let's go." And we did exactly as dad instructed us.

We got up, and left. We didn't even blink an eye or object to his command. We literally, all seven of us just walked out the door. Dad understandably, was very very upset.

What should have been a twenty-minute drive home, with dad's anger, took ten. Worrying about the risk of a car wreck was not on dad's priority list. He just wanted to get to his comfort zone, his house, his part of town and his friends.

Once inside the house dad went directly to the phone. It was no secret who he was calling. We already knew he was calling Ray.

Ray was the go to man. He's the one, if dad said, "do it," it got done. Ray never ever asked questions. He wasn't paid to think or ask questions, he was paid to act, as soon as he was told to do anything, Ray did it.

But this conversation was different, dad was yelling at Ray. I have no idea what Ray was saying, but he got to our house faster than dad drove from the south side of town to our north side.

Dad met Ray on the porch the second Ray jumped out of his car.

As calmly as he could, Ray said, "Ok Johnny, we will take care of it."

"Calm down, we will figure it out." Dad wasn't trying to hide any of his conversation with Ray from us as he usually did. Any other time we were told to go to our room or go outside while the grown ups talked. This was completely different. It was as if dad didn't care if we heard any of this or not.

"I don't give a fuck about my self." He yelled to Ray.

"Those mother fuckers can think what ever the hell they want about me, but no mother fucker is going to disrespect my kids... Ever."

For some odd reason, for the first time in my life I wasn't ashamed to be the daughter of a gangster. Dad was crying now. A bit of self-pity, perhaps. A lot of sadness for losing mom, definitely... but more so, a lot of anger towards his in-laws...

Ray did everything he could to keep dad calm. Then I heard it straight from the horse's mouth.

"I know them mother fuckers think I killed Shirley, I fucking know they do" Dad was all over the place at this time, seems like he was gonna explode into a million pieces.

"Ray I swear I did nothing to her. I don' give a fuck how it looks for me, or what they think of me, but for Shirley's mother, and all her family to ignore my kids like they did, I don't take that shit from no one, and you know it."

Ray looked towards all six of us who were ten feet behind dad and said. "Johnny."

Dad turned around, saw all of us, and just lost it.

We were crying, dad was crying, Ray was crying, everybody crying on the porch just as we had the day mom died.

Ray gathered us all together and said, "Kids, y'all go inside, I'm gonna talk to your dad for awhile."

He motioned for us to go to our room; fearing dad would get the machine gun the F.B.I had desperately searched for years ago, get in his car, go to grandmas in three minutes or less, and blast the place.

We kids knew our place, so we went to our room as Ray had instructed us to do, and sat on the beds, and waited.

I heard Ray call Helena and tell her to catch a ride from her sisters and get to our house... Now...

Ray's focus, always, was dad. Ray had no other position in dad's organization than to fulfill each and every one of dads' demands...

Dad was Ray's boss, his friend. He was like the brother dad never had. Keeping dad calm, making sure dad didn't try to leave and go make the biggest mistake of his life was Ray's immediate priority

Tonight Ray's job was going to prove to be the most difficult of his life.

## 54

Ray earned his pay that night and them some. He did what no one could've done, he kept dad calm. Maybe he got dad high on marijuana and mellowed him out, perhaps he made dad realize we were all he had left. Whatever Ray's strategy. Whatever he said or didn't say to dad, made him forget of his plan to take out all his in-laws, which I know damn good and well dad would never have done.

It's quite possible dad would've gone over to grandma's, cussed them all out, and I'm sure there would've been a lot of yelling, but to actually spray machine gun bullets all over the place, I don't think so. But then again, we will never know, because good ol loyal ass Ray had the situation under control.

Hell, I do believe I heard them laughing about it as they stood in the front yard passing their joint back and forth. Probably making jokes of what dad would have done and the expressions on every ones face.

Dad was not one of those, big talkers, he was a doer. He didn't boast about what he might do, he straight up did it. Never thinking of the consequences. Except this one time.

Leader of the pack or not, dad got his hands just as dirty as the men that served under him. Lead by example, so the saying goes. He was the meanest of them all, and to look at him, you'd never think it. That goes equally for Ray.

Any bad things dad did to support his family were not exactly conversations we had at the dinner table. However, today dad let his emotions get the best of him, and he blurted out his desire to fuck some people up. Also, he let it be known that he believed everyone thought him to be the murderer of his beautiful wife.

That's a hell of a burden if you're guilty and an even harder one if you're innocent. But now I heard it for myself. All the whispers and gossip at moms' funeral, and after the funeral. It was on everyone's mind, but none had the guts to confront dad and straight up accuse him of killing mom.

I mean, put yourself in every one else's place. Mom was young, healthy, and beautiful. She wasn't sick coughing or with fever. She had gone to sleep and didn't wake up. But how was that possible? How does a healthy thirty three year old woman, just lie down, go to sleep and never wake up? Then there was the fact dads trial was about to start, or should've already started.

Could he have killed her just to save his ass from going to jail? Could he have actually suffocated her, choke the life out of her. Could he actually have taken her away from her kids so he wouldn't have to go to jail?

Everyone thought it, I'm sure even dad's sisters and mom thought it, but what kind of family would they be if they actually accused him of it.

Then, there's dad's side. He could say he was innocent for the rest of his life, who the hell would believe him? Why would anyone believe him? Dad had only one thing on his side, other than Ray. He had the medical examiner. The medical examiner was going to be the only person to hand down a verdict of guilty or not guilty.

There was nothing physical on mom's body to say, *"Johnny you mother fucker, you killed her."* So dad, like everyone else, would have to wait, wait on a report that would save, or sink him.

Helena and Ray stayed with us that night. I suppose Ray just wanted to make sure dad didn't come down off his high and wander off in the middle of the night.

Helena tried her best to comfort us and be close to us, she was after all, moms' best friend.

I walked into the kitchen and saw her drinking a cup of coffee, remembering her being there for so many hours the night dad was in jail. I wondered what were all the secrets she was telling mom?

I wondered just what Helena really knew about dad? How much did mom actually know? What had the monster done that had him locked up? What was he really about to go on trial for?

All these were questions a normal twelve year old had no business thinking about, wondering about. But then again, I wasn't your normal twelve year old. I had seen and heard things only gangsters knew of.

This was my first night in our house since mom died. I couldn't sleep. Somewhere in my mind, I could hear my mom crying, gasping for air, pleading with dad.

Seems I played that night over and over in my mind, wondering why in the hell didn't I get up that night. If she really were gasping for air as Becky suggested, I could have helped her. I could have saved her. I buried my head under my pillow and I cried and cried and cried. This life was going to be so tough on me, how would I ever survive.

And if things couldn't get worse, just as I woke the next morning I heard someone enter the house. Dad and Ray already awake, drinking coffee and talking in the living room. Helena in the kitchen preparing breakfast. I recognized the voice, I cringed.

We all heard dad talking, and the loudest female voice talking over him, it was his sister Liz.

Now me, Malina, being just a kid, one has to realize we all inherited certain traits from other family members. Some I was proud to possess, some I was not. One of the inherited gifts I was not proud to possess was the one I inherited from my dad's sister Liz. I, unfortunately did not inherit my mom's kind ways of speech, rather the harsh tone of gutter mouth Liz. Hence, the story is being told. Yet I was still too young to voice my foul mouth thoughts, I, none-the-less thought them, and I cared less if anyone could actually read my mind.

Liz was the loud mouth in the family that didn't care whose feelings she hurt when she spoke. Three husbands had divorced her because she never shut the fuck up. I wondered how dad tolerated her mouth.

She lived out of state, luckily, so it was only on certain occasions we were forced to see her. She talked way too loud for a woman and cussed even more than almost any man did.

Every other word was fuck. Seems she couldn't control her words, or didn't care too. Though she was very pretty and looked younger than her actual years, you could hear her voice all over the house.

She made some sly remark to dad, which was just her style, funeral or no funeral, then worked her way to our room. She politely hugged each of us kids only because it was the respectful thing to do, and asked if we were ok?

I wanted to say, 'Shut up bitch, how can we be ok? Our mom is gone! Remember you're here for a funeral, not a party.'

She was looking around the room and managed to see herself in the mirror, which interrupted her concentration.

Liz always wore clothes that were to tight on her and she wore way too much makeup. She reminded me of the skanks in the bar I had seen those times dad took us there. She was louder and her clothes tighter and she shook her ass when she walked. And I mean shook. Becky used to imitate her to the Tee. You couldn't help but notice just how desperately she was starving for attention. I mean really, what descent woman shakes her ass, especially in front of a bunch of kids.

Liz carried a small bottle of perfume in her too tight fitting jeans, the second she couldn't smell it on her anymore, she doused herself again and again, gagging us over and over. Anytime she reached in her pocket, we already knew what was about to happen, and we'd run outside for fresh breathable air.

She would talk without thinking about what she were about to say, and if she hurt your feelings to bad to sad, the words had already left her mouth.

Liz spent a few minutes in our room looking around disgusted, at the raggedy room. When she realized we weren't over excited to see her she went to search out Helena in the kitchen.

She was trying to carry on a conversation with Helena, whom also wasn't crazy about Liz. I don't think Helena particularly liked Liz. Maybe she knew Ray, being a man, would look at Liz's ass every time she shook it, and it just made Helena uncomfortable.

Helena was secure in her marriage with Ray, she knew what Ray did, and the things he did, but stood by his side regardless.

I believe dad teased them both continuously, that they had met on a Thursday night, drove to Oklahoma the same night, and got married bright and early the next morning. I suppose that was real love at first sight, no courting, no dating, just got married, and had been together ever since.

Yes, Helena loved and trusted her husband; she just didn't appreciate Liz here at our house acting disrespectful.

Liz realized there would be no conversation for her with Helena so she shook her ass back to the living room where dad and Ray were talking about mom. Liz having the big mouth she had, and not caring what anyone thought of her said. "Ok Johnny, what happened?" As if dad had killed mom and he was going to straight up confess to her.

Dad, I suppose, not wanting this big mouth sister of his to think him guilty, told her everything. Then with the intensity of a hurricane, she opened her big mouth.

"I hear the girls heard Shirley crying that night."

"What?" Dad said.

"Yep I think it was Malina and Becky that said they heard Shirley crying."

At that moment, Helena walked into our room. She looked at me as tears filled my eyes.

"Did you Malina?" She asked with a soft tone to her voice.

"Yes." I said.

"Then you tell the truth, if your dad asks, don't lie, you tell anyone that asks exactly what you heard." Helena was folding clothes that were in a laundry basket, almost intentionally standing beside me just as dad, Ray and big mouth Liz walked in the room.

"Malina what is this I hear? Dad asked

My mouth wouldn't move, my eyes went from dad to Ray to Helena's, than focused on Liz, who seemed to have a little smirk on her face.

"What did you hear baby?" He asked in a calm voice.

"I heard mom crying and you telling her not to cry." I explained.

Dad said. "No baby that was the week before when she was crying."

Becky stood up and said. "I heard it too. I heard mom trying to breathe."

Dad looked like a deer in headlights.

"No girls y'all are mistaken."

He seemed to try to make us believe we were wrong. What the hell was he doing? He was making us out to be liars. He was twisting our words. He was making everyone believe we were mistaken about the dates.

Why was he lying? What was he doing?

There is no way I was mistaking anything. I know damn good and well what I heard and when I heard it.

Dad was lying, but why? There is no way me and Becky made any of this up. I didn't even know Becky woke up that night until she blurted it out at Aunt Gloria's.

There is no way both of us had made a mistake. Dad was lying and I knew it. He was straight up a fucking liar.

But why? Why did he have to lie?

Only one reason I could think of.

Oh my god! Did he really kill her?

My dad killed my mom? My dad killed my mom!

I was paralyzed and couldn't move.

Dad rambled on an on that we were just upset and what we had heard did actually happen, but it was the week before.

Everyone in the room, the kids, Helena, Liz were all looking at dad as he spoke, hanging on to his every word.

Everyone except Ray. Ray was looking at me.

All the times I pissed my pants in my life, just for the fact dad would walk through the door, even the day after he beat mom I was about to piss myself, but mom comforted me so I didn't. Now here I was faced with this monster, his big mouth sister, and his hired killer, all just staring at me.

I knew dad was lying, even Becky knew, though she seemed unaware of the things that were being said, other than the one sentence she was more than happy to tell...

Dad spoke up "Malina has taken Shirley's death very hard, worse than the other kids, she is just mistaken."

But I knew I was not mistaken, and as sure as I was that I was not mistaken, I also knew for a fact dad was lying through his damn teeth... I might mistake many things in my young life, but anything concerning my mom, I never would've made a mistake.

Standing there amongst a bunch of grown ups, ones that were compelled to believe Johnny G. before they would believe me. Should I now tell the world he had beat her, tell them how he pistol-whipped her as he would a man in a bar room brawl?

Would anyone believe me? My only witness other than my brothers and sisters was Bee, and she was nowhere to be found.

Ray worked for dad; surely, he would hear me out! Or would he? I know Ray would not have taken out the pistol he carried in his back belt.. .but he was also sworn to protect dad, do whatever it would take to protect this monster, so would he turn against dad to take my side if dad had killed mom.

People like Ray were replaceable, people like dad were not.

Helena, the loving friend of moms stepped in just at that second.

"Come on let's eat." She got me by my arm and took me to the kitchen. I desperately wanted to say to Helena. But you're the one who told me to tell the truth. I decided against it.

She saved the day for the moment. Dad and Ray went to the living room to eat. We kids ate in the kitchen, Helena sat with us. Liz pulled up a chair, sitting beside us but not getting herself a plate of food, leaving us with the impression she thought she was too good to eat Helena's cooking.

Liz looked around the kitchen, in pure disgust, starring at the ugly linoleum floors, at the beat up cabinets and the lack of paint on them. She looked at the old stove and icebox that looked older than the house its self, then opened her big ass mouth again.

"Damn, didn't Shirley ever clean this place?"

"Get the hell out of here." Helena stood up and was on Liz's ass ready to pull her hair out of her head.

Dad and Ray came running, holding Helena back.

"This bitch wants to come in here and disrespect Shirley and these kids." Helena screamed right in Liz's face.

It was more than obvious Liz was scared; she knew Helena could beat her ass without even trying.

Ray was the paid employee, though dad loved him like a brother, Helena was the wife of the paid killer. In the gangster life, Helena had crossed a line, and Liz knew it.

"Get her out of here Johnny." Liz tried to sound tough.

"How dare her talk to me like that?" Liz was trying to get dad to feel sorry for her.

We kids were again crying, hating Liz for everything she said, everything she stood for.

Helena was moms friend, she loved us kids, I'm sure more than Liz.

Helena said. "No you get out, you bitch. I'm here to take care of Shirley's kids, what the hell are you here for? To talk shit about this house and disrespect Shirley in front of her kids?"

Helena reached over to slap Liz. Liz looked at dad for help, wanting dad to take her side, step up and run Helena out of the house, by none other than Ray.

Dad was in a predicament. Run off his sister or run off the one friend that was helping him with his kids, while leaving her own kids alone with her sister to be here to help. Dad looked at the two women, looked at us crying, looked at Ray and said. "Damn Liz," and told her to get her things Ray was going to take her to Gloria's.

As pissed as Helena was she said. "No Johnny, you take her, Ray isn't leaving this house."

It was the first and last time anyone ever told dad what to do, and he did it.

When dad left to take Liz to Gloria's, Helena sat down with me and Becky and asked us exactly what we had heard. Ray stood beside Helena, never saying a word, just listening, and watching.

I told Helena everything I heard the night before mom died and what I had heard the week before that. I assured her I was not confusing the two dates. Ray listened, and watched me as I spoke. I was crying and I was scared, then Ray spoke.

"I love your dad." He began. "Not just because he is my boss, I love him like he is my brother. I love your mom also, and I love you kids."

"As bad as this looks for your dad, I know in my heart he did not, or could not ever kill your mom. He has done a lot of bad things to her, but he would not take her from you kids, so y'all could suffer. I don't know when or how, but one day you will know the truth, I'm sure of it."

"In a few weeks, the medical examiner will release your mom's cause of death, and we will know exactly what happened to her, but I know there is no way he would've killed her."

"I also want you kids to know that anything you need, if y'all ever need to talk or you just want us to come stay here with y'all, all you have to do is call and we'll be here."

"Malina, especially you. You are taking this very hard. I know you loved your mom so much, but please hear me; your dad did not kill her: I give you my word."

And with that, he walked out onto the porch to wait for dad.

I believed Ray. He would not give his opinion unless he believed what he said.

"Please trust him Malina." Helena said as she hugged me.

I was horrified of all the things that had just happened and I was confused to why dad would have lied, but I did trust Helena.

I was afraid of Ray, only because of who he was, what he was capable of, but I had no choice but to trust what he said.

As Helena got up to clean the kitchen, she said, "At least I got that bitch Liz out of here didn't I?" She laughed which made me smile.

Yes, she had done us a favor and got rid of that big mouth, and for that, I truly appreciated her being with us.

And she added. "Don't ever worry about anyone talking about this house. You kids know your mom took good care of it. It's not what the house looks like. It's the love inside it, never ever forget that."

She knew just what she was talking about. Mom had said it to us many times, but without mom there to share the love, it was just what that bitch Liz said it was... A dump.

That, I always knew.

# 55

    Every time I walked through mom's room, I cried. Helena helped me each time hugging me and telling me it was ok to cry.

    I saw her looking at moms dress, as if she too visualized mom there, in the dress, as she was the night she died.

    Helena told me it was a good reminder of mom and that she could smell mom's perfume, and powder and hair spray just standing near it.

    The dress hung on that door so I could see it every time I walked to or from mom's room.

    Dad came and went a lot after he took Liz to Aunt Gloria's. Ray took Helena for a few hours to tend to her own kids. Ray returned without Helena and dad and Ray went to run errands. Or, so they said.

    We found ourselves just us six kids home by ourselves. The little ones were watching TV. Sher in the little room listening to her radio. I went to see what she was doing because we really hadn't talked since the day mom died.

    There had been so much shuffling us here and there I actually didn't remember seeing any of my brothers or sisters...On occasion I saw Sher, but we hadn't said two words to each other in over a week.

    "I felt her pulse that day, I knew she was dead." Sher more or less blurted it out while looking directly at the floor. I didn't say anything.

    "I also felt to see if she were breathing, I knew she was dead." She said, still looking at the floor... Again, I did not say a word. Sher was lying on her stomach, arms folded, her chin rested on her arms.

    "Did you really hear her crying that night?" She asked.

    "Yes." I said, so afraid she was going to make me cry.

    "I didn't hear anything." Sher said. Her voice cracking.

"Do you think dad killed her Sher?" I asked, knowing how much she loved him, and horrified she would jump off her bed, beat the shit out of me, and throw me out of her room just on a mere insinuation.

She looked me right in my eyes, her beautiful green eyes, reminding me so much of mom.

"I really don't know. I don't think he would, because if he did, he would probably go to prison for the rest of his life, and we know he doesn't want to go to prison." Sher always talked as if she knew the answer to everything.

"Then what happened Sher?" I went on. "Mom wasn't sick, at all, we know that for sure." I tried not to cry.

"I know Malina, I really don't know, all we can do is wait and see what the doctors say." She tried to explain.

We both forgot the term Ray had used when he said Medical Examiner, so she referred to him as doctor.

She lay there looking right at me and she said. "Malina, I know this is tougher on you than any of us, because of what you saw that night, and I wish I knew how to make it better, but I don't. I don't even know how to deal with it myself."

"I know Sher." I interrupted. "And I know I cry a lot, but I just miss her, I want her to come home."

Sher started crying. "I know."

We were both crying when we heard J.J. yelling for Sher. We ran to the living room only to see Helena at the front door holding Babytoo. Danny was crying, J.J. was crying, as were Becky and Carrie.

"Tell mama see Babytoo." Danny yelled. "Tell her see Babytoo."

He was just a little kid who had no idea of death, he had no idea what had happened, none of the kids did. They didn't know they were never going to see mom again, or talk to her, or hug her, or kiss her. They just had no idea.

We all cried, sitting on the living room floor. Helena and Ray left all six of us on the floor with Babytoo, to spend time with one another, to spend time with Babytoo...

Helena and Ray stayed with us a total of four days, mostly it was Helena. Ray, well he came and went with dad. Business as usual I suppose. We were all glad Helena had run off Liz, she was disliked by us all and she was just so damn hateful talking shit about our mom.

I was so lost, so sad in so much pain over my mom I just didn't know what to do. I would sit on the front porch for hours and cry. Always trying to hide the fact that I was crying so no one would threaten to take me away.

I couldn't go anywhere near the little city mom had made, it was just to painful, so I sat on the front porch, knowing I would have to pass her room every time I would go inside.

When it was time for Helena and Ray to leave she cried as much as we did, and assured us she would be back every few days to check on us.

Sad as the good byes were, it was such a relief to know she would come back and not abandon us. She made sure we had her phone number and told us to call her no matter what we needed.

I didn't want her to leave, but knew she had to. As I watched them drive off I remember thinking. "Gosh, her kids are so lucky they still have her. What I would give to have my mom coming home."

Every day I would go to our room and sit, on the bed, or lay on the bed, close my eyes and visualize my mom in the next room, hear her voice or smell her cooking.

I convinced my self she was there, still in that dirty old house, smiling at all of us, playing outside with us. It's strange; you can create so much in your mind. You can have an entire separate life, if you just imagine it. I would get lost in my thoughts, my memories, and my dreams.

While I lay on the bed, not knowing what to do, I closed my eyes again, and when I did I saw mom laying there next to me, hugging me, the way she did the night dad had beat her.

She was holding me, comforting me, while I was crying, she said "Sssshhhh It's ok Malina." But this time she wasn't beat, she wasn't crying, and she wasn't throwing up blood. Her eyes weren't swollen, she was smiling at me and she looked so beautiful and peaceful, and then she said. "Shhhh Malina, don't cry, I'll be back."

I did not open my eyes; instead, I just cried and cried. If I told anyone what had happened, they would send me away to Aunt Gloria's. If I kept it bottled inside of me, I'd go crazy.

I lay there, eyes closed, tears gushing from my eyes. I couldn't breathe. My mom was right there with me, comforting me, assuring me she would be back.

My heart was pounding, my head was pounding, I was near hysteria, knowing any second dad or some one was going to come in and tell me to pack my bags, I was going to have to got to Aunt Gloria's'.

But, no one came; no one yelled at me, no one said a word to me.

I fell asleep. It may not have seemed possible to anyone else, but my mom was there in the room with me comforting me and hugging me and talking to me. It is what I needed.

I was afraid to open my eyes for fear she would be gone, in fact I knew she would be, but for just those few moments, she came and helped me. I knew she was gone from this life, but I also knew she would keep her word to me and she would come back....

# 56

At first dad would come and go. He would spend ten minutes here, ten minutes there with us, but to be perfectly honest, dad knew nothing about raising kids. He didn't know how to cook, he didn't know how to do laundry, he knew nothing, except to be a bad ass.

As quickly as he would come home, he would leave again. I mean really, what was he gonna do at home? Twiddle his thumbs, stare at the walls, take care of his children. No, he was gonna do nothing of the sort. He wasn't a domesticated dude; he was a mother fuckin gangster. And he sure wasn't gonna do that while babysitting six kids.

Slowly, again he was away more than he was at home.

Dad gave some miserable excuse about having to go to the garage everyday. Not exactly an excuse, we knew he would have to go to work eventually because he really wasn't the sit at home and mourn type of guy, but really now, already not coming home till after 2 am every morning!

We had never had to make breakfast lunch or dinner for ourselves, we didn't even know how to.

Dad had found himself a reason to leave, to walk away from his responsibilities, and he did. It was now up to me and Sher, well up to Sher, to take over.

I wasn't a leader, I was a follower. I would do what ever Sher told me to do; she just had to find the strength to take control. It was certain once we woke up in the mornings we would have to get the little kids up, dressed for the day, and fed. We knew for sure mom would help J.J. and Danny with everything. Becky and Carrie could dress themselves.

Sher would have the boys wash their faces, brush their hair, and brush their teeth. As short as mom kept their hair, fixing it would not be a problem; there wasn't much hair to comb anyway. Fixing Becky and Carries hair would be a different story all together; theirs was long and easily tangled.

There wasn't a huge selection of breakfast items to fix; it was oatmeal, or oatmeal.

It was obvious Sher had been in the kitchen watching mom cook more often than I thought she had. She managed to fix oatmeal that was pretty good. It definitely wasn't moms, but it was better than I had anticipated. She didn't burn the toast either.

Once we ate, it was time to clean up the place, making the beds and sweeping the floors. I couldn't go near moms' bed, so Sher agreed it would be her job. Cleaning that old house, though we had just swept the floors, and made the beds, it still looked trashy. At that second I wished that old bitch Liz would walk in running her mouth so I could have said, "Looky here big mouth, we just cleaned this place and it still looks like shit." I could see her point, it was a dump, but to insinuate mom never cleaned it. Well let's just say in my mind "Fuck you Liz."

A few days passed. Dad couldn't get out of bed fast enough to get to the garage. He would rush to take his bath, remember we had no shower that was a luxury we had been deprived of all our lives.

Just as he had every morning, he would yell "Shirley." Expecting mom to walk into the restroom with the clothes he would wear for the day. Yes, not only did she smother six kids with all her love, she catered to dad. All he had to do was get in the tub, she did everything else. Took his towel and wash cloth to him, took his socks and boxers, took him his freshly ironed clothes. Sometimes, I believe she even dressed him.

So he's calling moms name out loud for all of us to hear, and I'm sure he stood there a few minutes wondering what was taking her so long, and then realized she was gone, further realizing he was on his own.

I don't see how the hell he managed to run a garage and be a gangster, he couldn't even get himself out of the restroom without her assistance. Talk about being dependent.

Seems the bitching slowed down, mostly because he was never there. Once he would leave the house in the morning, he literally didn't come back until late. He would call, once or twice during the day, mostly to see if he had any mail. Was he waiting on Publishers Clearing House to send him a check?

I did not miss him at all.

At times, he would come home crying, sometimes drunk and crying, sometimes high and crying, other times drunk, high, and crying. Never could he just come home and be a dad.

Sher tried to get us on some kind of a schedule. Wake up, eat breakfast, clean up the house, eat lunch, clean the mess, send the kids to play outside, fix supper, clean the mess, play some more, bath time, everyone go to bed. It was not easy at all for her.

Sher had been doing everything she could to fix us meals the best she could, mostly soups and sandwiches, but our groceries were running low.

The first two days after Helena and Ray left, Aunt Gloria came by to bring food that had been left over from mom's funeral. She said she had kept it frozen so it wouldn't spoil. She would cry while she was there, but she seemed scared. I never knew why I got that impression, she just seemed hurried. I assumed it was because she had her own family to take care of.

She came three days, straight in a row. Aunt Mary came with her one of the three days. They didn't stay long, just enough time to warm the food for us, hug us, and then leave. It was very sad and lonely for us. We really had no idea how to function without adult supervision. Considering we were six kids fourteen years and under, I think we did extremely well.

Kids will be kids, and though they knew mom wasn't in the house and would never be coming back, they still had no concept of what death was.

J.J. approached me one afternoon, after about an hour of playing outside. He had fallen down and scraped his knee, and was crying and needed a band-aid on it.

"Malina will you tell mama to fix my knee?"

I looked at Sher; Sher looked at me and came to my rescue.

"J.J., come here, I'll fix it." Sher said.

She took him by his hand to the restroom to wash his knee and bandage it. I over heard her talking to him.

"J.J., mom is in heaven, she is with god, the angels, and she's with papa.

"Is she going to come back today?" He asked excitedly.

"No." Sher said. Mom is not coming back. She's asleep in heaven."

"Can I go with her?" He asked.

Oh my goodness, I couldn't stand this. I was gonna go crazy listening to my brothers innocence.

"No." Sher said. "Maybe someday, but not now."

"Can dad go with her?" He asked.

Sher had such patience; she would talk calmly to the kids as if she were reading them bedtime stories. Patience she inherited from mom.

"Why did she die Sher?" He asked as she finished up with his knee.

"I'm not sure J.J., but everything will be ok."

That seemed like a very stupid statement. I also remembered Helena and Ray saying the same thing, how does anyone possibly figure everything will be ok?

Ok for who? I wasn't mad that she said it; I understood she was comforting a small child; nonetheless, it seemed an inappropriate thing to say. I wasn't about to criticize her, she was doing what I couldn't, talking about mom dying, taking care of my little brother, taking care of five kids. Being mom and dad to all of us, cleaning, cooking. It was just so much work, so much responsibility. Perhaps Sher was at a loss for words, perhaps she really didn't know what to say to J.J. But she had the situation under control, more than I could have done.

Two days passed, three days passed. No one and I mean no one came to our house. Not one person came and checked on the kids, no one came to see if we were hungry, no one came to help us cope with our loss.

Periodically when some one did show up they always seemed rushed, in a hurry to get the heck out of there. What were they afraid of, that they were gonna see a ghost?

Maybe mom's family thought dad's side of the family was with us, maybe dad's side of the family thought mom's side was with us. Regardless, it was as though the entire world stopped existing except for us kids. I did nothing but cry all day. The memories of mom were overwhelming. It was a good thing, or was it too much for me? The smell of her lotions and sprays lingered throughout the house all day and night. I would deliberately spray her perfume on myself; spray it in the air, just to have her smell everywhere. If I wasn't crying, I was about to.

Sher would try to talk to me, but the result would always be the same. I would walk away crying uncontrollably. I do know the other kids cried also, just not to the extent that I did.

I was sitting on the porch, in a daze, not really watching the kids play, more like staring into space. Carrie and Becky on the porch, playing jacks. Danny and J.J., playing with their cars in the little city, a spot on our property I still hadn't been able to visit.

Sandy saw me and waved, then within minutes, walked over with a big pot of soup Jewel had made for us. Poor ol guy, he was so ugly with his missing nose, which, thankfully he had bandaged before walking over.

Chicken soup, a good home cooked meal. We finished the pot between lunch and dinner. Looking back, we must have looked like a pack of wolves devouring our prey, just so damn hungry.

Dad showed up on the fourth day, not as a father, but as a relative passing through town to see how the poor little orphaned kids were. I get it; he was depressed and missed mom and just couldn't handle his responsibilities.

Too fucking bad, dad.

He marched in as if he were raiding the place. Tossing things here and there. Sher got up the courage, no it wasn't courage, it was Sher being Sher, and being mom, dad ,sister, cook, house keeper, babysitter, friend, caregiver, all the above, that made her step up and say.

"Look, come in the kitchen." She didn't address him as dad, father, she just said. "We have no food; I don't know how to take care of your kids." She didn't say my brothers and sisters, she said your kids, like that was going to make him stop in his path and break down. Seemed he wasn't interested at all, as if he didn't want to hear her.

"Are you listening?" She snapped as dad grabbed another shirt and put it on.

"Dad, we need food. What am I supposed to do?"

He stopped fiddling around with his belongings long enough to look at her and say.

"I know baby, I'm trying to get some money together now."

Bullshit! I thought. That's just the kind of shit he would say to mom, over and over.

"Dad!" Sher yelled.

He stopped, opened his wallet, and handed her a ten-dollar bill, not a one hundred dollar bill, a ten-dollar bill, and said.

"Go the store and get groceries."

Groceries? Groceries? Are you fucking kidding me? I thought to myself.

Sher threw it on the dresser, and walked out of the room.

She was so damn pissed off.

Dad stood there a minute; any other time he would of beat the shit out of her for disrespecting him. He knew better this time.

If he alienated Sher, he would have no one to take care of his kids. He sure the hell wasn't about to do that...

He followed Sher to her room. She wasn't crying, she was too tough for that. She was throwing things around in her room, almost mimicking the father she loved so much.

Since the day dad brought new mattresses for our beds, Sher more or less took over the little room as her own. Hot as it was, she preferred the heat, as opposed to her other choice, sleep four to a bed, a tradition she had grown sick and tired of.

She was a teenager in high school and needed her own space. No one ever entered her room without her permission. Till now.

Dad just walked in almost like a bully barging in, then stopped in his path.

"I'm sorry Sher, I'm trying, I'm really trying." He pleaded with her.

No, you're not. I thought. You have an excuse now to stay away and you're taking full advantage here.

Sher said. "What do I do? I can't do this alone." Complete and utter frustration in her voice.

Not meaning to throw me under the bus, instead trying to make a point to her precious father. She knew I helped her a lot. It just was not enough.

"Ok, look, you take the ten dollars, go buy some things and I'll be back later."

The devil was trying to cut a deal….We both knew he was lying. Sher was fourteen. You just don't throw that kind of responsibility on a fourteen year old.

What was wrong with this man? Did he have no morals? Did he not realize what he was doing?

He was more loyal to the fucking gangsters than he ever was to his kids.

He talked a minute or two longer, hugged Sher, and was out of there. Almost like an escaped convict, not even looking back for fear of confinement.

I guess guilt was not a trait my dad shamed to carry. He just left us, pretty much just standing there.

Sher looked at that ten dollars in such disgust, it was a miracle she didn't tear it up and throw it out the door, but she didn't. She knew how badly we needed it.

Sher wrote a small list of things we needed, necessities, no junk, no lavishes like candy or ice cream. Just what we needed to survive for a day or two.

Me and Becky walked to the store, calculating how many candies I could buy with a ten-dollar bill. I laughed to my self-thinking, what fun it would be to buy candy. Sher would be pissed if I did, so I went against my better judgment, bought the designated items, and returned home with sixty-three cents.

To my horrified surprise, Sher sent me and Becky to Miss Dyes little corner grocery store and insisted we buy sixty-three cents worth of candy. .

# 57

The next day Aunt Gloria showed up with groceries. We were pretty sure dad had sent her shopping, and we also knew he wasn't going to be coming home every day. I mean think of it, he barely came home at all when mom was alive, and that was because he needed a punching bag, emotionally and physically. Common sense was telling me, he wasn't gonna be around, we were on our own, but it definitely made no sense that he would just walk away. Who does that shit?

My dad, that's who.

Aunt Gloria brought mostly can foods, things for us to prepare without a lot of hassle. Some cereals, milk, bread, you know the items we would need to make sandwiches. Fast food that wouldn't require a lot of preparing. At least our bellies would be full for a few days. Aunt Gloria visited a bit and just like that, she too was gone.

Over the next few weeks, a handful of relatives came and went, even Helena came only once.

I get it, I understood all the pain, the sorrow, the constant reminders, but we were not twenty-year-old adults that had lost our mom, we were kids ranging in age from four to fourteen.

How do you not come on a daily basis to check on kids?

Then there was moms family, they were so messed up over her death they all stopped coming over completely. No more coffee dates at all.

Understandable, her two sisters that lived out of town, we saw them on a limited basis anyway, but Uncle Bill, grandma, and Dolly they all lived here, ten minutes away. They were at our house almost every other day drinking coffee and talking. How could they just disappear? No visits anymore, not even a phone call.

Why were they all staying away? Because mom's death was too much for them? Or did they blame dad for her death and they didn't want to face him?

Common sense tells me if you think he killed her, then by all means, prove it. Send his ass to jail and take her kids away from him, but you just don't walk away and abandon kids.

Now it was as if mom never existed, or we kids didn't exist in any of their eyes. But we did? And I wanted to know why were they punishing us for what they may have thought dad did?

They were our family, we needed them too. I just didn't understand all this abandonment shit. You don't walk away from six kids, even if he had killed her, what kind of people just walk away.

But now, no one was coming, not even dad.

Where was he? I wondered did the main gangster know that big bad Johnny G. just abandoned his kids? Did gangsters punish such horrible crimes? I simply did not get it. Where was everyone? Why didn't anyone care? Why didn't someone, anyone call Child Protective Services and have us picked up? Put us in an orphanage? Anything besides abandon and ignore us.

I honestly didn't know how Sher did it. Being in shock all I ever did was cry. I would sit on the front porch for hours and hours just crying. It was just unbelievable to me that all this was happening to us.

Day after day, we six kids struggled on our own. At one time in our lives there were adults in and out of our house, seemingly every day for whatever reasons they were there. Now, no one. Not one adult in sight.

We had been home pretty much a month alone after mom died, with only an occasional visitor, and almost as few phone calls. Dad would come in, throw his weight around, and then leave.

Really, he was thirty-five years old, and literally had no one to worry about but himself.

We, it seemed now, were Sher's problem. How she ever did it all at the age of fourteen was beyond me. We were trapped and confined to that old house, no mother, no father, no relatives. We pretty much only had each other to depend on.

Then, one day, out of nowhere, Sher said. "Come on kids, let's go." No preparations, no discussion, no planning, just get up and go.

Where the heck were we going?

I knew exactly where we were going, the second she told J.J. and Danny to get their baseball bat, their gloves, and their baseball. I knew she was taking us to the park.

The park was eight blocks away, a distance we had never walked as a group of kids, but Sher said she was just tired of being cooped up in that house. We didn't even have a key to lock the door. So, we just shut the door behind us, up, and walked to the park. Paired off in our normal two by two's, we started on our new journey.

We had been to the park once or twice with mom. The kids were very excited about having somewhere different to go. About a block before we got there, we saw it. Beautiful green grass, swings, slides, everything kids could possibly want and need to have fun.

We formed groups of three and played an hour or so of baseball. Danny couldn't run fast enough. We deliberately didn't tag him out because we didn't want him to cry.

J.J. would hit the ball as hard as he possibly could, hitting home run after home run. We laughed, we ran, we played, we took the kids on the swings, and the merry go round and the slides. We stupidly forgot to take any water with us, so by the time we got home we were drained of all our energy.

The visit to the park is what Sher needed. She told the kids to get cleaned up as she prepared supper. Once everyone had bathed and got comfortable, we ate. Sher had been sad and mad and even started taking her frustrations out on us.

Then there was the fact she was going through the summer with no volunteer work, no friends, and no phone calls. She lost that part of her life the second mom died. She did not realize it then, but from the time mom died, she was no longer a freshman in high school, she was now a prisoner of our life.

She could go nowhere, no activities to take her away from that house and her brothers and sisters. She had a new role, caregiver, and it started taking its toll on her.

Danny and J.J. were not the problem. I personally was terrified of Sher. I knew she could kick my ass, and she knew I was afraid of her. It was Becky and Carrie. They formed a union against Sher.

At first, it was little things. Sher would tell them to put away their laundry, or do the dishes and they would disobey, or not do it all, pissing Sher off.

However, the problem was Becky. Being that she was the one that always had to have the last word, the last comment in a conversation. Sher would ask her to be quiet, don't talk back. Becky, a smart ass, would say something back to her then they would argue. Becky knew Sher could kick her ass, but it never deterred Becky's smart-ass ways. . She would talk back to Sher, tell her to do things herself, even yelling at Sher saying "You're not my mama."

Which, if that had been me, I would have just cried. Sher would wrestle Becky to the floor and say "Take it back Bucky," hence the fights.

Yes, being our parent wasn't easy at all for Sher. She had to be strong, yet comforting. She was the authority figure, yet the big sister. It was just Becky's nature to be difficult. And Carrie, just because she and Becky were always paired off, she would be on Becky's side just to go against Sher. Things were beginning to get out of hand, and there was no one there to control any of us.

The weeks drug slowly. I had headaches that started from the minute I woke until I went to bed late at night. It could only have been caused from all the crying I was doing.

I wanted my mom so badly, but no crying, begging pleading was ever going to bring her back.

Then, out of nowhere, dad came home one morning, rushing around, in a complete panic. Actually, it was quite funny to watch him in action. He'd put something down on his dresser, forget it was there, and then proceed to tear up all his own shit looking for the very thing he had just placed on the dresser.

So, he's scurrying around, like one of those wind up toys, you know, the toy you wind up as much as you possibly can, then put it down and watch it go every which way. That's exactly how he looked. Shit I got exhausted just watching him.

While he's bouncing off the walls, he told all of us to get dressed he was taking us downtown.

What the heck for, I wondered. He didn't say, "Hello kids, how are ya'll, is everything ok." Nope, just jumped right in with the demands.

Sher didn't talk to dad at first; she just did as he said.

Never asking how we were? If we had food in the house? Were the little ones okay? By the way, he didn't look like he was starving.

What man? What kind of man just walks away from his kids and leaves a pissed off fourteen year old child to handle such responsibility. No man I would ever know in my life would compare to this so-called man.

Sher got the boys ready, Becky and Carrie hurried and put on their shoes and changed their shirts. I was already dressed, so when dad demanded, "Let's go." We piled in the car as he ordered.

Downtown indeed, and of all places, he took all six of us with his jerk lawyer, to talk to a judge.

He was to go before a judge, the one that would be hearing the case he would go on trial for. The mystery case that he had gone to jail a few months back. The same case mom herself had warned dad, she wasn't sure how much more she could take.

So here he goes, all dressed up in his black suit, standing as the bailiff says. "All rise." And like robots, everyone in the courtroom stands up as a man, the judge, wearing a long black robe looking thing, enters the room.

Ok, Ok, I had never been in a courtroom, I had no idea what to expect. So dad's lawyer instructs us to stand, everyone stands and waits for this old guy to get to his seat, at the front of the courtroom, and sits down. Once he sits, we are allowed to sit back down. It was funny to see dad actually take orders from another man. I suppose when you're in a courtroom, you have to follow the rules. How difficult that must have been for the Great Johnny G.

Me and Sher look at one another like, what tha....

Dad is sitting beside his lawyer at a table, the defendant table; we are on the first row of the courtroom, just watching.

None of us kids made a sound. Then a young woman reads from a paper out loud for everyone to hear. "The State of Texas VS John Vincent Guetarro in the matter of attempted murder."

Whaaaaaaaat? He actually tried to kill someone, and was being blamed for it?

But, killing, or trying to kill someone was Ray's job, and by the way, why wasn't Ray here, I wondered? Hypothetically holding dads hand. . I turned and looked around the room. No sign of Ray what so ever.

Whoever dad had tried to kill or did kill or wanted to kill, was all part of the Gangster Life, this was dad's problem. The woman didn't say murder she said attempted murder. I knew that meant he was in big trouble, but why were we here?

We didn't know anything about any of this and if we had, there was no way we would've ratted him out.

Rotten father, it goes without saying, but there was no way any of Johnny G's kids would rat the rat out, we'd take the fall for his lousy ass before we would snitch on him, even four year old Danny would have "gone down the river" for this jerk.

Poor little Danny, just looking around like he was lost in space. I glanced over at J.J. comparing him to dad, hoping like hell, when he grew up that he would be the exact opposite of his hero, dad.

J.J. looked at me and smiled, a bit of fear I'm sure went through his little mind when he heard his name John Vincent Guetarro, being read off by the court reporter, not really realizing they were calling dad, not him. This was quite a scene.

I wanted to laugh as I looked over at my brothers and sisters, eyes bulging out, wondering who he killed.

Here we sat, watching our dad stand before this judge, hell he looked more like an attorney all dressed up, than a gangster. I didn't get it.

Then dad's lawyer read out all our names. Sher Guetarro, Malina Guetarro, so on and so on all the way to poor ol terrified Danny...

Ok, so the bastard knew all our names, so what....

The judge spoke again. "Mr. Guetarro, I'm going to postpone your trial for one year. One year so you can get your affairs in order. I sympathize with the loss of your wife and respect the fact you have taken on the role of mother and father...

Hold the heck on. Mother and father to whom? He wasn't no mama or daddy to us six kids, what the hell was going on? I couldn't believe this shit.

"In the event you are convicted in this case, you will need to make sure you have made proper arrangements for your children. If there are no suitable relatives or friends to parent your children during your absence, then it will be ordered they be placed in a children's home during your incarceration." The judge ordered.

Wait a gosh darn minute, this is too much. This here judge is predicting the outcome of his trial before he even has one, and wanting to send us away, and furthermore is postponing this trial for one year so dad can take care of us, but, hello stupid ass judge, he's not doing that now any way.

Sher's eyes filled with tears. Was she upset for dad or pissed because he drug us to court to plead his case knowing damn good and well once we went home we wouldn't see him for four or five more days. I do believe Sher was furious.

Dad's face, now a pale yellow, began to get its color back as we left the courtroom and walked back to his car. On the drive home Sher began to cry.

Dad had bought himself a year to wiggle his way out of this mess.

"Who did you attempt to kill? She snapped at dad.

"It's a long story, don't worry baby, everything will be ok." He sounded so relieved.

"Ok? Ok for who?" She asked him.

"All of us." Dad said.

"What do you mean all of us? You aren't ever home. I'm doing all the work myself, you don't help at all." She screamed.

Now, I got the picture. He used us kids to show the judge how six minor kids pathetically look without their mom. Put on an elaborate show, convincing the judge he was needed by us, was about to drop us off at home, then mosey on down the road and live his gangster life, without a care in the world.

How I wished I had a gun at that moment. Shoot that mother fucker in the back of his head. There ya go daddy, no trial for you. I laughed my silent laugh at the thought.

Now...Here sits Sher crying that this is too much for her and she's doing all the work...I agree, it was too much for her, but did we really want him at home twenty hours a day, bitching about everything under the sun from the time we wake up, till the time we go to bed. Me, personally, hell no I did not.

The thought of him being in control, us kids walking those egg shells again, everyday all day. No thanks. Stay gone fucker.

I know now, no matter how much bullshit dad talked to Sher, he was not going to be an active parent in our lives. He wouldn't even know how to be. Hell, he didn't even know most of our names.

Sher's name, yes, because she was the favorite. J.J of course because, aaahhh he was Junior. However, I'd bet a million dollars if that judge would have asked dad the rest of our names, the fucker would have said, "uuhh baby, son, baby, son." Because for sure he had no idea of our real names.

Something stupid like that. Now if my name had been Mary I bet he would remember me because of the Mary Jane, illegal marijuana he always carried in his cigarette pack, as if no stupid mother-fucking cop would think to look in his damn cigarette pack. Oh, I could not believe this day.

I wondered how in the world Sher would be able to handle it without any grown up help.

Mom's family hadn't been back since her funeral, not even grandma. Dad's family only came to bring groceries, but no one out of all the family and friends mom and dad had, no one stepped up to the plate. I thought about it very hard.

Aunt Gloria, already had seven kids, there was no way she could take on six more, thirteen kids, impossible. Uncle David was a good man; thirteen kids would have driven him to drinking, or worse. Nope.

Aunt Matty, she had one kid, but how do you ask a single parent of one kid, to take six more and by the way, you gotta support them alone, cause there was no way you're gonna get a fucking dime of child support. She lived in efficiency behind Aunt Mary's house, where would we sleep, on her roof?

Aunt Mary, well she already had three kids, did she want the burden of six more. Another uncle forced to do whatever to support six more kids, nine kids, did she really want to ask her husband to support nine kids. Not in this life.

If I had been either of my uncles and my aunts asked to raise that many kids, I'd leave on the first train out of town. Nope, there was no way anyone would take all six. I believe even an orphanage would have had second thoughts on that one.

Even though Sher tried, I already knew she was bitching for nothing. Dad wasn't gonna give up the single life for his kids, he wouldn't even do it for mom, he sure wasn't gonna do it for us.

I wanted to tell Sher to shut the hell up, quit wasting your time. You're his damn favorite and he doesn't give a shit what he's doing to you, he sure the hell won't care about the rest of us.

I was right, their conversation went absolutely nowhere.

Dad had come home after being gone so many days, because he needed something. He needed his kids to put on a pathetic show for a stupid judge that should have asked each and every one of us if we were ok.

No, I would not have ratted my dad out, but I sure as hell would have said how lonely and sad I was, and how much I missed my mom. Hey they have the witness protection program don't they? I think I would have qualified for that one.

So, as a useless father, he dropped us off in front of our house, shifted his car into drive, and hauled ass, dust trail and all.

I was glad to see him go. Now I had to figure how in the heck I was going to help Sher, with the kids, the house the meals. I believe she was near her breaking point, and with my emotional state, there was no way I could handle the responsibility.

We stood there a few seconds watching dad drive away, choking on the dust he literally blew in our faces with the screeching of his fucking tires. What a sight we must have been in his rear view mirror, if he had even bothered to look. I seriously doubt it.

Bitter sweet.
He was gone for now, Sweet.
No one was helping us, Bitter.
Again, in my life, I hated everyone.

## 58

Waking up in the middle of the night, I swear I could hear mom crying. Sometimes I could go back to sleep, then there were nights it was impossible. Seeing her dress hang on the closet door seemed to be what got me through it all.

Our Phantom father only came long enough to change clothes and bitch about something, anything. Never did he say,

"I miss you kids, are you kids ok?" Rather, he said absolutely nothing.

Crying for me never stopped. It was impossible to imagine what it was going to be like growing up without my mom. I wondered if and when I married and had kids of my own, if this same situation were to happen to me, would I, could I, just walk away from my own kids. Abandon them.

Only if I were a fucking animal could I ever consider such a thing. Any respect I may have had for dad was completely diminished.

Dad asked me once. "Do you love me because you respect me? Or, do you respect me because you love me?

Get the fuck outta here! That's a trick question and he knew it. It was also a loose, loose situation for me. If I say I love you because I respect you, I'm in trouble. If I say I respect you because I love you, I'm in trouble. How the hell do you answer such a question to someone whose reputation stems from respect?

I can't even remember how I got out of that situation, maybe the phone rang, maybe he saw the confused look on my face, and had a pretty good idea I'd piss myself trying to answer that question just to satisfy his curiosity. I wonder how many people he fucked with over that one.

Sher had decided to take us twice a week to the park. We all needed a break, and what better way then to run free at the park. Sher would watch the boys running everywhere, screaming and laughing and from time to time crack a smile herself. She would watch Becky and Carrie talking and laughing and briefly, she herself would relax, and enjoy the time we spent together at the park.

One day after we had been at the park for quite a long time, we arrived home and Liz was there, alone. It shocked the hell out of me to see her rummaging through moms things.

Sher said. "What do you think you're doing?"

Liz said. "I leant a lot of these clothes to your mom, they belong to me."

This was the first time we had heard that one. No one in my life ever came and said. "Shirley give me my clothes back."

But now, of all times, Liz wanted what she said was hers. Was this big mouth serious? Did she actually think we would just stand there and let her take what belonged to our mom?

This bitch lost her damn mind.

Now, I know cussing for a twelve year old is not acceptable behavior, and being that mom raised us properly, under most circumstances I would agree. Little kids have no business cussing, but no one was gonna tell me I could or could not cuss this bitch out in my mind. And as far as respecting my elders, well this bitch deserved no respect whatsoever.

It was ashamed really, because in spite of being such a bitch, Liz was a beautiful woman, I give her that. She dressed nice, her hair was always fixed, and she had money. But in reality, she was a straight up big mouth bitch. And though I would never admit this, I think my vocabulary was a direct hit from her. If I had to inherit one thing from her, why did it have to be her big fucking mouth? I'd knock a bitch out if she were to ever say, "Hey you remind me of Liz."

Catching Liz at our house, uninvited Sher went directly to the phone. She called the garage, dad wasn't there. She called Sal-E's, he wasn't there either. She was so furious she even called Helena to see if dad and Ray were at her house, by some chance, but there was no answer.

Sher began yelling at Liz, "You get out of here. You're not taking anything of our moms out of this house."

Liz yelled back, trying to act tough to a fourteen year old.

Since Helena wasn't there to beat the shit out of Liz, she yelled at Sher. "They are my clothes."

Sher said. "I don't give a damn, your not taking anything from this house."

I was crying, Sher started crying. Liz was about to say something then stopped herself, took the suitcase she had brought with her, hoping to steal mom's things till we caught her there, and stormed out empty handed.

"Damn bitch!" I heard Sher say.

Good for Sher. She stood up for mom and moms things, knowing that was all we had left.

Again, Sher called both places dad "lived." The garage and his precious bar and both times, she left messages for him to call his kids. She was extremely pissed; I was surprised she didn't cuss out Sal and the mechanics.

Sher called everywhere she could think of looking for him. If it had been a real emergency about one of the kids, he would never have known. She tried calling the same places over and over throughout the day but he was nowhere to be found. I wondered how many times mom went through this, trying to find him only to waste her time.

We were getting ready for bed, when the phone rang. Sher answered it yelling. I went to mom's room, to listen to Sher. She was crying as she said. "I don't know who she thinks she is, but she's not taking a damn thing out of this house that belongs to mom. You keep that big mouth away from here."

I have no idea what dad was saying to Sher, but if he was threatening her, she was not afraid of him at all. She hung up without saying good-bye.

It would be two more days before dad came to check on us and leave us some money. He had graduated from his pathetic ten-dollar bill to fifty dollars. Sher never looked at him when she talked to him anymore. Maybe it was the love-hate feeling she was having for him. Sher loved dad more than me, that's for sure, but she hated what he was doing to us and ignoring his responsibility of "raising his kids, being mother and father." As the judge had thought, he was doing. She seemed to hate him, but I know for sure her love for him was stronger than her hate. Mine on the other hand was not.

As a kid I would have been traumatized if I had been unfortunate to witness my dad beat down a grown ass man, instead I witnessed him brutally beating my mom. Perhaps it was mean of me, but I just couldn't love him, as I should have.

Now with all the new dramatic events, I hated him even more, because he not only walked away from us, but now he was allowing his sister to come in and take things that belonged to our mom. Sher could love him all she wanted. I couldn't get past my hate.

Then, I would think back of all the times I cried to stay home with mom. All the times he whipped me to make me go to school, knowing damn good and well I wanted to be with my mom. That is why I wanted to be with her.

Now, she was taken from me and I hated him for not allowing me to spend the time with her. I hated him for taking those moments from me. The more I thought of the mean things he did to me, even when mom was alive, the more I hated him.

I suppose dad told Sher some bullshit story about Liz and maybe she bought it. I have no idea.

We went to the park again on a Friday. It was the middle of the summer, and it was hot, very hot.

Sher decided it wasn't a good idea to have the kids out in the sun for too many hours, so we went home early. It was a slow walk home, not only it was so damn hot, but also we knew once we got home, that it would be even hotter inside our house. That old water cooler was no match for the summer heat, no matter how many times an hour we watered it down.

I thought of the wintertime, wishing it was snowing and we would be having snowball fights. My mind wandered on everything cold as we walked, drenched in sweat, hating the thought of entering the house and feeling the gush of heat as we passed the water cooler.

When I grow up I'm moving up north, somewhere cold, somewhere freezing cold, where its' cold six months out of the year and where the wind blows freezing cold blasts of air at you.

I'm moving to New York, or Chicago, hey I may even move to the North Pole just so I don't have to ever be so miserably hot again. What an incredible idea. I laughed to myself. Sher saw me smile and said. "Why you laughing Malina?"

"I wish it would snow." I said.

Sher also smiled at the thought of it snowing.

When we got home, the first thing I noticed, mom's dress wasn't hanging on the closet door.

I screamed.

Sher said, "What's wrong?"

"Mom's dress, it's gone."

Sher opened the closet and half mom's things were gone.

"That fucking bitch." She screamed.

She ran to the phone and called dads garage, he answered. She was screaming at him "That bitch came and took mom's clothes."

"Dad I want those clothes back in this house now. Malina is crying, dad I mean it." She screamed as loud as she could.

Hey, I say, screw the respect. He wasn't taking care of his own, and Sher was fed up. She almost sounded the way dad did when yelling at one of the gangsters. Again, I couldn't make out anything dad was saying.

Sher continued. "Those things are for us, when we grow up, not for that bitch. You know good and well those clothes aren't Liz's, they were moms. How can you allow her to come in here and take them, especially mom's blue and green dress?"

Sher was crying and yelling then she just hung up the phone. She walked away from the phone without saying a word to me.

What had he told her? Did he tell her it was ok that Liz came in our house and just took what ever she wanted? Sher stormed to her room, and started slamming things down to the floor. She was never one of those crybaby kids, and she definitely wasn't gonna let us see her cry. She was supposed to be the strong one.

I was afraid to follow her knowing she was in no shape to talk at that moment. So, instead of following her to her room, I sat on my bed looking around. Something was wrong, something was missing, but what was it? Something just was not right in our room.

Then I realized, moms old trunk was missing. Her big old trunk she kept all her personal things in, all her keepsakes. Like all the costumes, she had made for us every Halloween. Her personal things like letters her and dad wrote to one another while he was in the Air Force. Why in the hell would Liz want that those things? She knew damn good and well those items were not hers. And, if for some reason the troublemaking bitch were going to say the old trunk was hers, why would she take all moms personal things?

"Sher!" I screamed. "Sher!" I screamed again.

"What? She ran out of her room almost tripping over herself, to see why I was screaming so loud... When she appeared, I could tell she was very upset.

"She took moms trunk. All moms' things" I was screaming and almost hysterical as I pointed where the trunk used to be. She looked around the room for a second then she went from room to room, hoping, I guess that Liz had not taken the things that were in the trunk, instead only the trunk.

But why the hell would Liz want the trunk, or anything in it. We knew for a fact that was mom's trunk handed down from grandma, to be given to us when we grew up.

It made no damn sense. Again, Sher called dad yelling at him. Then she did something no normal rational, daughter of a gangster would ever do.

She said, "If she does not bring that trunk right back where she took it from tonight, I'm gonna call the police.

Dad was home in three minutes.

I'll tell you one thing for sure, if you ever want to get the attention of a gangster, threaten to call the police on them.

We could tell he was furious by the way he slammed the brakes of his car only inches from the steps. If Danny or J.J. had been playing in the front yard he would have run over them, luckily all four of the kids were on the porch. He didn't get out of the car right away, rather sat there a few minutes.

I pretty much figured he was either going to beat the shit out of Sher for such disrespect, or he was going to get stoned before he came inside, and try and sweet talk her.

One thing was for sure, he knew Liz took everything, because he wasn't on the phone bitching Liz out. However, if he knew she took it all, then why would he allow her too, especially the dress I loved so much, the love letters they had written to one other.

What business did Liz have with any of it? How does anyone hurt kids in such a manner as to take the memories of their mom, the mom that died so suddenly.

I already knew if Sher didn't call the police, I damn sure would.

# 59

I believe Sher mentally prepared herself for an ass whooping. Possibly, she didn't care anymore anyway. She was just so tired of everything. I had learned a valuable lesson. I will never let anyone in my family get beat and not try my best to protect them.

I had failed my mom because I did nothing to help her. My fear of a complete monster kept me from at least trying to help. I had such a guilty heart.

Maybe my mom would be here now if I had tried my best to help her. I hated myself for not doing anything that night. God, I hated myself.

Should dad start to hit Sher, there would be no other choice but to call the police. If, for some reason I couldn't get to the phone, my next choice would be to run past him and go to my friends' house and get her mom and dad.

It goes without saying dad wasn't about to let me get past him. And, if by some complete miracle I did, I'm almost positive there would be a ten-foot tall gangster blocking the door. Who the hell was I kidding?

I was sitting on my bed, Sher paced back and forth a few times. The kids had all gone to sleep already, so it was just me and Sher against him.

What a fucking sickening feeling. To wait to get your ass whooped. That wasn't a feeling I liked at all. Now, I remembered my mom crying the night he beat her. She was crying before he even got into the house, not because she had done anything wrong, but she already knew she was going to get beat for something she wouldn't do.

After Sher paced a few times, she said. "Oh, Fuck this." And went to bed. Just like that.

I'm not quite sure if dad tiptoed into the house that night not to wake us, or if he even came in at all. All I know is I woke the next day everyone was still asleep, and he was nowhere to be found.

What a relief. We had survived another day without him, and now it seemed, we had to worry about this day.

Something occurred to me, through all the bullshit in life, through all the neglect and hunger and crying and sadness and loneliness. My birthday had passed two weeks before.

I wasn't sad because I didn't get a big ol birthday party, I was sad because my mom wasn't there to see me become a teenager.

It wasn't like we ever had big birthday parties anyway. Simply put, there was never enough money for such things. Mom always made us a cake, and managed a little gift, usually something she made herself, but as far as friends, food, gifts, party favors, etc. I never once in my life had the experience of one... Actually, none of us did, but it didn't really matter, mom always made it feel like the happiest day of our lives.

No one had remembered it was my birthday, even I didn't, but it was ok. I surely wasn't going to go cry about it to Sher. She already had enough problems without me complaining about a birthday. Naw, I just as soon forget it anyway.

The end of July was near. We had some really hot days again, and all I could dream about was snow, and cold fresh air, and making snowmen... With only one water cooler to keep us cool, it seemed impossible.

Sandy and Jewel's snow cone stand was long gone, so we couldn't depend on them. Sher would let the kids play with the water hose from time to time just to get cool. All that did was make a muddy mess in the front yard and we couldn't go in the back yard to get wet, there were too many stickers all over the yard, and who wants to get wet with a water hose with their shoes on.

We learned to do what ever we could to help pass the days. Honestly, we could only watch so much TV. We would sit around and sing, just us four girls, harmonizing, making up songs, changing lyrics to songs we already knew.

Me, I just pretended mom was right there with us, watching us sing, and play, and talk. I could vision her beautiful smile, and hear her say, "Good job, girls."

Danny and J.J. would still go out and play in the little city; it just wasn't the same for me without mom there.

Poor Sher she tried so hard to make descent meals for us but she had no knowledge of anything besides shit on a shingle. I guess that's what it was called. Mom used to make it all the time. Hamburger meat, bread, and gravy. Poor people's meal mom used to say, but it was good and filling.

It was very easy to tire of the same meals, but then we had no concept of preparing meals. Ovaltine and bologna, day in and day out. Bologna, we ate more bologna than anything else. And I'm not talking fried bologna. I mean just bologna, at times with no bread at all. That was our entrée. Now, for dessert, nope not some elegant dessert prepared by a chef. Our sweets were sugar on bread. That's it! Get a slice of bread, sprinkle some sugar, and munch away. Times we really craved sweets; we would put an excessive amount of sugar on the bread... Hey! We were starving.

How I wanted a home cooked meal. But it just seemed everyone forgot us.

I wondered did everyone stay away because of dad.

Ok, I knew mom's family hated him because, in their eyes he killed her, guilty, hands down guilty. So rather, than help us and try to take us with them, they left us under the guidance of who they believed was a murderer.

Then there was dad's family. They were never around either, but I'm really not sure why.

For arguments sake let's say they were afraid to question him about our welfare. For Example, if one of them were to say, "Johnny, are you taking good care of the kids?" He might just blow up on them.

Naw, that made no sense. They were all mothers, and as mothers, why wouldn't they at least check on us, make sure we were ok?

Did dad tell them to leave us alone? Did he want us taken away from him so he didn't have to bother with us? Did he really not care?

Oh, it was obvious he didn't care, but did everyone else not care also. I just didn't get it. We were mourning for our mom.

Thinking on it maybe, I needed some type of counseling. Maybe I needed a mother figure in my life.

Poor, poor Sher. She couldn't be a mother figure; she was just a kid herself. She was only eighteen months older than I was.

She knew more than I did, that was obvious. She was, after all, the one that explained to me what an orgy was. She knew how to cook, a little. She did care for us, and she wasn't frightened to stay home alone without an adult there. So yes, she was better educated than I was.

But how is a fourteen year old trained to be mother, father, protector, cook, housekeeper, sister to five kids? How did she have the strength to take care of all of us? Why didn't she just throw her hands up and say fuck all this bull shit and call the operator and scream for help to have some kind of Children's home come take us away, so the burden could be lifted from her shoulders.

Why? Because she was Sher, she wasn't a quitter. She wasn't about to give up and say fuck all y'all brats, I'm done with this.

She was Sher, and she was in it for the long haul. I couldn't have done it. I was too sad, too scared, and too wimpy.

Sher was, of course, as sad and lonely as me, but she couldn't just break down every five minutes like I did.

What responsibility and strength she had. I never saw her crying, not only for mom, I knew she missed her, but she also lost her personal life, her friends, her books, her school. She didn't get to go to the library and sit there for hours in peace and read. There was no time. She had to be confined with five kids, that at times, didn't listen to her, disrespected her, and talked back to her.

I don't believe she took it to heart when we disrespected her; she just beat the crap out of us. Not the same way dad had beat mom, but Sher knew how to put us in our place. When dad would beat one of us, or whoop us, once he got stoned, he would come home and say, "I'm sorry baby, or I'm sorry son." Then hug and kiss us.

Not Sher, her apology would be, "You should've listened to me in the first place, and I wouldn't have hit you." Nothing more.

In her eyes, we were whooped from her because it was our fault. We didn't argue with that.

Dad came and went, and for a while, nothing was said about the trunk and mom's clothes. I still cried everyday for the dress. It was my mom's no matter what that bitch Liz said.

It had all the memories of mom on it, her perfume, and her powders. Then I realized, if Liz ever brought it back it would never be the same dress to me. It would now smell like Liz's powerful bar room cheap perfume. The thought that Liz even wore it took the love right out of it for me. I mean surely she took it so that she could wear it. What other reason would she even want the dress?

I was tormented over the dress, it was the first thing I had seen when I first entered the house after the funeral, of course I wanted it, but not if Liz had worn it.

She was a cheap loud mouth and I hated her and everything she stood for. How could a dress that looked so beautiful on my mom, even begin to compare on Liz's nasty self. Somehow, the dress would seem trashy with Liz having possession of it. I knew now I wouldn't even want to see it.

I hated Liz and knew I never wanted to see her again, especially if she had on the dress.

# 60

We began spending a lot of time at the park. I was always so sad to be at home, looking at moms' bed, picturing her in my mind the last time I saw her in our house, her blue lips, her eyes closed. If her lips hadn't been so blue, I would have just thought she was asleep.

I thought how dad was right next to her in bed asleep that night, yet it seemed he had no idea she had died. Was that possible at all? To lie next to someone and not know that they are dead. I knew for sure he lied about talking with her when she was crying that night. No matter what he said I was not confusing times or dates as he insinuated I was. He hadn't been fighting with mom that night, that I was one hundred percent positive about.

So if he wasn't fighting with her, why would he lie?

He only made one of us look very stupid, and I'm not the one everyone hated, he was. So why lie? I mean honestly, the things I had to say made him look innocent, he made himself look guilty with all the lies he was telling.

Then there was the court thing. He stood there and accepted the year to get his affairs in order, which he was not doing.

What was he up to? Who had he attempted to kill and why? Why would he risk his freedom on something he so easily could have ordered Ray or any of his other men to do? Why do it himself?

I think I had seen more and heard more horrible things in my short thirteen-year life, then most kids are even allowed to watch on TV. Yet I knew these things to be facts. I didn't make any of this up.

Perhaps that is why I seemed to jump the gun on occasions. I didn't think like a normal thirteen-year-old girl. I didn't even know what it felt like to be thirteen. I knew most, maybe even more things then my own mom did, yet there was not one person helping me figure life out.

So when Sher suggested, no demanded, we go to the park every day, I knew it was good for all of us.

The park really was so much fun. So much to do, so many different areas of the park to visit. We never got bored, actually if we could, we probably would have stayed there all night and sleep on the park benches.

At one end of the park was a public swimming pool. I personally would never go near it, after all the bullshit at the lake a few years back. I hated water and wanted nothing to do with it.

The boys would constantly beg Sher to let them swim, even though neither of them knew how... regardless if they knew or not they still begged her to let them get in the water, just to play, to stay cool, to have fun, maybe even learn to swim. There were three lifeguards on duty at any given time, and I'm sure if either of my brothers were to go under and not float back to the top, the lifeguards would save them, after all that was their job.

The issue was with money. It cost fifty cents each to get in the swimming pool area for the day, and with hardly any money, Sher knew she just couldn't spend what little money we did have, no matter how much they begged.

"We still have the water hose." Sher explained to them one afternoon as we were walking home. Nonetheless, they would beg, but Sher insisted there was not enough money for such luxuries.

Dad was home that when we got home that afternoon, which was so unusual because we only saw him every three or four days now.

He was in the restroom, shaving, or something, when we got there. We all went straight to our room. We, rather I, wanted to avoid him... Sher went to the kitchen, to wait on him so she could confront him when he got out of the restroom.

His freshly laundered clothes from the cleaners were laid out on his bed, his shoes appeared to have already been shined, and everything set up for him as if he was a prince, royalty, waiting to go to a formal ball.

I looked at all his things in complete disgust. It's ashamed, we barely had food in the house, yet this bastard afforded the luxury of freshly pressed clothes.

It had been a few days since the trunk incident. Sher had threatened to call the cops on Liz; dad had rushed home to bitch Sher out, but backed down once he got home.

He took the coward way out and just left that day, maybe it was the best thing. Not for dad, but for Sher. She would have been put in a tough spot, to call or not call the police.

No matter what he did, didn't do, said, didn't say, she still loved her precious dad, I'm sure she just didn't want a confrontation with him.

When dad finally came out of the restroom I heard them talking. At first, I couldn't make out what they were saying, and then I heard Sher say, "I need money to feed them, we're starving here. How do you expect me to take care of them with no money?"

Dad mumbled something, and then he began getting dressed.

Sher said. "Dad, why are you doing this? Why aren't you ever here? Why don't you take care of your own kids?"

It was so obvious Sher was sick and tired of doing dad's job.

"I'm working, I'm trying, I'm paying the bills, I'm doing all I can." He sounded absolutely pathetic.

"No you're not!" She yelled, "Why don't you stay home and take care of them, you answer all their questions, you"...

Without warning he turned and walked outside, he went to the trunk of his car, a bit of an intimidating move; you know how those gagsters go to their car to get something? A gun or what ever, and he came back with a big basket. "Here." He said.

"Here are some of your moms' things."

I walked in the room shaking, almost too damn afraid to speak. I looked toward the basket, noticed the letters, and just a few of mom's dresses.

"Where's moms green and blue dress?" I asked him.

He didn't answer me immediately. I mean really, I knew he didn't have to answer any of my questions; he was the bad ass in the family.

He looked directly into my eyes. "It really did belong to Liz, Malina." Almost apologetically looking for the right words to say.

I started crying.

Liz was his sister, he wasn't going to take my side, he was taking that bitches side.

"Even if it is her dress, mom has had it for years, why does Liz even want it?" I was crying louder. I was so upset, so mad I couldn't hear a word he said. I just walked away, letting him talk to himself.

I half expected him to creep up behind me, pull me by my hair back to his room and say, "Don't you disrespect me by walking away?" But he didn't. Instead, he left the basket on his bed, handed Sher some money and walked out the door.

He didn't say good-bye, didn't hug anyone, he just left.

This is no man I thought. This is far from a man.

I wondered what happened to the trunk. If he was able to get some of the things out of it, why didn't he bring the entire trunk back? It was moms, Liz didn't own that trunk. Why would dad allow Liz to keep it? Why was that bitch allowed to take our memories from us?

I had no feeling in me when dad left that day, no feeling for him at all. If I never saw him again, I would not have cared. He was doing everything possible to alienate us, and as far as I was concerned, he had accomplished just that.

For me I had no mother, now I had no father...

## 61

Sometimes the days were so hot in that old house it was almost unbearable. The big trees out in the front yard seemed to block a lot of the sun, but still, it would get so hot we could hardly stand it.

Sher let the kids use the water hose almost everyday now, not caring at all about the mud and puddles it would make. Not caring how high the water bill got. Even Sher and I would stand out in the sun and let the kids spray the water on us.

That old water cooler just couldn't keep anything cool at all. Watering it down every fifteen minutes didn't really help much, and the only room that stayed even a little cooler was moms' room, but not knowing when and if dad would come home at all, Sher didn't allow anyone to sleep in moms' bed...

We would sleep with the windows open, but then the mosquitoes would eat us up. Sometimes late at night I would fill the tub with cold water and just lay in the tub to cool down.

One thing for sure, I couldn't stand the hot weather. I would rather put on two sweaters and a jacket inside the house to keep warm in the winter, than to deal with the hot horrible summer. Sometimes when I would get up really late at night, imagine my mom in the kitchen sewing clothes for us or making doll clothes. I realized that would never ever happen again. She would never make another dress or short outfit for me again. So many wonderful things mom did for us. It was all over now.

The nights I would get up and lay in the cool tub of water I would think to myself, if I weren't so damn afraid of water, thanks to dad and his near drowning of me. I would lay in that tub and drown myself but I was afraid I would not succeed rather, I'd get a lot of water in my lungs and start to choke on it as I did that day at the lake.

Most nights Sher would be reading her books just as I would be ready to go to bed. Sometimes we would sit and talk, sometimes we would cry, hardly ever would we laugh. I would get sad thinking, not only of mom, but also of Sher and I would wonder how the heck she did all the things mom would do for us. She had the strength of ten kids her age. She was such an incredible teen, because she gave up so much to take care of us kids just so we wouldn't be left alone.

It was the beginning of August, about a month before school would start again. Two and a half months since mom had died. It seemed like years to me. I was always so sad, and with headaches day and night, and it seemed I hated so many people for what we had to go through.

Very few people came by to check on us. Mostly it would be dad's sisters, that would bring bags of groceries, sometimes dad's famous ten-dollar bill, but never did any one come and talk to us, see how we really were doing. Were we afraid at night? Did we have any problems we needed to talk about?

The more everyone stayed away, the more Sher and I resented that they even came at all.

I could not have imagined my mom would have acted like this if any of her sisters or sisters- in-law would have passed away. I imagined she would have done everything in her power to help their kids, no matter what kind of hell dad would have put her through. Yet no one was doing for her kids. Surely, she was a witness to this; even from her grave, she must have felt her kids were hurting.

We had finished lunch, and were cleaning the kitchen when dad appeared out of nowhere... He came in, got a few of his things out of his dresser drawers, and picked some things out of his closet, always in his famous fricken hurry. I could smell marijuana on him, so I turned and walked out of the room.

He went to find Sher in the kitchen. I heard her raise her voice to try and talk to him, but he just gave her some mumbo jumbo talk about respect.

Sher started crying while dad went to his closet and took something from the very back of the closet.

I watched him as he slithered around.

Instantly I recognized what it was. It was the pistol he had beat my mom with. Was this bastard kidding? He literally waltzes in the house, takes the gun he used as a weapon against my mom, talks shit to Sher and he ignores all of the kids.

And he wants to talk about respect. Yes, he and Liz were blood relatives for sure; they both had big mouths and cared only for themselves. Was it possible to hate a man any more than I hated him at that moment?

He was attempting to pack some of his things in a small bag, as if he were a man packing to go on a fishing trip, or an out of town business trip, not a worry in the world.

God, if there was one, was surely going to punish this bastard one day. All the crying in the world was never going to bring my mom back, but where does it say we kids have to be treated like shit by this fucking monster.

I could hear Sher crying and I was crying. Dad couldn't get out of there fast enough. He had apparently moved on with his life. That old saying "till death do us part," was so true. Once mom died, he was done with his family life, with his kids, with any kind of mourning mom. He couldn't even wait for the respectful one-year anniversary of her death.

I wondered why even come home? Why not take all his shit out of the house and never come back? He wasn't doing anything for us, beside his periodical ten dollars.

People get locked up for abandoning kids. That's child abuse, that's child neglect, but who was going to tell on him?

No one, because no one had the guts, everyone was afraid of him. The only person I knew had any guts at all, to talk shit to him was Sher, and even she backed down once he frightened her.

There was no way I would step up to him. I faithfully admit I was afraid and couldn't stand him being there for five minutes. There was no way in hell I would insist he stay home and be "Ward Cleaver" to us.

One thing stopped for me when my mom died. My heart from loving anyone and I stopped pissing myself. Seems like the biggest fear that always caused me to piss was the fear dad would hit mom or one of the kids. Now he could never ever hurt mom again, and for sure, he wasn't going to stick around long enough to hit anyone. He wasn't stupid, he was a free man.

His priority was himself. Sad as it sounds and as horrible, it seemed for Sher, I was glad he wasn't around.

Only because Sher loved him so much, was she able to go on, do all he expected of her. Ten minutes here, ten minutes there of his time. Twenty dollars here thirty dollars there, that's all he had to do, and pay the monthly utilities. He was no better than the rats he used to kill. Only thing, this rat had a name.

I watched him as he left the house. Sher still crying in the kitchen, my brothers playing in the front yard not even noticing him as he passed them in the yard.

Dad ignoring them as they threw the baseball that almost smacked him right in his face as they threw it... Carrie and Becky continued playing jacks without missing a beat, never even looking up at him as he almost stepped on their jacks.

Yes, no one seemed touched by his appear then disappear act, no one but me. I stood by the door to the little room and watched him as he opened his trunk of his car to put his bag in it. Noticing also, he didn't park his car right in front of the house as he always did, to disturb any game the kids might be playing.

No this time he parked his car in the street almost in front of Sandy and Jewels house, which seemed odd to me.

This bastard liked making his grand appearances and letting everyone know "Daddy's Home."

Not today! Today he seemed to be sneaking around.

What was he up to now?

I started to just walk away, go about my business, but the little bitch I was now, wouldn't allow me to shy away, so I opened the door and walked out onto the porch, as he was getting into the drivers side of his car. I stepped off the porch and walked toward the big oak tree and I saw it. What I really hadn't expected to see.

He was hiding the fact there was a woman with him. Of all things, he was with a woman and it was not just any woman. I couldn't believe what I saw. He was worst than a monster now.

If all the rumors and gossip were true, that he had killed my mom to go on with his life. If he killed her, so he had freedom to do as he pleased. And if he killed her, was this who he killed my mom for?

## 62

I stood there five minutes just thinking of my mom, wondering how many women dad had been with and just left her at home, while chasing women and staying out all night. I wondered how the heck mom could've stood it. Messed up shit like this, we kids had no idea of.

How the hell does anyone live like that? I personally could've cared less. If he stayed gone the rest of his miserable life it would not bother me one bit, but does he have no shame in front of his kids.

No, he didn't and it just put one more notch in my belt spelt hate. How much hate could I have bottled up inside me? Was hate a good emotion for me to have?

Through all this pain and anger, I was positive I didn't think I wanted to feel love for anyone, as sad as it may seem, I didn't even want to feel love for my brothers and sisters.

To feel love meant I would have to hurt by someone else's hands, and I just wasn't ready to hurt for any one, any time soon.

I would feel bad for anyone, but love was something I wanted to shy away from.

"Malina, Malina." Sher was yelling out my name from the porch. I turned around to see her looking at me. "What are you staring at?" She asked as I turned to walk toward her.

"Your damn daddy." I said in the most smart-ass tone possible. I walked right past her without crying, flung the screen door open, and stomped through the living room like a little kid having a temper tantrum. Then I stopped right in front of the closet that, at one time was the spot my moms dress once hung, and broke down crying.

Why was I crying? I wondered. Things would never be worse than loosing my mom, so to cry over any bullshit dad did seemed so minimal. I was a basket case of nerves, a roller coaster of emotion. It seemed nothing was ever gonna get better. And really, without my mom I didn't care, or even want things to get better.

A thought flashed in my brain. If things never get better, if things are always fucked up, then I'll never be disappointed, never have to cry or hurt for anything or anyone. But is that a way to live? What did I know about living? My life seemed to end before it even got started. To cry everyday for my mom was one thing, to cry over this useless father of mine, even I realized how stupid I might have looked.

Being the wonderful sister Sher was she followed me, as if she didn't have enough problems without me falling apart on her.

I went directly to the kitchen and poured me a big glass of Kool-aid, then a second glass. After I downed the second glass I realized, Sher finally learned how to make it just like mom.

"Malina what happened?" Sher asked.

"I hate him Sher, I swear I hate him." I screamed

"What did he do?" She wanted to know.

"He has a woman in the car with him." I was almost out of breath as I said it. Sher looked at me so serious like, really bitch, you're crying over that.

"Malina, surely you didn't think he didn't have a girlfriend?" She said as she looked at me, but as she looked at me she began to raise her right eyebrow, higher and higher. She just stood there looking at me with that incredibly raised brow, just staring, waiting on my reaction. I looked at her and could not help but laugh.

As I was laughing, she kinda did her lip like Elvis. She was standing there, one eyebrow arched to the high heaven, her lip quivering just like Elvis, then she began to shake her hips like Elvis.

She was singing, "I'm all shook up." I was laughing and crying at the same time. She stopped for a moment to laugh with me then she did it all over again. Almost three months of nothing but crying, I had my first real laugh. Sher, my hero, had done it again. She took a situation and made it into a joke.

Sher, though she loved him, made no excuses for him and surely, she didn't approve of the things he did to us, but with all her problems and responsibilities, still found time to cheer me up.

The saddest kid in the world finally had a smile on her face. I left Elvis in the kitchen, still singing, still laughing and went to the porch to check on the kids.

I was standing at the front door when a car pulled up, one I recognized as aunt Matty.

Aunt Matty, dad's youngest sister, was about ten years older than Sher, which put her right at twenty-four or twenty-five years old. Matty, a single mom with a five-year-old daughter Lori. As soon as aunt Matty opened the car door Lori jumped out of the car and ran to play with J.J. and Danny.

Aunt Matty looked up and saw me standing at the front door, as she climbed the stairs she said. "Oh my Malina, you look just like your mother standing there."

Mom would spend so much time standing in the doorway watching us play outside; she would also be standing there waiting for us on the days we walked home from school.

Sometimes she would just stand in the door way and stare. I always thought she was wondering where dad was, but maybe she was just staring out past the big old oak trees, dreaming what life could be like past those trees. It seemed everyone knew it to be her iconic pose.

Mom was usually the first person anyone would see upon arriving at our house.

A beautiful silhouette of a woman against the background of a trashy old house.

What a portrait Leonardo Da Vinci could have created.

With the words Matty spoke, I began to cry again.

Matty came in the house as Sher stepped in the living room.

"How are y'all? Matty asked.

"We're ok." Sher lied, but with a tone of being short tempered.

Matty sat on the sofa. "I want to say how proud I am of you girls for taking care of the kids, I'm sure your mom is very proud of you also."

Neither Sher nor I said one word. I guess Matty felt the tension in the room. We weren't necessarily upset with her, we were upset with everyone.

"Do ya'll have any food?" Matty asked, as she went to the kitchen.

Me and Sher looked at each other, and then followed her to the kitchen. Matty wasn't like Liz talking shit, she was, or seemed to be really concerned.

She looked in the icebox noticing what we already knew, there was very little food, shaking her head, almost as disgusted as we were.

"Has your dad been around?" She asked sounding rather pissed off.

"He just left." Sher said. I wanted to walk out of the room but didn't, rather staying in the kitchen to hear what Matty had to say.

"Girls I'm very sorry this happened to you kids and I really want to help, but I'm barely making it myself.

Started to sound like a sad song to me. I was just being a little bitch I guess.

"I get no help from Lori's dad but I wanted to know, (Ok, here it comes, I thought.)

"I wanted to know if it would be ok if we came and stayed with you kids for a few days."

"WHAAAAAAT?" I thought. Why? Why would anyone deliberately want to stay here?

Matty was young and hip and fun to be around but again, I couldn't help but wonder Why? No one in their right mind ever volunteered to stay in our dump. We kids were use to it so to us we could look past the dump aspect of it, but to have Matty ask to actually stay, seemed to be a joke.

I looked at Sher, she looked at me. "I guess so." Sher said shrugging her shoulders.

I really wanted to trust that Matty's motive was to help, not to come in and insult our mom as Liz had.

So, I bluntly blurted it all out to her, the way Liz had come in and disrespected our mom.

"Aunt Matty it's ok if you want to stay, but when Liz was here she said mean things about this house and mom not cleaning it." I wanted to call Liz a bitch, but Matty, after all was Liz's sister.

Still crying, Matty stood up and hugged me.

"Look Malina, me, my sisters, and mom have all lived here at one time or another.

"I know about the issues with this house. In all the years everyone lived here no one has ever put any money into fixing it or repairing it."

"Your mom was the only one to ever even paint it." She said. I looked past her at the lilac paint, remembering mom tirelessly painting the rooms, with only one paintbrush, not even a roller to assist her. Now, looking at the lilac paint, it actually looked nice. Then I thought of Uncle Bill and Papa who were actually painters, and wondered why they hadn't come in and painted it for her.

"I'm going to call your dad and tell him that me and Lori will be staying here a few days. Is that Ok?" She asked us both again.

Sher and I agreed.

After what I had just witnessed with dad, it was obvious he wouldn't be coming home anytime soon. It is certain it would be a relief that someone would be with his kids. God knows he wasn't going to. Matty informed us she would be back in a few days.

Her visit lasted about an hour, trying her best to cheer us up and possibly relieving her own guilt for not coming around sooner. To me sooner or later, the fact she was making the effort to help, was enough for me.

# 63

Matty left with Lori assuring us she would return on Friday. She didn't call dad from our house so I wasn't sure if she were sincere about staying with us or not. I had a lot of mixed emotions about it all, thinking it may be nice to have an adult with us, though considered quite young she was the only adult showing any type of interest in being with us.

Dad hadn't been back, only calling once or twice to talk to Sher. It became a joke to us, when we realized it was dad on the phone we would all make background noises to try to make Sher laugh.

Friday rolled around and just as she promised aunt Matty showed up, the trunk of her car loaded with things of hers and Lori's. Immediately Lori began playing with the boys while Carrie and Becky helped Matty unload her car.

Sher stayed in the kitchen making lunch while I went out to help Matty also.

Matty did some small talk with us mostly, "Put this box here, put this box there."

It took all of fifteen minutes to unload her car and by the looks of the things she brought, this was definitely not a long-term stay. But then again who ever said it was. I reminded my self of her conversation. She said she was going to spend a few days with us, not a few years.

"Do you girls think it will be ok if we sleep in your mom's room?"

That question had my head spinning. Why would she want to? I had to think on this, but had to think on it quickly, because she was standing there waiting on an answer so she would know where to put her things.

Oh my, no one had slept in mom's bed other than dad, not even to take an afternoon nap did Sher allow Danny to sleep there, or to get a tiny bit of sticky wet air from that horrid water cooler did Sher allow anyone on that bed. The bed always remained made up, at all times, unless dad stayed, which was seldom if ever anymore.

"What if dad comes home?" I asked her as she stood there.

"I doubt he will." Sher was quick to respond.

"Well Malina, if your dad comes home, then me and Lori will sleep in the living room on the sofa." Matty said.

Sher looked at me.

"Yep, sure aunt Matty, you can sleep in mom's bed." Sher said.

Still unable to say anything, because I was mentally preparing myself for waking up in the morning and seeing Matty lying there in moms bed. Wondering just how much of a shock it would be for me to see a female, any female lying in mom's bed.

Though Sher and Matty were talking, I really couldn't hear anything they said. Trying my best to do a visual in my mind, some eighteen hours before it would actually happen. Perhaps if I prepare myself now for waking up tomorrow, I will be able to handle the thought of what I might see.

"Come on Malina help out." Sher barked.

Help what? All she really had were their clothes, they didn't need my help for that, but did as I was told anyway.

Within an hour, Matty had some of her powders and hair spray and personal things on mom's dresser, dad's dresser now.

Even when mom was alive, it wasn't considered her dresser at all. Mom never kept anything of hers on top of the dresser; she only kept her personal things in the left side drawer. She couldn't, more like wasn't allowed to put anything on top of the dresser for fear dad wouldn't be able to find any of his precious personal things if the dresser was cluttered with moms' things.

How strange it looked, having Matty's, anybody's things visible on his dresser. Dad was very strict about his dresser, never allowing anything other than his damn wallet, piece of shit comb and his damn breath mints.

How easy it seemed it was for Matty to march in and take control. This would be quite interesting if dad showed up.

I had a quick vision of dad walking in the room and seeing Matty's things on his dresser, going psycho on her and throwing her things to the ground. Then I had a funnier vision of Matty saying. "Who the hell do you think you are?" Then smacking all his things right to the floor with just one swipe of her hand, clear across his dresser. Oh if only! I thought.

Matty had us water down that old water cooler several times within an hour. She put on some shorts and a thin cotton shirt because she was already so miserably hot.

Sher served her a glass of Kool-aid to help keep her cool, knowing damn good and well Matty very well might just gather all her things and get the "Hell out of Dodge" so to speak, just because it was too hot for her and Lori.

Finally, all her things were put away and she was sitting down in the living room relaxing.

The kids had eaten lunch and were outside getting wet with the water hose. Lori was so excited to do this, because, according to Matty, Lori had never even tried this.

The phone rang; it was dad demanding to talk to Matty. Demanding? How I wished just once, someone would slam the phone down, then not answer when he would call right back to cuss whoever was so brave.

Matty's responses on the phone were "Yes, ok, I know, yes, but you have to bring money. I need to feed these kids. Yes, no, yes, ok I'll be there in a few minutes."

She explained to us that she was going to dad's garage to get money and would return in a short while. Lori was overly excited to stay and get wet with the hose.

"What do you think?" Sher asked me once Matty left, as we sat on the sofa watching the kids get wet.

"I do like her being here."

"You know we're probably gonna have to baby-sit Lori while Matty works."

"I don't mind." I said.

"Me either, she's a fun happy kid, it'll be good for J.J. and Danny."

"You know I'm just afraid to wake up in the morning and see her lying in mom's bed."

"What are you afraid of?" Sher asked.

"I'm not sure, maybe just seeing a woman in the bed will bring back memories or, maybe I'm afraid Matty would die in her sleep as mom had, just from sleeping in that bed."

"Don't worry Malina, it won't be as bad as it would have been if Liz had stayed here, and it can't be as lonely as being here alone." Sher was just so wise.

"You're right Sher." I confessed

"Thank you very much." Sher said in her famous Elvis voice, making her lip quiver as every Elvis impersonator does.

We laughed and tossed cushions from the sofa at one another just as Matty drove up.

Though this was going to be for a few days only, perhaps it is what Sher and I needed. Mostly, I thought, this would be good for Sher. She needed a break from being an adult, a break from all the responsibilities. Maybe she could be a kid once again if for only a few days.

Matty must have robbed dad's garage or maybe she robbed the garage and the bar because she had some serious money when she returned.

"Sher, where are the utility bills? I told your dad I'd pay them." Matty said.

"Do you want to go to the grocery store with me Malina?" Matty asked, as Sher went to get the bills.

I didn't even have to think about it. Normally I would've jumped at the chance to go anywhere, especially in a car, but this was one trip I didn't think I should take.

"If it's ok aunt Matty, can you take Sher? She hasn't been out of here in two months." I suggested to Matty.

Matty smiled at me. "Ok." She said. I'll take Lori with us."

"That's ok, I'll watch her. Just take Sher." I said.

I knew Matty was just trying to lift all the responsibility from me possibly thinking it was too many kids for me to handle, but taking even one kid with them was the same as Sher having to baby-sit. I believe Matty understood my suggestion.

"You're right Malina, just me and Sher huh?"

"Yes." I said as I smiled at her.

Sher came in the room with the electric, water, gas and phone bills for Matty to pay.

"Come on Sher, it's me and you." Matty said.

Sher began to say, "I have to watch"... Matty interrupted her.

"No, Malina can watch the kids, we won't be gone very long, she can handle it."

Sher looked at me like! Yeah right, twerp. I looked at Sher, who looked so tired, and knew she may well be at her breaking point.

"Don't have to tell me twice." Sher said. With a great big smile on her face.

Matty explained to the kids that I was in charge while she was gone, and they were to mind me.

They all laughed, almost as if it was a joke and they didn't believe I was capable of watching five kids. Well I never had done it alone. Sher was always there to handle it. Now it was me against them.

Sher got in the car with Matty, a gigantic smile on her face. As they drove off, she waved at me, sort of like a beauty queen type of wave. She looked so happy escaping her self-made prison of constant demands and duties as mother and father to five kids.

She had done so much for us over the past two months, and no one had thanked her, not dad, not any relatives, not even us five kids.

This was such a small thanks for everything. Something so simple like going to the store, a minor incident it would've been to any other teenager, a seemingly milestone for Sher.

The weight of the world was lifted from her shoulders for an hour maybe two.

I watched the kids as they were playing, tug of war for the water hose, each so full of excitement. Though our lives had been turned upside down two months ago, they seemed so happy.

Matty and Sher were gone a bit longer than she had anticipated, but I didn't care. The kids played outside the entire time.

When they arrived we all helped bring the groceries in the house, even Danny and Lori did their share of hauling things back and forth, carrying the lightest bags.

Matty had bought quit a few groceries, even managed to buy some ice cream and cookies, treats we hadn't had the pleasure of in awhile.

It was time to for supper; Matty insisted she cook for us. We were more than happy to have someone else cook a good home cooked meal. Sher and I went into the kitchen to see if we could help, but Matty wouldn't hear of it.

What a wonderfully kind thing for Matty to do, step up and be a parent to six kids. It was a relief to see that she had made more food than we could've possibly eaten. Second helpings, and even cookies and ice cream for dessert.

Sher and I did the dishes while Matty sat with the kids and watched TV. Once finished, we went in to join everyone else in the living room. Matty pretty much just watched us to see what our daily routine was like. She didn't interfere and say "Do it this way or I think this or that." She just watched, noticing how we did things and the times we did them.

I cringed thinking if this was Liz here with us she would of ran her mouth the entire time, degrading us and talking crap to us about our house and about our mom. There is no doubt in my mind, if we had been unfortunate enough to deal with Liz, the gangster blood in all of us would've come out, forcing us to beat her ass, chunk her loud mouth out onto the porch, then lock her out. I knew we were blessed it was Matty here with us.

After the kids were in bed, Sher, and I were about to go to our room when Matty sat us down to talk.

"Tell me." She said. "How often does your dad come home?"

I wanted to blurt out never, but knowing dad was Sher's subject, I kept quiet, thinking she was going to lie to cover up for him.

"Maybe twice a week." Sher said.

I was so surprised she told the truth.

"Does he sleep here?"

"Not really, maybe once or twice a week." Sher said.

"Does anyone come to see y'all?

"No." I jumped in the conversation. "Only Aunt Gloria."

"What about your mom's family?"

"No." I said. "We haven't seen them since mom died."

"Not even your grandma?" She asked. A really sad look on her face.

"No, not even grandma." I said.

She shook her head in disbelief. "Well we won't worry about any of them right now. Let's just figure out what we can do for y'all now."

We said our goodnights and went to bed.

The next morning Matty was up making breakfast and getting all our dirty clothes together to take to the laundry mat.

Sher and I had figured out how to use mom's old wringer washing machine, which was a pain in the ass to fill with the water hose. Always making sure not to over fill the tub, and then drain the water with a bowl, one bowl at a time. It was such a long process just to do one load. Once we explained the tedious details of washing one load, Matty decided to do it all at one time at the laundry mat

I had never been to a laundry mat ever. Mom did all the laundry herself, asking only that we kids hang the clothes out on the clothesline.

When she died me and Sher did the best we could. Sometimes we preferred to just wash the clothes in the bathtub.

We would fill the tub with water, put the clothes and laundry soap in, and then get to stepping, just as "I Love Lucy" did to those grapes. Stomp, stomp, stomp. Sometimes we would get the boys to stomp the clothes other times Becky and Carrie would.

It was an event that took all of us to do, but then, they were our dirty clothes and they needed to be clean. So, we did it the best we could. The hardest part would be wringing out the water. We would literally get one of us on one end, someone on the other end and just twist the clothes, turning in opposite directions until all the water was wrung out.

Very, very tedious work. Luxuries are things we knew nothing about, so when we explained to Matty all the steps it took to wash just one load, she said to heck with that, we're going to the laundry.

Rather than take one or two of us, she took all of us, since none of us had ever been to the laundry, she wanted us to experience it all at the same time.

After eating breakfast and cleaning up, we loaded all the clothes in her trunk, then loaded the kids in the car and headed out to the nearest laundry mat... Matty stopped at the store and bought laundry detergent. Usually we just used dish soap if we couldn't afford the real thing.

Matty taught us how to load the clothes, separating everything first, which was something mom had taught us a few years back... It took six washers to get it all washed at the same time. After thirty minutes, the machines all stopped and Matty began putting things in the dryer. Our clothes had never been dried in a dryer before, instead, ours were always hung outside on the clothesline to dry or in winter weather or rainy weather, we hung them around the house to dry.

Such a prehistoric way of doing things.

Thirty minutes later the clothes were dry, then Matty taught us the proper way to fold things so they wouldn't need a lot of ironing. Our clothes were now so soft and smelled so good.

To think there were things we had never experienced in our lives. Something as simple as a laundry mat. It cost only a few dollars to do all our clothes and less than two hours. To do all those clothes in our machine would've been an all day event.

Modern conveniences, what an amazing thing, it seemed.

Simple things in life, things my mom should've had, but never dared to ask, never complained that she didn't have.

"Don't complain of what you don't have, be grateful for what you do have." Mom told us so many times.

I understood that so clearly now. I wasn't sad that we didn't have a washer and dryer at home, I was use to what we did have, because I knew once Matty left, things would go back to the way they were before. We could never afford a few dollars to go to a laundry. However, I realized there would be so many more things in my life I would wish my mom would be here to share with me.

Missing her more than ever now. Thinking of her life with that miserable excuse of a husband. Wanting so desperately to tell someone what I saw that night, but who would ever believe me.

Enjoying one experience in life with Matty would never compare to the years of loneliness I was going to have to experience. I missed mom so much. Why did this have to happen to us, to mom, such a beautiful loving woman? Why did she have to be taken from us?

On the drive home, I wondered just how much of life my mom had to sacrifice. It goes without saying she didn't possess nice material things, but to have a simple thing like a washer and dryer. Sure, many folks don't have them, that's what the laundry is for. But, other things, like a descent sweater, or even an air conditioner to keep her cool. So many sacrifices, yet she never ever complained. I wondered how many women there were like my mom.

# 64

Matty took control of everything for us. She did the cooking, cleaning, watching the kids. On Saturday, she suggested me and Sher go to the library, just me and Sher, no kids.

Libraries reminded me a lot of school and I particularly didn't like them, but I knew Sher did, and I really looked forward to going somewhere, anywhere.

After helping Matty with lunch, Sher and I set out for the library. It was the same distance as the park, so it took a few minutes to get there. Seems to me Sher walked faster than I did, or was it just because she had them great long legs, it just seemed harder for me to keep up with her.

Sher's eyes lit up when we got to the library. The second we opened the big double door I was overwhelmed with the wonderful smell, everything smelt new, nice and clean and cold. Unfamiliar grounds.

Sher did not hesitate to look through every aisle of books as if she were on a treasure hunt. Thousands of books and Sher literally tried to read the titles of every single one of them. Strolling from aisle to aisle, looking up and down from top to bottom of every shelf. She had a look on her face as if she was in paradise. I, on the other hand, got bored after awhile and went to sit at a table.

I grabbed the first book I saw and pretended to read it. I knew better than to bother or rush Sher, she was in her element here at the library. If she couldn't be in school then she was just as happy at the library.

I sat there looking at all the people. Why do people whisper in a library I wondered? I get it, everyone needs to be respectful and not talk loudly, but to whisper to someone, just drew that much more attention to that person.

Since it was Saturday, there were many students there.

Some, I noticed had been in the same school I went to...

Some were high school kids. Some kids were with their moms, others were with their apparent older siblings, like me.

Sher had a library card so I knew she was going to get as many books as she possibly could. I watched her as she went from aisle to aisle picking out just the perfect book for herself. I myself didn't like to read much, maybe I just couldn't concentrate as Sher could. I literally read only if I was forced to for school, but to do it on my own time, naw, wasn't for me.

Sher was on the other side of the library when I noticed, no heard, three teens enter the library. They were loud and laughing, not really caring about who they might disturb.

They looked to be older than Sher. When they entered the library, they were talking, not whispering. The librarian looked up as they entered and motioned them to be quiet.

There was a water fountain to the left as you entered the library and they gathered around it laughing and cutting up, splashing water on the floor. Again the librarian instructed them to be quiet, again they laughed at her. I wanted to laugh also, because they weren't obeying her, instead creating a scene. I watched them as their eyes scanned the library just to see who was there.

I continued watching them be disorderly wondering what were they up to. They looked like the type of guys that would take milk money from the schools geeks. I saw them scanning the crowd, possibly looking for a geek to rob.

Their eyes met mine, then past me and went straight to Sher's eyes. One of the guys said something and they started walking toward Sher. She noticed them walking toward her so she came to sit with me which was one table away from the librarians desk. Sher put four books on the table and sat down next to me.

"Are you going to read all of those now?" I asked, afraid she was going to say yes and we would have to sit there all day. To my relief she said no, about this time the three guys made their way to our table.

"Hey there Sher." One of them said. Sher ignored them.

Another one of them started to pull up a chair, and sit with us, but by this time the librarian was on her way to rescue us.

The three guys laughed when they saw her approaching.

"You gentlemen need to find a table and don't disturb these young ladies."

They all laughed at her and one said. "That ok, we outta here."

"Good day gentlemen." The librarian said.

"Good day Miss Sher, and is this little sis?" The tallest of the guys asked. Neither Sher nor I said a word.

"Good day gentlemen." The librarian said again.

They left laughing and talking as loudly as they had when they entered the library. Seems to me they were a little bit old to act so stupid, but then I really didn't know too much about boys.

We stayed at the library an hour longer, enough for Sher to pick a fifth book, the limit any one was allowed to check out from the library at any given time...

As we walked home, Sher began to tell me of the boys that were in the library making all the noise.

"Do you know them?" I asked.

"Yes they go to my school. Everyone calls them the Three Stooges." She said. I laughed because it was obvious why.

There was a white guy, a black guy and a Hispanic guy.

All so different, yet exactly the same.

Sher went on to tell me, the white guy Arnold (Arny) lives in a trailer with his drunken dad." She said. "His mom left his dad and didn't bother to take Arny with her. He wears the same clothes every other day. I guess he has nothing else to wear. Everyone teases him that he is white trash; they say he is lower than white trash because he doesn't live in the trailer, he lives underneath it with the rats and spiders. But he doesn't get mad, maybe because he thinks he is.

"The black guy Trey, nick named Whitey because, as you can see, he is so dark but has those beautiful white teeth that are absolutely perfect. He always, always has some kind of breath freshener or mints in his mouth, not only are his teeth so immaculate, but his breath is always fresh."

"They say his parents fight all the time, and every week he threatens to leave home but he says he has no where to go. All he ever talks about in school is how he is going to be a famous football player one day. He cares of nothing but football." Sher said.

"He talks so much about football the teachers put him right on the front row of the class room so he can't distract the other students. You can ask him any question about football and he can give you the correct answer every time... He knows every statistic about football from the very first professional game ever played, to a game played a month ago and he has all the answers. He knows everything and he knows every player ever played. He's a football genius."

"Then there's the third guy, Juanito. He is the one with a bit of a Mexican accent." Sher said. "His nickname is Ese, because he calls everyone he comes in contact with Ese."

"He even calls all the girls Ese. It's Ese this and Ese that." Sher went on. "It really is annoying to hear him talk because when he talks to the teachers or coaches he even calls them Ese. I heard he has about six brothers and no sisters. His mom died years ago and he has a big chip on his shoulder. Trey and Arny call him Juanito, Pablo. Jesus, Luis, and every Mexican name they can think of just to mess with him. He laughs it off saying " Gracias Mother fuckas."

"Are they trouble?" I asked.

"I've heard gossip at school, but I'm not really sure. I have never had a problem with any of them. They all met in elementary school and though they were three different nationalities, they hit it off very well. They are all dirt poor and from broken homes, they seemed to bond and have been friends for seven or eight years."

"Where one goes, the others go. The nicknames they each have I heard when they first met they sat around and made fun of each other, making up the nicknames, and those nicknames stuck with them ever since. I think they are just guys that like a lot of attention and they get it everywhere they go."

"The way they just acted at the library is the way they act at school. They aren't allowed to have any of their classes together because they bother everyone. The only class they are allowed to have together is football."

I looked at her like "What?"

"Yes, they are the star players." Sher said

We walked home slowly talking about the library, the books, the people in the library, The Three Stooges, and aunt Matty.

Matty had come and rescued us just when we needed help, for that, we were grateful for sure. Sher couldn't wait to start reading her books.

Supper was almost ready and the kids were glad to see us. Sher was more excited than any of us, not knowing exactly which of the five books to read first. Seemed she got just a tiny piece of her life back.

I was happy for her. All the responsibility on her shoulders and though I knew Matty wasn't going to stay too many more days, Sher had her escape for a little while. I wondered then why hadn't we gone to the library sooner. I guess Sher had so much to worry about she just never thought of it.

## 65

Dad came by Sunday afternoon, standing outside long enough to talk with Matty. I believe she was pissed off because I heard her tell him things like "Johnny this isn't right, I can't stay here forever."

She told dad she was moving to a one-bedroom apartment with her boyfriend in a week, and that something needed to be done about us spending so much time alone. Then out of nowhere she says "And what about school? These kids need school clothes."

"I'm sure if he had his way we would've all dropped out of school just so he didn't have to be bothered about such things like school clothes, school shoes and not to mention school supplies and lunch money.

Mom was the one that always took care of all that, never bothering him for anything. She made the clothes, she took her ironing money, and bought our shoes, she packed our lunch's everyday. Now he was forced to deal with it himself.

Dad would shake his head yes, then no then yes again. I wasn't sure what he was saying. It was obvious dad was living somewhere else, probably with the woman I had seen in the car with him that day. He sure wasn't living with us. So, unless he was living with a rich woman who was taking care of him, then he was the one supporting someone else.

He assured Matty he would take care of it. Just seemed to me Matty didn't believe a word he said.

We were all in the living room watching TV, I was watching them.

The phone rang, Sher got up to answer it. Just as she said, "Hello." Dad and Matty walked in the house.

All I heard Sher say was "What? Don't call here again." And she hung up the phone.

"Who was that?" Dad asked. Sher looked scared.

"I don't know." Sher answered.

"Why did you hang up?" Dad was drilling her.

Just then the phone rang again, dad picked it up, but before he could say hello, someone said something that sent him into a rage.

"Let me tell you something you mother fuckers, if this phone rings one more time I swear I will find you and by tomorrow morning there will be a couple of mother fuckers hanging by your mother fucking toes from the flag pole.

Now, because he said fuckers, plural and not fucker, singular, I would have bet my life he knew it was more than one person on the other end of the phone. Hell was about to break out!

He slammed the phone down, then turned to Sher.

"Who was it?" He yelled.

Sher again said, "I don't know."

"Were they cussing at you?" He yelled even louder.

"Yes." Sher said. Tears were now forming in her eyes.

"I could hear the mother fuckers laughing. What did they say to you?" Again, demanding Sher to tell him.

Sher didn't lie to him. "They were laughing and said they wanted to." She looked at Matty then at me then at dad.

"They said they wanted to fuck me." She was terrified.

"Who was it Sher?" He was yelling at her this time a lot louder and he even got up close to her face.

"Dad I don't know." Sher began.

Matty stepped in just when she saw that dad was getting more furious.

"Johnny she said she didn't know." Matty tried to calm the situation.

"That's fucking bull shit and you know it. Have you been talking to boys on the phone?" He yelled.

"No." Sher said, and as far as I knew, she really had not because she was too damn busy raising his kids.

"Don't fucking lie to me."

"I'm not lying" Then Sher began to cry.

"Johnny." Mattie yelled.

"Stay out of this Mattie." Dad yelled at her like she was one of his hired hands.

"I will not." She barked right back.

"If I find out your lying to me Sher, I swear I will beat the shit out of you."

At that moment I got so scared thinking of mom, thinking of poor Sher being so stressed, I literally had to cross my leg over the other to keep from pissing all over myself.

Why did he even come home, my mind was racing. Maybe if he stayed home he would see for himself Sher wasn't talking to boys. But I didn't want him at home. This is the exact reason I hated that he even came to pick his clothes up, to hear him bitching.

I give him the fact that some idiot was talking shit and it pissed him off, I'm sure it would piss off any father, but to torment his favorite daughter like that. He was literally bitching at the wrong person. Sher was crying while Matty was trying to comfort her.

"How many times have these mother fuckers called here?" He demanded to know.

"Just once." Sher cried.

"How did they get the number?" He yelled at her.

"I don't know daddy." Sher cried.

I could not help but think. "Sorry sista, but this is one time your little "Daddy" comment just ain't gonna work on this mad man."

"Did you give the number out?" He yelled.

"No, only to my girlfriends." Sher continued to cry.

He did not believe a word she said. I know he wanted to slap the truth out of her but didn't only because Matty was there.

Heartless bastard, his pet was crying right there in front of him and he couldn't just calm down, comfort her, then try and sort through this mess...

All six of us and Matty were no match for him. If he hit Sher then Matty would have to get in to defend Sher, then for what ever reason, I thought I'd have to try to help. I had a visual of all of us getting beat like mom. This monster made me so sick.

Dad kept on and on and on. Sher kept crying, while Matty stood by looking horrified, but knew if she called the cops and dad went to jail she may as well move to another planet because sister or no sister he would find her.

What a fucking mess! Some jerks called at the exact second dad entered the house, what horrible timing.

Who could it be? I'm not sure why, but screwy crossed my mind. Is he that damn stupid I wondered for a split second? Naw... I really didn't think so.

If screwy had called, I sure hoped Sher would have mercy and not tell dad, because he knew exactly where screwy and his family lived and there were a lot of them, and maybe just as badass as dad.

Sher cried, dad bitched, Matty paced not knowing what to do. Dad even called the operator to see if she could trace the call, fortunately she could not. It was obvious it was someone we knew, but who would be so damn stupid.

Sher kept quiet, she wasn't going to tell dad shit. Maybe if he had taken a different approach toward her, she would have told, but for him to bitch at her as if she was the one prank calling someone else. Nope, her lips were sealed.

Finally, after blowing a fuse for an hour he left. No goodbyes, no nothing. Sher had stopped crying by then.

Now her fear had turned into anger. Matty went to Sher's' room to talk to her. I didn't try to listen; I did good not to piss on myself.

Sher needed to talk one on one with Matty; I would be of no help to anyone. I had no friends and no one knew my number.

Another hour went by and Matty came out of Sher's' room to tend to Lori and the kids.

I was sitting on my bed staring at the ceiling looking for the angels Becky always claimed to talk to. I sure didn't see any.

"Malina." Sher called out to me.

"Yes?" I answered.

"Come here." I obeyed as if she were dad.

When I walked in her room, she looked at me and said.

"Shut the door." Again, I did as I was told.

"I know who it was." She confessed.

"Who?" I asked, just fearing she was going to say screwy.

"Those bastard Three Stooges."

"What? " I said in complete shock.

"Yep." Sher said.

"How do you know it was them?"

"Because that fucking idiot Juanito said Ese, I want too fuck you. Who the hell else says Ese? And I could hear the other two idiots laughing in the back ground."

"Are you sure?" I asked

"Yes." she said. "I'm positive."

"How did they get the number?" I asked.

"I have no idea, maybe the school directory or information or the operator, but I know for sure it was them." She said.

"Why didn't you tell on them?" I asked, but already knew the answer to that one. She looked at me like seriously.

"You know damn good and well if I told on them dad would find them, and what if, just what if he did find them and tomorrow there would be three teens hanging from a flag pole?"

I was getting a visual of this and realized it could get really bad.

Dad does whatever to three teens, and then their families come after us, worse than that dad goes after all their families.

No, we definitely didn't want that to happen.

Poor Sher, in a seconds notice she made up a lie, she kept the truth from her precious father, she had been threatened an ass whooping and actually, bold face lied to her gangster father, which in his eyes seemed to be a crime punishable by death. Yes, Sher saved everyone, what a terrible situation to be in. One thing was for sure, Sher could never be accused of being a rat. She didn't rat those idiots out. She could have, but she didn't. We weren't sure what dad hated worse, a rat or a liar.

Once Matty was sure dad had left, she sat with me and Sher and she cried. Not only for us, but also for the fact she was really in no position to help us. Financially she just couldn't take us all to live with hr. We understood that. However, even she knew leaving us with him was a mistake, but how could she just walk away after what she had just witnessed.

She was the baby in her family, and she could barely support herself and Lori. It would be very tough for her to walk away from us, but we all knew she would leave in a few days.

She cried, sadness, dislike for her brother, knowing Sher at fourteen was doing more than most grown women could do.

She apologized to us over and over. I think she racked her brain about what to do. There was no solution. She couldn't just come in and take his kids away from him, even though he wasn't being a father. She knew better then to put him in any type of spot to piss him off.

She cried a lot, I believe mostly for herself, maybe her own guilt that she knew she had to leave and she had to live with that decision.

Dad was mad, Sher was sad; Matty was overwhelmed with dad's behavior. And the three stooges, well they will never know have how close their lives came to being over that night, all over one prank call.

Would dad have really hurt them? Who knows, but with him and Ray together, with dad's anger anything was possible.

Once Sher and I went to bed, I heard Matty get on the phone. She was crying and though she was talking very quietly, I could hear cuss words, and her talking about dad.

Possibly, she was talking to her mom or Aunt Gloria, but I wasn't sure. Whoever she was talking to she was telling them everything that had happened.

Unable, still to come up with a solution.

Sher was in her room, though I couldn't see her, I knew her light was still on and I would've bet my life her nose was in a book, lost in her stories, her imagination of a life outside these walls.

The next morning Matty made breakfast and took us all to the park, she even paid for those of us who wanted to swim.

Everyone was excited, not me and I didn't even go near the pool, thanks to that messed up swimming lesson I had years ago. I vowed then never to get near the water and I stood by my decision even now.

We stayed at the park all day. Matty even left to get us something to eat. There were lifeguards to watch the kids, so she had no worry of them drowning. Seems we were there more hours than we needed to be. By the time we got home, it was getting dark.

Matty talked to us about her leaving in two days, knowing that we needed her, but we really weren't her responsibility.

She promised to come by every other day to check on us, and as soon as she moved and got a phone, we were to call her if we ever got in another situation with dad. It would be tough on us, we knew that, but we knew this was a temporary arrangement from the get go...

After unloading her car, Matty got the mail in from the mailbox. When she walked in the house, she was pale as a ghost.

"What's wrong aunt Matty?" I asked.

"It's here." She sounded like she was choking...

"What is?" I asked.

"The medical examiner report, it's here." She said

"What does that mean?"

"It means whatever is in here, in this envelope will explain how your mom died."

She blurted it out without realizing what she was saying. She immediately picked up the phone and called dad at the garage. She told him of the letter.

"Open it." He said so calmly.

I thought how strange? He doesn't want to come read it himself.

It was "the" paper telling him how his wife died, wasn't that something he should read himself, not have his sister read to him over the phone?

Matty sent the kids out of the room but allowed me and Sher to stay.

I was scared, I was shaking. Not really sure what I thought would be in the letter.

Dad was silent, as if he had nothing to worry about at all.

I had a visual of dad sitting at his desk at the garage, twittling his thumbs, like, can we get this over with.

Matty read out loud. "Dear Mr. Guetarro. After performing a complete and thorough autopsy, it is my professional opinion that Mrs. Shirley Ann Guetarro died on May 28th of bilateral bronchial pneumonia. Should you have any questions please feel free to call."

Complete silence from everyone, dad, Matty, Sher, me.

Dad, it seemed cleared his throat, then talked a minute with Matty, and hung up. The complete look of relief on Matty's face that it didn't say "Johnny G. watch out "mutha fucka," the cops are coming for you, because I can prove you killed your wife as she slept."

That's what mom's family thought, that's what dad's family thought, it's even what I thought, but I suppose dad was the only living person that knew he did not kill mom.

What did this change? He still wasn't a good father; he still abandoned us, as everyone else did. It still didn't get him released of his parental duties.

I asked Matty what did the letter mean.

"Well Malina, it proves on thing for sure. Your mom had pneumonia and she was sick, very sick."

"But she wasn't I explained. She didn't have a fever, she didn't cough, she wasn't on medication."

Does pneumonia just creep up on you and kill you in your sleep. Apparently, it does according to this paper. Or was the medical examiner wrong?

Did dad suffocate her and he only thought it was pneumonia. What if he were wrong? Then that meant dad was still a murderer.

But, if he didn't kill her, and he had the report, then why wasn't he on the phone calling all moms family saying.

"Here's the proof you bastards, I did not kill my wife."

But he wasn't doing that. This means mom's family abandoned us for nothing. They had no reason to hate dad. They had no reason to abandon us. How or who was going to fix this for our sakes?

Dad, Matty, who me?

I didn't understand any of it. My poor mom was not sick. She wasn't in pain. What had happened to her, I wanted someone to tell me.

Matty wasted no time calling all dads family, mostly so everyone could stop guessing and thinking the monster was also a murderer.

Dad showed up about an hour later, talked with Matty, got the letter, then went to apologize to Sher.

Matty was leaving tomorrow he needed to be on Sher's good side. After a few minutes, he got some of his things and again just left.

I didn't get it at all. But I guess he was the only person other than mom who knew what happened to her that night. It's almost as if he had an attitude like, "I told y'all mother fuckers I didn't do it."

More than likely, he blamed me and Becky for everyone hating him because we had told everyone what we heard that night. But those were facts, things we really did hear.

We had been raised to never lie, so many ass whoopings we got if he thought we lied to him. Now he was mad because me and Becky hadn't lied to make him look good.

Life made no sense to me.

Get beat for lying, get hated for not lying. Well he could hate me all he wanted. I did not lie about anything.

Now his life could go on. I was the one missing my mom so much, Sher was the one being mom and dad, and he was already toting some woman around, like he never had a wife.

If this letter proves he didn't kill mom then why wasn't he even trying to explain it all to us.

Be the father you never were you damn coward I thought. Less then three months had passed and he was doing nothing for us. That letter proved nothing to me, all it did was save dad's ass, but really, it did nothing.

Mom was gone and there was nothing gonna change that.

## 66

Matty was leaving, we were crying, she was crying. I wondered if she thought she should stay and tough it out with us. Though she had spent many years of her own child hood here in this house, this was no place for Lori. If she stayed, Matty would always think she would have to defend us against dad, though she had done good the one time, I knew she probably couldn't do it again. Then if her boyfriend moved in he would more than likely get into it with dad, thinking he had to defend Matty for defending us.

My head was spinning. Lori cried because she didn't want to leave the boys. Being an only child she loved being around other kids.

I believe I cried the most. Matty was so different from Liz. If it had been Liz, we couldn't have gotten rid of her quick enough. But Matty, with her kind ways, and all the help she gave us in just a few days, was just what we needed... Yes, it was sad to see her leave, but after losing mom, nothing could have been as tough on me ever again.

Once Matty and Lori left, Sher stayed in her room reading, the rest of us watching TV.

I thought of mom, knowing if she were here, she would be in her room making our school clothes. I thought of mom's family abandoning us because they thought dad killed her. How stupid they would feel when they read the medical examiners report. I thought a lot of Danny and J.J.

Danny would be starting school this year. How sad for him not to have his mom to share that with. I thought of J.J. and his love of baseball. Would he want to play sports in school, would he even be able too? I thought of Becky and Carrie, how they spent so much time together and hardly ever fought, how well behaved they all were. I thought of Sher, knowing school would be the one escape she finally would get to enjoy.

No one would tell her she had to stay home; no one would say she couldn't go to school. No one would put pressure on her to be mother and father, at least during the school hours. She would have approximately seven hours Monday through Friday, to be a teen, to enjoy her life, to be Sher. I knew she had to be the most excited of us all.

I thought of myself, my complete dislike for school. How all I ever wanted during school was to not be in school, but to be home with mom. And I thought of dad with his bitching and cussing and hatefulness, and his gangsters and the woman in the car.

I didn't tell Sher, but I knew who it was with him that day. I knew exactly who that woman was that day she was sitting in his car. She was the same woman I had seen at dad's garage both times I had been there. She was the same woman dad sat and talked to, with his own wife sitting outside the garage with all six of his kids watching him talk to that woman.

My mind flashed back to that day, remembering how dad was so deep in conversation with her that he hadn't even noticed us drive up, or he did notice he just didn't care. I think of that woman looking dad directly in his eyes as she talked to him. I remember dad's calmness as he talked to her, thinking of the times he talked to mom or us kids, if he weren't high on drugs, his conversations with us would be yelling and cussing, and pointing at things and moving his body around like a boxer trying to avoid being hit.

Remembering how he would always question us saying "Why, Why?" While moving about. How scary he looked and again how fucking stupid he looked. Almost in an intimidating manner to try to scare us. Really dude your stepping up to a bunch of kids and a frail woman.

How pathetic he was. And now we were left without the protection of Matty. I hope that he would never come back. However, I just knew that wasn't even an option.

Sher stayed up very late reading her books. Several times I woke and her light was still on. I wondered was she trying to read all five books in as many days. I'm sure she was capable.

I fell back asleep, but within an hour, I woke to J.J. crying.

Sher didn't hear him, so I got up to check on him. He was burning up with fever. We had no thermometer to check his temperature, so I felt of his forehead, which was extremely hot. I called out for Sher, she didn't answer. I knocked on her door.

"What?" She said.

"J.J. is sick." I said.

Just as I said that, J.J. threw up. Sher came out of her room and went straight to his side. We were choking cleaning his mess up, but we knew we had to do it.

Sher got a cold washcloth to wipe his face and forehead. He was crying, and shivering. She told me to fill the tub with cool water. Mom had taught us anytime we had a fever to get in a tub of cool water to cool the body down, because when Sher and I were much younger the theory of a fever was to sweat it out, wrap a kid up in blankets and sweat. Somewhere along the line, that theory changed.

J.J. sat in the tub for fifteen minutes or so. When he came out his body seemed a bit cooler, but he looked like shit. Sher got him some water to drink, and told him to go back to bed. Within a few minutes, he was asleep. Sher told me to sleep in her room so she could be near J.J.

Oh, hell no! I thought. That would be like sleeping in the oven. Though I initially considered putting up a fight about sleeping in Sher's room, I knew the best thing for everyone was to let Sher stay with J.J., so I grabbed my pillow and did as I was told, knowing she was the better doctor to help J.J. than me.

I have no idea how Sher could stand it being in that room as hot as it was. I could barely breathe, wondering what the hell is wrong with Sher. It is miserable in here. However, I suppose privacy was more important to her than comfort.

Not that the big room was much cooler, but it damn sure was cooler than the little room.

As I lay in her room I thought of the library of all places, which I didn't necessarily care for, the books and all, but thinking of the nice cold air. I sure wish I were there right now.

I had a vision of myself dragging Sher's mattress to the library in the middle of the night, placing it on the library floor and sleeping with all that cold cold air, falling into a deep sleep only waking to the librarian bitching at me for breaking in.

Poor Sher, she never complained about how hot it was for her. Besides, I had never been in her room in the middle of the night. How the hell did she ever fall asleep? This is what hell might feel like I thought.

Eventually, I fell asleep, then I heard Sher up with J.J. I got up to help but she was already putting him back to bed.

When we woke early the next morning, J.J. was crying a lot. I felt his forehead and he was hotter than he had been the night before..

My mind went back to the time I got real sick when I was eight yrs old. The nurse had sent me home from school in the middle of the day because my body was on fire with a terrible fever. Once home, mom put me directly to bed and gave me seven up. She tried sweating my fever by wrapping me in blankets. (That was definitely a no no.) An old wives tale they say. I only got worse. I'm not sure how high my fever was, but I do remember waking up, because I was mumbling so loudly. Someone used the word delirious, me not knowing what that meant. I was crying and talking to myself and I was in so much pain. I tried opening my eyes but was unable to. Tears rolling down my cheeks, but my eyelids were shut tight...

I could feel my mom beside me trying to wash me down with a cool washcloth and her giving me aspirin. I couldn't lie still because I was in so much pain, and so incredibly hot.

When I finally opened my eyes, I looked toward the little room and I saw a man. It was not my dad. This man was as tall as the room. I couldn't see his face only his turquoise shirt and dark slacks. It was as if he had no head, but he was tall and his turquoise pull over shirt had what appeared to be silver thread sewn in rows vertically on it. He stood there and I could hear him talking to someone but couldn't make out what he said. I would cry out to my mom,

"That man. That man." Pointing to the little room, saying "That man."

Mom would say, "Malina there is no one there."

But there was. I could see him. I saw his clothes and the frame of his body. I just saw no face or head. Even as sick as I was, I knew I was in bad shape.

I cried over and over out loud, because I wanted to get up and be healthy, wake up and that horrible sick feeling be over with. I'm not sure how long I was sick, two maybe three days, but I will never forget the fear on moms face when my fever broke and I finally woke.

She hugged and kissed me over and over and she cried.

She cried a lot. Who knows, possibly I almost fell into a coma. I really don't know. No one ever explained to me what had happened to me. To this day if I walk into a dark room, I fear I will see that man again.

Now, poor little J.J. was sick. He was hotter than he was when he went to bed a few hours prior. Sher was on the phone talking to dad telling him of J.J.'s condition.

Dad did not come right away, but eventually he did show up. You would think he would have tried to be calm and caring.

Really? You would think, huh?

He walked, no barged into the house. "Where is he?" He demanded.

"In the big room." Becky pointed.

Dad stormed into the room and said, "What's wrong with you?"

J.J. didn't answer he just started to cry.

Dad made him get out of bed, and said. "Let's go." With no feeling or concern at all.

Now, J.J. was a skinny child but he was strong for a little kid... Everyday to show off his strength he would stand in the doorway and put one hand on the left side of the door frame, and the other on the right side, one foot on one side, the other foot on the other, and like that he would climb up the door way and touch the top, then hang from the top of the door frame by his finger tips. Dad called him Spiderman, because he could climb so quickly then just hang from his fingertips.

He made us laugh everyday with this show of strength. We would even applaud him because no matter how hard the rest of us tried, we were unable to accomplish this ourselves...

So as this "Father" of ours is bitching, he stops in the doorway, picks up J.J. and says, "CLIMB!"

What? You fucking monster. Climb? I wanted to scream.

He put J.J. up to the top of the frame and tells him to.

"Hang there, like you always do" He barked at him.

He called J.J. "Chicken shit," when he fell to the floor, unable to hang there to please dad.

Thinking to myself, J.J. is a sick child and you're treating him like this. I cried for J.J.. He was so sick and dad was demanding him to do acrobatic tricks just because.

Dad got J.J. by the hand and literally drug him to the car. I thought to myself. You're doing all that shit just because you're the fucking dad and you're the only one that can take J.J. to the doctor.

God help this man.

Sher tried to comfort me after they left saying, "Don't cry Malina."

I cried all day wondering what was happening to J.J. while he was alone with dad. Was dad hitting him? Was dad cussing and yelling at him just because he had to take time out of his miserable life to tend to him.

J.J. was my "Baby" paired off by mom. He was my responsibility everywhere we ever went. It hurt me so bad to watch dad be a monster to his namesake, the son he wanted so badly, and now he was treating him worse than he would some punk off the street that may have disrespected him.

I was sick thinking of J.J. being afraid and alone with the most miserable man in the world.

Poor J.J., we had no idea where dad took him. Hospital, doctor, quack, or maybe he got him high. Who knows?

Hours passed no word from dad. I wanted to call Matty or Gloria, but Sher insisted we wait.

When they finally got home dad had some medicine for J.J. He gave Sher money to buy soups and seven up, as I wondered why he didn't drive his ass to the store and get it himself, but really, just to get rid of him was enough for me.

J.J. slept off and on all day. Sher gave him his medicines and kept him cool. She made him drink plenty of water and seven up.

Dad actually called once to check on him. I guess he figured if he didn't check to make sure he was ok, and J.J. were to have died he would have to answer for it.

It would be two days before he was well enough to sit up and joke around with us. I knew he was feeling much better when I heard him and Danny laughing about dad trying to force J.J. to climb the doorway and become Spiderman.

We were all in the room laughing about it. Though it was sad when it was happening, we could only laugh about it now.

Sher, with all her hard work, was definitely entitled to get her angel wings one day. Dad on the other hand was no George Bailey taking care of Zuzu and her petals.

Laugh, yes we could relax now, J.J. was well, and as scary as it all was, we got through it. We tried to make the best of everything, we were all we had.

# 67

Our routine continued, but now we had a new place to go. This was a place we could go daily, keep cold, and have fun. The Library. From now on, our library visits would not be just me and Sher; it would consist of all six of us going together. Not knowing exactly what we would be up against by taking all the kids, we knew we had to at least try.

Sher sat the kids down and explained the rules.

"Do y'all know what a library is?" Sher asked everyone as we sat in the living room.

Carrie and Becky raised their hands as if they were in school, indicating they did in fact know what a library was. Then J.J. slowly raised his hand remembering then, or wondering if the library at school was the same as the one Sher was talking about. Danny did not raise his hand because he had no earthly idea what she was talking about.

She explained, looking mostly at Danny as she spoke.

"It's a building with lots and lots of books, and you have to whisper when you talk. You must speak real quietly, so you won't bother anyone else." Sher even whispered as she spoke, to give the kids some sort of an idea how quietly thy must speak.

With Danny's deep voice, I wondered if it were even possible for him to whisper...

Sher continued to explain. "You can get any book there, and sit at a table, and read all day if you want."

"I can't read." Danny was quick to remind us.

"I know." Sher said very calmly. "But you can look at pictures."

"Ok." Danny said with an enormous smile on his face.

"Now, you can't run around in this place, and you can't make noise because there will be other people there so we have to be real quiet, and you have to mind me, no acting up at all."

"Agreed?" She asked.

With lots of excitement, all the kids agreed.

"You know if this doesn't work Malina, we're going to have to take turns taking the kids." Sher said.

It was agreed, if it didn't work out as Sher planned, Sher, Danny and Carrie would go one day, then me, J.J. and Becky the next, alternating every other day. We had found a new place to go. It was freezing cold in there, it was clean, and it had a water fountain where we could drink nice cold water.

It would be difficult to keep them quiet and still for any period of time, but possibly, their interest in books would be enough to keep them calm and well behaved.

We hoped.

So, excited to take the kids on our new journey, we set off for the library. As with anything new, the little kids were extremely excited.

The second Sher opened the door to the library, Becky and Carrie simultaneously let out a moan like "Aaahhh," indicating that the cold air had hit them like a ton of bricks.

Me and Sher smiled at one another, because just a few days prior we had experienced the same feeling.

We instantly paired off in our sets of two. Sher and Danny, me and J.J. Carrie and Becky, who Sher felt were old enough and responsible enough to venture off on their own.

I took J.J. to one of aisles that had nothing but kid's books. The shelves went from the floor to way above my head. J.J. got on the floor and looked at the books that were closest to the floor, sort of crawling and sliding on the floor to scoot himself about.

Sher and Danny were one aisle over from us, though I couldn't see them I could already hear Danny talking.

Sher kept saying "Sssshhhh Danny, whisper." He would try, but wind up right back talking loud again. I was thinking, oh my, we are gonna get thrown out of this place before we ever get started.

J.J. found himself a book and handed it to me.

"Do we pay for it now?" He whispered.

"No silly, we don't have to buy it, were going to look at it here." He smiled.

"You can get another if you want." I told him.

So, as I suggested, he got right back on the floor crawling around looking for another book. Within ten minutes we had four books for Danny and J.J..

We found a table that was near the kid book area. Becky and Carrie sat with us, each with one book. Sher had returned two of the books she had already read, which meant she could check out three new books for the kids if she wanted, bringing her limit back to five. I didn't get a book to read, I wasn't interested. The only thing that interested me was sucking up all that cold air, knowing darn good and well my love for this cold air was going to end at one point or another, when we had to lug ourselves back to our Sahara desert house.

Looking around, remembering my thoughts the night J.J. was sick and I imagined dragging Sher's mattress to the library. My eyes searched for the perfect spot I would, if it were ever possible, bring Sher's mattress and sleep on the floor. I closed my eyes, reliving my thought of making the library my secret place to sleep.

With my eyes closed I imagined being asleep, on the mattress, shaking because it was so cold. Smelling the cold fresh air, smelling only clean air, not hot sticky funky air. I kept my eyes closed for fifteen minutes opening them only because the librarian broke my chain of thought.

The librarian, the same one that was bitching at me the night I imagined sleeping in the library.

"Good afternoon ladies and gentlemen." She addressed us.

"Hello." We all said.

"What nice, well behaved children you are." She smiled and looked at each of us, her eyeglasses on the tip of her nose, so she could look over them and see each of our faces.

Ok, now you didn't think it would be a librarian without glasses did you? Me, and I'm sure Sher and the librarian remembering the loud teenagers that had been there a few days ago, comparing their grown ass selves to ours.

"Thank you." Sher said.

"Can I help you kids with anything?" She asked.

"No." Sher said. "We're fine."

"Is your mother here with you?" She asked looking around.

Now, old four eyes knew darn good and well we six kids came in alone, with no adult accompanying us. She was looking right at us as we walked in.

"No." Sher said.

"She died." Danny blurted out, not even knowing what dead really meant at this time.

She looked at Sher, I closed my eyes.

Well, really now, how was she to know? We didn't carry a sign with us announcing we were pretty much orphans.

Sher stood up and motioned the librarian away from our table. They spoke a few minutes, then Sher came back and sat with us.

I opened my eyes, I closed my eyes.

Danny and J.J. looked through their books with so much excitement. Couldn't blame them, most or pretty much all their toys were old and tattered. These books were clean, fresh, and brand new. J.J. tried to read the pages of his book but he had picked a book that had words bigger than he was accustomed.

I took him back to the aisle we had been earlier. He searched and searched until he found a book with words he could actually read which pleased Sher. With all the love she had for books and school, it was obvious she wanted at least one of us to follow in her footsteps. Everyone was either reading, or just looking at the pictures in the books. I again closed my eyes pretending I was in a mansion on the better side of town.

It really wasn't hard to pretend, considering my surroundings. If you try hard, you can let your imagination put you anywhere you want to be.

The library for most people was for reading, studying, and learning. For me it was an escape. It was free, you didn't have to pay to be there, and you could stay as long as you liked.

Yes, it's very fair to say I found me an escape. Sher's escape was the books in the library; my escape was the library itself.

We stayed a bit longer, and then the kids started complaining how hungry they were, so Sher checked a book for Danny, one for J.J. and one for Carrie, promising Becky she would get one on the next trip.

We took our time walking home, though it was so hot, but other than the kids being so hungry we had nothing to rush home to.

I couldn't believe my eyes when we turned the corner and saw dad was home. There was his car parked right in front of the little city. We started up the stairs, and from the stairs, we could already hear him yelling and cussing at someone.

Oh dear god, here we go again.

I wanted to turn around, go back to the library, and beg that woman to let me sleep there for just one night, but I knew that would never ever happen.

It was too late anyway, dad saw us, and he was furious.

Dad, with all his cussing and yelling had the same effect on me as fingernails on a chalk board, you know like you want to slap that person up side their head and say don't fucking do that.

We walked through his, or should I say, mom's room, trying our best to avoid him, he remained on the phone. But sure enough, he stopped his cussing at whoever he was cussing at and said.

"Don't ya'll know how to say hello?" As he covered the phone with his hand, like he didn't want who ever he was cussing at to hear him become an even bigger ass to his kids.

"Hello daddy." Sher, of course was the first to address him.

Danny and J.J. said hello then the rest of us did... As I passed him to say hello I looked on mom's bed and there was all his junk piled on the bed.

"Oh no!" I thought. "He's fricken back."

That was quick, less then three months and his new bitch got tired of him, and kicked him to the curb I assumed. Fourteen years and mom died to get away from him.

The bitching and yelling on the phone continued.

"Yeah mother fucker I have four of them, what the fuck is it to you?" I could also hear someone yelling on the other end of the phone, but couldn't make out what they were saying, only that their voice was just as loud as dads.

We hurried to get to our room, Sher to the kitchen.

Then I heard dad yell. "Yeah, I got four you son of a bitch, and they ain't whores." He yelled even louder.

What or who was he referring to?

It could be anyone. But, who ever they were referring to, he was one pissed off individual.

I went in to help Sher, the kids stayed in their rooms.

Dad slammed the phone down as hard as he possibly could. I heard him messing with the things on the bed hoping he was repacking and would be leaving soon.

Perhaps this was laundry day, and not him moving back in day. I did everything I possibly could to avoid him. Sher made soup and sandwiches for the kids, then stupidly asked dad if he wanted any.

Yikes, he said yes!

Oh please Sher, serve it to him in his room like a king being served by a peasant, so he won't come sit with us.

No such luck, here he comes. I thought.

And there he was, sitting at the head of the table just like I had imagined, only I didn't want him in the kitchen with us I wanted him somewhere else, anywhere but sitting in the chair he was sitting in. I watched as he panned the room. I already knew he was looking for something to bitch about. Our clothes, our hair, someone was slurping their soup too loud.

One minute passed, two minutes passed. I wondered if I could shove all my food in my mouth at once just to get the heck out of there, before he found something about me that would get him started.

Don't make eye contact Malina, don't make eye contact Malina. I kept saying to myself.

Then outta nowhere, like a brisk cool autumn breeze he says, "How ya feeling son?" As he looked at J.J.

WHAAAAAAAAAAAAAAAAAAAAAAAT??? I thought.

"Better." J.J. smiled.

"Good, good." Dad said.

Hey wait a minute; I didn't smell any weed on him. Isn't this normal family conversation? This was not our family conversation at all.

"Where did y'all go?" He asked, again with out the use of any cussing or bitching.

"Li-berry." Danny said. Not looking up at dad as he said it, rather looking down at his bowl of soup.

Dad smiled at him because he knew Danny said it wrong, so for a laugh he asked.

"Where Danny?"

"Li-brerry?" Danny was excited. Danny continued eating his soup then looked up at dad.

"I got me a book." Danny said. "Wanna see?" He started to get off his chair to get his book to show it off.

"No, no." Dad said. "Sit down and finish your food."

Dad never really sat facing the table to eat; he sat with his chair back to the wall so he could see everything around him.

That was an ol gangster move, never sit with your back to the crowd, and give any one the chance to creep up on you and bust a cap in your ass. Face the crowd, so you can see trouble coming.

But dude, you're in your own home. What? You afraid Danny gonna creep up on you and spray you with his water gun? Geez!

So dad sat there eating his soup and sandwich, his back to the wall. As we each finished our food, we got up, put our plates in the sink, cleaned off the table, and sent the kids to their rooms. Me and Becky did the dishes. Dad just sat there looking, staring, as though he were hypnotized.

I washed the dishes as quickly as I could, dad still sitting there. This was a bit uncomfortable to have him just sit there, and not say a word. But, with out a doubt better that he was quiet than bitching at every little thing.

Dishes were done and me and Becky were outta there. Dad was now in his room sorting through his things. We didn't ask, we assumed wherever he had been staying, whoever he had been staying with, had booted him out. So, he was back.

Crawled back to the rat whole in which you came from huh dad?

He looked clumsy trying to put his own things away. I'm sure he had no idea which was his sock drawer, which was his underwear drawer, because mom was the one that did all that for him.

Hell, we weren't gonna put his things away for him, he was a grown man he could do it himself. It took him awhile, but he managed.

Sher and I were in her room laughing at him, knowing if we went in his room and opened his drawer everything would be a crumpled mess.

We weren't fools. We knew best not to let him catch us laughing. It took another hour but he finally left. He didn't take anything with him so we knew at one point he would return.

As soon as he drove off, we did go check his dresser drawers and to our complete disbelief, everything in his drawer was perfect.

Sher went in to read one of her books, the kids were playing jacks in the living room and the boys were coloring. I was in my room lying on my bed. My stomach was hurting badly. I lay there awhile trying my best not to cry, but this was some pain I had never felt before. I tried to get comfortable but it was impossible.

It wasn't my entire stomach that was hurting, just one side. I didn't want to tell Sher, she had already been through so much with J.J., now to burden her with my problems; it seemed it was just too much. Thinking it was possibly something I ate, but when I got to the restroom I realized it wasn't anything I ate, it wasn't a tummy ache, it was Mother Nature.

I saw the blood and realized what was happening. I was scared, but not to the point of pulling a "Carrie."

When I left the restroom, I went directly to Sher's' room. Guess she saw something wrong with the look on my face the instant I walked in her room.

"What's wrong?" Couldn't hide anything from her, though I desperately tried not to cry

"I'm cramping." I said. She smiled, as she jumped up off her bed and ran to me.

"It's not funny." I said.

"I know it's not, are you sure its cramps?" She asked, as she reached to pat my tummy, as you would pat a woman's tummy that is expecting a baby.

"Yes, I went to the restroom." Pushing her hand away from my tummy, annoyed.

"Malina a woman now. Malina a woman." She did a little dance around me.

"Oh shut up." I started to laugh.

"Why does it hurt so much?" I asked her.

"Well, it's supposed to, that's just how it is." She laughed again.

"Why are you laughing? I never ever laughed at you." I demanded.

"Because your were my little sista, now you a woman like me." She teased.

I didn't laugh at all. There was nothing funny about this kind of physical pain.

"Come on." She took me to the restroom, got a pad, and told me how to put it on properly, while she waited outside the restroom door. I heard her giggling.

I locked her out and did my clumsy attempt at putting the pad on the proper way.

"Are you ok?" Sher knocked on the restroom door.

"Yes." I said.

When I finally came out of the restroom, she hugged me. That pad, which felt more like a big towel shoved in between my legs, was the most hideous feeling in the world. It seemed impossible to walk properly and I just knew everyone was going to see that big gigantic thing through my clothes. I wanted to go to bed so no one could see me.

"My little sista a grown ass woman now." She hugged me again.

"Be quiet big mouth, I don't want the kids to hear." I said

"Why?" She laughed.

"I don't want anyone to make fun of me."

"Oh shut up, cry baby." She teased.

"Now lay down and rest." She said.

"You will feel like shit the first day or two, but after that you'll be ok." Sher even went in the kitchen, brought me some seven up and crackers, and instructed me to eat them all and drink all my seven up. She was catering to me, as if I was as sick as J.J. had been. I wondered why she was doing so much for me. I never helped her when she started. I realized I had no idea until that very minute exactly how she felt. She, on the other hand knew how I felt. I even heard her go into the living room and tell all the kids to be as quiet as they had been at the library.

"Malina is sick and she needs to rest." They all did as Sher said.

I felt like shit, my body ached and I was hot. Being a woman was not at all like I thought it would be.

I was tired, hot, and bitchy like I wanted to cuss some one out or hit them.

Oh my goodness was this normal?

Now there would be two of us going through this every single month. What a horrible thought. Me and Sher going through all this woman stuff together.

I laughed to myself at the thought of us bitching non-stop at every one and having a perfectly legitimate excuse to be a bitch.

Ooohhh, was I in pain.

Woman, my fricken foot. This was feeling more like an evil crazed animal in pain.

Indeed, this pain, this body heat, this desire to cuss the hell out of everyone was not what I imagined. I didn't like this at all. I wanted to remain a child.

# 68

We didn't hear dad come in at all that night. Anytime he came in without making a sound usually meant he wasn't drunk. If he would've been drunk he would've woke us all up and terrorized us. So this meant only one thing, he was high.

Just as we woke the next morning, he was leaving. I was still in a lot of pain. I heard Sher tell the kids we wouldn't be going to the library because Malina is sick. I lay there a minute, and realized, yes I was in pain, but I'd rather be in pain at the library, where I could be comfortable, then to lie in that hot bed all day. No, I couldn't actually lie down at the library, as I had dreamed about. But, I could sit in comfort for a while.

I got out of bed and told Sher not to change our plans, I still wanted to go.

"Are you sure Malina?"

"Yes I'd rather be there where it is nice and cool, then to be here."

"Ok, you tha boss now." She laughed.

We fixed the kids breakfast, and then prepared them for our trip to the library. Dad had called wanting Sher to look for something in his drawer, some important paper he said. Who knows?

It took forever for her to find it, dad insisting all along he had put it right on top of his socks; this was his sock drawer she was looking in.

The kids were impatient while waiting, wanting to hurry up and get to the library. But we weren't going to leave Sher behind.

I was in pain but there was no way I was going to stay home alone. It would only be our second visit to the library with all four kids. They hadn't been there enough times to be bored and rowdy so we knew the kids would still be on their best behavior. This was a new and exciting adventure for the little kids.

They weren't about to ruin it by acting like brats.

Once Sher found the paper for dad and hung up the phone, we left on our second journey to the library. When we arrived, the librarian greeted us with a warm smile. Such happy smiles on the kids faces when we entered the library, smiles caused by the gush of cold air. You really couldn't help but smile.

I was already burning hot, inside and out, due to my new found woman hood, so being able to sit in the library, undisturbed, was like floating on a cloud for me.

Sher helped J.J. and Danny pick out new books. Becky and Carrie went off on their own.

I sat in my normal spot with my eyes closed, while my body ached. Several times, I heard Sher "Sssshhhh." Danny. Several times his little manly voice got louder. Finally, they came to the table and we sat and enjoyed the books, the air, the freshness, the quietness.

The boys were looking through a book about baseball players, loving every page of it. The girls picked out books of kids from other parts of the world, laughing at pictures of different kids, but not laughing so loudly as to get the attention of the librarian. And Sher, well she was happy reading anything. She could've read the dictionary and been content. She didn't care, as long as she had her nose stuck in a book.

Me, my eyes were shut, back into my imaginary world, my imaginary mansion, far far away.

Yes, we could learn to love this peace and quiet. But, as all things do, it was about to come to an abrupt halt.

Completely out of nowhere, we heard it.

"Sher, Sher, where the hell are you?" A voice was yelling.

Oh my goodness, Lucifer was here. The only words to describe that horrid demanding voice of his.

The librarian ran to the door where dad was standing, incidentally, looking like a mad man.

"Sir you can not come in here and" She was interrupted... Ray was with dad.

"Ma'am mind your own business." Ray was quick to protect dad.

"This is my business." She insisted, having no idea who these two men were. Sher stood up, my eyes popped open, and the kids all got up.

"Get over here all of you." Dad demanded.

The kids left the books just where they were reading them. Danny and J.J. ran as fast as they could to dad, ignoring any rules about not running in the library.

Sher said, walking as quickly as she could toward dad.

"What's wrong, what's wrong dad?" She kept saying.

"Let's go." He demanded of all of us.

The kids were damn near running to get to him, seeing the anger on his face. He grabbed Sher by her armed and pretty much forced her in the car as if he were kidnapping her.

He piled us all in the backseat of the car, Ray driving, dad on the passenger seat screaming at the top of his lungs. Ray didn't interrupt. He just let dad yell as much as he wanted. The words dad yelled did not faze Ray at all. The eight block drive could very well been a drive to China, that's how long it seemed to take to get home.

Dad was yelling so much I couldn't hear what the hell he was bitching about. Danny and J.J. were crying by this time, mostly because everything happened so quickly, I guess they thought crying was the solution for yet another episode in our lives. Becky was just staring as if she were in shock, and Carrie, well, she didn't even look at him, or any of us for that matter.

Sher kept saying, "What's wrong?" Wondering what the hell had happened now that had him so pissed. I wanted to cry but couldn't. Womanhood or not, though technically I had the right to be a bitch, trying my new found right as a woman to be a bitch, because it was acceptable once a month, I just didn't think that right applied to my hysterical monster father.

When we got home dad told Ray. "Stay in the fucking car." Ray did as he was ordered.

"Get out." Dad demanded all six of us as he opened the back seat car door. The boys ran into the house, Carrie and Becky followed; I was behind them, Sher behind me, and Hitler behind Sher.

"What the fuck is wrong with you?" He screamed in Sher's face

"What are you talking about?" Sher was crying.

"I fucking told you I was coming for that paper? Where the fuck is it?" He just couldn't calm down and stop screaming.

"In your drawer." Sher cried.

"Show me." He screamed.

"It's right here." Sher said as she opened the drawer. The paper wasn't there.

"Dad I put it right there." She cried as she pointed to the exact spot she had put it after she talked to dad on the phone not an hour ago. Still crying, trying her best to look for it through tear-filled eyes.

"Where?" He screamed. We were all just standing there looking at his drawer.

"I don't know dad, when I hung up with you I put it right there on top." She didn't even get to finish her sentence.

"Find it dammit." He demanded.

Now, I certainly admit when we peeked in dad's dresser drawer the previous day it was completely in order. But what we hadn't realized at the time, though his drawer was neat it was also jammed packed, and you know if you put something in a drawer that is jammed packed with things, and you place something on top then shut the drawer, what happens? Because it is so packed, the pressure of opening and closing the drawer forces the object to the back of the drawer.

Simple... It didn't take a genius to figure this out, only a fucking minute or two of patience.

Sher took out some of his items and there it was... his precious paper. Becky and Carrie had already left the room. It was Sher, dad and me. Once she handed dad the paper she started putting his things back in the drawer.

"What the hell were y'all doing at the library? Dad yelled.

Already having his paper in his hand, he just had to continue bitching. Why not just put your devil tail between your legs and leave, shame and all. Nope Not Him.

"Reading books." Sher snapped. My jaw fell to the floor.

What? I was horrified at Sher's' courage.

"Who the hell said y'all could go?" Sher didn't answer.

"Did you ask permission?" Dad yelled.

As far as I was concerned, now, he was just being a fucking jerk. He had his fucking lottery ticket or the Holy Grail, or whatever he was bitching for, why was he still carrying on?

"No, I didn't ask anyone's permission." Sher was pushing her luck.

"Who the hell do you think you are?"

Oh no, I thought. I'm right in the line of fire. I got teary eyed.

"Sher." I said her name trying to distract her.

"No, why do I have to ask you anything?" She yelled about to burst with all the anger built up in her.

At that very second, all I saw, in actual slow motion, was his hand go right past the tip of my nose and smack Sher right across her face.

"Dad." I screamed.

Sher grabbed her cheek. I believe to this day, if there had been a gun in the drawer rather than a piece of paper, she would have shot him.

"You don't ever leave this fucking house without asking me first. And you stay away from that fucking library."

"I will not." Sher argued back.

I wondered if I pretended to faint at that very second would he shut up. Nope, he wouldn't have even noticed, I'm sure.

Now, he was taking from her, what was giving her strength to be mom and dad to his kid She didn't care what he thought or said now. He probably would've beaten her as he had mom, but at that second Ray stepped in.

"Johnny." Ray yelled.

"Stay out of this Ray."

"Come on Johnny" Ray said. Getting dad by his arm and walking him out the front door.

Sher still holding her cheek and crying, a horribly sad look on her face. While I was still wondering how dad's hand managed to go right past my face without hitting me first. Sher just stared at him like, *I hate you motherfucker*. However, she didn't say the words.

Ray took dad on the porch, doing the second best thing Ray could do. First thing he was good at, was killing people, second thing, defusing situations.

He was defusing this one.

Ray, this is the same man not three months ago, him and his wife were here being like parents to us, and then just like everyone else they stopped. At the time, I didn't know why.

So in my eyes, Ray was no uncle, his wife no aunt, he was what he was. A hired killer.

I cared less about him, or his position.

They both went to get in dads car. Then I looked down, and there it was, the dumb ass had left the paper he was slapping the shit out of Sher for, right there on top of the dresser.

Sher was crying. She was more upset than I had ever seen her. For the first time in my life, I wasn't freaking out. I was actually very calm. I wondered why? Maybe it was the new woman hood I was experiencing.

Staring at the paper, I looked up as Ray was opening the door. My mind envisioned dad had sent him in, with a machine gun and he blasted us all to kingdom come so dad would have no more responsibilities. Dad obviously had sent him in for the paper. Me and Sher were standing near the dresser. Ray walked up to the dresser, picked up the paper, and asked. "You ok Sher?"

She shook her head yes.

"I know this isn't right, but just so y'all know, he called and called and when there was no answer, he got worried. We came over here and y'all were gone. He pretty much lost it. We rode up and down the streets looking for y'all, and then he remembered y'all had gone to the library yesterday.

"Girls, y'all know how he is."

Oh well, excuse the fuck out of us Ray, "Y'all know how he is." Well, now doesn't that just make everything peachy crème, because we know how he is. Fuck off Ray. Did I dare?

Nope, too chicken!

Dad honked the horn.

"I'm not saying it's your fault, or that any of this is right, but next time, at least try to call him and tell him where y'all are gonna be."

Sher continued to cry. "You have no idea." Sher cried to Ray.

"Yes I do Sher, I'm sorry."

Dad honked again, indicating just how impatient he was growing.

Ray couldn't be any kind of a father figure to us. He couldn't put kid's first, gangster duties second. He couldn't let our pain interfere with his obligation...Dad.

If Ray were to have stood up to dad, and taken our side, then Ray would no longer be needed in dad's organization, and Ray knew it. He was as pathetic a man as dad. He was an emotionless, heartless piece of shit in my eyes.

Ray left us standing there giving us whatever excuse he could come up with to protect dad. If Ray was nothing at all, he had one trait on his side. He was one loyal ass motherfucker. Because in my eyes, any man that can stand there and watch another man slap his daughter, then you are either one fucked up coward, or you are one loyal ass mother fucker.

One day I hoped they would both be in jail, cell mates, because neither man could ever claim to be a real father, a real man... I hated them both.

All the people that came and went since mom died, it was Ray and Helena that seemed to fade away. We would call Helena during the day but she never answered. She too had abandoned us, when we needed her the most. I got so tired asking, why, and where was everyone. It seems that's all I thought about was, where is everyone? Don't quite remember how I found out, but it turns out Helena got very very sick three days after she stayed with us. Nobody would tell us how or why only that she was sick and wouldn't be coming over.

Sher was pretty quiet all night. I asked her if she wanted to talk, she said no. I knew to leave her alone. I had my dislikes for dad, mostly because of what I witnessed when he beat mom. Sher still had a love hate relationship with him. Mostly love. I think her feelings that day were more hurt than anything else. I mean really, she was about the only one on dad's side and he dared hit her.

Yes, I believe he was destroying his relationship with her and being that he was the only parent we had left, she didn't want to damage it any further than it already was.

Me, I cared less at this point. The only ones I cared to have a relationship with were the kids and Sher. Everyone else didn't matter to me.

Dad came home late that night. He sat in his car for a long time. That meant, of course, he was smoking weed. I just knew he was going to apologize to Sher. Eventually he came in, as quiet as a mouse. I had a vision of him taking off his shoes and socks and literally tipppy toeing to his room, like a fuckin rat, and then I wished Susie our cat would have eaten the fuckin rat.

Sher was in her room, not asleep, not reading, probably just thinking. He called her into his room. I didn't get up to try and listen to their conversation, he had already done about the worst he could do to Sher, hit her. Whatever was going to happen now was between them.

I could've bet my life he wouldn't hit her or cuss her when he was high. This would have been the perfect time for Sher, if she so desired, to talk all the shit she wanted to him, but good ol Sher.

I could hear him apologizing, her talking to him, telling him she was tired of doing everything herself. She told him of her fears of getting the kids prepared for school and that she needed money to prepare them. He assured her by the weekend he would give her the money she needed to buy school clothes and whatever else we needed... He sweet-talked her and she accepted it.

Sher didn't want to hate him as I did, and I knew better than to make fun of her lack of discipline where he was concerned...

Dad needed her. I couldn't figure out how the heck he could dare be mean to her. She was his only real friend. Sure, the gangsters loved him because they were afraid of him. We were afraid of him also, but for some reason she couldn't abandon him. Sher couldn't abandon him, like he and everyone else had done to us.

Her heart was filled with sadness for him. Possibly the other kids felt the same as Sher, they just didn't know all the details. I think the kids saw it as, it's better to have one jacked up parent then no parent at all. I would agree, if I hadn't seen him beat my mom as if he were beating a man.

I couldn't change anything that had happened, any more than he could. And I couldn't make my heart just forgive and forget. Perhaps if he had been kind, just a little bit, I could have found it in my own heart to forgive, but I didn't have my mom anymore, and she was the only reason I needed to be able to forgive.

I felt sorry for Sher. She was in a very tough spot, but this was her beef with dad. She was a big girl, the only one that could handle him or half ass handle him. I did not envy her the privilege.

They talked awhile then Sher went to bed. I heard dad get on the phone, yes, talking to his lady friend. I covered my ears, not wanting to hear anything he said to any woman. He was talking kindly to her, not yelling or cussing as he normally did. I didn't want to hear this. I wanted to go to sleep. I put my pillow over my head as Sher did every night to drown out dad's voice.

It was too fricken hot for me to do that.

I went to the restroom to get toilet paper to stuff in my ears. Yes it worked! I fell asleep...

The next day Sher woke us all up and asked if we wanted to go back to the library. We could not get ready quick enough. Almost as if we had ants in our pants, we scurried around trying to hurry, even bumping into one another in the restroom as we brushed our teeth or brushed our hair. Eating breakfast took all of five minutes. The quicker we got ready, the quicker we could get out of the house. She called her dad and told him of her plans.

"Ok baby." Was his response

Get the fuck outta here! Was my evil thought for the moment. I mean seriously, that's all he needed to do the previous day, instead of all that hell raising. .

When we got to the library, the old librarian wasn't there. I hoped she hadn't had a heart attack or quit because of dad and Rays behavior.

We all did our same routine as we had done on previous visits.

My eyes were shut, dreading should I hear dad storm the place again. In my mind, I was building my self quite a secret life, with such comfortable surroundings. I could only imagine the things I could invent in my mind should we actually live in a place like this.

We stayed a few more hours then, as we were going home, we took a detour to the park, which was four blocks from the library. The kids ran and played on the swings. Sher and I sat and talked.

"Before you ask, I get it Sher. I understand that you love him and you can forgive, but I can't. What you feel for dad I always felt one hundred times that for mom. I just hate what he is." I tried my best to explain to her.

"I know Malina, and if I had woke up that night maybe I would feel differently, but something in me just feels sorry for him."

"But he doesn't feel sorry for us especially when he's hitting us." I told her.

"I know, I just can't explain it." She pleaded.

"One day I'm going to marry a man that is gonna love me and be so good to me." I said.

"Yeah right little Changa." Sher laughed. "Hell I'm never going to get married. Ever." Sher swore.

We gathered the kids and went home.

We had a peaceful night at home that night, just us kids. Sher made jell-o and gave us popcorn. Since I had heard dad on the phone the night before, I pretty much knew he wasn't coming home again. It didn't matter anymore. He wasted no time finding himself a replacement for mom. He only periodically came to throw his weight around to keep us in line. Without knowing, we kids were surviving times that would have been impossible for any other kids to survive.

Mom had taken such good care of us and sheltered and loved us, it was that love and strength that got us through all the bad times. There would never ever be another woman like her.

Dad may have his girlfriends and wild women but he could never ever have a woman like mom. He lost the only woman in the world that could do what she did, live with a monster. It cost her, but he's the one that had to live with himself.

Could he?

I couldn't, my heart hurt everyday of loneliness. It was a struggle to get from one day to the next. I really don't know what I would have done without my brother and sisters. Mostly Sher.

She was a mini mom, only Sher was tougher. She knew just how to keep us in line, though many times we didn't listen to her. But just like mom, she never gave up. I could not have survived those months if it weren't for Sher. Life was rotten as it possibly could have been.

I often wondered what God was thinking when he lay mom down that night put her to sleep and never allowed her to wake. Did he not realize the life six kids would have to live without her? Did he take the wrong parent by mistake? I'm not ashamed to admit it at all. He had to have taken the wrong parent. Did God need mom more than we did? I really don't know how we did it, but somehow we kept on, kept on trying to live.

We were whooped, hurt, sad, lonely, tired, hungry, scared, every emotion you could imagine. Something kept us going, something made us get up every morning and move on. It could only be one thing. Mom...

# 69

Over the next few days dad came and went, leaving only money for us to eat. I assumed he and his girlfriend made up, which got him out of our hair.

It was the weekend, two weeks before school would begin, and still no money from dad for the things we needed to start school as he had promised. There were also no boxes of clothes from mom's family that we normally received a month before school started, except this year.

Sher and I began going through all the clothes we owned laying everything out on the big bed trying to figure out what was salvageable for the kids. Hand me downs, it's a given, though for us it wasn't humiliating, we were used to it.

We didn't care if our friends said. "Hey I saw that on your sister, last year, or yesterday."

"Up yours." I would think toward them.

I was upset with moms family for not sending us their hand me downs. Perhaps it was done every year for mom's sake rather than ours, but when you think about it, they were going to hand them to down to someone anyway, why not us. So Sher and I emptied out the closets and had each kid try on whatever we could find that might be suitable as school wear...

We figured if we could get five separate outfits for each kid then we would be doing good.

It would be easy to give J.J.'s hand me downs to Danny. But then there were no hand me down for J.J.. Sher wrote a list of what we needed, one kid at a time. J.J. would need everything. Becky's things would go to Carrie, my things to Becky, Sher's things to me.

Now Sher was left out. She continued with her list, consisting of clothes, shoes, socks, and underwear.

Her rough estimates we would need about three hundred dollars, which didn't even include school supplies or lunches.

Sher called dad and laid it all out. "This is what we must have."

He listened as Sher explained the things we each needed, he said something the rest of us couldn't hear, then they hung up.

"He said he'll be here in a bit." Sher explained to us.

Dad had never had to go through this before and we weren't sure if he was going to come through for us now. Always, mom the provider. It was rather embarrassing, I mean really, you're a so-called gangster, and you can't afford school clothes for your kids. I thought. What a fricken disgusting shame.

Sher had us load the clothes we managed to gather for school in a basket saying. "We're not using that damn old washing machine. Let's go." And off we all went to the laundry mat. Sher was determined to clean the clothes real good, starch them, and get them to look the best she could. She did call dad and tell him we were going to the laundry just so he wouldn't pitch a fit. We spent two hours at the laundry washing, drying and folding clothes.

When we got home, Sher went directly to moms' old sewing machine.

She looked at it a few minutes then said. "I gotta figure this out."

"It looks simple." She said.

She got a washcloth and attempted to sew on it to see just how difficult it might be to operate. She did very well I must say.

"What would be the easiest thing to make?" She asked me.

"That's easy." I answered. "A skirt."

"You're right." She said with a smile.

"But what material do we use?" She asked me.

"Well." I said. "Mom made me that dress out of a red curtain, remember?"

Sher looked around at everything. Towels, sheets, old clothes, there was nothing.

"Dammit." She said. "There has to be something I can work with."

Almost at the exact same time, we looked toward the back door and there hung a beige colored curtain with a light brown border on it.

"That's it." I told her.

Sher took it down from where it was hanging. She didn't take the time to wash it, why waste the time if it didn't work there would be no need.

"Who is the easiest to make something for?" She asked.

"Easy again." I said. "Carrie, she is the smallest."

Sher went into her own closet, got one of her skirts and turned it inside out to see how it was made.

There would be no zipper for sure, that was impossible to attempt this time. She needed elastic, again no elastic, she searched and searched. Finally, she found an old fitted sheet that had four areas of elastic, we began cutting it out.

"Ok, come here Carrie." Sher said.

Sher stood Carrie on a chair and did her finest attempt of measuring her. She got the scissors and cut the material just to the shape she needed. She followed the pattern of her own skirt gathering the material as she sewed it, to make the skirt appear full, rather than a skintight skirt.

What a wonderfully sad sound that old machine operating again, it was exciting, it was sad.

Sher went as slow as she possibly could, taking her time wanting to do this the best she could. Within twenty minutes she had the skirt made, all she needed was the elastic put in for the waistband.

Sher took her sweet time again, trying so carefully to make this as good a skirt as she could possibly make. An hour and twenty minutes later, she had Carrie trying it on.

All five of us stood in the kitchen waiting for Carrie to come out and model her new skirt for us.

How beautiful the skirt looked. Sher had made it with the little brown border all around the bottom of the skirt. Carrie was smiling the entire time. She even spun around about twenty times showing off her new skirt.

"You did good big sista." I complimented her.

"I sure did, didn't I?" She said as she blew on her fingernails and rubbed them on her upper shoulder.

We all laughed. I think if Sher had a bundle of material, she would've stayed up all night and made us each a skirt.
She was very proud of herself, we were all very proud of her.

We waited and waited all weekend for dad. He was a no show. One thing we weren't going to do was call and beg any of the relatives for anything. They all knew what we needed, but no one showed up. It was no surprise. We were down to the last weekend of summer. Last weekend before school would start.

Sher and I planned exactly what we were gonna do about getting the kids to and from school. We would walk J.J., Danny and Carrie first, get them there a little bit early giving us enough time to walk Becky also. Luckily, Sher and I didn't have to be at our school until eight forty five, which, if we walked quickly enough, we could get there in time. We just knew we had to do it. It was up to me and Sher. No one was calling and volunteering to help. We had a plan and we were going to stick to it.

Sher had been concerned all summer that she was going to have to repeat ninth grade because she had missed all her final exams, but we had found out all our teachers passed all of us to the next grade, we didn't have to take the final exams after all...

I suppose to each teacher the death of our mom warranted being promoted to the next grade, I'm sure it was a tremendous relief to Sher.

We were all going to start school with what ever we had. To everyone it was better to go to school no matter how we looked, than to stay home.

It was Saturday and dad appeared out of no where. He was rushed as usual, parking his car down the block indicating he had his girlfriend with him. We all went to our room, because he was rushing so badly he just rather blurted out, "Here Sher, here's some money.

"I'll get you kids some more in a few days." And with that, he left.

It was early afternoon and we had plenty of time to go to the department store.

Sher unrolled the wad of money and to our complete surprise; he gave us four hundred fifty dollars. I honestly wanted to cry. I couldn't believe it. It must be a mistake; maybe he accidentally gave us his dope money?

Sher sat us down as she always did when she wanted to have a serious talk with us.

"Ok kiddos." She began. "I was going to go to the store alone, but it's impossible to pick just the right thing for all y'all. So were all going to go together, and we are going to start with Danny and work our way up. Y'all might get bored but we have to do this, all of us together."

"Ok? And please don't ask me for toys and junk, even though dad gave me extra money, we have to make it last."

"Agreed?"

We all agreed.

We ate a quick lunch and started out on our school clothes journey. Sher called the garage to inform dad we were leaving the house, but he wasn't there, so she left a message.

The nearest dept store was twice as far as the park and library, but we knew we just had to do it. We were exhausted and excited at the same time. It was the same department store I had gone with mom at Christmas time.

We finally arrived. It was cold and clean just like the library.

Oh, I was going to enjoy this for sure. First thing we did, we went to the shoe department, since we all needed shoes.

We would get to pick out one pair each. Sher told each of us to pick what we liked and if we could afford them, she would buy them. Two store employees helped us fit the kids and get the right sizes. The boys were so excited, laughing and carrying on.

We spent maybe an hour picking just the right shoe for each of us. Next Sher got the boy's socks and underwear, each girl a pack of panties and a bra each for me, Sher and Becky. Carrie didn't need one yet. Sher had a pen and paper to keep tally of what we were going to spend.

Next, we went to the little boy's dept to get the boys clothes.

The jeans were on sale so Sher was able to get six pairs each for J.J. and Danny. Then Sher went to find the boys some shirts. We managed to find seven shirts each for them. They were so excited, but still obeyed everything Sher told them to do.

Next, we went to the girls department for us girls. It took about two hours to get all the girls to try on all the clothes, but Sher insisted we try them all on, because she didn't want to have to come back. She got three jeans each for the girls and me and herself, four shirts each, one dress each, one skirt each, and four blouses each.

Sher searched and searched for all the sales and the cheap priced clothes. She was determined to get the most for her money same as mom had done that at Christmas.

We had our buggy full of clothes, and were headed to the check out register when I saw the material dept.

"Sher." I said.

"What?" She asked.

"Look." And I pointed to the material dept.

"Oh my." Sher said.

"Sher buy some so you can make skirts for all of us." I said as her eyes lit up. We went through all the material but it was just so expensive.

The attendant showed us the clearance material that was two for the price of one. Sher absolutely couldn't believe it.

Sher got what material she could; trying to match material with the blouses she had picked for each of us, knowing she could attempt to make a skirt to match each blouse. She picked out material, elastic, thread, needles, pretty much every thing she would need to make something for all of us. She was as excited as the boys were.

We got to the check out stand, I was about to cringe thinking we wouldn't have enough money and would have to put some of the things back. To our complete surprise, it came up to two hundred forty three dollars.

We were so excited because for once we had money for groceries, some real groceries.

Each of us had a bag or two to carry the long haul home, but we didn't care, it was worth it...

As we walked home, Sher said. "Malina will you stay with the kids when we get home so I can go to the grocery store? I need to buy lunch meat and stuff for our lunches."

"No problem." I said.

"I told Sher I knew she was a better shopper than me, and besides she already knew exactly what she wanted to buy.

We got about half way home; Danny and J.J. were tired so we stopped at the park to rest.

Really, I think Sher was so excited she didn't want to stop, but the little kids couldn't go on and carry all the bags any further without resting. We stayed at the park for thirty minutes, then we went home.

Sher instructed all of us to leave the bags alone so she could separate everything once she returned from the store. Sher, Becky and Carrie all went to the store together.

I thought they were going to carry all the bags themselves. Nope, Sher pushed that grocery cart full of food right to our front door. She was not ashamed at all. Either was I. We were all like kids at Christmas. We carried in bag after bag, just loving everything she bought.

She had lunchmeat and chips for our lunches and grapes. She bought hamburger meat and chicken for us to cook. She bought potatoes and eggs and beans and bread and Kool-Aid, and soups. We had more food in that one day than we had scraped up all summer.

We were happy, we were excited, and most of all we were doing this together, with help from no one.

I couldn't help but think of dad, finally he did something good. He came through for us. Though he wasn't there to enjoy our happiness, I couldn't help but thank him for the one good thing he had done in a long time. Some of the bad he had put us through faded for the moment.

# 70

It was now the night before school was to start. Sher had the kids pick out what they wanted to wear for the first day of school. Danny couldn't stop talking. I didn't think he was gonna be one of them kids that cried the first day. He was just too excited, but then he had never been away from home, alone.

It was going to be interesting. I already thought it out in my mind, if Danny, or J.J. for that matter, cried, I would stay with them. Sorry, as much as I hated school, I wasn't about to let those two kids suffer. Besides, Sher would be so excited about getting her self to school, she wasn't about to put up a fight with me.

We had an early supper and were taking turns with our baths and such. Everyone was lounging around watching TV pretty much just waiting for the clock to strike ten so we could call it a night. Just as we were turning off the TV dad drove up.

He was sitting in his car and we believed he was crying. He was alone and had the music turned up really loud. I suppose it was time for him to feel sorry for himself, or maybe he really was missing mom. You would not think so since he already had himself a girlfriend. I heard Sher finally go to her room, but never heard dad come inside. Knowing the excitement of getting to go to school again was overwhelming for Sher, I wondered how the heck was she going to be able to go to sleep. She looked forward to going back ever since school had let out; missing everything she loved about school and her friends.

We pretty much had figured everything out as far as getting the kids to school, but we weren't sure what to do about getting them home. Becky could wait on me and Sher to walk by her school, once we got out of our school.

She would be getting out about fifteen minutes before me and Sher would, so we knew she would be ok waiting for us. But Danny, J.J. and Carrie would get out an hour before we did so we just weren't sure what to do.

The plan was to get everyone in school, then Sher was going to get herself dismissed early and walk to get the smaller kids, then I would walk and get Becky, all of us meeting at home.

We knew it was impossible for Sher to get an early dismissal every day, so her plan was to get to the elementary school early and see if she could find anyone to pick them up everyday and keep them until we could pick them up. Ideal situation would be for dad to pick them up and keep them until we got home, but somehow we knew he wouldn't, why even suggest it.

We woke up early, fixed the kids breakfast, and assisted the youngest ones to get ready. We helped the girls with their hair and packed their lunches. Dad was no where to be found, you would've thought he would at least try, but I remembered last year all the difficulty mom had getting us to school and the fuss he made about it. At least we weren't trying to get the kids to school on a cold rainy day.

The clothes dad had been wearing the day before were on his bed, so we knew he had come in at some point during the night. He did his disappearing act long before we woke up, reminding myself, don't be such a bitch Malina, at least he came through with money for school clothes.

Danny was very excited. I wondered, really, I hoped, he wouldn't cry when we got him to school. Also, I wondered would he be scared, or lonely.

J.J. had already been in school, he knew what to expect.

Me, being the biggest crybaby of all, wondering how Danny would react, just had me so sad. My goodness he was just a baby. How in the world would he do this without his mom? I was entering ninth grade and I wondered about my own adjustments. To go to school was one thing, to come home to an empty house, no mom waiting, no hugs when we got home, no snacks waiting on the table, no love. It just seemed unbearable for all of us. How the heck was I going to prepare myself for any of this? There was a suffocating feeling in me just walking to school, now I had to figure out, how to deal with that same feeling once I got out of school, and face the fact there was no mom to go home to.

I wanted so badly to cry as we were walking toward the elementary school, knowing if any of the three little kids cried, or even looked like they would cry; it possibly would push me over the edge. Should one of them cry it would take me back to my own days of crying because I never wanted to be in school, but rather at home with my mom. I know I had to be strong for the little kid's sake.

As we approached the elementary school I saw the idiot Principal Mr. Mann, the same principal that griped at me everyday that I cried in the first grade, insisting I couldn't be with my mom, but that I had to be at school just because him and my fricken dad thought I should be there. I still hated the old fart.

He said hello to me and Sher as we walked past him to go to the office to see what class each of the kids would be in. He called us by name, still remembering each of our names.

Rumor has it Mr. Mann remembered every kids name from the very first year he became principal, which I estimated was about fifteen years.

Mr. Mann followed us as we approached the secretary to discuss the kid's classes. He instructed us to go into his office.

"Can I please have the kid's files?" He asked the secretary. She handed him three files that were already on her desk as if she knew exactly what "kids" files to hand him.

He didn't say our names or the kid's names, which made me think "hum" they must of already discussed us. He opened the door to his office and told us to go in.

We did, as he walked around his desk, sat down, with a big smile on his face, and said "Good morning."

We said "Good morning."

"Let's see." He began. "First I want you each to know I'm very sorry about your mom." He looked us all directly in our eyes.

"Thank you." Sher said.

"I see you kids are alone." He continued.

"Yes." Sher interrupted. "Dad had to work."

Mr. Mann looked at her but said nothing at first. Then after a short pause, he said. "Ok Sher I want to ask how are you kids doing?"

Oh my, I thought, this was my opportunity to tell him everything we were going through. I so wanted to blurt it all out but the look on Sher's face told me otherwise.

"We are doing fine Mr. Mann." Sher said.

"Well I must say, you kids look good and I can't express my sympathy enough for y'all."

I wanted so badly to cry, but didn't want to start the day off for the kids being a teary one, because they were all so excited.

"Ok let's see." He continued. Danny how are you?" As he looked at Danny, with his little white buttoned up shirt so neatly pressed, and a bit of a frightened look on his face.

"Ok." Danny said a bit shyly.

"Good." He said as he reached for Danny's hand. Danny extended his and shook Mr. Mann's hand, looking absolutely adorable and grown up. My eyes teared up

"And you J.J.? How are you?"

"Good." J.J. said.

"Carrie you look lovely today." He said. She smiled.

"Ok let's see." As he read the files.

"Danny, you are going to be in Miss Hanna's class in the lower level. J.J. you are in Miss Martin's class which is right across the hall." He said as he pointed to a classroom opposite the office. "And Carrie, you are in Mrs. Roberts's class, third floor."

"Now." He said looking at the three youngest kids. "I want to let each of you kids know that if, at any time you need anything, anything at all, all you have to do is come directly to me and I'll do everything I can for you. Ok?"

The bell rang at that exact second and kids were, everywhere, and being that it was the first day of school there were parents all over the place also.

Mr. Mann stood up and walked to the door. "Come on kids I'll take ya'll to your classrooms."

First, we took J.J. since his class was right across from the office. As we entered the room, J.J. saw one of his friends from the neighborhood and smiled. Mr. Mann introduced J.J. to his teacher Miss Martin. She shook J.J.'s hand, said "Welcome J.J." Then showed him to his desk. Before he sat in his desk, he came back and hugged me and Sher.

I got teary eyed. *Please, God, I don't want to cry, please don't let me cry.*

He was so grown up, not crying, him also wearing a white buttoned up shirt, looking just as adorable as Danny. We assured him we would pick him up when school was over. He seemed to be ok, so we went to take Carrie to her class, on the third floor.

Miss Roberts was standing at the door and greeted Carrie with a big smile on her face. We repeated the hugs with Carrie as she stepped into her classroom. I noticed Mr. Mann wink at Mrs. Roberts as he said. "Take special care of Carrie for us Mrs. Roberts."

"Most definitely" Mrs. Roberts said with another big smile.

Then we went to the basement to meet Danny's teacher. He looked so scared with his big brown eyes. He moved close to Sher. The closer we got to his class the closer he got to Sher... I hoped he didn't cry, I knew if he did, it would only push me over the edge.

Sher knelt down to talk to him.

"Now Danny, I want you to be a big boy ok?"

"Ok." Danny said. He looked around. I honestly think he was looking for mom or J.J... Sher continued. "Now these kids are all gonna be your new friends." As she pointed to all the little kids in his classroom. Miss Hanna reached for his hand. She had a remarkable resemblance to mom, not as beautiful, but the dark hair and light skin. Danny took her hand, looking at Sher for approval.

"What do I do with my lunch?" He asked Sher and Miss Hanna.

"It's ok sweetie, I'll show you." Miss Hanna smiled, talking to him with such kindness.

God I wanted to cry. Danny, like J.J., came back to us for a hug. Sher and I both hugged him and assured him everything would be ok. He was being such a big boy, amazing us that he didn't shed a tear.

We left his classroom before it caused us to cry. I took three steps out of his class, turned around to go back and stand at his classroom door to see if he was crying. He wasn't he was just staring at Miss Hanna. I wondered if his little mind was making the comparison of mom. I hoped the fact that she did resemble mom, would be easy for him.

At that second, a little girl walked up to him and began talking to him. It was my cue to leave before I did cry.

"Come back to my office ladies, I want to talk to y'all." Mr. Mann said.

"We have to get Becky to school." Sher insisted, knowing also that she couldn't wait to get to school herself.

"This will only take a few moments." He said.

I looked at Mr. Mann remembering how he was not able to comfort me in the first grade, hoping he treated my brothers and Carrie better than he had treated me. I really hoped he would. When I was in first grade, I cried to be with my mom, if the kids cried now it would be because they had no mom

My heart was breaking in two for my brothers and sisters, but there was nothing I could do. How the heck was I going to get through the day myself? My heart was breaking for my family knowing not only were we going to school without our mom, and then we had to go home to an empty house with no mom.

God this just wasn't fair. Again, my eyes were full of tears. How the heck was I going to get through this day, how was I going to get through the rest of my life?

# 71

Mr. Mann instructed Becky and me to sit on one of the chars in front of the office. Becky did as she was told, I did not. I wanted to hear whatever Mr. Mann had to say to Sher.

"It's ok Mr. Mann." Sher began to say, as Mr. Mann turned and saw me right behind Sher. Even if he wanted to object to me being there, Sher wouldn't allow his objection.

"Malina needs to hear what ever is said, she does a lot for us." Sher said.

"Ok ladies, have a seat." He began.

"I'm very well aware of your family situation, and I know you kids must be having a very tough time adjusting."

"Yes." Sher said. "It has been tough."

"I mean no disrespect when I say I'm aware of your dads past."

No disrespect? I thought. That's an understatement. Really, Mr. Mann wasn't disrespecting me; it was Sher he had to worry about. Sher said nothing.

"I see that you girls accompanied the kids to school this morning, that's very admiral, but I'm sure it is very confusing for all of you. You ladies have definitely been raised properly, and I know your mom would be very proud of you all. So, here's what I suggest. Why don't we let the school bus pick up the kids in the mornings, so you don't have to walk every day?"

Wow, I thought. That's a good idea.

"I will have the bus driver pick up Carrie, Danny and J.J. right in front of your house at seven forty five every morning."

Sher thought for a minute. What the hell was there for her to think about? It just means she gets to go to her school that much earlier. I was confused about her hesitation.

Then it hit me like a ton of bricks.

I know damn good and well I read her mind. What would her precious dad say? Really? I thought.

He should have been the one bringing us to school, yet he pulled a Houdini on us this morning.

I continued thinking to myself. Gosh, it would be so convenient for the kids, and also when it rains or is cold, we won't have to worry about them getting sick.

"Yes." Sher said, finally. "That will be nice."

"Now, I really am sorry, but our bus driver can not take you two to the High school or Becky to the Junior High." Mr. Mann was apologetic.

"We understand." Sher said.

"What are y'all doing about the kid's lunches?" Mr. Mann asked.

Sher held up her sack lunch. "We're taking our lunches."

"I'll tell you what, how about we give the kid free lunches for the year?" Sher looked completely surprised.

"We have arranged for the kids to get their lunch for free so you ladies don't have to worry about fixing them a lunch everyday."

Sher smiled. "Thank you Mr. Mann."

"And Sher, if you talk to the principal at Becky's school and your own school, I believe arrangements have been made for all of you to have free lunches.

Hurrah! Hurrah! No more fricken bologna every single day. I was laughing to myself.

That answered it, that's how the secretary knew who we were without him saying our names. There had been a meeting and, more than likely everyone already knew our situation.

"Now about after school, have you made any arrangements for the kids yet?" He asked.

"Well." Sher said. "I was planning on getting myself an early dismissal today to come and see what I could do."

"I believe we may have found an answer for you there also. We have a program; this is our second year for this program. It's actually more like a tutoring program. We take only a select group of kids. It's from two thirty until five. Of course, you can come get the kids anytime before five, but it gives you time to get Becky and not have to worry about J.J. Danny and Carrie sitting outside waiting, and Sher, if you have any after school activities, then it gives u a little bit of time to get here and pick them up."

Sher had a smile on her face I had never seen before.

"I know you young ladies are carrying a tremendous load, so we're trying to ease a little bit of your pain.

"Gosh Mr. Mann, I don't even know what to say."

"Just say yes." He smiled.

"Oh yes, yes." Sher said almost crying.

I was speechless with tears in my eyes.

"I honestly can't imagine what you kids have been through." Mr. Mann said.

Personally, I knew that remark was intended, not only about mom, but about dad also. Dad's name and picture had been plastered all over the newspapers over the years, and I'm pretty damn sure Mr. Mann had read about dad's activities and knew what kind of man he was. .

"So whatever you kids need, please feel free to come see me. I have known you kids for many many, years, and I admired your mom very much, she will truly be missed."

"Yes sir." Sher said.

"And Malina, I am very sorry for all the times I insisted you stay in school, I realize now you just wanted to be…" He didn't even get to finish his sentence, I was already crying. He came around from his desk and hugged us both.

"Now you ladies can run along to school. Talk to the principals, ok?

"Ok." We both said. "Mr. Mann, thank you so very much. You have no idea how much this is going to help us." Sher said, trying to fight back tears of her own.

"Yes Sher, I'm sure I do. My door is always open to you girls, and don't worry about the kids, I'll explain to them about the after school tutoring, they will be fine."

"Thank you Mr. Mann." I said. Remembering how cruel I had thought he was nine years earlier, insisting I stay in school, not allowing me to go home and be with my mom.

Now it seemed, Mr. Mann was doing all he possibly could for the kids.

Yes, I felt I owed him a big apology for thinking he was being mean, when in fact he was just doing his job at the time.

I just took it so damn personal.

We left the elementary school and went to the junior high with Becky. She was so grown up now in the eighth grade, and would be the only one of us in a school all alone, and I worried if she would be ok.

We went to the principal's office to talk to him as Mr. Mann had suggested. Becky was also offered free lunches, and being that she was in the eighth grade, the principal, Mr. Prince had arranged for her last class of the day to be her elective class, which he also arranged her to be an assistant in the attendance office. Just in case she needed to wait at the school for me or Sher, she would not have to wait outside of the school alone; she could remain in the office and help the attendance lady with whatever help she may need.

Becky was both excited and happy. We hugged her goodbye, and set off to our high school.

During our fifteen minute or so walk from Becky's school, Sher began telling me what to expect, where to go, things to do, people to try to avoid, the "snobby bitches," she called them. I was scared, then I wasn't. The more she talked the faster we walked, I thought for a second she was gonna take off full speed running just to get there quicker. I wanted to laugh at her, but I knew she'd stop in her tracks and beat the crap out of me.

Once we arrived, the bell had already rung, but I didn't care, Sher did, that was twenty minutes less she would be able to stay at school. It would all be new to me. But, in reality, it was no different for me than any other ninth grader. I wondered if any of the kids in this big school, and it was enormous, might not have a mother or a father. I wondered if any of them were as emotional as me. Sher livened up the second we walked into the building. She literally became a different person. Saying hello to ever boy, girl, and teacher we passed on our way to the office to see what homerooms we had. Looking at Sher in this school, to see her smiling and so friendly, you would never have known she spent the entire summer stressing over being mother and father to us. You would never know just a few short days ago dad slapped the shit out of her, and to look at her you would not think she was a mere teen, rather looking like a woman in her twenties.

"Hello Sher, nice to see you." Said the very thin woman behind the counter.

"Hello Miss." Sher said.

At that moment the principal, Mr. Brey walked out of his office. He recognized Sher immediately.

"Hello there Miss Sher." He looked like he didn't know whether to smile or cry. Mr. Brey was a very handsome man. Maybe mid forties, looking more like a movie actor than a principal. He walked over and hugged her.

"Hello Mr. Brey." She hugged him back.

"And is this your little sister Malina?" He asked with his soft-spoken voice.

"Yes sir, this is Malina." Sher said

"Hello Malina." He hugged me also.

"Have you ladies found your home rooms yet?" He asked

"No Mr. Brey, we just got here." Sher said.

"Well well, come into my office and we'll see what we have for you ladies." He said as he smiled at us and opened the door to his office. We followed.

The office was crowded and by the looks of the other teens in the room, it wasn't so customary for anyone to be allowed in his office unless you were in trouble, or you had important business with Mr. Brey.

He gave us his sympathies and assured us if we ever needed him, we were welcome to come see him. He was very kind and he made me feel very welcome. I didn't want to cry.

I wanted to be an adult, but being an adult doesn't mean I can't cry does it?

The morning had been a very emotional morning for us, especially me. People were reaching out to us, which we weren't accustomed to. Other than Matty and Gloria, no one had come to our aide.

Mr. Brey showed us our schedules, and went over the normal routines with us. Sher already knew what he was talking about; she had heard it all last year when she was a freshman. I knew she didn't want to be there in the principal's office, she wanted to get on with her day. But, out of a courtesy to me, she stayed right by my side just as she had the little kids. I suppose to her we were all little kids and her obligation to us all was to get us into school, make sure we were ok, and then get busy with her own day.

Mr. Brey reminded us because of our grade level, we were not able to have lunch together. It was no big deal for Sher; she already knew she had tons of friends to sit with at lunch. I was horrified of having lunch alone. But again, I reminded myself, I'm not in kindergarten.

We visited with Mr. Brey about thirty minutes, missing homeroom completely, so he instructed us to go to our first period class.

As he walked us down the hall, Sher said, "Ok Malina, I'll meet you right out in front when school lets out."

"Ok." I said. She hugged me, said goodbye to Mr. Brey and ran off. Literally ran off.

She was just too excited about getting back to school. Sher knew exactly where to go. Me, I had no idea what I was doing and where I was going.

One hundred one was the number of the classroom. "It's right down the hall, there on the corner," Mr. Brey pointed to the classroom at the very end of the hall.

"Thank you Mr. Brey." I said as I walked toward the class. Embarrassed, I thought, oh this is going to be such a long day.

"You're so welcome Malina, and just remember my offer."

"Yes sir." I smiled at him as he walked away.

Even before I got to the classroom door, I could hear all the students laughing and talking. I got the lump out of my throat by swallowing. I tried to smile and opened the door to my very first class in high school. I was so afraid, and sure hoped I didn't start crying.

You know that horrible embarrassing feeling when you open the door and everyone turns to look at you, and it's obvious someone is talking shit about you, because you can hear the slight giggles and "Hey I know her."

Well, that's what I felt. I wanted to turn around and run out of there, but my feet weren't cooperating...

The teacher, an old woman that looked as if she should have already retired said. "Yes ma'am can I help you?"

"Yes." I began to say.

"What is your name?" She asked, almost yelling.

*Do I really have to answer that out loud?* I thought to my self.

"Your name dear, your name?" She said again so damn loudly as if I were deaf and didn't hear her the first time, which caused everyone to stop what they were doing and look up at me.

"Malina." I said, then like an echo I could hear kids saying, Malina, Malina, (someone started the name game song. Malina Malina Bo bena, banana fanna Fo fina, fe fi … you know tha fricken song, right.) These jerks were already about to make me cry and I had only taken three steps into the classroom.

"Have a seat miss Malina." She ordered me.

I looked around, in complete horror, knowing this class full of smart asses was just waiting for me to fuck up so they could laugh and torment me. I had a vision of pulling a "Carrie" on all of them if they fucked with me. Pigs blood my fuckin foot.

My eyes roamed the entire classroom, looking for an empty seat, still hearing kids whisper things like Malina, sit here by me Malina, don't sit by me, sit out side, sit on my lap. Not looking at anyone's face only concentrating on finding an empty seat. There were no empty seats, except one. I focused on the seat, too embarrassed to look at whoever the nearest student was. I headed toward the seat, and, not having a locker yet my sack lunch rattled as I walked. I was so fucking embarrassed.

I remained looking at the floor, like a damn zombie, until I got to my seat, then, once seated I focused my attention on the teacher and the chalkboard.

I was the only nerd doing that, all the other kids were walking around, talking to one another, and cutting up.

What the hell I thought. Even the teacher was looking at a magazine, not even paying attention to her students. Would it be possible for me to run out of the class and no one notice. Naw, with my luck I'd trip and fall right on my face giving all these fuckers something to really laugh at.

"Well, well, if it isn't miss Sher's little sister. Malina is it?"

I was too horrified to look to my left, the direction of the voice talking to me and before I could, I heard it.

"Hey ese, what's up?" And then, without me even looking at them, I heard Arney's stupid laugh. I looked over and all three of them were in the same class, something Sher said was impossible to ever happen.

I saw Whitey first, with his beautiful white teeth smiling at me, Juanito and Arney sitting at their desks, one in front of Whitey, the other sitting behind him. Three Stooges, all together, all in a row. I still didn't say a word.

"First off." Whitey said. "Computer mess up. We." Pointing to all three of the stooges, "should not be in this class at all, at least not together, but by tomorrow, the computer will correct it's mistake and there will, unfortunately be only one of us left."

"Yea ese, probably me." Said Juanito. All three of them laughed. What one did, all three did, I remembered Sher saying.

"Hey where's Sher?" Arney asked.

"Be quiet." Whitey said. "Sooooo miss Malina, just want you to know we cool, right guys? He said.

They all agreed. Shaking their heads yes.

"Yeah." Juanito added Ese to the end of his "yeah right."

*Cool about what*? I wondered.

"So." Whitey continued. "We cool Malina, and we ain't gonna hold it against you that your daddy wants to hang us up on that there flag pole." As Whitey turned and pointed at a flagpole that was right outside our classroom window, with the great U. S of A flag blowing in the wind.

My face turned red, completely red.

Arncy and Juanito were laughing, Whitey was not but… He was smiling.

"Hey I didn't." I started to say in my own defense.

Whitey stopped me. He did a, thumbs up, looking right in my eyes.

"Hey we messed up, we were acting like fools. I got the low down on your daddy, I respect him. And if the things I hear bout him are true. He a bad mutha .. And he damn sure would've done it too, So hey, thanks, thanks for not snitching on us. And, we really are sorry for talking smack; ya know I wouldn't want no fools talkin shit to my daughters, if I had some. So, y'all some cool ass chicks." He smiled the entire time he was talking.

I could see that he was the leader of the pack. Arney and Juanito were followers. And I'm sure it was Whitey that suggested they call that day.

"I didn't know it was y'all, Sher did." I confessed. Sounded more like I was snitching on her.

"How? Whitey asked.

Without saying a word, I pointed at Juanito. They were all laughing.

"He said ese, Sher knew it was him." I said.

"Damn fool." Whitey said. I was laughing because there was no way not to.

"Hey we cool, ok?" Whitey asked.

"Yes, we cool." I said.

"And tell Sher thanks for not snitching." Whitey smiled again.

"Sure." I said.

Then another thumb up from Whitey, and a very nice smile. He popped a breath mint in his mouth, then turned and started talking smack to one of the geeks in the classroom.

What a beginning for my first day in high school. Would I get through it ok? Who knows? But, the day had already begun with the guys my dad wanted to hang on a pole for talking shit to Sher. Though all was forgiven for three class clowns, could it have possibly gotten any worse?

# 72

Class after class, teacher after teacher, I got lost a few times, was tardy once and saw Sher twice. She didn't ignore me as if she were ashamed; she simply did not see me. She was just so much into her own world.

I pretty much did the first part of my day in slow motion. I got overwhelmed twice and went directly to the rest room to cry. Thinking of going home and my mom not being there, would be my first time in ten years of going to school, then to go home and not see her.. I didn't know how to handle all this.

I cried and cried, not caring who might hear or see me. I couldn't help but think of mom and all we were missing, all she was missing, mostly Danny's first day of school. I wondered if mom was alive and all six of her kids would be in school, what would her day be like. Would dad be mean to her because for once in her life, she had a minute to herself? Would he make her sit at the garage all day just so he could control her? No, thinking on that issue, he couldn't have his wife and his mistress at the garage at the same time...

I wondered just what mom would be doing at that very second. Would she have lunch with Danny? Would she sew all day? It's for sure she would have time to herself; she had never had in her life. Sure, she may have gotten bored, but I could only imagine the look on her face when we would all be home from school. The look of love.

It was time for lunch, with the option to either eat my sack lunch that had been in my hand pretty much all day, or indulge on a hot meal, which reminded me that I really wanted a hot meal.

When I got to the cafeteria, kids were everywhere. So damn much commotion. It was not at all like elementary school, everyone sitting at their designated tables, with their entire class. All the little kids actually eating their food quietly and obeying the cafeteria workers.

No this was a lot different. Some kids getting their lunches, some sitting here and there in their own clicks, kids getting their lunch and running outside to eat. Boyfriends and girlfriends sitting in the corner, trying to sneak a kiss before the cafeteria lady caught them.

I could smell the delicious aroma from the area of the cafeteria where the food was being served, and my nose led me in that direction. Before I got in line I wanted to make sure I was able to get a free meal as the principal had promised. I mean really, there was no way I wanted to stand in that long ass line, get to the front of the line, only to find out I had to pay for the meal, which would have been impossible to do considering I had not one cent to my name. Then proceed to get the crap embarrassed out of me thus making myself look like a bigger nerd than the real nerds.

So as I began to tell my story "The principal." I began.

The cafeteria lady said, "What's your name?"

Oh goodness, I didn't want her to embarrass me as my first class teacher had. I tried to say my name real softly, standing close enough to her for her to get the name correct on the first attempt.

"Yes Malina, you're here. Get in line." She said as a command rather than a suggestion. What a relief, and what a wonderful relief for my tummy. I could not wait to get my tray and sit down to a good meal. Meat loaf, mashed potatoes and green beans, with a roll, and a glass of tea is what was being served... Now... this is a meal I thought as I took my first bite of food.

Mashed potatoes melting in my mouth. I admit no one could cook like my mom, but this, after three months of bologna, was a very close second.

I was sitting alone, something I knew Sher definitely was not going to have to deal with, when a girl and guy came and joined me.

I had seen her before in Junior High several times, but it seems she changed a lot. She was much prettier, older looking somehow. Her name was Donna, his was Greg.

I thought they were boyfriend and girlfriend because they carried on laughing and touching each other's arms, turns out they were cousins, just hanging out.

"Where's your next class?" She asked.

"I'm not sure." I told her, as I handed her my schedule.

"Home Ec." She said so happily. "Me too ha, what's the odds? I'll take you when the bell rings." She said as excited as a kid at Christmas.

"Better hurry Malina." Greg said. "Cause the bell will ring in, three, two, one, he pointed, and with that the bell rang.

"Ha ha ha ha ha." He said, actually saying the words ha ha.

"How did he do that? I asked Donna.

"He's a real nerd." She laughed.

"Come on I'll help you with your tray, we only have five minutes to get to class." She said, as she ran to the trash to throw my things in the proper container, put the tray in the appropriate spot and then Donna said, "Throw your sack away." I did as she told me, without thinking of the food I was throwing away, knowing Sher would beat the crap out of me if she knew I had just thrown away a perfectly good sack lunch.

We ran, no walked quickly to our class. It was fun to have a new friend, someone that didn't know of all the things I had been through, that wouldn't think of me as sad or unhappy.

Donna was an extremely funny girl. We laughed all through home Ec, which was fun.

By the end of the day, Donna and I had two classes together. It was three thirty, time to go home. I waited ten minutes, at our designated spot, for Sher. She came out with her big smile, almost a glow on her face. As we walked for Becky, I told her of Donna and Greg and of my wonderful lunch. I told her of my visits to the restroom to cry, which made her sad.

"I know Malina, I know it's gonna be tough."

Then she told me of her day and also her love of her lunch.

We walked to get Becky who also had a big smile on her face when we walked into the attendance office to get her.

Becky told us of her classes and how she just loved working in the attendance office.

She had a good day, which made Sher very happy because a lot of times in the past, Becky would come home from school, very upset because kids would make fun of her buckteeth.

Once she got into a fight in seventh grade, just before mom died, because a girl was teasing her and pointing at her teeth, so Becky bit her finger. She had been suspended from school for that, which mom had to pretend Becky was sick so dad wouldn't beat her ass. Becky was used to her teeth and rather than cry about it, as I would have, she fought back. She didn't care what any of the kids said. She was like Sher, ready to beat anyone's ass for anything they ever said mean to her.

It took another fifteen minutes to get to the elementary school. Upon arriving, we went to the office to see where the kids were and to our surprise dad had picked them up about ten minutes before we got there.

This was very strange, why would he do that? We weren't sure, so we hurried home. Sure enough they were there, outside with dad, on the front porch.

Was he high? I wondered.

Danny ran to hug Sher, J.J. to me, and Carrie to Becky, just as we always had. A touching moment, even for a tough ass gangster. Dad sat there watching us.

We all said hi to him, and started into the house. He called us all back out side.

"Well, how was all your day?"

I almost choked, almost fainted. Almost fainted and choked.

Danny began first telling of the pictures he colored and the letters he learned a "D" for Danny.

J.J. talked about nothing but recess.

Carrie talked of her teacher, and Becky talked of her duties in the attendance office

Dad listened as if he were really interested.

"And you Malina?" He asked of me.

"It was fine." I said, while in my mind I wanted to say," I met the idiots you wanted to hang from the flag pole, knowing if I did, he would accompany me to class the next morning and yank those three fools right out of their desk and follow through with his threat.

Naw, I'm not stupid.

Sher told dad that the bus was going to pick the kids up in the mornings, and about the after school tutoring. "Just in case you're too busy to get them." Sher said, not wanting to piss him off.

While me and my bitchy little mind thought, your an idiot and can't be depended on, knowing he had just gone out of his way to get the kids.

She didn't mention the free lunches, thinking maybe we should save that news for another day.

Too much news at once might just piss him off thinking we went and begged for help, then turn it on us. And believe me I wasn't giving up that wonderful lunch for anybody...

Think of it, we had been all alone all this time, and now he shows up to pick up the little kids, just like a normal dad. Being "Ward Cleaver" for the day, picking up "Tha Beav" doesn't make you a father. Try doing it every day.

Sher talked with him for quite awhile on the porch while the rest of us went inside. Danny and J.J. were so excited and even more excited to see each other, after the long day apart.

As soon as Becky and Carrie put their school things away, they began playing jacks When Sher and dad finished their conversation dad left, Sher came inside, went straight to the kitchen, looked through the cabinets to see what to cook for supper. She decided she was going to make chilidogs and chips, simple enough. No matter what she made and as hard as she tried, her supper could not compare to the cafeteria lunch, that we had both admitted loving...

I made a stupid comment about our supper compared to our lunch in the cafeteria, and to my surprise, she agreed. After we ate, cleaned the kitchen and the kids were getting ready for bed, I told Sher of my run in with the stooges.

"I just knew it." She said. "Damn fools." She said as she laughed. I told her they thanked her for not snitching them off to dad, she laughed again.

"Well when I see them I'll say, "You welcome She said Ese trying to mock Juanito.

We couldn't stop laughing.

I looked towards mom's bed, it was a good day, but nothing compared to the days we would enjoy if we had mom.

I went to bed crying, wishing so bad mom was there, dad was not. Even when I try to smile my heart goes back to the sadness and the loneliness. I desperately wanted to see my mom, see her smile watch her take Danny to his first day of school, remembering how hateful dad was the first day J.J. went to school. The more I thought of mom the sadder I became.

I prayed so hard to dream of her that night. I did 'Make believe' as I tried falling asleep, hoping, if I thought of her long enough, she would come back, just as she had promised.

I was crying again, whispering my moms name so no one could hear me, pretending she was there in the next room, pretending like magic she would appear.

# 73

The school bus arrived just as Mr. Mann had promised. We hugged the kid's goodbye and wished them a fun day.

Dad hadn't come home the night before. We finished our breakfast cleaned the dishes and set off to walk Becky to school.

Sher and I arrived at school on time and Sher ran off with her friends, as I found my homeroom and was given a locker.

This would be the busy day at school, getting our books and supply lists, which, to a high school student were mostly paper, folders, and pens, not really much more than that.

It was the little kids that would have big supply lists. Sher said she still had money left from the money dad had given her for school clothes, to buy their supplies.

I didn't see Sher at all, but I was sure she was busy with her friends. Me, Donna and Greg ate lunch together again, another wonderful meal of spaghetti and garlic bread.

The day seemed to go faster than the first day, again me getting sad for my mom and going to the restroom to cry.

Donna managed to cheer me up through each class we had together. Once school let out, we walked for Becky, and then went to the elementary school to get the kids, this time the kids were there. It figures, dad only did his grand appearance for the one day.

Danny was so excited to show Sher his supply list. J.J. and Carries lists just as large as Danny's. When we got home, we started supper, tonight being hamburgers and French fries.

Sher told me she was going to the store to see what supplies might be there for the kids so she wouldn't have to go all the way to the department store.

Me and Becky cleaned the supper dishes while Sher and Carrie went to the store to shop for school supplies. Gone only a short while, Sher came back with maybe half of what the kids needed. She separated and bagged each kid's things for them to take the next day to school.

Again no sign of dad, so we did our daily routine. Sher stayed up late that night trying to make a skirt for Becky. Sher vowed to make one skirt a week, because she knew we would need clothes throughout the school year. I wondered why she didn't wait until the weekend, when she would have more time. I suppose she was just so excited about being back in school, she couldn't sleep anyway.

Aunt Matty called to see how the kids were adjusting in school, Sher told her of the bus picking up the kids and the free lunches. They talked a bit, Matty reminding Sher she had to have Aunt Mary take Lori to school, because Matty was already at work by the time Lori went to school.

I fell asleep early that night, trying so hard to dream of my mom. The days we had spent at the library, with the cool comforting air, taught me how to relax. Relax my mind, think good thoughts. I was learning to control my mind, my thoughts. I felt the only way for me to survive so much negative shit it my life was to create nice things in my mind. Rather than say, "This mother fucker is back, referring to my father. I would create, in my mind, a happy life; a life still filled with mom love, the kids, Sher beating us up, everything I wanted in my life, but on a happy note. Though I would be wide-awake, my mind would make me believe I had a good, happy life. It's ok to do this I told myself over and over.

This or drive myself crazy.

Sometime late that night dad showed up, cussing and throwing things around. He wasn't happy until he knew he woke us all up. He cried for a while, and then went out side to smoke his weed. Is an overdose of weed even possible? I wondered.

Someone tell me please, what is the fucking point of waking all of us kids up? He was not sadder than me, he didn't miss mom more than me. He already had a girl friend, that must be it.

One week later, after their first fight, she broke it off with him again. Damn, I couldn't blame her, look how he acts.

I tried and tried to go to sleep, entirely impossible, so I got up to go to the restroom and noticed the time 4 a.m. and here he was making an ass of himself.

Now, if he had woke us up to cry, of how he missed mom, I could have understood his unhappiness. But this shit, this was not him missing anyone, this was his anger and hate, but for who, who was he hating on now? Why couldn't he be normal?

I suppose he stayed out side until daylight, because when we woke the next morning, he was in his room.

The bus arrived and because the bus driver honked his horn for the kids dad was up and bitching. How fucking stupid, he was bitching because a bus driver woke him up, after he had come in and woke us up just a few hours earlier. He was cussing, telling Sher to "Tell that mother fucker to never honk again, get off his lazy ass and knock!"

Was he serious, this wasn't a boyfriend calling to take Sher on a date you idiot, I thought. This is a man doing his job, honking was part of his job. Was this jerk serious?

He cussed saying, "You better tell that mother fucker."

Sher hurried the kids past him so he wouldn't find a reason, any reason to bitch at them and thus ruining their day further.

Of course, Sher did not tell the bus driver what dad said. Was that wise though? What if your "Daddy" is home tomorrow morning and the bus driver honks again. Dad is going to kick your ass tomorrow for not obeying his commands today.

Seems to me Sher couldn't catch a break... There was no way Sher was going to repeat dads demand to the bus driver or anyone for that matter.. Sher walked past him, as she came back in the house after getting the kids to the bus..

This is no way for kids to begin their day.

Then he saw Becky wearing a skirt and started bitching that the skirt was too short.

"Pull that damn skirt down some, or go change your clothes." He yelled at her.

She walked in the room where I was brushing my hair and said, "Ok daddy, I'll pull it down some, and when I get to school I'm gonna pull it right back up." Which made me laugh, not out loud, I knew better.

Talk about starting the day off horribly. How the heck were we gonna get past him without having to hear more bitching.

And, just as I predicted, "Where's your lunches?" He barked.

Now the proverbial "Lie by not telling him everything" was upon us.

"We are all getting free lunches." Sher said.

"Why free? He barked, knowing he had given Sher money a few short days ago. I guess the fucker forgot we needed to eat, and we needed clothes, and supplies.

"A lot of kids get lunch for free; we're not the only ones." Sher tried to explain. He didn't believe her, hoping to catch her in some sort of a lie.

Goodness it was time to leave and Sher is having to explain the meaning of "free" to this common criminal.

Come on jerk, no one is saying you're a pathetic ass, and you're poor kids need free lunches cause you're so fucking cheap..

No it is, Sir, all the kids or most of the kids get free lunches, its a program provided by the schools to make sure all kids get a healthy meal not just a fucking bologna sandwich everyday of the summer you fucking jerk. How wonderful my mind was working this morning... He had fucked with everyone this morning, so I just knew my turn was coming. All this fucker had to do was say "Boo" to me and it would be over for me.

How I wish I could talk shit right back to him, knowing damn good and well if I did I damn sure better know how to out run his car, cause as soon as I attempt to leave, he's gonna chase me down with his new Cadillac.

Then I had a vision of dad standing in the hallway at school and hollering for Sher as he did at the library. My mind was going to fast for me, I felt faint. Should I piss myself just to give him something to really bitch about?

This bitching seemed to go on forever, but I knew if Sher said just the wrong thing he would go off on all of us.

Then it happened. "I'm going to take y'all to school." He screamed.

Why? I wondered. Why? Lord, why? Doesn't he have someone he can go kill nice and early this morning, anything besides take us to school.

Oh, this day was only getting worse. Here I go with my visions.

I could only imagine him driving up to school to drop us off and seeing teenage boys and girls holding hands or worse sneaking a kiss from each other...

This man would have jumped out of the car and kicked the boy's asses. Better yet dad would more likely go up to every boy and say "Are you the mother fuckers that called my daughter talking nasty?" Then taking every boy he saw and hang them by there feet up on the pole.

Now I really didn't want to go to school, but it was impossible to fake it, I had no mom to protect me...

I wondered why his ass wasn't at work. Why was he home? I wish his bitch would quit breaking up with him. What kind of a woman was she anyway? She couldn't stand him but for three months, what a fucking weakling she was.

Dad was putting on his shirt as the phone rang.

Who ever it was on the other end, really made dad blow his fuse.

He yelled "You stupid mother fuckers."

Now, dad didn't say stupid like most people, he said stuuuuupid, more or less dragging the stuuuuu for a long ass time. If this bastard weren't so fucking mean he would have been comical because some of the shit he said and did was actually funny.

Well who ever stuuuuupid was, he, or a she got him out of our hair.

I have wished the Candid Camera Crew would pop out of nowhere and bust this fucker. Ashton Kutcher where the hell your "Punked" ass when you need him.

Though dad was a fricken jerk about almost everything he did, some of the shit he said and did was actually very funny, cruel but funny, and he had no idea just how much we laughed at him for being so fuckin stuuuuuupid himself.

"Go on, go on walk, I have to go to the fucking station."

Better for him to ruin his workers day further, than ours. As we walked, quickly so we wouldn't be late, or he changed his mind, Sher and I couldn't resist saying "Stuuuuupid" non-stop, which made all three of us, laugh. I wanted to suggest that we walk streets we had never been on, but knew better. I would not put it past this crazy man to drive up and down every street in north side until he found us.

We took Becky, than walked even faster to get ourselves to school on time. Once at school, I didn't go to my homeroom, I went to the restroom, and cried and cried, I was just so tired of everything. Sure, I laughed with the girls; it was the only way to cope with all this. But once alone I was filled with so much hate and emotions, I couldn't help but cry.

As I cried, I heard someone in the restroom. I looked up to see the assistant vice principal. Mrs. Crow.

"Are you ok?" I was frozen. I honestly didn't know what to say. Instead, I just cried and cried.

She comforted me as long as I cried, not once trying to stop me, or interrupt my tears. Even as I was crying, I was trying to figure out what I would tell her, knowing damn good and well I couldn't tell her about dad.

# 74

The assistant vice principal stayed with me until I stopped crying. I cried so much my eyes were swollen, so when I finally did stop, she took me to her office. She didn't rush me to talk, she knew who I was, and she knew of the ordeal we had been through.

Every few minutes someone would knock on her door to ask a question or get a tardy slip signed. Phone call after phone call from whoever needed her for whatever reason.

Then she called her assistant into her office.

"I do not want to be disturbed. I will be busy for a bit, so please, put everything else on hold, unless Mr. Brey asks for me."

"Ok Mrs. Crow." Her assistant said.

Mrs. Crow handed me some Kleenex and asked, "Do you feel like talking about it?"

My mind was confused. Should I tell her everything? Should I trust her? What was I going to say to this complete stranger? She wasn't a priest! Anything I told her wouldn't be between me, her and god. Only a priest could keep your deepest darkest confessions. Anything I told her would be between me, her, and all the fricken school district.

How could I explain to her, a mere stranger, what a monster my dad was? Was it possible she would listen to everything, without calling the police? And then here's all the situations with my dad. If I did tell her just how badly he treated us, she would call Child Protective Services, and they would go after him for sure. My biggest worry was not CPS, my biggest worry was the fact if I ratted my own father, he would go ballistic. Gangsters hate rats. And for his own daughter to actually rat him out. Unforgivable. So, I cried again.

Finally, I told her. "I just want my mom. I don't know how to get through the days without her." She got teary eyed herself.

"It has to be very hard for you, I know, and being that my own mom is still with me I can't possibly imagine what you are going through." She was comforting.

I said, "I cry here at school because I hate going home and she is not there."

"Is anyone there when you get home?" She asked

"Well," I really wasn't lying, "My dad, sometimes."

"And how is he handling this?" She asked.

Oh no, now there was the open invitation for me to tell all.

Say it Malina, say it. Tell her everything. My conscience was telling me. No Malina shut up, he will beat your ass. My other conscience was beating into my brain. I just didn't know this woman .Yes, she was nice, and she was comforting, but not even to Matty my aunt, could I tell all.

What was I going to do?

I changed the subject. "When I'm here I'm sad because I want to be at home with my mom, but I know she isn't there, and when I'm at home I can't hardly stand it cause I want to see her again." She listened to every word I said. Her dark brown eyes looking directly into mine. She had an uncanny resemblance to Maya Angelou, just as soft spoken as Miss Angelou also.

"Ok Malina, I'll tell you what. I'm going to inform all your teachers if at anytime you don't feel well or you're sad and just need to get away from everyone and everything; I want you to be excused from class and go directly to the nurse's office. Come I'll show you."

She took me to the end of the hall and knocked on the door to the nurse's office. When we went in the office an older lady greeted us, she looked like a real nurse from the old movies with her white outfit and white stockings, only thing missing was her white nurses hat, which, was sitting on her desk.

"Mrs. Reese, this is Malina. Malina this is Mrs. Reese."

"Mrs. Reese, I want you to know that anytime Malina comes to you, you are to take her to the "Comfort Room."

The office we were in at the moment had Mrs. Reese desk, two small beds, army cots similar to J.J.'s and Danny's bed, a scale, which to weigh students, and a table. Quite a simple room, no pictures on the wall or plants. Not even a photo on Mrs. Reese desk.

There was a door that led to another room, Mrs. Crow opened the door. This was an unbelievably beautiful room that didn't look like a hospital room or nurses office, rather a bedroom in a nice home or a hotel.

A quick rush of the Wizard Of Oz flashed in my mind when Dorothy opens the door to leave her house that had been blown all over the place, and steps out of the old black and white scene to the beautiful colors of Munchkin land. Immediately, I felt as if I was in another place, another time.

A very large bed, with a comforter on it that looked more comfortable than any bed I could have ever imagined. Four or five pillows on it, with matching pillow covers. There was a vanity double sink, with a mirror. There was even a big colored TV.

Beautiful warm pictures on every wall that gave me the sensation I was about to walk right into a beautiful snow covered mountain. Another picture of a waterfall so real, I imagined seeing the water actually flowing. Pictures of landscapes so beautiful I had no ideas such places even existed. Thick dark drapes covering the windows to block the rays of the sun from entering the room.

Mrs. Crow went on to say this room was for special students.

She said. "I'm sorry to say Malina, but we have other students like you and Sher."

"We have a few students that have suffered losses similar to yours and at such a young age. We have students that have lost their fathers in the war; we have students that have lost friends in car accidents. And this is where they come to rest. Not to be sent home, but to get their thoughts together, so they can return to class when they feel they are a bit better. This is where I want you to come any time of the day you get overwhelmed and need to have a good cry. You do not need to go to the restroom and hold back your tears, instead come here, relax, get your thoughts together."

"Before we established this room, students would have to go home when they had a crisis in their family, and we found most of those students would go home and be alone because their parent would be at work. So we created this room so you can mourn, cry, rest, get your self together then go back to class if you so desire. And should you feel you can't go back to class, well then it is quite all right for you to stay here. This room was founded for students just like you and Sher."

"Do you think you would like to come here when you get sad?"

"Yes." I said.

"Fine, then I will instruct your teachers to allow you to just walk out of the classroom if you should get overwhelmed."

"Does that sound ok with you?"

"Oh yes Mrs. Crow." I said.

"Ok Miss Malina, this is where you can come anytime of the school day to get your thoughts together and no one will bother you or tell you to hurry back to class, is that fair?" She asked.

"Yes." I said.

"Would you like to stay here now?" She asked

"No." I said. "I think I'm ok now." I said.

"Ok." Mrs. Crow said. "Just remember, anytime you need to, just knock on Mrs. Reese door and when she sees you, she will already know why you're here. Unless of course you are sick, then just tell her and she will take care of you."

"Ok." I said. "And thank you so much Mrs. Crow.

"Now, I believe it will be ok if we go to class now, but please don't tell the other students of this room. As I said this is a special room. You may tell Sher if you like."

"Ok Mrs. Crow and thank you again." She hugged me as I went to my class.

Sher saw me with Mrs. Crow and asked if I was ok?

"Yes." I said and went to my class.

My day was confused, but just knowing I had a place to go when things got too much for me, or even if I got sad, made it all a bit easier to handle...

When we left school that day, I told Sher of the room Mrs. Crow took me to. Sher was amazed because she did not know of this room and told me she was glad Mrs. Crow had been in the restroom when I was crying. Yes, even I thought of that as a small blessing.

We picked up Becky and went for the little kids, walked home and again dad was there. How I wish there was a room to hide in any time he showed up. I dreaded walking into the house.

Dad wasn't high he was drunk, falling over drunk, at five in the afternoon. This wasn't going to be good.

Just as all six of us walked up the stairs, a kid passed on a bike and said. "Hey Bucky." Spontaneous reaction from Becky was to flip that little fucker off. She did it without batting an eye. Dad didn't see or hear the kid on the bike, he only saw Becky's finger and he went crazy.

"What the fuck are you doing?" He yelled at her. Then grabbed her by her arm and threw her to the floor. The little kids ran to their room crying. Dad picked up Becky and hit her in the face so hard it knocked her to the floor again.

Sher yelled "Dad," but he didn't hear her, instead he picked up Becky and hit her again this time he threw her across the room, she looked like a rag doll being tossed by an angry child.

"What the fuck are you doing sticking your finger?... He didn't even know why she did it. His eyes were blood shot red, not from crying, but from drinking all day.

"I'm sorry dad." Becky screamed.

"What the fuck is wrong with you?" He hit her again.

Sher tried to pull Becky away from him.

"Dad don't." Sher yelled as Becky pissed all over herself. Sher was crying.

He hit Becky again, this time she stayed on the floor holding her cheek.

Sher was screaming. "Stop, stop, please stop." As she picked Becky up off the floor.

"Get that little bitch to the restroom to take a bath." He demanded.

Sher did as she was told. I was crying, I was paralyzed.

There was no one there to help. The phone was out of reach to any of us. I heard Becky crying uncontrollably as Sher started the bath water.

"Take a bath Becky." Sher said crying. I'll get you some clean clothes."

Becky did as Sher said. When Sher left the bathroom Becky was getting undressed, dad was yelling and cussing the entire time, then he pushed open the restroom door, just as Becky was getting into the tub he hit her, but this time he was hitting her with his belt. I heard her body hit the tub, as she fell, he continued cussing and hitting her...

Becky was crying saying, "I'm sorry daddy." His yelling continued as the hitting continued, it was non-stop. I was panicked as to what I was witnessing, with the restroom door open, my naked little sister was getting bombarded with hits, by an angry drunk crazed man.

The belt, and the belt buckle striking Becky's body with his belt, over and over with the same pounding force he had the day he pistol whipped mom. But this time, it was a belt and he was beating a child with it, striking every part of her naked body and face. It seemed as if he had no control over how hard or how many times his belt struck Becky.

Unable to beg enough, or protect herself from him, she literally crawled into a fetal position in the tub, trying to protect her body and face, from what was an endless stream of power blows from the belt... I believe Becky gave up helping herself. Dad was over come with evil intentions. It appeared he was so drunk he could not stop beating her. I was hysterical. He was going crazy. I screamed as loud as I could for Sher.

Sher, heading for the phone to call the police I'm sure, was stopped by the phone ringing.

Sher screamed into it, "What..." I'm sure she was hoping it was someone calling to rescue us. It was Sal. There was some kind of emergency at the garage.

"Dad." Sher yelled.

"Dad." Sher screamed again, trying to get his attention.

"It's Sal, something happened." Sher knew something was happening in the rest room; she just had no idea what.

Possibly, we were really just that horrified of our dad. I'm sure any other family in the country would have called the police. But we were just too afraid of him.

Me and Sher ran to the restroom, wrapped a towel around Becky, and took her to Sher's room. She had marks on her face where he had slapped her and whelps from the belt buckle on her face and all over her body. We could hear him yelling on the phone.

He got his keys and ran out of the house, got in his car and hauled ass towards the garage.

Sher helped Becky get dressed, as I tended to the smaller kids that were all crying uncontrollably. We were all scared now. More scared than we had ever been.

What if that phone hadn't rang? What would have happened to Becky? Would he have just beaten her to death?

It all happened so quickly, Sher had gone to get clothes for Becky, within a few seconds dad was in the restroom viciously hitting Becky with his belt. He was out of control. Being a ruthless badass gangster is one thing, this was beyond beating the shit out of someone...

Being drunk gave him no right, made no excuse for what he was doing. Child neglect was one thing; he had gotten away with that. This was literally child abuse.

Sher was hysterical; she knew she had very little options now. What the hell were we gong to do? He had gone too far. Now he had to be stopped.

# 75

He was drunk, violent drunk. Argument could have it he was so drunk he didn't know what he was doing. It didn't matter; we knew what he was up to. Becky was saved by a phone call; we might not be so lucky next time.

Cry? We did a lot. We knew what would happen if we called the police. We would all be separated that night and we weren't about to let that happen. Sher was in charge, now she needed to make the right decision. She did what she thought was best. She called Matty first.

Sher was crying. All she could say to Matty was. "Will you come over?"

At first Matty said she would be over tomorrow, thinking we were crying because we were sad.

Then Sher told her, "If you don't come tonight, I'm gonna call the cops on your brother."

Matty was at our house within five minutes.

Sher made the little kids go to bed, and then she sat with me, Becky, and Matty, and told her everything.

I was so scared I literally threw up.

Matty was crying. It was a lot for her to take in. She couldn't do this alone, but she knew if she called Gloria and told her to come over, and dad showed up, he would beat their asses too, just for getting in his business. So Matty did what she thought was right.

Becky fell asleep on the sofa, her head on Sher's lap, so badly beaten, her face swollen, and whelps from the belt all over her face and body. Matty told Gloria the entire story word for word as Sher had told Matty.

It was obvious my aunts thought alike. There was no way to leave us with him anymore.

Enough was enough.

"We can't just take them out of here overnight, so I'm gonna call Johnny and tell him I have no electricity at my apartment until tomorrow, and that I'm going to stay here tonight." Matty said.

"Do you think it's safe?" Gloria asked

"No." Matty said. "But I'm not going to leave the kids here alone. But if he does show up and starts raising hell I'm going to call the police."

Gloria was crying. We knew they weren't trying to protect him for what he had done; they were trying to protect their own families from his wrath. Gloria called Aunt Mary to tell her what had happened, meanwhile Matty called dad at the garage.

"Johnny are you busy?" She played it off. Wiping her tears away.

"Hey I just got here and I wanted to ask you if it would be ok if me and Lori could stay here tonight, I don't have electricity yet, and I needed a place to stay for the night."

He agreed, possibly his sick fuck drunken mind didn't realize how bad he had beat Becky. And our hope was that he wouldn't come back all night.

Gloria called back and said her and Mary figured what they could all do.

Matty listened to Gloria, we listened to Matty. They talked for a long time. Sher was very upset. Her life was crumbling again, but no worse than any of ours. After a long while, Matty hung up the phone.

"Ok girls, here is what we are going to do." Matty said.

"J.J. and Danny are going to stay with Aunt Mary. Becky and Carrie are going with Aunt Gloria, and you two are coming with me."

"Why in pairs like that?" Sher asked.

"Mary and Gloria don't work, so it's easier for them to take the little kids. I work and you two are old enough, should I not be there, y'all can take care of yourselves until I get home."

It made sense. There was no way any one family could take all six of us, so it was final we would be split up, but better to be split amongst our family then to be taken to an orphanage.

We stayed up most of the night; dad never showed up, Matty vowing to call the cops on him should he show up starting shit... The plan, according to Matty, was for all of us to go to school the next day, except Becky, her face and body to swollen to explain.

The three sisters had gotten their story together. They were going to go to the garage and ask, not tell him, if we kids could move in with them.

He would object of course, but they would say "Johnny it just isn't right for the kids to go home from school to an empty home."

They would do the sympathy thing to him explaining how we would be paired off.

Then if all else failed, they would say "You don't need the judge to find out the kids are alone." Which, they believed would seal the deal.

Now it's a given dad was not a fricken idiot, and possibly he would think this was some bullshit story his sister conjured up. Possibly, I said. But, for arguments sake let's say he really didn't remember what he did to Becky. If, and I say if he did not remember, then he should agree with his sisters plans, but, another big, But, if he did remember, then this jerk would realize his sisters were fucking with him. Double edged sword. It was a lot of If's and butt's and who, what, what the fuck ever. Everyone was walking a thin line here.

Dad was a scrupulous, conniving motherfucker. He'd let you hang yourself with your own lies, and even though he would be wrong for what he did, he'd flip it and blame everyone else for whatever was fucked up. I knew these three aunts had to have their shit together if they were going to approach him with any kind of deal.

It was impossible for me to go to school the next day, so I went with Becky to Aunt Gloria's house. Over and over I relived Becky's ordeal in my mind. The way he just flung her in the tub, banging her head on the side of the tub as she fell. And the endless stream of blows with the belt. God help this monster should karma ever get to him.

Matty, Gloria and Mary all went to see dad at the garage.

Now, though I wasn't there, I had a vision of my dad's face when his three sisters approached him. I agree he was a low down dirty motherfucker for everything he had ever done in his life that was wrong, but, right or wrong, and it don't mean she was weak, but Aunt Gloria always had a soft spot in her heart for dad just as Sher did. I wished I could have seen the look on his face when these three women walked in the garage unannounced. I could have bet my life he already knew they were not going to say one word about Becky. Which they didn't.

They gave him a way out. Yes, they gave him the song and dance about us being alone, and not eating home cooked meals, and how sad it was for us. But, somewhere in the back of his mind, I can't help but wonder, was dad laughing inside at these three women, as they gave him their rehearsed speeches.

Well, no one will ever know will they?

So after an hour of all three sisters explaining how horrible it was for us to be alone he agreed. He actually agreed to let us move out of that house and with our aunts.

Actually, I always thought since the day he slapped the hell out of Sher over a fucking piece of paper, we should have been taken out of that house.

What's the saying, "too much, too little, too late?" Snowball effect, one bad event, the next gets worse, then the next worse after that. Snow ball rolling down hill. I wondered did any of my aunt's want to tell him what we had told them. Maybe it crossed their mind, but as dad was no idiot, either were his sisters. I would almost bet, just before the three sisters left dad at the garage that day Aunt Gloria still blessed him, that's just how she was.

My Aunts had all seen their brother in action; they knew exactly how bad he could be. Sometimes that evilness was on their side, when they needed his help. Other times they only heard of just how mean he was, but now, they saw the after effects of his viciousness, and it goes without saying, they knew for a fact they had to intervene. You can't just walk away from that kind of physical abuse on a child.

So, just as they were all getting out of school, Matty picked all the kids up. Mary took me and Becky to the house to start packing our things. Matty, Gloria, and Mary all drove their own cars to take their new additions to their families and each of our belongings.

Sher and I helped Danny and J.J .pack. We collected all their clothes and toys. I'm really not sure if the boys understood what was going on. It didn't seem the appropriate time to give them details just yet. They would be right across the street from where Sher and I would be. We would have plenty of time to explain things later. Right now, the important thing was to get everyone away from that house.

Becky and Carrie packed their own things. They were old enough to understand. Becky's face was more swollen now than it had been overnight. Her whelps twice as big. Aunt Gloria cried several times as she helped the kids get their things.

Becky looked confused and scared. Carrie, helping as much as she could, doing what ever Becky did. By the time we all got every thing we each owned, it looked as if no kids had ever lived there.

Danny and J.J. would be right across from where me and Sher would be living with Matty and Lori. Becky and Carrie, five minutes away at Gloria's house. We would not be far from one another, we just wouldn't be all together in the same house, but hopefully we would all be safe.

After we loaded all J.J. and Danny's things in Mary's car we hugged them, knowing we would just be across the street from them, we kissed them good-by and they drove off with Aunt Mary.

Becky and Carrie finished loading their things, hugged us, and left with Aunt Gloria.

Sher was still loading our things in the car, not really talking to anyone. All the love she had for her dad, even she knew how close he came to being arrested. She loved him, but I believe yesterday, she hated him. Though Sher could not take the really big items like her sewing machine, she knew she could go back anytime to get whatever she wanted.

It was obvious to everyone, even Sher; we could not stay there anymore. Dad had gone too far. He was doing the unforgivable the unthinkable to one of his children. No one could just sit back and pretend as if this wasn't happening.

This was the second time I had to tell of my dads actions. Who could just walk away from us now? Dad's family couldn't turn their backs, they wouldn't dare accuse him. Actually, they wouldn't even mention it to him. Ever.

It was obvious dad was not my favorite person in the world, and this was not a proud feeling I had telling on my dad for beating my sister the way he did.

Again, this monster father had done something horrible to hurt someone, and got away with it.

A sick horrible monster left alone with six kids. After what happened to Becky, anything would've been possible. Maybe that was the thought that made my three aunts decide it's time to step in. Step in before it really was too late.

# 76

Life was going to be different now. For better? Of course. It goes without saying. It definitely could never get worse.

Mom would never have wanted her kids split up, such a responsibility for anyone, raising another woman's children.

We weren't just any ones kids though.

You really gotta love my aunts and uncles for stepping up. They were about to inherit a few more mouths to feed, though they didn't seem to mind at all.

Our lives were definitely gonna change, we would now be allowed to be kids, not have to worry so much, perhaps breathe again.

For me life would never ever be the same, though poor, I was rich with the love of a wonderful mother. What I would give to have my mommy, but all the pleading in the world would not have my prayer answered.

Dad wasn't there when we left. He had believed his sisters story about his kids coming home to an empty house. It was probably the only excuse he would've ever believed.

Him not being there when we left was easier for him, us also.

He had stayed away for the past three months, coming home only when it suited him. There was no reason for him to be there now.

Fear of him and his capabilities had kept his family loyal to him. Isn't that the concept of a man like that?

Once Sher put all our stuff in the car, she came in one last time to look around. She looked sad, but didn't cry.

Her responsibilities for five kids was now lifted, she could be a normal teenager, if that were possible. Sher walked out of the house and got in the car just as Matty did.

I was left alone, in that house. No one there just me.

I walked first through the kitchen, there I actually saw my mom cooking, and making her famous Kool-aid saying, "Come on kids, time to eat."

Then I walked past the restroom, where I saw dad beating Becky, my eyes filled with tears.

I walked to our room, there it seemed in my mind were all us kids, confined to that one room, most of our lives.

Walking from our room to mom's room, I saw my mom lying on the floor-begging dad to stop beating her. Just as I had seen the night he beat her, I saw dad on top of her, hitting her with the butt of his pistol over and over

Now, from where I was standing, I could have almost pushed him off of her.

Just my imagination.

Then I was in mom's room. I looked around one last time. In my mind, I saw her lying in her bed. Sleeping peacefully, as she had the morning I found her. She was asleep; there was no more pain for her, no ass whoopings, no cussing, and no crying.

I wanted to wake her, to hug her, to tell her one last time how much I loved her.

I walked past her bed to the living room, and there I could see her dancing and laughing with all of us, as she did so many times before. That beautiful smile, her happy laugh, all the kids laughing with her, her ponytail bouncing around as she danced. I could even hear the music she was dancing too.

She was so happy. So full of life, so full of love.

I got to the front door, turned around, and said "Goodbye mommy. I miss you so much; I just don't know how to go on without you. I'm sorry I didn't help you get away. I will never forget you and I will never ever stop loving you."

I was one hundred percent crying now, almost hysterical again. "Mommmmmmy" I screamed.
I did not know what to do. I turned and walked out of that old house, shutting the door behind me.
All the bad memories. Now behind me when I closed the door. I took my mom's love with me in my heart. All the sorrow and pain was left behind.

I could hardly see where I was going with so many tears flowing from my eyes. A pain in my heart I couldn't describe even if I tried.
I walked to Matty's car, opened the door, and got in the backseat. I looked toward the house.

From the corner of my eye, I saw the little city. I looked, and there we all were, sitting on the ground-helping mom create a city for my little brothers, mom laughing, having fun and loving every second of her kids. So much laughter, so much fun, so much love with her as she created the "Little City."

I was crying even more now, the thought of never seeing my mom that I loved so much. I was hurting so badly, wanting to scream at the top of my lungs. I want my mom so bad I can't stand it; I just can't stand this empty feeling.

I shut the car door, and just before we drove off, I looked toward the house and there stood my mom, in the doorway, as she had almost everyday of my life.
Standing there, that beautiful pose of hers, just standing in the doorway, as she did everyday watching her kids play outside, smiling that beautiful, beautiful smile.

Now, she was watching all of us leave, saying goodbye.
Goodbye to all of us, and saying goodbye to her pain.
Her beautiful green eyes looked directly into mine.
Her kids were safe now. She could rest.

I looked down to wipe my tears away, when I looked up again, she was gone.

www.ingramcontent.com/pod-product-compliance
Lightning Source LLC
Chambersburg PA
CBHW021138160426
43194CB00007B/617